CULTURE, PLACE, AND NATURE

STUDIES IN ANTHROPOLOGY AND ENVIRONMENT

K. Sivaramakrishnan, Series Editor

1) See comments in CES Books file

2) Does not take as complex or subtle a
look at global environmentalists as might. E.G.:
Can be seen as an anti-globaliz movement
against homogenization of world landscapes under
global cultural + economic forces

CULTURE, PLACE, AND NATURE

Centered in anthropology, the Culture, Place, and Nature series encompasses new interdisciplinary social science research on environmental issues, focusing on the intersection of culture, ecology, and politics in global, national, and local contexts. Contributors to the series view environmental knowledge and issues from the multiple and often conflicting perspectives of various cultural systems.

WILD SARDINIA

INDIGENEITY AND THE GLOBAL DREAMTIMES

OF ENVIRONMENTALISM

TRACEY HEATHERINGTON

A McLELLAN BOOK

UNIVERSITY OF WASHINGTON PRESS
SEATTLE AND LONDON

This book is published with the assistance of a grant from the McLellan Endowed Series Fund, established through the generosity of Martha McCleary McLellan and Mary McLellan Williams.

University of Washington Press
PO Box 50096, Seattle, WA 98145, USA
www.washington.edu/uwpress

All photos are by the author unless otherwise noted.

Library of Congress Cataloging-in-Publication Data
Heatherington, Tracey.
Wild Sardinia : indigeneity and the global dreamtimes of environmentalism / Tracey Heatherington.
    p. cm. — (Culture, place, and nature)
Includes bibliographical references and index.
ISBN 978-0-295-98998-3 (hardback : alk. paper) — ISBN 978-0-295-98999-0 (pbk. : alk. paper)
    1. Human ecology—Italy—Orgosolo.   2. Ethnology—Italy—Orgosolo.   3. Sustainable development—Italy—Orgosolo.   4. Orgosolo (Italy)—Environmental conditions.   5. Sardinia—Environmental conditions.   I. Title.
  GF587.S3H43 2010
  304.20945'92—dc22   2009035338

For Tziu Pepinu Marotto,
1925–2007

CONTENTS

around the world hope to benefit from the growth of sustainably managed ecotourism associated with nature parks.

The European Union, too, has been concerned to preserve biodiversity and sponsor sustainable development by promoting systems of parks and protected areas. Yet on the Italian island of Sardinia, the greatest source of environmental conflict and debate has been the plan to establish a national park in an area of dramatic, austere beauty and rich biological diversity, in the highlands of central Sardinia. Traditionally used for subsistence cultivation and extensive animal herding, this area contains mature forests and scrublands now thought to be representative of important, rare, and increasingly threatened Mediterranean biotopes. Given the apparent marginality of subsistence agriculture today, and the pressing need to protect remaining green spaces from "wild capitalism," one might ask: who could possibly object to a system for environmental conservation? Why should some Sardinians be so wayward as to reject the opportunities promised by the creation of a national park?

At a moment when environmental advocacy has achieved significant moral authority in international politics, I explore how and why some rural Sardinians have become what we might call the "black sheep" of environment and development efforts in Italy. Sardinians living in the highland towns of the interior have systematically opposed erosions of local autonomy over land and resource use and development. Many of them perceive a broad category of "environmentalists" as the architects of government-mediated and usually corrupt dispossessions. Outsiders to these towns, including urban-based Sardinians, the Italian media, and spokespersons for international environmental organizations, have tended to explain local antipathy to environmental initiatives as cultural backwardness and a lack of education. In contrast, I develop an anthropological case study to explore the ambivalent and open-ended meanings of these Sardinians' "resistance" on their own terms. There is an important parallel between my project and Michael Herzfeld's (1985, 1987a) well-known discussions of "aboriginal Europeans" in relation to the politics of identity on the Greek island of Crete. In the margins of Europe, encounters with biodiversity conservation and ecological management compel us to question assumptions about the nature of indigeneity.

Revisiting the question of the commons and models for sustainable development, I focus on the central Sardinian town of Orgosolo to explore the formation of political subjectivities articulated in response to discourses of global biodiversity conservation and to the regional, national, and European policy initiatives that have had an impact on this Mediterranean island. I reflect upon ethnographic fieldwork from 1996–98 and subsequent visits to Sardinia to complicate assumptions about culture and community in relation to both ecological and political practice. Orgosolo is noted for refusing to sell or privatize its traditional common lands during the nineteenth century, and for exercising vehement opposition since then to any projects that would put areas of the Commons under the control of outsiders or in private hands. Orgosolo is also known for its notorious bandits, its left-wing activism during the 1960s, its blood feuds ongoing through the 1970s, its rare climax forest of Mediterranean oak, and its famed artistic murals throughout the streets of the town. Above all, Orgosolo is perceived to exhibit a particular fidelity to indigenous cultural traditions, such as Sardinian language practices and transhumant herding. There is, paradoxically, no unifying story of "resistance" here. My account contradicts a number of strategic political narratives that have reified two-sided oppositions such as "community" vs. the "state" or "traditional" vs. progressive or "modern" citizens. Instead, I have attempted to describe a set of contingent, transitional narratives about environment, development, and cultural identity in Sardinia during the main period of my research in the late 1990s.

In many ways, the research reflected in this book comes out of a fairly conventional ethnographic project, centered in a small, out-of-the-way place.[1] Yet as ethnographers take account of increasingly fluid geo-economic contexts, fieldwork is no longer bounded by place but guided instead by thematic engagements and particular questions (Gupta and Ferguson 1997a; Marcus 1998). By the 1990s, anthropologists (see Brosius 1997, 1999a, 1999b) began to theorize the ways in which ethnographic standpoints could be used to assess and critique global environmental campaigns. An unusual feature of the project discussed in this book is that it bridges debates in European ethnography and political ecology. Some gaps in analysis are perhaps inevitable, since there are relatively few precedents here. In southern Europe today, global environmentalism helps to both reproduce and subordinate ethnicities linked to "resistance." Recent debates about indigenous identity and ecological relations are surprisingly provocative in analyzing this case. To understand the cultural politics of so-called resistance in Sardinia, one must grasp how the global discourses of environmentalism tend to essentialize, primitivize, exoticize, and even fetishize cultural minorities around the world, ultimately undermining rooted sovereignty over landscapes and ecosystems. It is through the lens of implicitly biologized "otherness" that the agents of nation-states evaluate the capacity for these cultural minorities to maintain or participate in environmental guardianship. In a neoliberal world, global environmental discourses can reify racisms and exacerbate embedded structural inequalities. What Sardinians share with indigenous peoples and traditional cultures in many parts of the world is an experience of marginalization, re-created in part through the moral and symbolic frameworks associated with global environmentalism.

Understanding the complex story of a national park in Sardinia requires both an effort to grasp the structures and processes associated with larger contexts, and an appreciation for the ways in which a profound sense of rootedness can shape local perspectives. I was introduced to the nuances of place in rural Sardinia almost in spite of myself. As a graduate student, I went to the town of Orgosolo to undertake ethnographic research from 1996 to 1998, quite focused on environmental politics. Yet a number of senior women wanted to tell me the story of their youths, about the hard days spent harvesting the fields for landowners, gathering wood in the mountains, and washing clothes in the river. My gentle landlady wanted to take me to see her garden where she still worked daily, and offered me all the local recipes that remain a testament to Orgosolo's good traditions. She wanted to be sure I had the opportunity to see all the festivals and photograph the processions. An anthropologist should do these things, she knew; an anthropologist should learn customs and traditions and interview older people to find out what the town had once really been like. The mother of a friend told me to sit and watch *Banditi a Orgosolo* (Bandits of Orgosolo), the famous film made in the 1960s and enacted by actual shepherds from the town. My own age peers often wanted to take me to the bars, where the "real" discussions of current events of friendships that constantly affirmed we are never merely "fieldworkers" and "informants," but also human, interdependent, and delightfully unique individuals. The fact that good ethnography is actually based on getting to know people can no longer be very contentious, and fictions of ethnographic distance would represent the Sardinian context poorly. When I speak about the many people who taught me something about the place, it should not come as a surprise that I refer to quite a few of them as "friends" or "acquaintances." In the context of ongoing collaborations with six or eight extended families across multiple households in a small town, over the course of years, it seems the most correct and respectful phrasing to adopt.

This book brings together some themes from conventional political economy approaches to environment and development, as well as approaches that privilege subjectivity and reflexivity as central to understanding the ethnographic process and its results. It does not closely follow the literary or subject narrative-oriented model of "postmodern" ethnographies, although in common with many anthropologists who came of age during the vivacious experimentation of the 1990s, I believe we have learned something fundamental about both fieldwork and writing from the so-called "postmodern moment"[5] of anthropological critique. This is reflected in elements of my stylistic judgment, including the choice to make inter-subjectivity and self-awareness conscientiously present within the analytical discussion. It is also reflected in the rather playful organization of the text, in my attention to critical theory, and in my preference for a somewhat open-ended conclusion that acknowledges the innate contingency, complexity, and contradictions of Sardinian experience. Given the colorful spectrum of ethnographic writing styles emerging among my colleagues working in environmental anthropology today, and the wide variety of intellectual traditions being brought into the larger domain of environmental studies, it is challenging to speak in meaningful terms to such a diverse audience. My synthesis of what some would call "objectivist" and "culturalist" elements is necessarily a work in progress.

This book is partly based on research originally undertaken for my doctoral dissertation at Harvard University in Cambridge, Massachusetts. Portions of some chapters included here were previously published, but have been extensively revised. I am grateful to audiences, co-panelists, and discussants at a number of conferences and invited seminars where drafts of these essays were originally presented. Conversations with Beth Conklin, Sarah Green, Yuson Jung, Kim Clark, Werner Krauss, Laurie Medina, Jon Mitchell, Katja Neves-Graca, Kenneth Olwig, Darren Ranco, Sarah Robinson, Colin Scott, Ed Snajdr, and Christine Walley have been particularly helpful. I extend my appreciation to the Anthropology and Environment section of the AAA, as well as the Society for the Anthropology of Europe, for providing wonderful forums and resources, and for their ongoing support of junior scholars. I thank all the anonymous reviewers and outstanding editors who generously contributed their thoughts, critiques, and encouragements, and particularly Lorri Hagman and K. Sivaramakrishnan ("Shivi"), as editors for the Press and the series, whose attentive support has been invaluable.

I owe sincere recognition and thanks to friends, teachers, loved ones, hosts, critics, and companions in self-reflection back in Sardinia. Since my second year in the field, Francesco Pili's thoughtful conversation and miraculous sense of humor enriched this work immeasurably. The Pili-Spanu family gave me a true home. I owe profound debts of gratitude to my accomplished Sardinian twin, Rosa Maria Usai, and her whole family. For many kinds of help and support during fieldwork, I sincerely thank Pasqualina Menneas, Ciriaco Fronteddu, Maria-Adelina Patteri, Giovanna Menneas, Maurizio Bassu, Pietro Manca, Titina Congiargiu, Luisa Muravera, Santina Cossu, Malena Mesina, Maura Lovicu, Agostina Garippa, Pasqua Corraine, Silvia Lombardini, and all of their generous families and friends. The delightful feminists who gave me sanctuary with the "women's cricca" of Orgosolo, and my Orgosolo age-mates, the children of 1967, who adopted me into the "leva '67" the year we all turned thirty, have inspired me in more ways than I can count. There are far more personal, professional, and intellectual debts to acknowledge in Sardinia than I can begin to list here, including all of those who graciously permitted interviews and assisted my work. I can only hope to persuade them that I have never forgotten their kindnesses and insights by treating their concerns seriously in the body of the text.

I appreciate the support of many institutions that facilitated developments of this project over the past fifteen years. I wish to acknowledge the assistance of Fonds FCAR, the MARE team project funded by SSHRC at McGill University, and the Mellon Foundation during preliminary phases of research in Sardinia prior to 1996. Intensive research for a Ph.D. was undertaken on the basis of grants from the Wenner-Gren Foundation for Anthropological Research and the Krupp Foundation, administered by the Minda de Gunzburg Center for European Studies at Harvard University, as well as a Harvard Merit Fellowship. The Town of Orgosolo and the Orgosolo Town Library provided generous practical and administrative assistance in the field. The Mellon Foundation and the Weatherhead Center for International Affairs at Harvard University supported follow-up research and the write-up of the dissertation. The Social Science Faculty of the University of Western Ontario and the Graduate School Research Committee of the University of Wisconsin–Milwaukee supported my recent returns to Sardinia in 2004 and 2006, respectively.

My prodigious mentors deserve unbounded thanks for their many contributions. As supervisor of my Ph.D. and a continuing sponsor of intellectual mischief, Michael Herzfeld has been the most benevolent and delightfully fierce of critics. Mary Steedly and Sally Falk Moore merit special thanks for invaluable input at formative moments, as do all the members of the research team led by Philip Salzman, which first took me to Sardinia. I remember Begoña Aretxaga both for her own provocative work and for the voice of critique and encouragement that helped inspire revisions and rethinking beyond the dissertation. Kay Milton, Thomas Wilson, Larry Taylor, Regna Darnell, and "Shivi," my series editor, have been among the extraordinary senior colleagues who have helped me find my way since graduate school. This book has taken shape over the course of my participation in three truly vibrant anthropology departments, the School of Anthropological Studies at Queen's University Belfast, the University of Western Ontario, and the University of Wisconsin–Milwaukee. I thank all of my amazing students and colleagues for their many helpful conversations. Research assistants Matthew Tobiasz and Maurizio Murru helped gather documents and assemble the bibliography. Amanda Gibson did a superb job of copyediting, under the supervision of Mary Ribesky. The intrepid Martha Van Devender undertook indexing with thoughtfulness, patience, and skillful judgement. I have particular obligations to thank Igor Ayora-

Diaz, Dan Bradburd, Mary Bouquet, Lissa Caldwell, Tom Carter, Jack Conley, Douglas Holmes, Luisa Muravera, Matt Robinson, Gino Satta, Maruska Svašek, Robin Whittaker, Kim Clark, Gaby Vargas-Cetina, and above all, Bernard Perley, for truly insightful comments and questions on various versions and portions of this work.

While there are perhaps better means of thanking family members for being there through the trials of academic life, my father, Marshall Heatherington, deserves heartfelt acknowledgement here for his unfailing encouragement and support through fourteen years of university and well beyond. He has lent me extraordinary strength, integrity, courage, and patience. Cornelia Fuykschot, my late friend and teacher, cared enough to inspire academic excellence back in high school. I fondly thank Phil and Lorrie Lancaster, Henrietta Black, Wendell Perley, and all the members of my fabulous extended family, for indulging and encouraging my work. Bernard Perley, my husband, has honored my stories and offered so many insights into anthropological theory, indigeneity, and the Sardinian experience. To Bernie, Dad, my wise friend Catherine Andress, and my intrepid birth mother Linda Watson, thank you, thank you, for sharing some of my journeys in Sardinia.

PART I Beginnings

The Orgosolo Commons, view toward Monte San Giovanni (2000).

Introduction

Paradoxes of Advocacy

During my first months of ethnographic research on the island of Sardinia, Italy, in 1990–91, I found myself one afternoon in a restaurant in a town near the eastern coast, the guest of six men who had befriended another Canadian student the year before. The men were workers in their thirties and forties whose economic strategies included flexible combinations of informal and formal construction jobs, herding, bartending, and entrepreneurial tourism. None of these men possessed the university degrees and political connections that would allow them to contend for steady, salaried government positions. Over a communal dish of *fave con lardo*, a traditional bean and pork recipe often enjoyed at festive gatherings, they brought up the subject of my fieldwork interests in environmental management with a certain amount of suspicion.

One of them asked me with a sideways look, and perhaps a little aggressively, "Are you happy that we are cutting wood?"

I was aware that there had been episodes of tension between townspeople and the regional government's Forest Ranger Corps the previous year, over access to winter fuelwood quotas from the woodlands under communal management. There had even been a public demonstration in the streets. I shrugged and said to him, "Yes, why not?"

He did not discuss it, but continued to interrogate, "What does WWF stand for?"

Grumbles sounded around the table as I stumbled tentatively over the words, "World Wildlife Fund."

Immediately my inquisitor demanded to know, "Are you in favor of the Gennargentu Park?"

3

Before I could answer, a passionate debate had flared up about the government plan to establish a national park. The men raced from point to point, shouting their positions to one another in Sardinian, and occasionally to me, in simple Italian. In this muddled and energetic debate, nobody seemed to agree with anyone else about exactly how the town should approach environment and development. What emerged nonetheless was a tacit consensus that the proposed national park would be bad for local residents because it would prevent the free continuation of hunting, woodcutting, tourism development, and pastoral herding on the Commons. All these uses of the local territory were recognized by people in that town as essential to their aspirations for the future.

The point in demanding to know whether I agreed with their right to take wood from their communal territory was therefore essentially the same, for them, as asking if I agreed with the creation of a national park. With each question, these men were requesting me to clarify whether I supported their rights to use and benefit from the local commons. And if I was "for" these rights, "for" the exercise of traditional rights of usufruct,[1] then I could be considered to be on their side. Only on these terms, I suspected, were they prepared to accept me into their social world, whether as an ethnographer, an intellectual ally, or a friend. By contrast, if I were seen to support the WWF or the national park, then I would be persona non grata working against their interests. I had already met a number of forest rangers recently stationed in the town who were pointedly denied some of the customary privileges of local hospitality, precisely because they were taken to be associated with both "environmentalists" and "the state."

"You cannot be an anthropologist and an environmentalist at the same time!"[2] one of them insisted emphatically.

I remember asking quite timidly, "But why not?"

This reductive dualism continued to haunt me, expressing what seemed to be a classic conflict between anthropocentric and biocentric values and perspectives. In retrospect, I see that this brusque warning against divided loyalties was more astute and provocative than I realized at the time. For both anthropology and environmentalism imply ethical orientations of advocacy. In the first case, a fieldworker is ethically committed not only to uphold the critical function of the discipline, but also to consider what role her work may play in the broader context of social justice. Many anthropologists accept moral obligations that go beyond fundamental issues of disclosure, consent, safety, and privacy. In a field historically engaged with encounters between groups of unequal power, we strive to transcend structural complicity and bear witness to poverty, distress, suffering, creativity, integrity, humanity, and hope. We listen for other voices and learn to question our own. An environmental scholar, meanwhile, must bear witness for those entirely without human language, at a time of undeniable and growing urgency. To advocate on behalf of non-human species and their homelands, to speak on behalf of seas and skies and winds and tides, demands a very distinctive form of attentiveness and understanding. So it is a paradox of environmental anthropology that we must be tuned simultaneously into different registers, spoken and silent, sometimes perceiving one only faintly through the other, and vice versa, so that we continually discover discomforts and contradictions.

Until recently, it was often taken for granted that the aims of biodiversity conservation would converge quite simply with the best interests of local and indigenous peoples, by protecting the ecosystems and resources upon which they depend, and even by sustaining their rights to sovereignty over homelands and sacred places. Anthropological work on traditional environmental knowledge in tribal and peasant societies has surely made significant contributions to cultural recognition in many contexts.[3] Yet it remains problematic for local groups to lay claim to authority over landscapes and biodiversity resources without essentializing their cultural heritage and identity. For example, as Darrell Posey (2003) pointed out, the guidelines of the Convention on Biological Diversity (CBD) left government elites to arbitrate which local communities truly embody "traditional lifestyles relevant for the conservation and sustainable use of biological diversity" (UNCED 1992). Given such stakes, the representation of "authentic" or "traditional" orientations to environmental management has become more fraught. It is problematic for many minority groups to be recognized for their cultural knowledge traditions as a result of their growing participation in a global economy, resulting in patterns of change in contemporary natural resource use and a symbolic failure of authenticity. As anthropology is directed to familiar, Western contexts, and as we move toward more nuanced assessments of political ecology in a changing world, the boundaries between cultural advocacy and cultural critique become harder to gauge. I faced these quandaries in my work on Sardinia. On this notorious island in southern Italy, the projects of ecological modernity associated with European nation-states, and more diffusely with the global campaigns of international organizations and environmental lobbies, encounter the culturally rooted life projects of people from traditional pastoral communities. The paradoxes of environmental and cultural advocacy here are as tangled as ever they might be.

Conservation and Development

The story of the Gennargentu Park (a gloss used to refer to what was once proposed as the Parco Nazionale del Gennargentu and is now called the Parco Nazionale del Golfo di Orosei e del Gennargentu) is one microcosm of the history of development initiatives that government authorities devised to boost the economy and transform the island of Sardinia after World War II. Almost in tandem with sweeping efforts to modernize agriculture and create poles of industrialization throughout southern Italy, several national parks were proposed during the 1960s. These focused on areas that were recognized to preserve important endemic species and ecosystems, often including exemplary megafauna and large birds that made for striking visual emblems. These areas also featured rural landscapes that appeared unspoiled to the city-dwellers, nature enthusiasts, and foreign travelers who might be expected to make regular excursions to visit the new parks. From the perspective of Italian government coalitions, setting aside lands for conservation was part and parcel of a larger vision for rational resource management. Above all, the object was to remake the economically marginal, agriculturally based areas of southern Italy in the image of modernity, in the hopes of replicating the "economic miracle" that had allowed a boom of small- to medium-scale industrialization in northern Italy during the postwar period. The Region of Sardinia, granted special autonomous status in 1948, has actively supported and solicited a variety of development initiatives, including the plan for the national park. Tourism in particular has been viewed as a promising alternative for development on an island rich with attractive beaches and striking natural settings. Conventionally, national parks not only provide important destination points for domestic and international tourism, but also energize commercial enterprises in proximity by bringing in special development funds and contracts, and by allowing the launch of recognizable brand names associated with the parks. The commercial visibility of whole regions can be elevated. Where successful national parks can be established, they may inspire higher levels of private economic investment and other ancillary economic benefits. At the political level, they reinscribe regional and national identities, and reflect well upon governmental commitments to environmental stewardship, in fulfillment of citizens' expectations as well as international agreements. Thus at the regional and national levels, the probable advantages of a national park in Sardinia appeared substantial. By looking at this case we can better perceive the curious role of parks in Western European nation-building, and in the process of constructing the European Union during the latter half of the twentieth century.

From another vantage point, the campaign to create a Gennargentu Park can also be seen as a microcosm of mounting efforts at an international level to protect global ecological resources as public goods. Building on the nineteenth-century nature preservation movements that established areas to be protected from the environmental destruction associated with the early industrial revolution, postwar environmental movements were powered by narratives of nostalgia inherently engaged with contemporary visions of modernization and development. After the hardship of two world wars, Western science and technology seemed to burst forward, achieving dramatic results in many domains, from agricultural production to space exploration and communications. All of these developments supported new forms of international awareness and engagement. Eventually, questions began to be asked about the possible limits of economic growth because of the ultimate scarcity of the earth's resources and the negative impacts on resource quality resulting from industrialization.[4] Advancing studies in natural ecology were both a phenomenon of continuing scientific optimism and an antidote to it. They encouraged us to value first "wildlife" and "ecosystems," and then later "biological diversity" and "habitats," not only as pragmatic objects of management, but also as bases for moral and cultural orientations. "Green politics" emerged to champion precautionary approaches to environmental risk, address cross-border environmental problems, and sponsor collaborations to conserve the global commons. Global interconnections came to underpin arguments in favor of instituting new parks and protected areas, just as they became integral to the mechanisms of lobbying for conservation. An examination of the campaign for a Gennargentu Park, then, can highlight historical and current elements of the discourses, institutional articulations, and postmodern practices associated with global environmentalism. These are increasingly strategic aspects of power.

For four decades, political debates about the creation of a national park in the central, highland region of Sardinia have been ongoing. For four decades, overwhelming opposition was rallied in the towns most affected by these plans, despite apparently generous funding for "sustainable development." This has puzzled many advocates of environmental conservation, who sometimes see the implementation of parks and protected areas as the only reliable way to stand against a tide of brazenly unsustainable development and shelter remaining "natural" landscapes and ecosystems from irrevocable harm. Yet despite widespread assumptions that parks are inherently well-adapted institutional solutions for community development, this kind of environmental advocacy quickly runs aground on the question of autochthonous cultural sovereignty. When one takes seriously the life projects of the Sardinians I met, salient historical contexts of colonial power and contemporary contexts of political economic marginality emerge forcefully. With them come fundamentally different, culturally rooted but also dynamically changing ways of relating to nature, community, and place. Sardinian aboriginality, if it can be taken to exist, is an identity fraught with layers of hybridity and ambivalence, ensnared by the tricky shadows of Italian and European cosmopolitanism. To examine the problem of evident resistance to Gennargentu Park, then, must be to pose provocative and unsettling questions about trajectories of "indigenousness" and the ways that both anthropologists and environmentalists can deal with it honestly.

Themes

This is the story of a park that has, at least for the moment, failed in important respects. An analysis of why and how it has been repeatedly projected, and why and how it has repeatedly fallen through, tells us something important about how locally defined needs and aspirations come into articulation, and disarticulation, with dominant global concerns (cf. Paulson and Gezon 2005). It guides us beyond facile accusations of local ignorance and complicates the role of parks in international conservation today. It challenges us to discover alternative modalities of meaning and feeling, alternative senses of history and community, which give form and context to resistance "from the bottom up." It also problematizes the models of nostalgia still broadly associated with environmental campaigns. Looking at why the Gennargentu Park project has now apparently been abandoned, and what has been offered in its place, tells us something about how the stakes of environmental politics might be changing in the twenty-first century. Yet Gennargentu Park arguably still lingers in the dreamtime of global environmental imagination as a moral imperative. Its fitful traces offer us a glimpse into processes of uneven development that continue to circumscribe the most sustainable futures we can envision.[5] This draws biodiversity conservation movements themselves within the purview of questions that we are now beginning to ask about global environmental justice. Following important research on the theme of political ecology,[6] I encounter discussions about science, culture, and environment embedded within contingent, often part-hidden, material and social agendas associated with governance over contested resources. Knowledge construction in the domain of environment and development, as in other domains of "science as practice," generates representations that cannot be taken at face value (Latour 1987, 1998, 2004; cf. Lowe 2006).[7]

Environmental conservation in the margins of the European Union, a political entity still in a process of self-definition and expansion, is a problem that involves the interplay of many levels and dimensions of cultural identity. These identities are precariously and contingently sited in the global, the European, the national, the regional, and the local. While traditional ecological knowledge in Sardinia is unquestionably very rich, my purpose is not to describe it in detail, nor to objectify and define the cultural ecology of Sardinia today. Instead, I attempt to sketch out perspectives on ecological politics "from the bottom up," and complicate them sincerely. I explore how visions of landscape are expressed, and the tensions between them negotiated, all in relation to understandings of history and cultural identity. This book presents the complex engagements between people of different occupational groups in one small town, between men and women, between practicing Catholics and left-wing supporters, and between the educated and the structurally disadvantaged. All of these untidy relationships are embedded within larger projects of storytelling through which representations of both local culture and local ecology are negotiated with the larger world. In concert with efforts to interpret the dynamics of "nature in the making" (Tsing 2001), I explore how narrative authority about the Sardinian environment has been crafted and contested in political action as well as everyday practice.

The ethnographic materials presented support a renewed examination of the problem of "resistance" to ecodevelopment in central Sardinia, revealing how standard explanations for environmental and political contestation in this context have been deeply inflected by cosmopolitan ethnocentrisms. A nuanced approach to this problem requires sustained attention to the voices of real people from central Sardinia, as well as a fundamental grasp of their immediate social and economic context that comes only from sharing some aspects of their daily experience for a time. Small-scale ethnography is therefore the staple methodological strategy of this exercise. Accordingly, the reported speech and anecdotal narratives included here record more than mere local color; they constitute a primary layer of qualitative data that energizes the hermeneutic reframing of analysis. More about what this entails is explained below.

The organization of this book follows three major themes: ecology, alterity, and resistance. In Sardinia, these themes are so mutually embedded that a discussion of one inevitably leads back to the others. This is so not only at a descriptive level, but also with respect to a critical theoretical framework, as I begin to explore in the next chapter. I argue that the objectifying discourses of both ecology and resistance are always fundamentally embedded in, and regenerative of, understandings about cultural identity and cultural difference. This is a salient feature of debates about nature and conservation not only in the case I study here, but also in countless other cases where more or less conventional definitions of "indigenousness," "aboriginality," or "tradition" are found at the center of conflicting claims to ownership and authority over land and biological wealth. Paradoxes of anthropological advocacy therefore remain at the heart of this project. They compel me to remember that cultural representations cannot be innocent, regardless of origin. If the ethical bonds of respect and support for the life projects of highland Sardinians predispose me to privilege local understandings of culture and environment, those same bonds obligate me to think critically about how well these same visions serve the interests of social justice and environmental sustainability for contemporary and future communities. Anthropocentric and biocentric interests are neither directly opposed nor simplistically convergent; they are mutually embedded in complex ways.

So too with the local and the global: as limited heuristic devices, these terms can lead us to forget that rural highland Sardinians are cosmopolitan actors themselves, with a stake in the global commons. The political and civic leaders acting on behalf of wider imagined communities are simultaneously embedded in and empowered by their own "local" social spheres and networks. Yet without genuine dialogue and collaboration across different scales of community-making and different ways of knowing landscapes, the prospects for sustainability are bleak. To this dialogue I offer my own account of Sardinian political ecology during the 1990s in the hope of making space for fresh and open conversations.

Contexts

Sardinia is located in the Tyrrhenian Sea, immediately south of Corsica and west of the Italian peninsula. With a land area of over 24,000 square kilometers (about 9,300 square miles), it is second only to Sicily as the largest island in the Mediterranean. Based on the 2006 census, the island of Sardinia is currently home to 1,655,677 people, with an average population density of sixty-nine inhabitants per square kilometer.[8] Most of the cities, including the capital, Cagliari, as well as Sassari, Olbia, Alghero, and Oristano, lie close to the coast in lowland areas. The island has been part of the Italian nation-state since the time of its unification in 1861, and it became an Autonomous Region in 1948, just after World War II ended and Italy became a democratic Republic. The Region was divided into the four administrative provinces of Cagliari, Sassari, Nuoro, and Oristano, roughly echoing the for-

Map of Italy in the context of the Mediterranean (map prepared by
B. C. Perley and T. Heatherington).

mer organization of jurisdictions during Sardinia's only brief period of
independence, in the medieval period. After 2004, provincial administration was decentralized when these units were broken down to create
four new provinces, Carbonia-Iglesias, Medio Campidano, Ogliastra,
and Olbia-Tempio. Some of the policy shifts that coincided with this
political-administrative reorganization will be the subject of discussion
at the end of the book. Ethnographic research presented here is primarily concerned with the province of Nuoro. My initial fieldwork there
was undertaken prior to the redivision of administrative units, when the
province of Nuoro encompassed an area of approximately 7,000 square

kilometers and incorporated the towns that are now found within the province of Ogliastra. Ogliastra and Nuoro continue to collaborate on a number of policy initiatives. The new province of Nuoro serves fifty-two towns in the Sardinian interior and has a territory of 3,934 square kilometers. As of 2006, with 164,260 inhabitants, the population density of Nuoro was just under forty-two people per square kilometer, only about 60 percent of the regional average. Over 35 percent of Nuoro's inhabitants are located either in the provincial capital, Nuoro, or in the large towns of Siniscola and Macomer, where some industry has taken root. Another 17 percent are found in the four coastal towns that remain within the provincial territory. These benefit from some limited tourism development and secondary sector activities. The rest of Nuoro's people are spread across small towns, among which are some of the poorest in the Region. Small-scale agricultural enterprises afford most of the occupational opportunities in these areas. Government-supported forestry and conservation activities have also come to play a role in the generation of livelihoods, together with labor migration strategies.

Sardinia features a high number of rare and endemic species and priority habitats for conservation, listed in the birds and habitats directives of the European Community (Directive 79/409/EEC and Directive 92/43/EEC), now the European Union. The island has very hot, dry summers and cool, wet winters; it is considered to have a semi-arid climate that may experience more intense heat waves and periods of drought as global climate patterns shift. Its fragile coastal areas include biodiversity-rich wetlands and marine ecosystems, as well as spectacular beaches and geological formations. Endangered species such as the pink flamingo can be found in some of these coastal habitats. There are many small, hidden bays and tiny inlets. Along the eastern coast, these are often framed like gems between dramatic cliff faces and steep slopes that crowd up to the water. In contrast to the Mediterranean coast along the European mainland, the majority of Sardinia's seaside land has not been built over, making it of significant scientific, ecological, aesthetic, and economic value.

Many areas of the island's interior, particularly the mountains and highland plateaux located in the central and eastern zones, are also considered to have very high conservation value. Highland Sardinia is characterized by calcareous rock formations, several of which have been recognized as natural monuments. These create extremely attractive destinations for photography, hiking, mountain climbing, and spelunking (cave-diving), for example. A profusion of species, including indigenous and/or rare plant, animal, reptile, insect, and bird species, exist in a variety of highland habitats, just as they do along the coasts. Vegetation is considered to be characteristic of the Mediterranean region, with spontaneous garrigue and maquis covering rangelands on the high plateau. There are many kinds of wild orchid and mushrooms, as well as myrtle, oak, olive, and strawberry trees.[9] Just below 800 meters, some climax forest area can be found, comprising sweet chestnut, cork oak, holm oak, and sessile oak. About three-quarters of Sardinian woodlands like these were denuded during the nineteenth century. The remaining areas are highly valued by scientists and environmentalists for their distinctiveness. Visiting wildlife enthusiasts can see rare mammals and birds, including the Sardinian deer, the albino donkey of Asinara, the Sardinian mouflon, the Sardinian wild cat, the griffon, the royal eagle, and the endangered Bonelli eagle.[10] A relatively low population density and low levels of intensive production or extraction, industry, or construction activities have supported the endurance of distinctive and increasingly rare examples of "traditional" Mediterranean forests and scrub. Some would say that it was, ironically, the very poverty of highland Sardinia that allowed the Region to conserve the natural resources that have now become so priceless in an era of concern about the global heritage of biological diversity. Others offer more credit, as I do, to the role of rural people themselves, who actively worked to maintain their extensive, semi-traditional forms of primary production and historically rooted visions of landscape, community, and common property ownership. Agencies such as the State Forestry Service have played roles in both resource extraction and resource management, since the birth of the Italian nation-state. Institutional governance measures, large-scale economic processes, and the social agency of rural Sardinians have all helped to define the "natural" ecology of the island as it exists today.

Sociologist Bruno Latour (2004) has urged the advocates of "green politics" to move away from any understanding of ecology that assumes a basic separation between nature and culture, or between science and society, since the logic of these specious dualities undermines vital mandates for deep-seated political change. In the disciplinary tradition of anthropology, cultural ecologists have long examined how local religions and ways of "being in the world" have informed nuanced and responsive cultural engagements with nature and environment.[11] Geographers Noel Castree and Bruce Braun (2001) have emphasized that all nature is inherently "social nature." Yet typical descriptions of "biodiversity and habitats" privilege certain perspectives on Sardinian landscapes and leave out evidence of traditional societies in environmental history. This compels us to reflect on the ways that ideas about global nature are typically imbricated in structural relationships of inequality, as well as the cultural discourses that sustain them. A new generation of anthropologists has contributed to the insights of political ecology by interrogating the ethnocentrism of narratives about culture and environment, by tracing the outlines of institutional structures or assemblages in which they are anchored, and by putting the perspectives of real people and communities as much as possible at the center of debates about global nature.

Approaches

The chapters that form the main body of this book focus on ethnographic fieldwork from the rural Sardinian town of Orgosolo, in Nuoro province. It is located eighteen kilometers from the provincial capital and is linked to it by relatively good (though brutally winding) roads, so that it is possible to commute there daily to work or go to school. Most households now have access to motor vehicles, but public transportation by bus is also available. The town has moderately easy access to the provincial highways, which have slowly been extended and improved, so that day-trips to or from cities like Cagliari, Sassari, and Olbia are gradually becoming less onerous. The town of Orgosolo has a population of approximately 4,900 people, and an elevation of roughly 620 meters above sea level. Most of its common lands lie above the town, on the mountainous high plateau referred to as "the Supramonte." This relatively large territory of approximately 22,400 square hectares has traditionally sustained subsistence-oriented herding, agriculture, and gathering. Over the course of the twentieth century, agro-pastoral activities were somewhat integrated into the market economy, so that family enterprises often straddle the

Map of Orgosolo in relation to Sardinian cities and an approximate outline of Gennargentu Park as it was proposed in 1998 (map prepared by B. C. Perley and T. Heatherington).

formal and informal sectors. During the postwar period, labor migration to continental Europe provided some alternatives to marginal agriculture, but out-migration was less pronounced here than in nearby towns with fewer territorial resources to draw upon. Forestry, agriculture, and tourism activities on the Commons have also contributed to the local economy. Historians have written about the town's historic acts to protect the local Commons from enclosure and privatization. Campaigns to protect nature and endangered species in highland Sardinia have envisioned incorporating significant parts of Orgosolo's historic territory within the proposed Gennargentu Park. There is considerable biological wealth there, represented by an old-growth oak forest, distinctive geological features, the relative abundance of indigenous wildlife, and a diversity of habitats. There is also immense cultural wealth in the form of archaeological sites, historic places and points of religious pilgrimage, a thriving indigenous language community and oral traditions, pastoral heritage, craft skills, political murals, a reputation for authentic cuisine, and unparalleled hospitality.

According to the 2006 census, however, Orgosolo fell into the category of towns that had the lowest levels of formal income and material wealth, highest unemployment, poorest access to services, and the lowest indicators of socioeconomic development. It was considered one of the "most deprived" and "most disadvantaged" towns in all of Sardinia. Orgosolo also falls within the area of Nuoro that has been associated with relatively high rates of political intimidation, homicides, and theft (with the objects of choice shifting historically from sheep to automobiles). Forest fires and links to kidnapping rings have, similarly, provided cause for concern. Orgosolo has borne a burden of particular notoriety as the hometown of several well-known bandits and kidnappers, from the nineteenth century to living memory. As the setting of several famous scholarly studies, works of literature, and films about banditry and pastoral life in Sardinia, it has taken on a consummate role in the imagination of cultural difference marking the interior of the island. It has also been at the forefront of repeated grassroots mobilizations to oppose legislation creating the new Gennargentu Park. It is not my intention to claim that Orgosolo represents the most extreme form of marginality and social distress on the island. Nor is it a typical Sardinian town. It does, however, condense and highlight a particular space of cultural "otherness." It is from the standpoint of Orgosolo's highly eccentric experience that we can perceive the form of ecological alterity that has gathered force here, and how it undermines the life projects of rural Sardinians, as well as projects of conservation.

Global approaches to environmental conservation have consistently promoted parks and protected areas around the world. Up until the mid-1980s, both national governments and environmental non-governmental organizations (ENGOs) usually favored biocentric and technocentric approaches to eco-management. Rising critiques of "top-down" development[12] and the growth of indigenous social movements, however, wrought a gradual change in the discourses of conservation. With the Brundtland Report (WCED 1987) and the Rio Earth Summit in 1992, the reconciliation of the international human rights agenda with the agenda for global conservation gradually became a focus for new programs in sustainable development. Funding initiatives for parks and protected areas increasingly highlighted "community participation," "partnerships," "co-management," and appreciation for "indigenous knowledge." Many anthropologists, geographers, conservation biologists, engaged NGO workers, and local advocates have been involved with the paradigm shift that envisioned a convergence of interests on behalf of environmentalists and local peoples. Arguably, however, the divide between "globally oriented" and "locally oriented" visions of the environment (Milton 1996) has not been resolved. Environment and development projects are often organized on a large scale and mediated by sizeable official bureaucracies in association with various consultants and NGOs (Goldman 2005; Agrawal 2005; cf. Gupta and Ferguson 2002).

Ideas of pristine "wilderness" continue to prove durable. Entrenched models of "fortress conservation" still frequently overshadow fledgling experiments with United Nations Biosphere Reserves and Integrated Conservation and Development.[13] Despite their colonial taint, national parks managed by scientific experts have evidently maintained the greatest attraction for tourists, nation-states, and environmental lobbies. The largest environmental NGOs have been indicted (Chapin 2004) for their failure to sustain respect for indigenous and traditional peoples' sovereignty over natural resources, and their failure to give them a primary role in the design and management of protected areas. Representatives at the top levels of the International Union for the Conservation of Nature (IUCN), the World Wide Fund for Nature (WWF), The Nature Conservancy (TNC), and Conservation International (CI), among others, have expressed limited confidence in local peoples' commitment to environmental values. Mac Chapin points out that these particular ENGOs grew enormously large, rich, and powerful during the 1990s. Today, they establish the parameters for many conservation initiatives and work internationally to popularize their own ideals of global environmentalism. Ironically, their campaigns for environmental education can misappropriate cultural identities.[14] These organizations wield trained political voices, and we count on them to goad the most conservative nation-states toward crucial goals, such as limiting their weapons testing, greenhouse gas emissions, and extractive industries. If these very organizations have answered the demands of cultural relativism half-heartedly, then anthropologists must learn new ways to intercede in the education of environmental advocates.

Recent ethnographic writing resists stereotypical images of indigeneity that encourage sustainable development experts to imagine culture as a mechanical black box.[15] Instead, it confirms a need to study empirically the variety of cultural and institutional engagements entailed in environmental governance. As Charles Zerner noted,

> All nature conservation and environmental management efforts are inevitably projects in politics. . . . Certain species, landscapes and environmental outcomes are privileged, while others are peripheralized or disenfranchised. . . . The task of critical scholarship and advocacy for international environmental justice is, in part, to examine regimes of nature management, to identify what kinds of politics and governance are imagined and implemented, and to assess the consequences. It is to place nature management on the scales of justice. (2000, 16–17)

Ethnographic critiques of global conservation carry concerns about social equity and distributive justice into the analysis of environment and development situations in different national contexts, with direct attention to the implications of cross-cultural and transnational engagements. One of the challenges for a politically committed anthropology today is to present ethnographically informed works that address issues relevant to the growing transnational ENGOs. The largest of these organizations have come to define and manage so many of the projects associated with global environmentalism that their ideological effects now obscure the true multiplicity of environmental movements around the world (Chapin 2004). Extended case studies, based on long-term research in situ, provide important opportunities to address complexities that might otherwise be glossed over. At the same time, they demonstrate how innovative forms of ethnography can be put to work in the real world.

The work I present here brings conventional Sardinian ethnography into juxtaposition with the para-ethnographic analysis of virtual and imagined spaces. As I explained in the preface, ethnographers today advocate sophisticated understandings of fieldwork "location" that no longer assume culture and place to be mutually contained. Rather, cultural phenomena may travel in curious ways, and we must follow them as we can. In order to glimpse the range of cultural engagements that shape debates about nature conservation in Sardinia, we must consider the dialogical play that takes place around the images and stories disseminated via mass communications media such as televisions, newspapers, magazines, and the Internet. Given the ongoing transformation and exponential growth of information and communications systems, new frontiers of human interaction and experience have opened up to progressively complicate the nature of the "places" where we choose to "ground" our fieldwork. The physical materiality of Sardinia, as I have known it, is not universally definitive of others' experiences. Technologically mediated encounters with Sardinia and Sardinians are available everywhere.[16] Increasingly, one wonders whether the "real" Sardinia is in fact the place that one can actually touch and smell and taste, or an island of images, fantasies, and desires suspended in a sea of electrons flowing ceaselessly across the World Wide Web. So much have our cherished Mediterranean landscapes been reduplicated and recolonized as expansive new virtual territories that the original seems to have diminished to a mere vestige (cf. Baudrillard 1983), irrelevant to policy decisions or international debates. How could I undertake ethnography with regard to one Sardinia, without considering its interdependence with the other? An experimental anthropological location in quixotic virtual Sardinia therefore both complements and complicates the "real Sardinia" of my fieldwork.

Dreamings, Nightmares, and Post-environmentalisms

In particular, I have been fascinated by visions of global society and the global commons portrayed in the websites associated with large ENGOs. These visual and narrative pieces make creative links between the local and the global, mediating the public understanding of cultural ecology in Sardinia. The fragments of environmental discourses produced here are not the ultimate objects of analysis, but rather the visible instruments and effects of ongoing hegemonic processes. Although the representations of Sardinian environmental issues found online cannot be taken as monolithic, they frequently come together in affirming the value of institutional, professional, scientific, technological, and "global" expertise. The tendency to privilege universal categories associated with ecology, civil society, and neoliberal governance is telling. These categories are defined and applied under the authority of relatively privileged cosmopolitan actors, and (falsely) appear to transcend mere cultural experience. They implicitly reify the subordinate status of local knowledge and those who embody cultural perspectives from the margins (cf. Herzfeld 2004).

Global approaches to ecology and environment constitute a strategic field of imagination within which social and political relations of power are negotiated and naturalized. I understand them collectively as "dreamtimes," a metaphor explained below.[17] The virtual landscapes of Sardinia that have now become so compelling exist in these global dreamtimes of environmentalism. They are the evocations of remembered and potential journeys through highly crafted spaces of transcendent imagination, spaces in which the signs of locality are remapped and transmuted into potent universals.

In the indigenous religious systems of Australia, the Dreamings are ancestral journeys that link people, place, and nature in Aboriginal deep time, or transcendant time, called the Dreamtime.[18] Powerful creation stories must be sung and enacted at sacred sites to retrace the paths of Dreaming ancestors; in this way, "songlines" map out landscapes and enfold them within living Aboriginal memory, identity, and experience. The songlines are not a seamless, monological narrative, but rather a cluttering of stories with similar epistemological roots. Despite their quality of "timelessness," of being rooted outside time, the songlines do not remain static. They are dynamically engaged with the meaningful current environmental, cultural, political, and economic contexts of Aboriginal life, in the ongoing remaking of the world. In this sense, they are "tellings" rather than overstructured and determined narratives. Even while they inscribe particular ways of being upon physical spaces, transforming them into places thickly textured with meaning and history, they remain potently open-ended and multi-vocal.

Anthropologists have long studied the role of the Dreamtimes in mediating Aboriginal relationships with non-human species and the environment.[19] Today, the cosmopolitans who undertake environmental campaigns deliberately seek to reorganize human-environment relations and reinscribe the sacredness of landscapes as a source of post/modern identity. Self-identified environmentalists, too, often look to the historic journeys of Henry David Thoreau, John Muir, Aldo Leopold, and others in their search for paradigmatic natural landscapes and the meanings they might yield for the contemporary world. In the Aboriginal Dreamtimes, emblematic non-human species or physical features of the landscape, sometimes called "totems,"[20] are believed to share kinship with particular human groups. The emergence of social movements and communities articulating ecological values, environmental philosophies, love of nature, and earth politics suggests a cultural project with strong elements of totemism. By suggesting this, I do not intend to equate all environmentalist practice with "new age" or "neo-primitivist" beliefs. Rather, there is evidence of an epistemological shift broadly associated with "environmentalism" that invokes a spiritual dimension in its orientation to the non-human world (cf. Sponsel 2001; Milton 2002). Access to this spiritual dimension is prominently referenced in environmentalist narratives of place. The idea of the global dreamtime makes explicit the ritual orientations, moral claims, and social and political identity constructions that are intrinsically associated with environmentalist narratives (even though these features cannot be considered unitary or identical across the wide range of social movements encompassed by the term "environmentalism"). The contemporary prominence of "cyborg" environmentalism, with its emphasis on global citizenship and online activism, suggests also the peculiar salience of new information and communication technologies to the enactment of "green" moralities.

Political sociologist Sheila Jasanoff (1999) has written about the "songlines of environmental risk" as an example of the cultural construction of environmental problems. Jasanoff understands that scientific debates are analogous to the songlines as "ways of constructing reality" (1999, 141). She uses the metaphor to highlight how cultural assumptions shape strategies used for environmental risk assessment, explaining that "judgments about the nature and severity of environmental risk inevitably incorporate tacit understandings concerning causality, agency, and uncertainty" (150). The argument that seemingly objective, quantitative interpretations of environmental risk are always embedded within specific social and cultural contexts takes us beyond an objectivist view of environmental science and its relationship to environmental advocacy. My discussion here both appreciates and explores beyond Jasanoff's analogy.[21] The dreamtime metaphor reminds us that the stories told by environmental advocates cannot be considered free of culture, history, class, religious sentiment, or real-world political contexts, although they may tend to obscure or efface some of these connections. Instead, we can recognize that globally oriented environmentalisms are largely rooted in Western, ethnocentric, Christian-influenced, modernist, liberal, and romantic inspirations (cf. Ingold 1993; Milton 1996; Argyrou 2005). I argue that we can understand the dreamtimes of environmentalism as a supple dimension of cultural imagination which overlays regional geographies with stories evoking the presence of a universal, sacred, transcendant, timeless, and global Nature—a Nature now increasingly at risk, apparently demanding new forms of reverence.

What the emerging global dreamtimes of environmentalism may mean for the life projects of indigenous peoples with very different conceptions of place remains problematic. In fact, the dreamtime metaphor is useful in underscoring the tendency of environmentalist narratives to borrow from and appropriate indigenous cultural forms. Cosmopolitan dreamtimes may well become the nightmares of indigenous peoples, as discourses of primordialism now reconstrue elements of "local" culture and place for the purposes of privileged, often urban-based, elites. At the same time, new technologies of visualization, information, and communication can engender new modalities of representing "otherness." In Sardinia, the global dreamtime of environmentalism is deeply implicated in the reproduction of ecological alterity. For this reason, it constitutes an object of critical discussion throughout the book, particularly in chapters 5 and 9. Yet global environmentalism itself still has a vitally important role to play in the critique of neoliberal models for unhampered economic growth. It also retains potential to support social justice, including indigenous sovereignties and other aspects of community development. In the spirit of enduring optimism, my own ethnographic witnessing and writing is situated within the context of auto-critique within this larger movement.

In the chapter to follow, I outline a theoretical framework for the book and reflect on the larger significance of the Sardinian case in a global context. Noting the problematic relationship of Sardinian identity vis-à-vis conventional models of indigeneity, I argue that the abject failure of Sardinian shepherds to embody naïve visions of tradition has delegitimized their communities' claims to authentic cultural authority over the environment. This highlights processes contributing to a larger, worldwide pattern of eroded indigenous sovereignty over landscapes and the epistemic erasure of indigenous knowledge and inhabitation of nature—a pattern that has developed despite the discourses of international organizations that appear to strongly support the role of native peoples in biodiversity conservation. My comparison of rural Sardinians to indigenous peoples is deliberately provocative, but not simplistic. It is true that Europe's pastoral groups, particularly transhumant herders like the Sarakatsani of Greece and the Saami in northern Europe, have occupied prominent places in the anthropological literature. This is precisely because they are typically identified as culturally distinct and historically rooted ethnic enclaves. As one reviewer suggested, such "transhumant indigenes" play the role of "Europe's Nuer." Yet Sardinians today, both as Europeans and as active participants in the "modern" world, occupy such an ambivalent space vis-à-vis conventional definitions of indigeneity that this case reveals the paradoxes embedded in representations of how cultural diversity underpins the conservation of biological diversity. The questions emerging from this quandary demonstrate the significance of Sardinia as a case study in environmental anthropology. At the same time, this work demonstrates the relevance of environmental anthropology to broader debates about nationalism, identity, aboriginality, and humanitarian discourse.

In the next three sections of this book, the interrelationships between themes of ecology, alterity, and resistance are discussed in relation to central Sardinia. The first section establishes a critical approach to political ecology by exploring the context of Orgosolo. Chapters 2 and 3 introduce cultural perspectives on the landscape and ecology of the Sardinian Supramonte, the high plains associated with a heritage of pastoral herding and religious life. Chapter 2 illustrates the way this landscape is seen through the lens of global environmentalism and the environmental sciences, in contrast to the ways that people in the community of Orgosolo understand their inherent engagement with the land. It highlights "social nature" as well as the impacts of the global dreamtimes of environmentalism, in the erasure of social inhabitation. Chapter 3 explores and complicates models of culture and environment by reflecting on how historically inflected senses of belonging to the Sardinian landscape have shaped reactions to initiatives to appropriate or transform the Orgosolo Commons. It draws on discussions of subjectivity and emotion that have been important in European ethnography to consider how local narratives about the landscape have been articulated. It also briefly introduces the theme of gender in relation to political practice.

The section on alterity illustrates how the story of Gennargentu Park is complicated by discourses of cultural essentialism. Chapter 4 explores historical objectifications of central Sardinia as a dark frontier: a culture of "otherness" that is characterized by violence and resistance. It documents how perceptions of cultural alterity in central Sardinia have informed economic and environmental policy in Italy, and how stereotypes of backwardness continue to be reified in media representations. In particular, it looks at a television documentary on kidnappings that broadcast "live" from Orgosolo in 1997. Chapter 5 carries forward the discussion of Sardinia as a dark frontier. It considers how visions of alterity are generated by processes of cultural translation associated with the work of both government agencies and non-governmental organizations in environmental governance. This chapter sketches a brief account of interactions between Orgosolo residents and the World Wide Fund for Nature (WWF), and looks at the WWF's representations of central Sardinian culture in its online campaigns to support the creation of parks and protected areas. Returning to consider the global dreamtimes of environmentalism, I argue that the "dreamings" of environmental experts and activists have contributed to "Oriental thinking" about Sardinia, with results that tend to undermine the life projects of Sardinians as well as projects of environmental conservation.

The third section undertakes the ethnography of so-called resistance to the state in Orgosolo, and to environmental initiatives in particular. Chapter 6 looks at the romanticizing of resistance ensuing from events in the late 1960s, accentuated by the legacy of Gramsci in Sardinia. The social memory of a demonstration against a NATO base on the Commons of Orgosolo shaped events that followed the ratification of legislation to create Gennargentu Park in April 1998. Chapter 7 illustrates how visions of authentic tradition, community, hospitality, and pastoral heritage were put into play to engage the projects of imagination related to global environmentalism. It presents an ethnographically informed case study of contemporary "resistance." It also complicates understandings of community by looking at the social divides that create tensions within Orgosolo. Finally, it reflects on the problem of hegemony by exploring the double-binds of resistance in relation to gender and occupational class.

The last section of this book explores critical perspectives on the global dreamtime of environmentalism in Sardinia. Introducing a gentle stylistic shift to intensify reflexivity, it looks for ways to transcend visions of ecological alterity and cultural essentialism, while taking account of specific contexts, conflicts, and problems in environmental management. Chapter 8 reconsiders my experience as an ethnographer with a conflicting sense of ethical obligation to projects of both environmentalism and cultural representation. Close attention to subjective voices suggests a firmer ground for cultural relativism by acknowledging rural Sardinians themselves as accomplished analysts in their own right. Focusing on local auto-critiques of contemporary ecological and political practice, I see evidence of revitalizing cultural knowledge and community in the efforts of local residents to respond to both social and structural violence. In chapter 9 I reflect on more recent fieldwork and consider policy shifts in Sardinian environmental governance, including the apparent loss of interest since 2004 in completing the institutional framework for Gennargentu Park. I evaluate trajectories of "ecological nationalism" in the context of neoliberal partnerships; these suggest ongoing conflicts over projects of landscape and identity in Sardinia. Finally, I relate these developments to the problematic global dreamtime of environmentalism and suggest alternative orientations for the future of environmental advocacy that anthropologists may support through their ethnographic writing.

This book is dedicated to the ongoing work of imagining new possibilities of environmental thinking for the twenty-first century. Nora

Haenn (2005), for example, suggests that we might best rethink the work of protected areas not through the rhetoric of sustainable development, but rather in terms of a "sustaining conservation." With her sensitive and ethnographically nuanced discussion of how we might look at issues of social justice and environmental governance associated with conservation and ecotourism at Mexico's Calakmul site, Haenn joins the call to reconceptualize the role of culturally rooted human communities in the protection of natural biological wealth. In this she echoes and develops the insight of authors such as the late Alexander Wilson, who insisted,

> We must build landscapes that heal, connect and empower, that make intelligible our relations with each other and with the natural world: places that welcome and enclose, whose breaks and edges are never without meaning. Nature parks cannot do this work. We urgently need people living on the land, caring for it, working out an idea of nature that includes human culture and human livelihood. All of that calls for a new culture of nature, and it cannot come soon enough. (Wilson 1991, 17)

To do this, it is crucial that we learn to reinvent environmentalism through richer, more respectful dialogues with indigenous and local cultures. I frame this as a fundamental move toward "post-environmentalisms" that might ultimately heal, enrich, and empower the global dreamtimes. In contrast to the conflicted moral legacy of naïve multiculturalism embedded in the global dreamtimes today, I understand "post-environmentalisms" as a path of optimism that might be followed, if we can find ways to support positive interactions among deeply rooted cultural perspectives, environmental science, and visions of global environmentalism. To do so requires the recognition of vital indigenous legacies in the dynamic cultural forms we often find to be deeply enmeshed in the global culture, economy, and political world today. At the same time, it means exercising humility and critical self-reflection on behalf of the environmental movements in which we participate. This can only be achieved if we can overcome the dark legacy of ecological alterity and encounter indigenous life projects on respectful terms. Fundamentally, I contend that the people involved at the heart of conservation projects should be viewed not as subordinate "participants" or "stakeholders," but rather as the intellectual and creative equals of technical personnel, researchers, or scientific experts. The deliberate craft of ethnographic writing is engaged here to reframe the "nature" of indigeneity as an open-ended story, to be told and retold from the bottom up.

Chapter 1

Ecology, Alterity, and Resistance

Sea and Sardinia

When we came up, the faint shape of land appeared ahead, more transparent than thin pearl. Already Sardinia. Magic are high lands seen from the sea, when they are far, far off, and ghostly translucent like ice-bergs. This was Sardinia, looming like fascinating shadows in mid-sea. (Lawrence 2002, 48)

And suddenly there is Cagliari: a naked town rising steep, steep, golden-looking, piled naked to the sky from the plain at the head of the formless hollow bay. It is strange and rather wonderful, not a bit like Italy. The city piles up lofty and almost miniature, and makes me think of Jerusalem: without trees, without cover, rising rather bare and proud, remote as if back in history, like a town in a monkish, illuminated missal. . . . The air is cold, blowing bleak and bitter, the sky is all curd. And that is Cagliari. It has that curious look, as if it could be seen, but not entered. It is like some vision, some memory, something that has passed away. (53)

Strange, stony Cagliari. We climbed up a street like a corkscrew stair-way. . . . Down below is the little circle of the harbour. To the left a low, malarial-looking sea plain, with tufts of palm trees and Arab-looking houses. From this runs out the long spit of land towards that black-and-white watch-fort, the white road trailing forth. On the right, most curiously, a long strange spit of sand runs in a causeway far across the shallows of the bay, with the open sea on one hand, and vast, end-of-the-world lagoons on the other. There are peaky, dark mountains beyond this—just as across the vast bay are gloomy hills. It is a strange, strange landscape: as if here the world left off. (56–57)

But it still reminds me of Malta: lost between Europe and Africa and belonging to nowhere. Belonging to nowhere, never having belonged to anywhere. To Spain and the Arabs and the Phoenicians most. But as if it had never really had a fate. No fate. Left outside of time and history. (57)

In the famous travel diaries of D. H. Lawrence, recording the British author's sea voyage to Sardinia and journey across it in 1921, we are introduced to an orientalist vision of cultural difference (cf. Said 1978).[1] Lawrence's candid, quasi-ethnographic account of conversations, travails, and wonders along the way reveals his own culturally based assumptions about civilization and backwardness. His evocative descriptions denied the movement of Sardinian history and located the island and its people in the past, or even beyond time. Indeed, some Sardinians seemed to him to look like "esquimos" (Lawrence 2002, 57). Lawrence essentialized Sardinian culture as bound to "the spirit of place" (57), and he saw around him a harsh, mysterious, deeply strange, and ultimately unknowable landscape. Perhaps in compensation for unhomely discomforts suffered on the trip, he could not resist the temptation to exoticize and eroticize the setting. He imagined the capital city, Cagliari, to be rising up naked against the coastline. His gaze rested admiringly upon "the full-petticoated peasant woman" with a tight bodice, moving "bird-like" through the streets (66).[2]

When Lawrence embarked with his wife upon the journey north overland into highland central Sardinia, on their way to the smaller city of Nuoro, his metaphors of distance, wildness, and isolation became even more accentuated.

Wild, narrow valleys, with trees, and brown-legged cork-trees. Across the other side a black-and-white peasant is working alone on a tiny terrace of the hill-side, a small, solitary figure, for all the world like a magpie in the distance. These people like being alone — solitary — one sees a single creature so often isolated among the wilds. (122)

Whenever we come to a village we stop and get down, and our little conductor disappears into the post-office for the post-bag. This is usually a limp affair, containing about three letters. The people crowd round — and many of them in very ragged costume. They look poor, and not attractive: perhaps a bit degenerate. . . . For in these villages that have been isolated since time began from any life-centre, there is an almost sordid look on the faces of the people. We must remember that the motor-bus is a great innovation. It has been running for five weeks only. (122)

Lawrence gives us an outsider's perspective on early twentieth-century Sardinia. His account has the grace of detailed observation and thoughtful curiosity. It displays a rueful self-awareness from time to time, but yet little understanding of the author's own fundamental cultural bias. While I am neither the first nor the last ethnographer to remark upon this, I do have a particular purpose in using an early twentieth-century English literary figure to frame and complicate the romantic landscape narratives later associated with global environmentalism in Sardinia. The author's poetic vision of the island introduces us to the theme of "alterity," sometimes glossed as "otherness," that is, the perception of innate cultural difference.

To D. H. Lawrence, Sardinia and Sardinians seemed profoundly distant and different from the modern Europe of his day, and conditioned by conventional thinking, he looked for the source of this deep alterity in the Mediterranean Sea itself.[3] Iain Chambers (2008, 12) tells us that "the contemporary theatre of European power" had been crucial to the framing of the Mediterranean as an object of study during the nineteenth century. The gendered, eroticized ethnocentrism of Lawrence's gaze reflects the hegemonic structures that sustained colonial power relations. By this time, the science and literature of Western Europe had already naturalized a model of unilineal social and cultural evolution. The place of any given culture along an idealized path of progress was thought to be partially determined by relations with the natural environment. Over the course of the twentieth century, such ideas were widely criticized and rejected, yet by then they had become so deeply ingrained in the logic of European nation-building, in Western literary genres, in a burgeoning international tourist industry, and in the environmental imagination, that they could not be easily purged.[4] Narratives like that of D. H. Lawrence have stayed with us, shaping common misperceptions of Sardinia as an isolated wilderness frontier, rising out of the sea like a figment of the past.

This chapter pursues the intertwined themes of ecology, alterity, and resistance as a means of setting Sardinian ethnography into comparative context. It begins with an examination of environmental conservation initiatives for the region of the Mediterranean Sea. Like the Amazon River basin or the coastal zones of the South Pacific, the Mediterranean Sea is a salient icon to both natural and human history. The island of Sardinia is found at the heart of a region whose natural biological heritage is recognized to be of immense global value and concern. The design and legitimacy of frameworks for conservation in the Mediterranean today are based in studies of scientific ecology. Yet ecological science is, like other enterprises in the production of knowledge, bound up with the zeitgeist of our time (Kuhn 1971). In a neoliberal era, conservation initiatives are based upon fluid assemblages of institutions and organizations, financing, and contingent cultural constructions, including narratives of ecological science and advocacy. This chapter and the section to follow emphasize the problems inherent in the idea of "ecology" as uncomplicated, transcendent, objective knowledge about the environment. Rather, the production of discourses about ecology is understood to be part of political processes deeply intertwined with rooted dialogues about modernity, tradition, and essentialized culture in specific nations and regions. The Euro-Mediterranean context is evocative and contributes to an evolving cultural critique of conservation.

The issue of resistance is examined as a problem in environmental governance. Just as "ecology" is often mistaken for a natural fact, so "resistance" to the state in marginal areas is often taken for granted as a social fact. In contrast to a number of case studies that emerged during the 1980s and 1990s, my work in central Sardinia demonstrates that "resistance" cannot be assessed as a simple descriptive type. The category itself has been reproduced and naturalized through a series of contingent cultural discourses that proceed in parallel and intertwined with the discourses of ecology and environmentalism. This leads us to challenge conventional assumptions about why Sardinians have raised so-called resistance to ecodevelopment projects such as the creation of Gennargentu Park. A theoretical discussion of resistance is further developed through an analysis of recent Sardinian ethnography in section 3 of the book. In the present chapter, I explain the basis of an approach that considers resistance as an object of ideology and cultural imagination that has been mutually engaged with social practice and political life in Sardinia.

Finally, I consider how potent representations of difference in culture and society continue to shape environmental governance even in Western "First World" settings. The descriptions of Sardinia's cultural otherness by D. H. Lawrence, for example, shared many elements with policy discourses of the day, and even with narratives of environmental advocacy that were to come much later. Historical writings that essentialized various aspects of Sardinian cultural identity will be examined in detail in the section dealing with the theme of alterity. Before going on to this, however, some comparative framing is useful. In this chapter, I attempt to show how processes similar to the cultural politics of indigeneity found in many "Third World" or post-colonial settings in fact mediate the relationship of rural central Sardinia with metropolitan centers in Cagliari, Rome, and even Brussels or Paris.

Frameworks for Conservation in the Mediterranean

Mediterranean ecosystems have been placed recently among the priority "hotspots" or "ecoregions" for biodiversity conservation by two of the world's largest environmental non-governmental organizations.[5] The distinctiveness and importance of Mediterranean ecosystems have been well established by now. The terrestrial Mediterranean region includes areas of southern Europe, northern Africa, the western Near East, and Asia Minor. According to the World Wide Fund for Nature (WWF), Mediterranean forests, woodlands, and scrub host more than 25,000 species of plants, more than half of which are endemic to the area. A set of common plants in this region is known collectively as Mediterranean macquis, or in Italian, *macchia*, characterized by evergreen shrubs and oak trees. Each year, between 600,000 and 800,000 hectares of Mediterranean forest and scrub are damaged by fires, which are caused by human negligence or arson.[6] In addition, these ecological systems have sustained impacts from agricultural and extractive activities, tourism, and economic development, particularly over the past forty years. A WWF online information site states, "most large mammals within the region are considered endangered."[7] The Mediterranean Sea itself has a significant number of habitats and species and is considered as a whole to be biologically distinctive from the adjacent Atlantic Ocean.[8] Rocky reefs and seagrass meadows, for example, support fish, crustaceans, and marine turtles. A number of the sea grasses that stabilize marine ecosystems in the Mediterranean are considered endangered. Sea mammals and sea birds also depend upon these coastal habitats. Industrial pollution and sewage effluents, tourism, and coastal development are understood to threaten the integrity of aquatic ecosystems in the Mediterranean region.

Environmental disasters, like the oil spill off the Lebanese coast near Beirut after an Israeli air attack in July 2006, have occasionally dramatized the vulnerability of biological diversity in the Mediterranean. About 15,000 tons of oil spilled when fuel tanks were bombarded at a power plant south of Beirut; when the oil drifted northward, about 150 kilometers of seaside were contaminated, including beaches, rocky shores, and seabed. This presented significant risks to loggerhead turtles, monk seals, seabirds, and fish stocks, among other species. It was clear that threats to biodiversity as well as human health crossed the boundaries between nation-states and called for urgent international cooperation. The European Union acted in this case to provide emergency technical assistance for environmental remediation. The United Nations Environment Programme recognized the need to collaborate on the protection of environmental resources in the Mediterranean Sea as early as 1976, when it launched its Mediterranean Action Programme (referred to below as UNEP/MAP). After two decades of sporadic progress, initiatives to encourage European and pan-Mediterranean collaboration on environmental problems in the region began to gain ground. A Euro-Mediterranean partnership launched in 1995 has increasingly looked to the importance of sustainability issues.[9] Euro-Mediterranean Ministerial Conferences on the Environment were held in 1997 and 2002. Between 1995 and 2004, the European Investment Bank provided approximately 2.6 billion Euros for environmental projects in the Mediterranean. In 2004, the Convention for the Protection of the Marine Environment and the Coastal Region of the Mediterranean entered into force, building on collaboration with UNEP/MAP.

When member countries met in 2005 to renew their commitment to the Euro-Mediterranean Partnership, they agreed on a series of goals and a timetable outlined as "Horizon 2020." The first five-year plan aims to reduce major sources of pollution in the Mediterranean Sea, including municipal waste, urban wastewater, and industrial effluents.

Both the World Bank and the European Investment Bank made major financial commitments to support the Horizon 2020 initiative. Europe's investments are made under the auspices of its Mediterranean European Technical Assistance Program (METAP). METAP was responsible for activating and funding Europe's emergency assistance to Lebanon after the oil spill in July 2006. Shortly after that, in September 2006, the European Commission published a communication to the European Council and European Parliament reaffirming the need for an integrated and cohesive "Environment Strategy for the Mediterranean," citing both the economic costs of forecasted trends in environmental degradation and the potential for environmental health hazards. In November 2006, the third Euro-Mediterranean Ministerial Conference on the Environment committed to implement a Mediterranean Strategy for Sustainable Development (MSSD) outlined under the auspices of UNEP/MAP. The Cairo Declaration emerging from this meeting looked to partnerships among governmental bodies, non-governmental organizations, international financial institutions, bilateral donors, and the business sector to meet the commitments of Horizon 2020.

Over the course of such continual high-level conferences, meetings, communications, declarations, agreements, regulations, and initiatives, there has emerged a series of what anthropologists have referred to as "global assemblages" (Collier and Ong 2005).[10] Geographer Bruce Braun has recognized in this idea an important possible approach to the study of environmental issues in relation to processes of neoliberal globalization. According to him,

> Nature, as is now commonly asserted, is inextricably social. . . . Likewise, the "global" is an effect not a condition, and uneven rather than uniform, perhaps best understood in terms of specific connections and encounters that work across and through difference. . . . Global natures are always specific: this configuration here, that network there. Nor do I imagine a global scale that pre-exists its construction. (Braun 2006, 644)

Common abstractions about both global and Mediterranean biodiversity, then, can be understood as the outcome of such specific connections and encounters. Within the shifting assemblages represented by the policy instruments, financing structures, modes of collaboration, and the somewhat convergent discourses of UNEP and the European Commission since 1992, some assumptions and priorities are privileged over those that fail to convincingly portray themselves as linked to "global" or progressive orientations (cf. Gupta and Ferguson 2002). Models of governance increasingly emphasize the power and legitimacy of "free market" enterprise as the cornerstone of socioeconomic development, while civil society itself takes shape as non-governmental organizations (NGOs) that must function in enterprise-like fashion. The ambiguous, business-friendly language of "partnerships" facilitates a blurring of boundaries between public and private, governmental and non-governmental. The partnerships envisioned for environmental protection and governance in the Mediterranean both reify and reproduce visions of the global, as they include inherently transnational corporate actors and organizations in the design and implementation of regional initiatives.

An example of this is LIFE-NATURE financing in Europe. The LIFE-NATURE 98 program was launched to support the European Union's Natura 2000 initiative, concerned with the guardianship of biodiversity and habitats, principally through the creation and management of parks and protected areas. The program gives a prominent role to partnerships with NGOs in conservation management, and the WWF was involved in a number of co-management schemes in the first phases of funding, including a project to support the implementation of legislation creating Gennargentu Park. In 2005, the Association of Italian Provinces (UPI) signed an "alliance" with the WWF, so that the NGO would play an active role in implementing a joint vision for "eco-regional conservation." By adopting the WWF's interpretation of current ecological science, Italian governmental bodies acquire the legitimacy of an ostensibly global, scientific, and civil-society-based orientation to ecosystem management. Simultaneously, they draw attention to natural resources attractive to investors in a new era of eco-development and satisfy the pride of Italian nationals. Environmental priorities in Italy now focus on two different eco-regions, the Alps and the Mediterranean. Sardinia will continue to be a focus for biodiversity conservation with regard to the Mediterranean eco-region.

Discourses of environmental governance, from qualitative descriptions to measurements, map-making, and data flows exchanging monitoring information, are presented as objective scientific assessments and rational planning for conservation and development. Yet the continuing assembly of institutional partnerships, legitimate knowledge, funding priorities, and implementation strategies for environmental governance is also a form of cultural production. Scientists, planners, entrepreneurs, activists, and technical personnel with recognized expertise now mediate new models of environmental governance in the Mediterranean. A class of professional environmental experts is emerging to articulate and sanction the technical and moral discourses that both obscure and legitimate the political ecology of power. This process is foreseen in Antonio Gramsci's (1971) famous notion of "organic intellectuals," the embedded cadre of intelligentsia that would grow up in service of any substantially new political-economic formation. Gramsci's description of such classes offers enough slippage to support both individual and collective agency; they may help produce hegemonies, and they may themselves struggle against them. Gramsci himself was a disadvantaged child of rural Sardinia, whose struggles—to obtain an education and play a role in Italian political transformation—were never scripted. He became a notorious political dissident, whose life work was later honored by compatriots and Marxists abroad. If other Sardinians from rural zones have now become ecotourism operators and forest rangers, partners in environmental initiatives and governance strategies, might they not also act to challenge the hegemonic structures that marginalize rural Sardinians?

Yet here the subtly entrenched divide between urban and rural plays a role, and not even Gramsci could throw off an enduring distaste for the agrarian values and aesthetics that shaped his childhood, although his critical work on the politics of southern Italian development recognized the cycle of subaltern reproduction. Even a hundred years ago, cosmopolitan expectations intruded upon the periphery to keep rude locals—including leaders and intellectuals—in their (subordinate) place, and ethnicize the politics of resistance. The socialization of intellectuals in itself cultivated a disdainful distance from the mundane brutality, aggression, and ignorance thought to inhere in peasant life. How much more so do the cultural artifacts of global sensibility intrude upon local worlds today, given the ubiquity of mass media technologies and institutional presences? Drawing upon Gramsci's work to explore the globalization of a neoliberal value system, Michael Herzfeld points out,

"Notions such as efficiency, fair play, civility, civil society, human rights, transparency, cooperation, and tolerance serve as global yardsticks for particular patterns of interaction" (2004, 2). Hegemony, he says, is suggested in the unmarked backdrop of categories whose contingent origin is hidden. Against the vast neutral background of modernity, local worlds bloom too indelicately. Local traditions may define some quaint and prosperous niches in modern society, but those who enact them must play out the roles assigned to living ethnic stereotypes, and risk indignity lest they embody them too well.[11]

We might also add a commitment to nature protection and even cultural diversity to this list of standards now taken to define pan-human progress. The hegemony of neoliberal expectation is ever more inscribed in the global dreamtimes of environmentalism. Hegemony is engendered in the "common sense" that we need global information, organization, and action on all our environmental problems. Hegemony is produced in the unreflective appeal to "the environment" as a universal value, and in the unsubtle equation of indigeneity with primitive nature. Hegemony is evident in the voice of shame that judges one's own failure of cultural authenticity by Western archetypes, as it is also in the voice of bravado that denies that failure by virtue of performances calculated to indulge those very fantasies. Acts of "resistance" may strain against the cooptation of local identity yet assist the hegemonic process that transforms them into evidence of brutish incomprehension. Let us not, then, take the power and hegemony associated with environmental governance too lightly, nor assume we truly perceive the "nature" of resistance in Mediterranean Europe.

Resistance

Most Sardinians I met were thoughtfully critical of "ecodevelopment" that painted a rosy picture of social impacts associated with efforts at environmental conservation. They were not unique in their suspicions of the politicians, bureaucrats, and environmental advocates who promote the management of natural resources through the institution of national parks. In Greece, Portugal, and Latvia, similar tensions have unfolded between relatively poor fishermen, farmers, or herders and "environmentalists" who wish to see wild species and habitats managed by experts (Theodossopoulos 2003; Neves-Graca 2004; Krauss 2005; Schwartz 2006). Conflicts have emerged over the making and management of parks around the world, from Tanzania,[12] for example, to Malaysia (Doolittle 2005) and Mexico (Haenn 2005). Some scholars have linked such conflicts with patterns of resistance to "the enclosure of the commons" (see Goldman 1998; Neumann 2004). Yet social movements that mobilize resistance to conservation policies in particular contexts are not activated by economic or material interests alone; rather, they encompass complex social histories, and are often tied to broader challenges to systems of power, privilege, and prejudice that are embedded in the structures and discourses of nation-states (Moore 1998, 1999). They motivate us to question how national parks actually work in the production and reproduction of power relations, and at the same time, to consider how acts of "resistance" to conservation initiatives are both conditioned by and implicated within that very process (see Agrawal 2005; Cederlöf and Sivaramakrishnan 2006).

Following Sherry Ortner (1995), I undertake an ethnographic project here that eschews assumptions about the nature of resistance in favor of empirical research. This book describes how a cultural politics of "resistance" related to environmental conservation has emerged since the 1960s on the island of Sardinia. Understandings of "resistance" as a cultural phenomenon often imply an essentialist approach to collective action. James C. Scott's (1985) classic work on "everyday forms of resistance" assumed relatively homogeneous cultural dispositions associated with community and class, and did not question the ways that subjectivity and experience may shape social action within a complex nation-state. In contrast, my approach to the problem takes seriously the ways that gender and historicity, for example, mediate political subjectivity in a marginal area of southern Europe. Here I am able to take advantage of a rich vein of ethnographic study distinctive to southern Europe. This has interrogated the role of embodiment and the senses in identity practices as well as the ambiguous mischief of resistance.

The optimism of apparently "community-based" projects in ecodevelopment—that now imperfectly overwrite many older plans for centralized, large-scale, highly protectionist nature conservation—tends to obscure the enduring disjuncture between dominant models of environmental governance and views of resource issues "from the bottom up"

(Brechin et al. 2003; see also West et al. 2006). Given this, it is tempting to frame the debate over Gennargentu Park as a straightforward contrast between those who attempt to use scientific ecology to render natural resources and land use more amenable to centralized governance, and those who deploy various forms of resistance against top-down schemes for development (see Scott 1985, 1991, 1998). This simple tale of power and resistance becomes more uncertain, however, if we use ethnographic evidence to survey the ambiguous array of institutions, people, and moral discourses implicated in environmental governance today.[13] On one hand, a diverse array of clientelist networks, public-private partnerships, and mediators complicates all attempts to define "the state" as clearly distinct from "local" interests. On the other, the idea of resistance is itself socially produced.

Sardinian scholars and earlier ethnographers have highlighted the forms of resistance practiced by rural Sardinians in response to foreign rule. Over its long history as a strategic point in the Mediterranean, the island of Sardinia was subject to colonization by the Carthaginians, the Romans, the Byzantines, the Spanish, Piedmontese, and Genoans, with a brief period of independence in medieval times. While the economic and development goals of external powers have contextualized most of Sardinia's historical development, particularly during the modern period,[14] the presumed links between pastoral heritage, banditry, and resistance in central Sardinia are celebrated in romantic narratives of ethnonationalism.[15] On the island that was once the home of political dissident and writer Antonio Gramsci, theories of resistance have acquired a social life of their own (cf. Appadurai 1988). In my research site, the Marxist legacies of Gramsci (1971, 1995), as well as Italian anthropologist Franco Cagnetta (1954) and prominent historian Eric Hobsbawm (1959), informed daily conversations in the bar as well as grassroots critiques of conservation. Ideas about resistance as an innate aspect of Sardinian culture were constantly reiterated and reproduced in emergent contexts.

To recognize that resistance is socially constructed does not deny that social practices of resistance may be discovered, but it does require a self-reflexive effort to reject a priori assumptions and explanations about them. In Sardinia, Nuoro province has long been associated with relatively high rates of theft, homicide, and banditry. Forces of order have also been concerned about recent patterns of bombings, kidnappings, and anthropogenic forest fires in this area.[16] A study analyzing the period 2000-2004 (Mazzette 2006, xli–xlii) reports no evidence of organized, mafia-style criminal activity in Sardinia, currently or in the past. Nor does it find conclusive correlations between socioeconomic deprivation and criminal phenomena. Instead, it suggests that patterns of criminal statistics in north-central Sardinia appear linked to questions of control over territory. For example, recent administrative reorganizations have vested increasing authority over natural resources in the hands of state agencies, and this phenomenon can be correlated with increased signs of tension and criminality. This finding provides an important context for the discussions to follow. As I explain in chapter 3, earlier attempts to theorize central Sardinian criminality have sometimes equated transgressive activities with an unreflexive, culturally based resistance against the state. Studies of criminality have contributed to the troubling public perception that the rural, highland areas of Sardinia where herding traditions remain important are not only rather distinct from other areas of the island—not to mention Italy and Europe as a whole—they are also definitively exotic, perplexingly backward, and inherently dangerous. Although Sardinian nationalists romanticize the resistance of legendary Nuorese bandits, contemporary outlaws are more likely to be seen as simply violent and deviant. Each time opposition to government-sponsored ecodevelopment projects has catalyzed, the diffuse perception of cultural otherness in highland central Sardinia has cast a particular light on environmental politics and governance, discrediting that opposition as a reasonable democratic response.

Alterity and the European Imagination

One important way that we can contextualize the study of political ecology is through critical attention to ongoing discussions about cultural identity and the "nature" of differences that are perceived to mark minority populations.[17] A maelstrom of claims about cultural traditions, authenticities, and innate bio-cultural differences come into play, as authoritative and interested actors present their interpretations of environmental issues. Donald S. Moore, Jake Kosek, and Anand Pandian (2003, 16) have argued that there are always both material and symbolic aspects to struggles over resources and territory. They recognize the importance of critical literature on environmental justice that attempts to map out race-based inequities in the distribution of both access to resources and exposure to environmental health risks.[18] They suggest, however, that "race" and "nature" cannot be taken for granted as objective categories in themselves, because their linked ideological production is integral to the cultural process through which such modern power relations have been — and continue to be — constituted. During the colonial period, scientific scholarship concerned with the classification of species, on the one hand, and the orderly classification of human cultures, on the other, linked models of race with ideas about the evolutionary progress of civilizations. In this way, "discourses of savagery and barbarism . . . often defined normative European humanity in relation to an imagined 'constitutive outside' that located racialized alterity in bodies and landscapes at once wild, uncultivated, and prehistorical" (ibid., 12). In areas of the world that became subject to colonial rule and occupation, ethnocentric perceptions of primeval nature, primitive culture, and racial inferiority informed the systematic displacement and dispossession of local peoples by Europeans.

Cases from the Amazonian Oriente supply dramatic examples. Candace Slater (2003) has given a nuanced account of the cultural construction of visions of the Brazilian Amazon, and how these were intertwined with strategies for resource extraction, control of labor, and repression of native insurrection in the New World. In the sixteenth century, legends of the golden city of El Dorado reported by Europeans magnified their ideas of "spectacular natural riches, mystery and elusiveness" (ibid., 40) associated with the Amazon. Images of El Dorado motivated colonial explorations for gold and later infused the writings of nineteenth-century naturalists. Similarly, ideas about the unfamiliarity, immensity, and dangerousness of the New World became crystallized in accounts of barbaric, giant warrior women they called Amazons (ibid., 86) and the vast, uncharted, and hostile landscapes they were said to inhabit. Slater suggests that the Amazons and their jungle home — represented as both "virgin forests" and "green hells" — became iconic images that would endure in visions of a hostile and feminized wilderness. This ultimately contributed to Brazilian government projects to open, tame, and modernize the Amazonian interior, with little or no regard for the impacts on remaining tribal communities. Today, Slater explains, the image of the Amazonian rainforest is magnified in the global discourses of environmental protection, and memories of El Dorado persist in the visions of rich genetic biodiversity that drive contemporary bio-prospecting quests.

Hugh Raffles's (2002) provocative rethinking of "natural history" in the Brazilian Amazon underscores the thoroughly anthropogenic character of the "wilderness" and "biodiversity" that can be found there. This exposes the fault lines embedded in environmentalist narratives that have typically presented history, biology, ecology, and culture as uncomplicated objects of knowledge and advocacy. During the 1980s and 1990s, the images of Kayapo Indians and Brazilian rubber tappers became iconic of traditional environmental knowledge. These images were presented largely in positive light by the environmentalists who perceived them as allies in the fight against logging, oil extraction, and other activities that would wreak ecological havoc on their rainforest homes. These images depended, nevertheless, upon the reification and essentialism of traditional culture, which amplified the presumed divide between an industrialized, capitalist "Western" heritage, and innocent, isolated, subsistence-oriented indigenous cultures. Paradoxically, the intellectual agency inherent in the complex ecological adaptations of rainforest communities was often undermined by visual representations of childlike simplicity and purity. Particularly in documentaries about the Amazon,[19] the people of the rainforest were often portrayed as the product of their environment, rather than reciprocally shaping and shaped by it. The exotic appearance of Brazilian native dress (and perceived nudity) contributed to a visual "thinning" or obscuring of colonial and postcolonial experience, and a parallel magnification of apparent primitiveness. Historical visions of cultural "otherness" in the Brazilian rainforest have not only shaped ongoing dialogues over conservation policy in the Amazon, but also visions of authenticity, tradition, and indigeneity that drive global dialogues about our environmental past and future (cf. Conklin and Graham 1995).

While historical discourses of alterity now seem obvious in the context of iconic landscapes in the New World, as in other colonial outposts in Africa or "the Orient," they are no less abundant within Europe itself. In the taxonomy of species created by the Swedish naturalist Linnaeus in 1753, "wild men" in the margins of Europe were considered to share some innately inferior characteristics with indigenous counterparts elsewhere (Moore et al. 2003, 12). Linnaeus drew upon images of Native American, Inuit, Indian, and West African peoples to describe the "Saami savage" he encountered during his travels in rural Lapland. Michael Herzfeld[20] has pointed out that the "scientific" typologies of culture devised by nineteenth-century anthropologists E. B. Tylor and J. G. Frazer compared European folk practices to exotic practices from other areas of the world, and from ancient civilizations.

> European peasants appeared to validate the survivalist thesis in two complementary ways: first, by demonstrating the persistence of traits from the childhood of the human race even in the most civilized countries; and second, by showing that only the intellectual independence of the educated classes could achieve final escape from the burden of superstition and ignorance. This created a double hierarchy: the European intellectual emerged as the peasant's superior; but the European peasant claimed pride of place over all exotic peoples. (Herzfeld 1987a, 10)

European cultural geography was not conceptualized as homogeneous; rather, internal divides based on perceived differences between people in urban and rural areas, east and west, north and south, were part of a global geography of difference grounded in related concepts of race, culture, and environment (cf. Harvey 1996). Iain Chambers suggests that the Mediterranean acquired a resonant marginality in this emerging cultural schema. From Napoleonic expeditions in Egypt to perceptions of a declining Ottoman empire, the idea of the Mediterranean as a boundary object of Europe took shape.

> In this history the Mediterranean comes to be suspended in a net woven by the objectification of alterity and the civilizing mission with which modern, "progressive" Europe has taken possession of the rest of the world. Within this frame the Mediterranean is transformed into an aesthetic and cultural measure: Its very "backwardness" and difference hold up to modern Europe the mirror of a lost world of antiquity, uncontaminated nature, and pristine "origins." (Chambers 2008, 12–13)

The vivid metaphors of D. H. Lawrence quoted earlier in this chapter show how Sardinia became evocative of the Mediterranean imaginary. The second section of this book examines past scientific studies linking biology, economy, and criminality in Sardinia. As earlier perceptions of identity and alterity in Sardinia are thrown into relief, it is possible to interrogate the cultural representations that reify central Sardinian towns as surviving examples of a backwardly traditional "culture of resistance" or "culture of violence." A more nuanced, anthropologically informed understanding of Sardinian identity requires broader insight into the daily practices, aesthetics, aspirations, critical reflections, and life experiences that shape creolized and heterogeneous subjectivities in the area. This perspective suggests the need to reflect back upon how national and global concerns about biodiversity and habitat conservation are often entangled with discourses that essentialize cultural alterity and reinscribe cultural racisms. Discourses about environmental governance in a European context often parallel the discourses of racism and cultural alterity that are deeply embedded in debates about immigration and ethnic minorities in European nation-states (cf. Cole 1998; Holmes 2000).

Ecology and the Nation-State

There are considerable stakes involved for nation-states in the linked representation of race, culture, nature, environment, and history. A variety of "ecological nationalisms" (Cederlöf and Sivaramakrishnan 2006) rest upon visions of deep national links to nature, place, and territory. Governmental and bureaucratic discourses often depict environmental governance as the moral monopoly of nation-states, serving the public interests of modern citizens, and celebrating distinctive national landscapes. These dominant ecological nationalisms appropriate the symbolic capital of particular indigenous and regional minorities to buttress the sovereignty of nation-states. Particular regional and local histories of cultural inhabitation are thus erased by official discourses, as we saw in many of the cases reviewed above.

Cosmopolitan-secular ecological nationalism actively weds the self-conscious newness of the modern nation to the antiquity of its lands by arguing for the nation-state, for its leaders as the repository of all the wisdom needed to hold an ancient heritage within a beneficial relationship of service to the new citizenry. (ibid., 8)

Not for nothing were the first national parks of Italy created during the 1920s and 1930s, under the aegis of fascist modernism. Italian initiatives for the institution of parks proved less successful under the democratic state, until just before European unification, when rhetoric of environmental sustainability began to proliferate in the context of extensive political and economic restructuring. Paradoxically, representations of national landscapes and nature were never more significant to political identity construction than at the end of the twentieth century, in the age of apparent deterritorialization. As nation-states sought to reconsolidate and enhance their legitimate sovereignty within a new world order, landscapes remained a premier site for the negotiation of identity at all levels. The European case suggests that a growing convergence of regional, national, and post-national representations of nature and environment underpins the rearticulation of political units with emerging neoliberal frameworks of authority. How this process has unfolded in Sardinia is part of what I describe in the chapters to follow. Here, romantic visions of Sardinian identity find roots in the harsh, beautiful mountains and high plains where indigenous islanders sought relative safety and independence from the various intruders and conquerors who landed upon their shores again and again. Rural townspeople in central Sardinia are typically proud of this history, but the imageries associated with it have been largely co-opted to serve the identity-making practices of the Region of Sardinia, not least of all in its promotional tourism campaigns. As legitimate control over traditional communal lands was disputed for the purposes of creating a system of parks and reserves, the authenticity and sustainability of pastoral traditions still practiced in highland Sardinia emerged as a focus of debate.

Reinventing Alterity

As ideas about ethnic and racial difference are increasingly glossed in terms of cultural difference, understandings of alterity are reinvented and "naturalized" through new discursive formations. The continuing racialization and exoticization of indigenous identities in relation to recent debates about the role of indigenous nations/cultures in biodiversity management should concern advocates of environmental justice. Mainstream cultural discourses about indigenous identities, even when benevolently intended, are typically fraught with double-binds that allow conventional power relationships to be enacted. Speaking to the Australian context, Elizabeth Povinelli (2002) argues that the liberal dream of multiculturalism is inherently shot through with paternalisms and encroachments on Aboriginal (indigenous) identity. The trouble with mainstream liberal admonitions to cultural tolerance, she says, is that in the face of "intractable social difference," white liberals themselves ultimately cannot put aside their own cultural values.

> They encounter instances of what they experience as moments of fundamental and uncanny alterity: encounters with differences they consider abhorrent, inhuman, and bestial, or with differences they consider too hauntingly similar to themselves to warrant social entitlements—for example, land claims by indigenous people who dress, act, and sound like the suburban neighbors they are. Moments in which subjects are prompted to calibrate the forms and modes of difference confronting them occur in large and small scales, in political and intimate settings. . . . They mark the site where indigenous persons struggle to inhabit the tensions and torsions of competing incitements to be and identify differentially. (Povinelli 2002, 13)

Australian Aboriginals cannot simply step outside the institutional and cultural setting of the nation-state, including naïve visions of multiculturalism, as they construe meaningful experience and enact their own senses of identity. Povinelli argues that to support marginalized minorities, we should acknowledge the power-laden contexts that frame strategic efforts toward both self-making and the fulfillment of material needs. If we can put aside expectations that indigenous peoples should behave according to predetermined stereotypes of innocent precolonial "others," we can go further and more sincerely along the path to real cultural recognition.[21]

Global and national discourses on biodiversity and culture reinscribe the liberal dream of multiculturalism in a different, but connected, political domain. The recognition entailed in the Convention on Biological

Diversity—that traditional cultures have supported the maintenance of genetic biological diversity and habitats—on the surface at least seems to work in favor of cultural recognition and indigenous sovereignty. Many indigenous peoples and their advocates have looked to environmental groups as allies. Yet the discomfort entailed in recent critiques of the idea of a "noble ecological savage" highlights the heritage of Western paternalism inherent in the dominant cultural imaginary associated with environmentalism (Nasdady 2005).[22] This universal stereotype has been applied to indigenous—particularly tribal—peoples whose contributions to ecological sustainability were perceived as the passive outcome of either cultural and economic isolation or failed modernization. The imagination of indigenous ecological alterities, very much in the vein of classic orientalism (Said 1978), has conditioned the widespread expectation that traditional lifestyles must eventually lose their integrity to the exigencies and temptations of the modern world, undermining the sustainability of indigenous cultural ecologies.[23] The cultural production of ecological alterity continues under the auspices of diverse organizations, governments, sciences, and popular genres. Visions of ecological alterity flourish in the age of globalization and environmental crisis.

Looking back at the Australian example, we can see that visions of ecological alterity support continuing processes of marginalization and dispossession. Indigenous and traditional peoples now suffer encroachments that even supercede those of the imperial era, as global markets commodify wilderness, wildlife, and genetic diversity in new ways (Langton 2003). Aboriginal rights to landscapes and resources are increasingly circumscribed by definitions of "tradition" that seek to exclude indigenous peoples' participation in the market economy, even as losses of biodiversity, environmental degradation, and a variety of ongoing intrusions force them to seek new options for maintaining livelihoods. Traditional hunter-gatherers face impoverishment today not only as a result of continuing loss of territory linked to large-scale developments and the extinction of species that once contributed to subsistence economies, but also as a result of wildlife conservation programs. Although "the biological integrity of the indigenous domain has suffered considerably less than that of the lands which have been radically altered to suit the imported management systems and understandings of the settler society" (Langton 2003, 146), during the late 1990s, concerns about the protection of endangered species on biodiversity-rich indigenous lands severely limited Aboriginal hunting. On the other hand, the Australian government awarded contracts for bio-prospecting activities for commercial gain on indigenous land. By 2003, only a few indigenous people were able to negotiate agreements with bio-prospecting firms or launch their own legitimate harvesting enterprises. It was "the primitivist conception of Aboriginal life" that stood in the way of recognizing indigenous groups as possessing customary proprietary interests in wild resources (ibid., 149). This case suggests that the naïve multiculturalism entailed in global biodiversity conservation has worked to undermine the positive cultural recognition of Aboriginal hunter-gatherers, and their role as active agents of ecological management.[24]

Campaigns to conserve the biodiversity of temperate rainforests on the west coast of Canada present a similar example (see Braun 2002). Many of British Columbia's old-growth forests have been clear-cut or subject to over-exploitation under the guise of scientific forestry. The Nuu-chah-nulth First Nations[25] of Clayoquot Sound suffered dispossessions during the colonial period and after, both through the loss of territory and through the depletion of environmental quality as a result of non-native development and unsustainable resource use. Ironically, the making of the Canadian nation-state entailed the symbolic celebration of its vast natural wilderness as well as romantic visions of "Indians" that early settlers displaced.[26] Notions of pristine or primeval nature, matched by misleading stereotypes of primitive culture, have come to mediate contemporary discourses of nostalgia that are crucial to both Canadian nationalism and environmentalist critiques of forestry policy. The "environmental imaginary" associated with forest politics in postcolonial British Columbia remains contained within established discourses of primitiveness and fails to recognize either the life-projects of Nuu-chah-nulth peoples, or the authenticity of Nuu-chah-nulth identities as they are dynamically engaged with the larger Canadian society today. This fundamentally limits indigenous claims to sovereignty or resource rights by continuing to erase from mind the native presence in the forest ecology of Clayoquot Sound. According to geographer Bruce Braun,

There can be little doubt that particular concepts of nature, culture, indigeneity, modernity, and progress have been deeply implicated in institutional and state practices in the region, and that a series of cognitive failures and discursive displacements have made it immensely difficult to recognize the political presence and environmental practices of the Nuu-chah-nulth, or to register hopes and plans for modern social and environmental futures that diverge from non-Native Canadian norms. (2002, 8)

We can see this case as another example of ecological alterity in practice. Braun reminds us that First Nations in Canada have experienced alliances with environmental campaigns and non-governmental organizations with ambivalence.[27] Although scientific forestry and environmental campaigns are politically opposed, they both reify the divide between modern and traditional, or between development and conservation, and so effectively obscure the social inhabitation of natural landscapes by First Nations. This is what Braun refers to as "epistemic erasure,"[28] because the holistic social experience and philosophies of First Nations peoples are largely overwritten by the mainstream visual and narrative discourses appropriating the representation of indigenous identity.

Some Nuu-chah-nulth individuals attempt to emphasize their own concerns about forestry management issues by reframing narratives about the social landscape outside discourses of primitiveness, and lay claim to alternative, indigenous forms of modernity. Such narratives are often marginalized when they fail to conform to the "tribal slot" established by more familiar, nostalgic representations of indigenous identity. Braun suggests,

This holds an important lesson for any antiracist environmentalism that seeks to move beyond the instinctive romanticism that pervades North American culture. Not only do many environmentalists posit an equivalence between natives and nature, they also tend to foreground Native activists who properly fit this image. (2002, 212)

The double-binds involved with attempting to conform to environmentalist ideals of indigeneity confirm the prevalence of alterity as a cultural frame for understanding ecological problems today. As I discuss in chapter 5, environmental partnerships with NGOs are transforming visions of Sardinian culture. In this case, the WWF has taken on a role in mediating the identities of central Sardinians, who are seen as providing obstacles to the realization of environmentalist goals. Much like the cultural erasures highlighted by Braun for the case of western Canada, the WWF's "globalist approach"[29] to biodiversity conservation in Sardinia systematically erases evidence of social and historical complexity from landscapes.[30] The anthropogenic nature of Sardinian environments tends to be forgotten. The subtle, changing contexts of nation-making, postwar rebuilding, region-making, Europeanization, and neoliberal globalization are erased from consciousness, and with them the hidden agendas of governments and ENGOs themselves. The implicit racism of bureaucratic discourses, which naturalize relative poverty, marginality, and violence in Southern Italy as the effect of corruption and innate cultural psychology,[31] is rendered invisible. In short, NGO narratives of environmentalism in the media and on the World Wide Web profoundly affect how both nature and culture in Sardinia come to be viewed. In the global dreamtimes of environmentalism, where imagined futures germinate in the hegemonic medium of neoliberal "common sense," debates over resource ownership and development rights are often reduced to debates about culture.

Identity, Ambiguity, and Environmental Justice

Efforts to critique the cultural essentialisms privileged in globally oriented discourses should not be confused with the simplistic deconstruction of indigenous identities. Beth Conklin (1997, 2006), Michael Asch and Colin Sampson (2004), Terence Turner (2004), Renee Sylvain (2006), and Richard Lee (2006a, 2006b) are among those who have recently commented on the problem of cultural deconstructions that undermine indigenous efforts of self-representation. There is no doubt that "strategic essentialisms" have been important to indigenous movements for resource rights and self-determination, precisely because the powerful rhetoric of liberal multiculturalism restricts possibilities to recognize authenticity in many diverse, fluid, and hybrid cultural forms. Yet the double-binds inherent in self-representations of indigeneity are significant. When the "pulp fictions of indigenousness" have been leveraged by native Amazonians in Brazil, these often proved to undermine the very people seeking to embody them (Ramos 2005). Discussion of Brazilian cases by both Ramos and Conklin (2002) note that some Amazonian groups invented more fluid paradigms for ecological authenticity in order to reappropriate visions of indigeneity and take active charge of self-representation. The subtle power of the global dreamtime, however, is that it continually reframes and translates such mischievous interventions to fit the structure of Western expectation.

Indigeneity eludes absolute definition. In Indonesia, notions of indigeneity are inherently mobile, but within a given regional array of state and activist discourses, "if they are to fit the preconfigured slot of indigenous people, [rural people] must be ready and able to articulate their identity in terms of a set of characteristics recognized by their allies and by the media that presents their case to the public" (Li 2000, 157). Tania Li suggests, "The tribal slot fits ambiguously with the lives and livelihoods of people living in frontier areas. It is not an identity space that every local group is able or willing to occupy" (170). The essential attributes of indigenous identity have been much debated across parts of Asia with regard to shifting cultivators, pastoralists, and settled rural peasants.

Akhil Gupta (1998), for example, asks how we should understand the case of north Indian agriculturalists who blend mutually contradictory and incommensurable forms of knowing and being on a daily basis.

> How does one theorize a condition in which disparate epistemologies and practices coexist and interpenetrate with such disarming ease? The farmers of Alipur, aggressively utilizing hybrid seeds, biochemical inputs, tube well technology, and state institutions, hardly correspond to depictions of "the traditional farmer." At the same time, they are not "essentially the same" as farmers in the United States or Europe. . . . Alipur's farmers neither fit the mold of indigenous people who have been uncontaminated by modernity nor that of progressive farmers on the brink of entering the takeoff stage of capitalist development. (1998, 156–57)

Gupta suggests that indigeneity has been produced as a residual category, defined by contrast to archetypes of modernity. As nation-state narratives of modern progress foretold the inevitable erasure of the traditional by the modern, icons of indigeneity came to embody an implicit challenge to scripted order, while the terrain of indigenous authenticity became increasingly circumscribed. For Gupta, the ambiguity of indigeneity must be considered inherent to the postcolonial experience.

This ongoing discussion is useful in reflecting on the implications of dynamic cultural hybridity. In the case of northeast India, those who criticize contemporary tribal groups as failed traditionalists often miss the point that claims to indigenous stewardship of nature may often empower forms of cultural revitalization that dramatically improve the prospects for sustainability, along with self-determination (Karlsson 2006, 190–91). The mutually constitutive relationship between discourses of indigeneity or aboriginality and discourses of modern environmentalism offers up not only the double-binds of essentialism, but also opportunities for creative cultural adaptation. If only the ambiguities of indigeneity can be recognized as wholesome possibilities, the global dreamtimes of environmentalism can be healed with optimism.

Undeniably, there is considerable awkwardness involved with using the category of "indigenous" to think about cultural heritage in Sardinia. Yet this is precisely the reason it is useful to do so. Many readers might be disinclined to confer "aboriginal" status upon any rural Europeans, who apparently were once (and perhaps still are?) virtually at the heart of Empire. Many Sardinians themselves may hardly wish to be cast in the same category with tribal groups in Africa and Australia, whose histories and cultural inclinations apparently differ so greatly from their own. Nevertheless, there is a deep history of cultural inhabitation in Sardinia. The island peoples of the Mediterranean suffered many successive waves of colonial occupation; however, Sardinians, particularly those who live in rural mountain towns, have maintained autochthonous cultural traditions that are recognized by UNESCO.[32] There are profound local attachments to place, and commitments to maintain and transmit key elements of a rooted agro-pastoral heritage. These are good reasons for considering highland Sardinia's "ecological alterity" in light of a complicated relationship to discourses defining aboriginality or indigeneity. I return to this theme in the final section of the book, to reflect on possibilities for a paradigm shift in dominant "global" approaches to issues in culture and environment.

From Enclosures to Partnerships: The Role of Cultural Critique

In the twentieth century, it has been suggested, conservation management operated as a tool of "bioaccumulation" resembling an enclosure movement (see Katz 1998). It favored those who already held the symbolic and economic resources associated with modern Western society and concentrated control over newly recognized categories of natural wealth in private hands. The corporate environmentalism that emerged in the 1980s (embodied in large environmental organizations such as The Nature Conservancy) retained a focus on parks and protected areas as the chief priority for environmental politics; this had overwhelming significance to—and largely negative impacts on—poor people and poor regions of the developing world. Models of conservation that emerged in the 1990s and thereafter have generally been professed to support indigenous participation, community co-management, and possibilities for sustainable development. They bring international discourses about humanitarian and indigenous rights together with discourses about safeguarding the environment. Yet the path to conservation with social justice has been a winding road, and we have certainly not yet arrived at our longed-for destination (Fortwangler 2003). Where structural violence continues to undermine the possibility for local communities to achieve cultural recognition and encounter environmental experts and policy makers as equals, the journey seems long indeed.[33]

The continued exclusion of indigenous peoples from many conservation areas around the world vividly demonstrates how visions of cultural alterity come to bear on readings of ecology and understandings of appropriate strategies of environmental governance. Embedded systems of cultural prejudice and racism act to shape and undermine projects to protect wildlife habitats and biodiversity today. While many historical cases are well documented,[34] environmental racism did not end with the colonial period. Rather, historical contexts and imaginaries have continued to shape conservation efforts.[35] A study of participatory ecodevelopment at the Mafia Island Marine Park in Tanzania suggests that despite rhetoric of social inclusion, technocentric approaches embedded in conservation practice tend to exclude the poor and disenfranchised, continuing historically embedded patterns of socioeconomic disparity between ethnic groups (Walley 2004). In cases such as this, we also see how the moral rhetoric of conservation priorities largely overwrites the "social nature" (Castree and Braun 2001) of African landscapes,[36] just as we have seen in other cases. It does so by reproducing the ecological alterity of indigenous cultures. African tribes, peasant communities, and pastoral groups are made to appear at once primitive and backward, dangerous and uneducated, basically unsuited to play active positive roles in ecological management. By extension, their roles in the conservation of ecological systems are minimized, effaced, shorn of deliberation and technique, or relegated to long-dead history. Such representations are the basis of racial and cultural disinheritance; they help to inflict structural violence by encroaching on both the resource base and the sovereignty of indigenous minorities.[37]

Cultural politics and environmental debates continue to shape one another in intimate ways. The nuances of ongoing identity- and alterity-making are therefore significant, and ethnographic insights are invaluable.[38] Attention to the problem of alterity highlights the connection between structural (political-economic) contexts of inequality and the historically embedded symbolic systems, discourses, or hegemonies that legitimate them. Visions of orientalism or cultural otherness function in terms of an essential ambivalence, so that exotic stereotypes of cultural groups are structured in positive or negative terms inherently prone to inversion. Both valences tend to reify a natural, implicitly or explicitly biologized, cultural identity with inherent links to iconic environments and landscapes, as well as a cultural distance between the marked category and the dominant group. The case study developed throughout the chapters to follow illustrates that perceived innate cultural differences structure relations between central Sardinia and its metropoles. Broad-based cultural discourses about national or ethnic identity often shape the design and implementation of initiatives in environmental governance and ecodevelopment such as those designed for Sardinia and the Mediterranean Sea. My efforts to offer critical perspective upon these discourses are aimed at the hopeful possibility of transforming them, so that both changing contexts of power and dynamic adaptations of culture can be recognized in service of environmental justice.

PART II Ecology

Companies of *Priorissas* lead a Roman Catholic procession to a chapel on the Orgosolo Commons (1998).

Chapter 2

Envisioning the Supramonte

The View from Monte San Giovanni

Gino is a partner in a thriving ecotourism enterprise that provides out-door lunches for large groups, as well as small charter tours of the high plateau, near the town of Orgosolo, in central Sardinia. Cultural tour-ism began to play a role in Orgosolo's economy after the Second World War, and two or three guiding businesses with Jeeps began to promote "ecotourism" during the 1990s (Satta 2001). In July of 1998, Gino picked up four foreign tourists and myself; I was invited along as a friend and an English-Italian translator. Gino drove us all out of town, continuing on past the end of the paved highway to navigate the rug-ged roads that begin near the foot of Monte San Giovanni. We trundled through forested areas and along steep slopes. The visitors were enthu-siastic, assured of penetrating hidden landscapes.

The itinerary included sites of prehistoric archaeology—the Mereu nuragh, a "Janus house," a "tomb of the giants"—and geographic land-marks such as Monte San Giovanni and the source of the Cedrino River. Gino presented the cultural and natural wonders of the communal ter-ritory as intrinsically bound together throughout history. He pointed out both wild and semi-domesticated animals as we passed near their haunting grounds. He offered us a lively, well-informed account of local ecology, particularly the cycles of vegetation involving juniper. He drew attention to eagles overhead, spoke with reverence of the beauty of wild mouflons that range through the area, and told us about the adaptive characteristics of indigenous cattle kept on natural pastures. Our guide presented the landscape itself as a testament to pastoral traditions.

According to Gino, Orgosolo's old oak forest was "the only true forest," in the area designated to become a national park. Orgosolo's Sar Vaddes is a very rare example of a mature Mediterranean oak forest.[1] About three-quarters of Sardinian woodlands like these were denuded during the nineteenth century, but Orgosolo's forest has long been treasured, used, and guarded by shepherds and the town administration. It lies at the heart of the local communal territory. When we reached this area of living sanctuary, we found oak trees of astonishing size, a few small cows of indigenous breed, a sow with a litter sired by an indigenous wild boar, and a handful of animal enclosures. Some of these showed us the "traditional" form built by local herders, fashioned from rock and juniper, while others were modified with newer materials. A couple of quaint old stone shelters were now roofed by garish plastic. Gino believed that this was the result of a mistake on the part of the forestry service, which had forbidden the herders to cut juniper branches for the construction of traditional-style roofs. The traditional and modified traditional animal shelters and shepherd's huts marked ongoing ecological bonds between the people and the land. When the tourists marveled at a dead trunk of magnificent girth, Gino explained that this "patriarch" oak had been hit by lightning in 1994.

"There are herders who cried for that tree when it died," he told us. The authentic symbiosis of herders and forest was a key theme in Gino's narrative. The shepherds had made the place "a garden," he said, since by pruning juniper branches for their enclosures and shelters they rendered the shape of the trees aesthetically pleasing, without harm to the ecology. The picnic lunch provided by our guide featured distinctive local meats and cheeses to further persuade us that pastoral traditions at Orgosolo remained authentic. The perception of inherent blending of nature and culture on the local landscape informed Gino's subtle argument against the institution of a centralized, government-administrated national park incorporating Orgosolo's Supramonte.

"There is already a park," he said. "We have made the park ourselves."[2]

The climactic finale of the day trip was the view from Monte San Giovanni. We left the Jeep and climbed on foot up toward the peak. Midway up the mountain slope there was an animal shelter still in use, built from natural materials by contemporary herders. Once we attained the view from the summit, Gino described how evidence of Orgosolo's "traditional" pastoral life was spread out for the eye to see, since around the base of the mountain there are high plateau areas of the Commons used for extensive pasture. He showed us the outlines of a chapel on the mountain crest used during medieval times and noted that Catholic processions were made on foot to visit the mountain once a year until just after the Second World War. Gino also introduced us to local men stationed by the forestry service to watch for fires. The visitors were offered local wine by the men and shown around the lookout, transformed from tourists into guests by the cultural magic of hospitality.

How does a landscape become a story, a narrative testament to the structure of time and the "nature" of history itself? Where strangers' eyes have seen wild spaces, rare species, the odd anachronistic shepherd, and the potential to "preserve" a historically significant ecosystem, Gino saw signs of deeply rooted cultural habitation not only in prehistoric architecture and old-fashioned shepherds' huts, but also in the rich forests, the pure springs, and the profusion of wildlife. Gino did not see the Supramonte of Orgosolo in a state of historical isolation, where the impacts of the world system have led to the abandonment and degradation of the rural countryside. Rather, his vision of the landscape powerfully situated Orgosolo's communal territory, the Commons, in the context of a self-regenerating, custodial, and fluidly adapting pastoral community. Our view from the peak of Monte San Giovanni was not the distanced vision of a wilderness from on high, but a social vision anchored within a web of ongoing, distinctively localized and personalized relationships.

This chapter introduces the landscape of the Sardinian Supramonte from two rather different, somewhat conflicting perspectives. It explores, on the one hand, a landscape of rich but fragile ecosystems and biological diversity, highly valued by ecologists and nature enthusiasts. A brief history of the project to create Gennargentu Park suggests that this is also a landscape of great value to the twentieth-century architects of Sardinian, Italian, and European identities. Yet attachments to landscape described by the residents of Orgosolo are of a different order. They derive from both a sense of history and a sense of community. Evidence of an epistemological gap emerges from the comparison of these viewpoints. I describe this in terms of the "museum effect" associated with putting elements of landscape on display in connection with ecotourism. Perceptions of legitimate authority and the nature of the landscape have varied according to perspective. The success of so-called "ecodevelopment" has been drawn into doubt by the basic failure to negotiate a respectful middle ground between autochthonous Sardinian and globally oriented, "environmentalist" conceptions of landscape. The failure of consensus is exacerbated by the transposition of ecotourism to virtual landscapes, where local "ways of seeing" the landscape that are rooted in historicity and social experience are virtually erased. This process supports the problematic appropriations of local culture and nature that are associated with the global dreamtime of environmentalism.

Nature on Display

Monte San Giovanni is one of the most celebrated peaks of central Sardinia. On a clear day, they told me in Orgosolo, from its height of 1,316 meters, you can see all the way across "from Arbatax to Oristano," the Mediterranean coasts on both sides of the island. This panorama already attracts tourists and local residents. A forestry lookout is maintained there throughout the summer, when fires can quickly threaten the landscape. Monte San Giovanni is also Orgosolo's gateway to the famous Sardinian Supramonte, the high plateau linked to a romantic history of anti-colonial resistance, rugged shepherds, outlaws, and kidnappers. With its dramatic calcareous formations, Monte San Giovanni has long been a distinctive symbol of the town of Orgosolo, and in 1997, the town council petitioned to have the peak named a national monument. Its image is also frequently adopted as an emblem of the delineated "National Park of the Gulf of Orosei and the Gennargentu." Today, the peak is managed under the auspices of the government forestry services of Sardinia, flanked on one side by state reforestation zones, and on the other by areas of communally owned lands still managed by the town. If the park plan is implemented, Monte San Giovanni will constitute an important designated visitor area, and most of the immediate surrounding Supramonte will fall under the centralized control of a park authority.

Sardinia is largely mountainous through the central and eastern portions of the island, with very few lakes. Its natural caves and significant underground formations are still being explored. The Gennargentu range is clustered in central Sardinia, reaching over 1,800 meters at its highest peak. The rural landscapes of the high plateau are valued for a profusion of wild flora, fauna, and avian species, as well as their geological complexity. The regional and national governments first began planning to create a Gennargentu national park in the late 1960s. This was related to a European Economic Community campaign to increase the percentage of land devoted to natural reserves, and it was expected that a national park would promote economic development through increased tourism to the Sardinian interior.

In Orgosolo, most households still included one or more full-time herders who depended upon access to communally owned lands, *su cumonale*, "the Commons," including the valleys flanking Monte San Giovanni. These same lands, as well as the forestry service–managed area of Montes, including Monte San Giovanni itself, were targeted for incorporation into the new park, and herders quickly became alarmed at their potential exclusion from these areas. Residents of Orgosolo contested the imminent loss of the Commons in 1969 and ultimately maintained control over it (Moro 1982). Local authority over land management was nevertheless gradually eroded through legislation and, in the late 1980s, the decisive expansion of the regional forest ranger corps. Although the economy of Orgosolo has transformed and diversified, many residents continue to view the Commons as a source of economic security and potential economic development. In 1989, the regional law 394 was passed, outlining a system of new parks and reserves to be created in Sardinia. Gennargentu Park reappeared in this framework, with some adjustments made to the management plans and the areas to be included. Although the revised project won tentative support from some local residents who hoped to take advantage of new socioeconomic programs associated with sustainable development, many others perceived specters of clientelism and corruption looming in the background. In 1998, the region and the state signed the final agreement defining the Parco Nazionale del Golfo di Orosei e del Gennargentu (still widely glossed as il Parco del Gennargentu, or Gennargentu Park). The legislation was suspended for review after another large demonstration at Orgosolo highlighted ongoing local controversy, particularly some disputes over park perimeters.

Orgosolo's leading citizens have found themselves in unenviable positions negotiating the politics of landscape. In general, experts associated with government institutions and politicians from the provincial level up have supported the creation of this park. The project has also been supported by some Italian university researchers and organized environmental lobbies. The World Wide Fund for Nature (wwf) has remained particularly active in promoting the park through its Internet campaigns and other attempts at public education (wwf 1998). Some moderate advocates of the park, such as the Italian-based environmental movement Legambiente, supported calls to renegotiate the 1998 agreement in a way that would better acknowledge the democratic process in local communities.[3] The wwf of Italy has agreed that some negotiations should be pursued, but its spokespersons insisted that the project should not have to be redesigned from scratch.[4]

Troubles with Wilderness in Sardinia

National parks were originally based, as William Cronon (1995) points out, upon the strict symbolic bifurcation of inhabited and wild spaces. In his noted essay on "the trouble with wilderness," Cronon crystallized several important critiques of the environmental philosophy entailed in the American national park model that many other countries tried to emulate. First, visions of sublime, uncontaminated nature in the New World were the ethnocentric misapprehensions of colonial Europeans. Perceptions of wilderness in the American "Old West" belied the cultural ecology of a landscape that was in fact peopled by indigenous First Nations. Second, the "preservation" of wilderness in the form of national parks entailed the dispossession of these indigenous populations. Third, the fiction of wilderness inscribed upon the landscapes of national parks today strategically sustains nationalist origin narratives about the conquering of the American frontier. Finally, the priorities set on wilderness conservation tend to mean fewer resources and attentions devoted to improving urban, industrialized, or otherwise "disturbed" landscapes. According to Cronon, the Western cultural system that affirms essential distinctions between natural and cultural landscapes continues to undermine a more holistic approach to the care of the environment.

None of these critical points would come as a surprise to my acquaintances in rural Sardinia, who used to ask me what had happened to the Native American Indians when national parks like Yellowstone were first made.[5] Long before I had read Cronon's work, or thought about the many parallels between Sardinia and the American West, they were the first to insist that I should pay close attention to the colonial histories that had shaped the ideologies and tactics of nature "preservation." The appropriation of indigenous lands in North America was instrumental to the creation of national parks and forests as public use spaces during the nineteenth and early twentieth centuries. As in the Canadian, Australian, and Tanzanian cases discussed in the introduction to this book, a number of conflicts emerged over access to resources and landscapes designated for conservation in the western United States. Even where there was not a wholesale expulsion of Native Americans from public lands devoted to wilderness protection, the subordination of traditional conservation practices to modern science, twinned with the subordination of indigenous religious concerns and economic needs to the perception of general public interest, served to erode connections of ecological guardianship between Native American nations and the landscapes that were historically important to them.[6] In my Sardinian fieldsite, residents in several of the highland towns had struggled for over thirty years against the plan to consolidate areas of their communally owned herding lands into a national park. Gino, the ecotourism guide, would sometimes explain ruefully that people in Orgosolo were just like the Indians, about to be closed up on a reserve when the park was made, and no longer allowed access to their traditional lands. He implied they might have preferred to be the cowboys in this scenario.

The growth of the parks system throughout Italy is an important focus of the "moral rationality" (Prato 1993) cultivated by various "green" lobbies in the Italian context. Italy's first national park was inaugurated in Abruzzo in 1922. Its exhibition leaflet, "Park Effect," illustrates the narratives of environmental citizenship current during the late 1990s. After several expansions, Abruzzo National Park now occupies 44,000 hectares and receives about two million visitors per year. Its work to protect areas of primary forest, endangered species, and biodiversity is represented as having positive links to various levels of cultural identity. The leaflet celebrates the park's beneficial influence on local culture, as "ecodevelopment" is shown to have provided markets for traditional cheese, biscuits, and honey (shown in photographs with the "DOC" mark of the national park) (Centro Parchi 1997, 8). It asserts the park's centrality to a flourishing national culture of environmentalism, noting its accessibility from Rome and Naples, and the many NGOs and individual volunteers in Italy who collaborate in park improvement. Finally, the leaflet sets the park within the context of ongoing Europeanization by noting its official status as a "green region of Europe" and calling it "a splendid jewel in the European Crown" (Centro Parchi 1997, 12). As in the American example described by Cronon (1995), the story told about nature conservation both subsumes and reifies a narrative about cultural and political identity. It also takes for granted an inherently modernist vision of progress, in which ecodevelopment has merely replaced the kind of industrial development advocated during the 1960s, as a panacea for socioeconomic needs and aspirations.

Sardinia's contested national park involves an area of Italy that is stereotypically associated with "banditry" and "backwardness." Monte San Giovanni constitutes a focus of several alternative narratives about how "culture" shapes the local environment. The area around the peak is used by different groups of people, including local herders, foreign visitors, urban nature seekers, ecotourism entrepreneurs, local hikers, herb collectors, state forestry employees, biologists, and others. As an important historical and geographic feature of the rural landscape, Monte San Giovanni is integrated into various patterns of cultural, political, and economic practice in ways that evoke vastly disparate expectations about the categories of social belonging, exclusion, and legitimate entitlement.

What Is a Park?

A park is designed to superimpose order on the way natural landscapes are managed. It necessarily imposes order upon the way that visitors "see" a landscape and in so doing, it affirms a particular set of stories about environment, history, and citizenship. These visions of "nature" are instruments used to negotiate cultural and political identities.[7] Today contemporary advocates of protected areas have become concerned about the connections between parks and their peripheries, and "resident peoples" are increasingly appreciated as participants in habitat conservation. Yet "national parks" continue to be defined by the idea of spaces "set apart" from human use (IUCN 1980).[8] It is this very act of setting a place apart from normal land use and development that establishes the landscape of a park as a kind of sacred space. Like other kinds of official narratives, the environmental discourses of nation-states entail moral and symbolic dimensions that come to be legitimized or even taken for granted through the enactment of "secular rituals" (Moore and Myerhoff 1977; see also Moore 1993). National parks create contexts within which the relationships enacted among individuals, communities, and the environment become idealized and ritualized as well as regulated and controlled. Landscapes that are "set apart" as protected areas ultimately become part of strategic debates about cultural identity and difference.

A national park resembles a museum in the way that components of an open landscape are made available to the social and the ecological imagination. Svetlana Alpers has argued that museums are characterized by "a way of seeing" that releases objects from their original, locally defined frames of meaning and history and heightens the power of aesthetic imagination (Alpers 1990). I suggest that in a national park, an ecosystem is deliberately decontextualized from its cultural milieu, displaying local species and geographic features as aesthetic objects and objects of knowledge in themselves. This "museum effect" is, I suggest, structured by three qualities: authority, authenticity, and ritual. I discuss these aspects further below. The museum effect tends to privilege universal knowledge over specific, local visions of the landscape. Parks and protected areas often function to support the global dreamtimes of environmentalism and undermine the ecological guardianship of indigenous communities.

Great educational and scientific value is perceived to reside in national parks.[9] These "ecological museums" derive authority from scientific models of vision, that is, from epistemological models that isolate specific objects of inquiry and celebrate empirical observation as the means of legitimate knowledge. One biologist from the University of Florence, for example, exhorted the value of central Sardinia as an "open book" of science:

The relatively uninhabited landscape of the territory of the park is a book open to the naturalistic perception, [open] to ecological reading, to the reflection and admonishment of that which nature can be and often, unfortunately, no longer is. (Professor Pier Virgilio Arrigoni in APN 1999)

This Florentine scientist apparently shares an understanding with the WWF (see Colomo and Ticca 1987; WWF 1998) that the ecological wealth of indigenous flora and fauna in the Supramonte has flourished in relative isolation from human activities, rather than benefited from the custodianship of local communities. The landscape is described as resisting human influence. It is the powerful visibility of accepted symbols of authentic nature, and the equally powerful invisibility of contrasting signs of modern human inhabitation, which render the tourist's experience of the local environment genuine and transformative from this kind of environmentalist perspective. There are very few elements of recognizably modern architecture visible upon the landscape around Monte San Giovanni. Apart from some springs, picnic areas, and special animal enclosures maintained on the Commons by the town, there are only a few simple cement shelters and animal enclosures built by herders themselves and scattered thinly, out of view from the road. There are some buildings maintained by the forestry service at the foot of Monte San Giovanni, where the government has already been supervising the planting and harvesting of trees for several decades. There are no houses, since Sardinians continue to favor a pattern of aggregated villages and there are legal restrictions to any construction in the highland countryside. The area around Monte San Giovanni, for example, is considered by experts to be both representative of central Sardinian wilderness and a memorable example of it.

If a museum is a place of pilgrimage made powerful by human art and science, a park is a site where the features of a "natural" landscape are taken to enshrine, without apparent artifice, a potent source of knowledge and aesthetics. The "authenticity" of "nature" is essential to the idea of a national park, since it is designed as a means of "protecting" or "preserving" what are considered to be "typical" examples of physical features and biogenetic resources. The techniques of park management—zoning, trail making, monitoring of flora and fauna, and so on—are imagined as custodial techniques, techniques that simply discipline human intervention in the ecosystem and facilitate the natural balance of local ecologies.

At Monte San Giovanni, a range of geological formations and indigenous wild plants and animals can be found in a striking, beautiful setting. Orgosolo's own nature enthusiasts—members of the hiking club, ecotourism guides, forest rangers, as well as herders and others—talk about the naturally occurring "botanic garden" in the forest at the foot of the mountain and comment on the inspiring presence of rare mouflon herds and royal eagles. The objects of scientific and aesthetic discourses of ecology are thus directly available to the senses. Monte San Giovanni is frequently chosen for school excursions from all over the island, as a relatively accessible and educational day trip. The immediate, vivid experience of authentic nature can be framed by a meaningful discourse of environmentalism.

Nature excursions engage the mind and the senses in the manifestation of ecological self-identities. In the Abruzzo National Park leaflet, for example, the park is seen as an opportunity for "discovering nature: with your eyes, with your heart and with your hands" (Centro Parchi 1997, 10). In the promotional literature and conferences on Gennargentu Park (Camboni 1991; Colomo and Ticca 1987; Scuola di Pubblica Amministrazione et al. 1993; WWF 1998), there are, similarly, repeated references to how people may become "closer" to Sardinian "nature" by visiting, seeing, learning about, and appreciating places like Monte San Giovanni. Pictures in an information leaflet featured campers in the Supramonte, while the text implied the quasi-ritual context of their experience by describing the aesthetic and spiritual rewards to be derived from "entering silently into the solemn and intact temple of nature" (APN 1999, 2). A park visitor who seeks out visual and sensory knowledge of plant and animal species ritually emulates scientific processes of empirical observation and, through self-monitoring against littering, lighting fires, or disturbing plants, shares in the project of scientific conservation. The bodies and the senses of park visitors can be directly engaged with the surrounding "wilderness" and metonymically aligned with the larger project of scientific ecology.[10] Excursions within a national park, then, can be seen as a means of ritually structuring direct contact with a richly imagined and often personified "nature" in a special domain "where nature is sovereign" (Centro Parchi 1997, 4).

Advocates of Gennargentu Park favor the creation of a single, centralized institution for environmental management. Environmental lobbies and members of government bureaucracies often recognize the ongoing work of the forestry service and the corps of forest rangers, as well as the innovative, scientifically informed initiatives of Orgosolo's agricultural cooperative, in maintaining and improving the quality of the local environment. References to scientific authority, however, support calls for more comprehensive and systematic ecological management techniques.

Technical discourses of environmentalism tend to model time in a linear way, gathering agency and moral authority over the landscape into the expert hands of institutions. They presume the history of human cultural ecology to have progressed from naïve resource management by isolated traditional rural cultures to inadequate resource management by transforming and economically developing societies as they become more open to the outside world. For example, a technical report for the U.N.'s Man and Biosphere Project indicated that traditional methods of pastoral production in the Mediterranean had been subverted by a new cultural-economic context, and so transformed into the source of ecological disequilibrium (Tomaselli 1977). Some government sources have contended (see, for example, IASM 1983) that local institutions for common property management fostered "irrational" resource use in central Sardinia. The ongoing problem of forest fires is often linked to pastoral traditions and local "ignorance." Small-scale, community-based ecological management systems are typically dismissed as an aspect of the cultural past which no longer "work" within the contemporary world.

The perceived failure of local management structures has been used to legitimize the appropriation of rural environmental resources by centralized institutions in order to satisfy the needs of a larger, national community with a large urban population. Alfonso Alessandrini, national director for the mountain economy and for forests in Italy during the late 1980s, claimed that the public interest in forests transcends the immediate needs of those who depend upon exploiting them in "traditional" ways (Cerrina 1987, 87). Modernist tropes often represent authentic environmentalism to be the outcome only of public institutions supported by an educated, forward-looking, urban citizenship. In Italian national park literature, landscapes become enwrapped in a scientifically authorized discourse about large-scale changes in cultural ecology.

These sweeping historical narratives often obscure the variety of structural possibilities for co-management and decentralized rural ecodevelopment. The creation of national parks highlights archetypal representations of historical landscapes and often reduces living cultures to the status of folklore survivals. Michael Herzfeld (1991) has persuasively argued that efforts at historic conservation in Greece enable institutions and governments to affirm ideologized, monolithic versions of history. These narratives, which Herzfeld calls "monumental time," can be inscribed in physical spaces. State bureaucracies can therefore attempt to reify nationalist visions of history and progress by controlling the preservation, reconstruction, and conversion of architectural landscapes. The linear histories told to explain and support initiatives to "conserve" ecosystems are similarly inscribed, I argue, upon the "natural" landscape, through the exercise of "ways of seeing" that are organized by state agencies and legitimized by reference to environmental science.

In contrast, residents of Orgosolo often discussed ways to preserve, reauthorize, and gradually transform an existing traditional ecology. Their everyday social practices enveloped the Commons in a reforging of dynamic ties between past, present, and future. These practices fixed the landscape not in history, but rather, within a definitive cultural space. The fluid time of Orgolese "tradition" corresponds rather well to what Michael Herzfeld (1991) described as "social time": the unkempt flow of experience, managed and remembered by pragmatically and socially oriented actors. He has suggested that this social time, just like the monumental time constructed by the nation-state, comes to be written into material spaces. Local protagonists reappropriate the telling of history and continually inscribe their own more flexible, personalized narratives of the past upon the landscape (cf. Hirsch and O'Hanlon 1995; Sutton 2000; Nazarea 2006). Gino's tour of the Commons provides an example of this in Sardinia. We can see how rural residents contested the national park by articulating their own narratives about culture, ecology, and history on the Orgosolo Commons.

The Cathedral of Orgosolo

Local residents think of Monte San Giovanni as a special place inscribed with deep traces of autochthonous human history. Archaeological ruins in the neighborhood of the mountain are a source of interest and pride for local people, and the ruins of the Catholic chapel tie the mountaintop to still vibrant traditions of festival procession from the town into sacred places in the landscape. In their own visits to the site, residents ritually embody their own perceptions of the past: by going out to the mountain, they sample and reenact the experience of traditional Catholic pilgrims, or that of herders who once lived for months at a time in the surrounding countryside. They also reconfirm the ongoing presence of the community, and thus their own part in shaping the aesthetic landscape. The centrality of local meats and cheeses to frequent picnic gatherings in the countryside emphasizes how the landscape is incorporated within a local system of social reciprocity and cultural practice that self-consciously celebrates its pastoral roots.

During the late nineties, my friend Santina served as president of the nature-hiking and spelunking (cave-diving) club at Orgosolo. She attempted to persuade others that the group should function not only to coordinate leisure activities, but also to engage the community intellectually and politically. She herself was an avid reader on the subject of local ecology, and she later helped sponsor an ecological exhibit in town. Like Gino, Santina was highly critical of the project to create a national park. In 2000, she became an independent member of the town council. I asked her at that time what she could tell me about Monte San Giovanni.

"Monte San Giovanni," she said, "is the cathedral of Orgosolo."
"Why?" I asked. She explained,

In general, everyone presents the most precious things to their friends. We take them to Monte San Giovanni if time and the weather permit. It has a high symbolic value, [an aesthetic] landscape value, also [it is the focus of] an attachment to the land. I mean to say that it is the most vital site of, let us say, the feeling of being owners of the land. Here it becomes most manifest. There is a symbiosis between man and the environment that here, at least, is more marked than in other places. . . . It is the most representative part of the whole territory in this particular sense. The "cathedral" would be the point where a citizenship gathers, let us say, in the deepest, most spiritual moments, and so we have Monte San Giovanni, though of course we also have churches. . . . [It is] the most beautiful thing that I can show, that I can offer [to guests], and with a great, great sense of pride.

Her eloquent comments suggest that we can see the mountain as a special place to which the people of Orgosolo are drawn to confirm meaningful relationships to a community, a cultural tradition, and the land itself. Cultural identity is strongly invested in places like Monte San Giovanni, so that the very "purity" of nature itself is seen to bear witness and tribute to cultural authenticity. Both the air and the water (from the Funtana Bona, "good spring") at the foot of Monte San Giovanni are considered salubrious, and people make family excursions to the area for picnics in summertime. Popular magical lore also specifies how to gather herbs around the mountain at auspicious times, to make natural medicines. From a local perspective, true Sardinian history—a history based in pastoralism and the commons—becomes manifest in the taste of springwater, the freshness of the air, and the healing properties of herbal remedies. Just as bodies and physical senses mediate knowledge and understanding of the environment for outside visitors, they also mediate the cultural discourses of environment generated in the town.[11]

Entangled Authenticities

One may "see" Monte San Giovanni as a symbol of the global environment, or as a symbol of local culture, or as a mixture thereof, depending on how one is introduced to the spectacle. Legitimate authority over "nature" is not currently taken for granted—rather, the decades-old debate about whether to create a national park in Sardinia has generated a range of narratives about the Sardinian environment that engage wider discourses about "science" and "culture" in very different ways. Visitors to Monte San Giovanni may position themselves (or find themselves positioned by their guides and companions) in relation to two different kinds of authority over landscape and ecology: scientific authority and cultural authority.

Reference to cultural authority recognizes the historical importance of local ecological knowledge and the role of local commitment to pastoral and communitarian traditions in maintaining the quality of the environment. In particular, some ethnonationalist-style discourses have emphasized that the resistance of local communities to the land privatization schemes of the nineteenth century functioned to protect areas of common land from deforestation (see Salis 1990; Zucca 1992). Orgosolo's rare old-growth forest, for example, lies in a remote area of the municipally controlled Commons rather than the area of Montes (around Monte San Giovanni and Monte Fumai) that has been managed by the government forestry service. Local opponents of the park scheme sometimes argue that a park authority would be guided not by science, but by a corrupt politics they believe to be ubiquitous throughout Italian public institutions. In contrast, residents say, they themselves depend upon the Commons and it is their custodianship that has made the landscape desirable for a national park.

Ideas about both scientific and cultural authority over the environment frame our visions of the mountain and its surroundings. Although the creation of Gennargentu Park may immanently privilege scientific authority over how this landscape is envisioned, it is important to recognize that local residents, tourist guides, and forest rangers with sensitivity to issues of local identity and welfare will continue to play a role in mediating the experience of Monte San Giovanni to visitors. Many of these individuals blend discourses of scientific and cultural authority together in their stories and explanations to outsiders, as Santina and Gino have done. Visitors themselves may arrive predisposed to witness elements of either nature or culture in the panorama before them. The museum-like experience associated with going to a park is therefore as much a product of processual negotiations over self-identity and representation as in any more conventional museum.

The authenticity of "nature" is deeply complicated by the way that local history and culture continue to be inscribed upon the landscape. Orgosolo's public image as a "traditional" shepherd village inevitably heightens the historical mystique of the landscape. One typically encounters cattle, sheep, pigs, goats, horses, and herders themselves in the environs of Monte San Giovanni, and they are easily visible along the main road followed by tourists seeking to visit the peak. Still more thrilling for some tourists is the idea that the undomesticated landscape below also harbors the secrets of historical and contemporary bandits, outlaws, and kidnappers. What is the link between ideas about the authenticity of "nature" and the prevailing stereotypes of local culture? Notions of "wilderness" in Sardinia are intrinsically connected to a vision of cultural wildness associated with shepherds and bandits. Environmental discourses commonly represent the landscapes associated with "traditional," rural societies as more "natural" than those associated with "modern" industrial or urban societies. Representations of cultural authenticity can reinforce the idea that the landscape itself remains much as it was in the past.

The Museum Effect

Inasmuch as Monte San Giovanni constitutes a prominent feature for "display," whether as part of a national park or as a part of Orgosolo's communal heritage, it is located at the center of continuing debate. Berardino Palumbo (2001) argues that museums in Italy are foci of social tactics and social poetics mediating relations between nation-state and local community, as well as public and private spaces. Sharon Macdonald's (1996) analysis of several case studies has shown that visitors' experiences of museum displays are not predetermined but open to negotiations of meaning. As Kevin Hetherington (1996) has convincingly shown for Stonehenge in that same volume, the creation of open-air museums can carry with it a particularly dynamic, ongoing process of negotiation over symbolic power. Parks and natural reserves are open to a play of discourses and cultural practices with regard to history and environmentalism, generated within a range of political, institutional, and social contexts.

Monte San Giovanni suggests an example of the museum effect possible with a landscape on display. In museums, objects are physically taken out of their original social and cultural contexts; the creation of a national park entails a similar process by setting legal and symbolic boundaries between park and community, "nature" and "culture," and excluding some traditional activities such as hunting from the reserve area. It is a powerful alchemy to set apart a place perceived to embody genuine nature and evoke discourses of scientific authority with which to give it meaning. The sensuality of immersion in the "wilderness" adds a special quality to what Steven Greenblatt (1990) has called the "resonance and wonder" of museums. And, because our cultural relationship to "the environment" is increasingly important to our ideas about who we are (or would like to be) as moral persons and citizens, our visits to parks and nature reserves often acknowledge a sacred character to the landscape.

Yet issues of authority, authenticity, and ritual experience structure the museum effect at Monte San Giovanni in ambivalent ways, cautioning us against a simplistic idea of how what we might call the "museumization" of the landscape actually works. Monte San Giovanni constitutes a key symbolic space for local residents and tourists, as well as environmentalists. Ritual action is clearly a component of their visits to the mountain, as they perform politically relevant self-identities and seek the sensual affirmation of an imagined connection to history or the environment. Some visitors may seek a tourism experience that allows them to appropriate and consume cultural "otherness" by means of pilgrimage to an exotic cultural landscape. A community of nature lovers and environmentalists and a cultural tradition of conservation may well be the most important points of reference for some visitors, so that the sensory appreciation of the landscape is linked to a discursive framework of scientific ecology. For them, a Sardinian nature excursion enacts a journey through the global dreamtime of environmentalism.

Within Orgosolo itself, not all residents continue to work on the land, and there is considerable diversity in how they envision their pastoral heritage. Despite the tendency to represent "local culture" as a reified whole, various interpretations of tradition diverge. Among these are of course some familiar rhetorics of central Sardinians being "close to nature" by merit of history, necessity, and cultural inclination. Dialogues on local cuisine often invoked this strategic virtue. In such examples we may possibly discern a willingness to conform to outsiders' expectations in exchange for livelihood or simply more hopeful relations of moral reciprocity. These identity constructions, however, are often subtly nuanced. Santina and Gino had extensive reading knowledge of local flora and fauna and were outspoken critics of pollution, arson, and overgrazing in their own community. They represent a growing nucleus of home-grown environmentalists who found value and authority in local knowledge and objected to the museumization of the landscape. They defined a space of authentic cultural hybridity within which global discourses might be challenged and reframed.

The symbolic boundary between "cultural" and "natural" landscapes in central Sardinia continues to be highly permeable. The museum effect is thus a paradox: although aspects of local ecology have been objectified and abstracted in the public imagination, they are never irrevocably deprived of their sociocultural context. The area designated to become a park is actually fixed in space relative to local communities, and local people frequently play a role in mediating the "naturalistic perceptions" of visitors. Visions of nature ultimately remain embedded in multiple frames of experience, including those of local historical self-identities. Monte San Giovanni casts many different spells upon its wondering visitors. While some are intent upon reading the scientific secrets of ecology, others celebrate an intrinsic symbiosis of pastoral culture and the Sardinian environment.

Ecotourism in Cyberspace

I arrived at the gates of Gennargentu Park under the auspices of the World Wide Fund for Nature–Italia in October 2001, three years after completing the main body of fieldwork for doctoral research in central Sardinia. Through the window I saw a woman and man wearing the folk costumes of a Nuorese town. My gaze slid easily past their impenetrable faces to the lush foliage of the forest and the mountaintop thundering up against a dry yellow sky. Muted colors and shadows suggested a dreamlike murmur of stories that could unfold with intimate glimpses.[12] The sign Parco Nazionale del Golfo di Orosei e del Gennargentu framed the scene before me. An Italian caption below announced, "A great opportunity for the future of the Ogliastra and the Barbagia."

I was visitor number 3,662 at this slick website.[13] The page was connected to the official "portal for Italian parks"[14] and another site describing the participation of the WWF in a range of Italian environment and development initiatives supported by European Union funds.[15] Paths branching out from the homepage offered an introduction to the park and details on the environment, the local communities, tourist itineraries, the organization of the protected area, the ecodevelopment project

"Life Natura," and a mysterious "adventure in the Gennargentu." Step through this page and visit the virtual park, the once and future park, the park that existed briefly on paper in 1969 and again in 1998, until evidence of overwhelming local opposition each time convinced government authorities to rescind the legislation creating it. It is the park that should be, according to WWF campaigns, if only a "minority of local stakeholders" could be made aware that environmental protection brings economic and cultural benefits for everyone. This is the national park that existed (still exists) in the global dreamtime of environmentalism—that is, in the imagination of environmentalists at the WWF, and particularly of the website authors at the local headquarters in the Sardinian capital of Cagliari. Here I wandered at length, a little breathless with excitement at my computer, trying to catch a glimpse of the Sardinia I had known through the eyes of people in Orgosolo. Yet this landscape was very different.

Narratives featured on the website were dominated by images evoking sublime nature. These present many magnificent landscapes and intimate portraits of wild species. For example, a branch of juniper coils poetically against blue sky, its individuality unmistakable. In another image, backpackers tramp along an attractive beach toward caves that open out where the mountain cliffs meet the shoreline. A text running alongside in Italian outlines the history of legislative initiatives and failures to institute a protected area.[16] In a section devoted to details about the park plan,[17] there are many more striking images. A deer pauses from its grazing amidst tufts of green. Wildflowers are captured up close by the camera. A pair of sheep range on a slope beneath a tree, with a vista of mountains in the distance. A tiny unusual bird alights on the sun-dappled earth. These photographs and others inspire a sense of relationship with landscapes and non-human species. The only people featured in them are anonymous, mysterious, and distant; these are examples of folklore photography. The mask and heavy bells of the carnival figure Mamuthone are shown up close; we see a sheepskin coat but not his head.[18] Another photo shows a herder dressed in old-fashioned velvet trousers, cap, and high boots. He walks away from the camera, into a shepherd's hut covered over by juniper branches. Another shepherd bends over the hindquarters of a sheep, squeezing streams of milk into a metal bucket. From this angle, once again, the man's face is hidden, although we can look an animal in the eye. What does it mean when people fade into the background like this?

In contrast to elaborate descriptions of flora, fauna, and geological features, there are only brief entries for each of the eighteen towns contributing areas of communal lands to the national park. Orgosolo's entry is longer than most. The town's reputation for criminality is understated in ways that pointedly recall it to anyone familiar with ongoing national newscasts—as many site visitors would be, since the pages are entirely in Italian.

> Fantastic natural landscapes, attractive [folk] costumes and fragments of the oldest story of the Barbagia characterize the [town] that reflects the bitter, savage world of the Supramonte. "Orgosolo is known across the island for its indocility and the notoriety of its inhabitants," remarked La Marmora in his Itinerario. There were others in the eighteenth century, however, who recognized the merits and moral qualities [of Orgosolo]. "Considering their better side, they are men of intelligence," wrote Vittorio Angus in his Dizionario, "most courteous in hospitality, delicate in certain points of honor and religious." (WWF 2000)

With this dubious admission of merit, the entry goes on to list points of interest for tourists and nature seekers at Orgosolo. These include murals, unusual plants and animals for which one can look, archaeological and geological landmarks, and a number of religious festivals. There is nothing in the contemporary lifestyles, concerns, and initiatives of residents to interest the WWF, except perhaps in so much as they might satisfy the exotic imagination and "reflect the bitter and savage world of the Supramonte."

Like the environmentalist pamphlets studied by Bruce Braun (2002) for the Canadian case examined in the last chapter, these narratives facilitate the epistemic erasure of Sardinian "ways of seeing" the landscape of the Supramonte. Such mundane symbolic violence to local life worlds often goes unremarked, bracketed off as it is in the ethereal world of the internet, where any individual or organization with the wherewithal to do so may have freedom of say. Increasingly, ethnographers recognize online interactions as relevant fields of social and economic life. Virtual networks and communities, computer-mediated work environments, "massively multiplayer online games," intensely social online constructs like "Second Life," and lively blogging exchanges have drawn the attention of anthropologists. Yet we sometimes overlook "the ephemera of everyday life" (Malinowski 1922) to be found on the internet. Mere websites often lack clear authorship, and we view them in individual isolation. We rarely know anything about fellow visitors. How can we ascertain the significance of websites like the one designed for Gennargentu Park?

I have approached these sites as alternate landscapes, situated in a transcendent everywhere and nowhere, seemingly monumental—as though they had always existed—and yet appearing, growing, changing, breeding, moving, petrifying (as hyperlinks "die"), and ultimately vanishing without warning. The "nature" of this electronic world beguiles us into taking much for granted: the space of global privilege that is our point of access to both technology and the skills to use it, disdain for physical barriers and political borders, a giddy disembodiment, and our own ethnocentric assumptions. An opulent luxury of resources and entertainments encourages us to forget what and who is not there, who guides us, and where we cannot reach. Visions of other places may seem so real to our eyes that we presume our understanding of them to be complete. The selectivity and partiality of representation is easily dismissed. Like the imaginative constructs present in other forms of media, representations on the web are discourses with hidden dimensions of social production and consumption. Yet the sense of englobement, of "being there," is unparalleled. Unlike television's clearly scripted tours, online interactivity gives us the illusion of control, personal agency, and freedom of movement through this landscape. Despite possibilities for social interaction, a sense of individual autonomy is usually unquestioned. Here we travel, each unto ourselves, exploring frontiers of knowledge and imagination that transform us as we go (though surely not always the same way).[19] A global perspective seems obvious. The ethnography of organizational websites is not simply the analysis of discourses. It must map out a dubious geography of enchantment so well known to us that it already appears unremarkable. It must recognize the mutually constitutive effects of virtual and material worlds and question what hegemonic processes are embedded in the emerging senses of place associated with locations "in cyberia" (Escobar 1994).

In virtual Sardinia, images and texts molded by the poetics of global environmentalism are invoked to simulate the ritual experience of eco-tourism. One can now visit the "natural temple" (APN 1999) of the Sardinian Supramonte online and never realize that residents like Santina look at it differently, as "the cathedral of Orgosolo." Dominant structures of authority, authenticity, and ritual accordingly fall in line with the priorities associated with global environmentalism. These condition feelings of attachment and protectiveness with regard to "wilderness" and wild species. Mass media visual technologies such as magazine photography, films, television broadcasts, and now websites often work to efface locally inflected evocations of history and cultural experience from the romantic landscape of Monte San Giovanni and its environs (cf. Vivanco 2002). Rural residents' voices and experiences are not well represented in the stories told about the landscape. Evidence of cultural authenticity is appropriated to authenticate the fiction of unspoiled nature. The "way of seeing" reflected by the WWF website undermines cultural authority over environmental resources by trivializing and exoticizing local communities, while obscuring class histories, property regimes, and issues of social justice in southern Italy. The growing importance of virtual landscapes deeply intensifies the "museum effect" of Monte San Giovanni, in ways that the constitution of a national park could not by itself achieve. Here we can perceive the growing power of actors associated with large, international ENGOs to overwrite locally rooted narratives of place, and inscribe highly crafted accounts about the Sardinian Supramonte in the global dreamtime of environmentalism. Online ecotourism at the WWF website is structured to mimic an experience of pilgrimage that evokes and affirms reverence for primeval Nature, transcendent Science, and a Global Commons at risk. This is not accidental; rather, it supports the neoliberal projects of landscape and identity construction managed by politicians, government agencies, and their ENGO partners. It also implicitly affirms that civil society, privately organized to bridge beyond nation-states and enroll individuals from around the world in postmodern forms of citizenship, has a vital—perhaps sacred—role to play in mediating the proper human relationship with Nature.

Comments drawn from a public feedback page ("virtual bulletin board") attached to the wwf–*Sardegna website for Gennargentu Park (consulted May 2002).* The wwf website claims to provide not only its own viewpoint, but also an open forum. A number of entries posted on the bulletin board or archived online in May 2002 (Gennargentu Park Forum maintained by Yahoo! Geocities for wwf–Sardegna, http://www.parcogennargentu.it/forum. html) showed a range of responses to the question of Gennargentu National Park (see table opposite). It is here, however, that both the "digital divide" (Compaine 2001) as well as the more subtle linguistic divides associated with written Italian and self-selecting interest in the wwf website itself are apt to bias the range of viewpoints represented, simply because of the manner of the forum. The reading of Sardinian history and modernity was in dispute. A handful of comments in favor of the park associated categories of modernity, progress, and civilization with environmentalism, while "traditional" culture in Sardinia was connected with "backwardness." In contrast, comments indicating a position against the creation of a centralized national park often conflated environmentalists with privileged, urban classes working to marginalize and dispossess rural Sardinians.

While some local advocates in Sardinia thought environmentalism cloaked a renewal of colonial power relations, others have seen Gennargentu Park as an opportunity to foster locally based development, if the control of municipal councils over decisions about conservation management were enhanced.[20] In the years anticipating the consolidation of the European Union, when regional structural development became a priority, both the power and potential of ecodevelopment discourses were strongly felt (Tsetsi and Cironis 1993). Yet the implications of ecodevelopment remain in doubt. The park initiative may have quite different impacts for different social categories in rural Sardinia,

TABLE 1.

Voices in favor of Gennargentu Park, 2002

"Yes to the park. . . . I would like modern progress for my children."
   Malva in the city of Kassel, Germany

"To think that the Park would mean 'selling our lands' to the Italian
   colonizers . . . but it's ludicrous . . . we're still in the middle ages if
   we think these stupid things." Roberto from the city of Sassari,
   Sardinia

"The institution and maintenance of a park are fundamental acts and
   milestones along the [evolutionary] path of civilization." Anna Maria
   from Mantova, a WWF member.

Voices against Gennargentu Park, 2002

"The park, understood as environmental management, has existed for
   millennia at Baunei because it was created by nature and by the
   inhabitants who have always managed it. We are not interested in
   management by the park authority. We want to continue to manage
   it." Rosa from the town of Baunei, Sardinia

"Sardinia is for the Sardinians! Leave the conventions in fashionable
   restaurants to the WWF. The herders haven't been invited there . . ."
   An anonymous Sardinian in Rome

"No to the park, where will the last Indians go to live? What kind of
   development will the money bring to these areas?" "Antipark" from
   the town of Orgosolo, Sardinia.

including relative prospects for control over meaningful cultural identities. Most people in Orgosolo might be considered to be relatively marginal, in that they occupy "distinctive and unequal subject positions within common fields of knowledge and power" (Tsing 1993, xi). It requires thoughtful analysis to understand just how different people have managed their experiences of marginality. Over the course of the following chapters, I explore forms of social agency and political practice associated with Sardinian responses to the global dreamtime of environmentalism. These are best understood not as objective manifestations of "resistance," but rather as "frictions" (Tsing 2005) that may disrupt and transform in subtle ways both power relationships and the hegemonies that support them, but yet at the same time may be implicated in the very processes that regenerate and extend them.

Anthropological dimensions of the debate over Gennargentu Park take us well beyond the analysis of superficially bipolar viewpoints. We can learn to question the whole range of ways that various groups of Sardinians themselves interpret, renegotiate, promote, appropriate, transform, subvert, resist, and circumvent the policy initiatives related to environment and development. I consider how marginal actors can contingently transfigure sociocultural contexts of political engagement. Public environmental debates are ordinarily framed by language, language style, and access to public media in ways that tend to limit the participation and authority of local voices. Such political discourses are rarely as open to popular intervention as they are made to appear.[21] While references to scientific knowledge and expertise are a staple of environmentalist arguments about how to manage resources,[22] local knowledges about sustainable resource use frequently go unrecognized because they are expressed in unfamiliar idioms of cultural experience (Ridington 1990; Brosius 1997). Simply put, the dialogues of Sardinians with respect to the environment do not always produce the genres of story that we expect, particularly in contrast to the narratives we encounter on the World Wide Web. To interpret them, we must be interested not merely in what local people have to say about environmental initiatives, but also in how they seek to communicate distinctive perspectives. It is in this way that the "ethnography of the margins,"[23] rooted as it is in the study of social practices and poetics that dynamically engage larger structural contexts, contributes striking insights into "nature in the making" (Tsing 2001). The next chapter pursues these insights by exploring the links between historicity and political subjectivity in central Sardinia.

Chapter 3

Intimate Landscapes

"As If Someone Dear to Me Had Died"

Maria is a lively and intelligent grandmother at the height of life, who has now reached the age of seniority and respect. In Orgosolo, she is usually called Zia Maria (or "Aunt" Maria), a customary kinship title offered to show respect for elders. Her husband is a shepherd, and she herself is active in the local organizations of the Roman Catholic Church, and in the community as a whole. When a provocative debate about the implications of Gennargentu Park emerged in the spring of 1998, Zia Maria and many of her female peers had something to say about it. Open political assemblies were held in the rural Sardinian towns that had been designated to contribute large areas of their traditional commons to the project. The park plan was designed to be quite in tune with mainstream philosophies of modern ecological management coupled with economic growth; it looked promising to many officials. Yet when news emerged that the agreement to make the park had been ratified by higher levels of government, Orgosolo residents were, on the whole, deeply upset and distressed. During a town meeting held that March to discuss the imminent creation of the park, Zia Maria said she felt "as if someone dear to me had died."[1] In a context where residential ties and familial relationships signify important social, economic, and political collaborations, the implicit kinship metaphor was redolent with meaning. The land itself, a cultural and economic space belonging to the community, was caught up in the natural, social bonds of a family defined by the boundaries of Orgosolo. This was particularly poignant for rural Sardinian women, who perform primary roles in the guardianship of faith and family. What was for Zia Maria as morally, experientially, and emotionally compelling as a family tie must necessarily also become persuasive for outsiders, she was convinced, if only the depth and legitimacy of this communal feeling for the landscape could be articulated in political debate.

In contrast to visions of wilderness, indigenous Sardinian visions of landscape draw upon both an encompassing sense of community and a deep sense of history. A number of ethnographers have written about the importance of "historicity" as the key to understanding cultural practice across southern Europe.[2] Historicity can be thought of as an ongoing relationship with history that shapes social and phenomenological experience rooted in particular places (Sutton 2000). What Nadia Seremetakis (1994a, 1994b) has called "the alternative sensual epistemologies" of the margins emphasizes that a place is not merely a geographic location, but also an embodied system of meaning and feeling with implications for political practice.[3] Rural Sardinians interpreted history in ways that reopened environmentalist accounts of past and ongoing events to fluid, sensuous, heartfelt, and immediate experience. The discussions that they wished to articulate about the environment were often stories that could "ride the gaps" of other narratives, opening alternative spaces for subjective knowledge and experience.[4] The Supramonte safeguarded generative social memories that enchanted the landscape with "the senses of the past."

In the previous chapter, I broadly introduced perspectives on ecology and landscape "from the bottom up." Here, I explore these perspectives in greater detail, examining social memories of the past and making an initial sketch of some gender distinctions that frame rural Sardinians' own narratives of intimacy with the landscape. Recent conservation initiatives in central Sardinia have often provoked overwhelmingly negative local responses. In the case of Gennargentu Park, this was forceful enough to result in the organization of grassroots demonstrations, and throw the legislation into question. This "resistance" was interpreted by outsiders largely on the basis of perceived cultural psychology, rather than treated as an organized, critically informed initiative. The emotional expressions embedded in the Sardinian anti-park movement have frequently been primitivized and dismissed by Italian politicians as dangerous and unsuitable to civilized political process. This chapter considers the strategic implications of the imagined divide between thinking and feeling as it has played out in scholarly and political discourses associated with ecodevelopment in central Sardinia.

Historicity and Hunger

Memories of wartime and postwar poverty in Orgosolo are significant, not only for the senior generations, but also for young men and women who referred to the harsh lives of their parents when they spoke about their own perspectives on the problem of Gennargentu Park. Their informal accounts highlighted tropes of "sacrifice" and "suffering" associated with daily work. Because the contemporary formal economy remains fragile, many local residents drew on narratives about work, suffering, and personal sacrifice to highlight the cultural continuity of past and present in Orgosolo. This contradicted visions of cultural decline following a shift toward "modern" economic practices in the postwar era. Above all, it asserted the authenticity of cultural tradition and legitimate, enduring connections to the local landscape of the Commons.

One day during World War II, when the fascist authorities sent German troops to stay in Sardinia, a young woman named Grazia went with another woman companion and a donkey to buy potatoes on the black market in the neighboring town of Mamoiada. The town was full of people from Orgosolo buying things that couldn't be found in the town. All the goods were contraband, and they paid a high price for everything. On their return, at the border of Orgosolo and Mamoiada, the police stopped them. They sent a few people back to Mamoiada, but when they saw how many there were, they arrested everyone and took them to the police station. Goods were confiscated from seventeen people, and they were all put on trial. Eventually they were released, but the potatoes rotted in storage while their families continued to feel hunger. Zia Grazia told me about this event in 1997, and the memory of this waste still haunted her.

Throughout the war, hunger, lack of supplies, and the absence of many men—and therefore of agro-pastoral labor—made life difficult, and this suffering was exacerbated by the sly caprice of fascist authorities. Zia Grazia, who had been a teenager in this period, said that people were forced by scarcity to buy the military rations of flour, potatoes, cigarettes, and other things put on the black market by the German soldiers stationed nearby. Her daughter, who was present at the interview, commented that nothing had changed in the way the *carabinieri*, the state police, deal with people. She referred me to Emilio Lussu's book about the period of anti-fascist resistance. Lussu was a Marxist political activist who had been sent to the *confini*, a form of internal exile, during this period. He founded a Sardinian nationalist party and later served as an elected representative to Rome for the Socialist Party.

Women who tell about the 1940s and 1950s in Orgosolo speak of hard physical labor and scarcity, and their plight in trying to care for family members. Zia Grazia was nineteen in 1944, when she began to work long days at temporary jobs harvesting grain, for which she was paid with a small portion of wheat flour. She explained that a few women went out to work as servants for the few landowning families, and might return home after a day's work with only a piece of lard or a small piece of cheese to divide among their own families. After the war, she said, people were buying rags left over by the military for clothes, for there was no merchandise in the stores.

> At the end of the war there were no more dishes, probably we had broken them all: people who had them in wrought iron were well off because they didn't break, even though small pieces broke off that were easy to swallow. People went to Nuoro to buy cloth to make clothes for the smallest children. I remember that we bought very stiff curtain cloth to make trousers for the men and to get thread for sewing and mending; we [unwove the cloth].
>
> Another curious thing was that summer and winter we put on sheepswool sweaters, wool that I spun myself, and [these sweaters] were made for the whole family. Once I went to harvest grain and I was wearing a sweater . . . and to give it some color they had given me a small tube of "talchina" that was a malaria medicine: it came out a beautiful lemon yellow, gorgeous, and everyone admired me, except I couldn't say what I had used to dye it because at that time the medicine was in great demand, given the high percentage of [malaria]. (personal interview 1997 [It])

Women's stories like this one often highlighted ingenious coping strategies, but also the shared local experience of *sacrifici*, "sacrifices," and *malessere*, "suffering." The gendered historical memories of women like Zia Grazia drew upon master narratives of the Roman Catholic Church, and themes of hard work and suffering also evoke a critique of structural violence and marginality. This was also apparent in some of the narratives generated by men, particularly by those few who are active, practicing Catholics. For example, local author Antonio Maria Manca (1995) wrote a fictionalized account of an Orgosolo man destined to suffer a series of *disgrazie*, a term that ambiguously connotes both "disgraces" and "misfortunes." The main character is a boy sent out to the Supramonte to become a shepherd; he discovers a body[5] in the countryside and is accused of homicide. He goes to prison. When the trial is held, he is soon found guilty and sentenced to death. Manca's novel borrows themes familiar from *Padre Padrone* (Ledda 1975) and *Banditi a Orgosolo* (Cagnetta 1954) to explore the relationship between herding and criminality. This story, however, highlights the state as a potent source of suffering that affects not only the main character, but also his family as a whole. What shines through Manca's simple prose is a representation of poetic subjectivity that enables the protagonist to find joy in sharing festive times with loved ones, despite lifelong asperity, and accept misfortunes with critical recognition, but without bitterness.

In experiential terms, women's narratives about the past were strongly located in the home, the town, and the gardens, and sometimes wage work in fields or households nearby and brief errands or pilgrimages to other towns. In contrast, though their themes were similar, male-centered narratives about the same time frame in Orgosolo were located outside the home and the town, in sites of pastoral work, war, prison, and exile. The difficulties faced by herders in particular were often vividly presented in relation to the material landscape of the Supramonte. Old shepherds in Orgosolo remembered the harsh conditions of work they once carried out in the highland countryside. Banne Sio[6] undertook a number of interviews with retired pastoralists, who had habitually remained with the herds for weeks or months at a time. The primary tropes found in men's narratives of the pastoral past are again those of "suffering" and "sacrifice," but these are set in a landscape of isolation and exposure to the elements. Sio asked a man born in 1918 when he had begun herding, and the man answered,

At eleven years [of age], with my cousins, [I was a] shepherd and in summer a pigherd. In November we left with the sheep and we came back in May, no pay, just food for the belly and some shoes, that's how it was. (Sio 1996–97, 146 [It])

Another man born in 1917, who became a shepherd around age ten, said,

Before, when it snowed we slept outside . . . we were always wet for whole days. . . . Before, there wasn't any work, it was a life of sacrifices because you were badly off, you ate badly, you had the same life as the sheep, you were worse off than a dog. (Ibid., 144)

Conditions of pastoral labor remained very difficult right into the 1960s. A younger informant told Sio,

When we were little, they sent us out [to pasture the sheep at night]. We were children of ten or twelve years, they didn't leave [the animals] penned up, whether [the weather] was good or bad you had to go. [The sheep were left to graze] from eleven o'clock for three or four hours every night . . . we were like the beasts. When I started in '61 I didn't spend a night under a roof, and in '62 it was the same thing, always outside all winter. (Ibid., 165)

Anthropologist Franco Cagnetta (1954) perceived a gradual proletarianization of pastoralists in central Sardinia, from the late nineteenth century until the time of his own ethnographic work in the period following World War II. After 1880, pasture rents ruined many men with small and mid-size herds. At Orgosolo, the communal territory remained vast and private pastures few, and not many shepherds gave their milk to emerging industrial cheese plants, so the impacts of market penetration were less severe than in many other Sardinian towns (1954, 213–14). Yet because the highland pastures were seasonally poor, herders still practiced reverse transhumance[7] and they needed to pay rents outside Orgosolo; Cagnetta suggested that about the time of World War II, conditions deteriorated and traditional contracts between herd owners and servant-shepherds were altered so that a new underclass of shepherds came into being (ibid., 215). Only the existence of free pastures in

Orgosolo, to which all the shepherds returned in the spring, assured that some income could be derived from herding activities. As long as the herds had to pasture outside the Commons, most of the product went to pay rent to the landowners (Sio 1996–97).

In the period following World War II, men's widespread, embodied experience of hard pastoral work shaped perceptions of a cohesive, locally shared past and future tied to the communal territory. *Su cumonale* was a crucial economic resource to most, but it also constituted a symbolic focus for collective identity. Memories of successful collective action affirmed that *su cumonale* implied a unique heritage of social agency. Many men had also garnered experience of wartime and of the *confini*, the camps of exile, which fired the politicization of local historical memory. The First World War constituted an important crucible for the Sardinian Autonomy Movement led by protagonists like Emilio Lussu. The Second World War sent a new wave of men off the island for a time, while the hardship of those left behind in the rural towns intensified, as women's memories reflect. Cagnetta wrote that many male Sardinians had their first exposure to communist thought during their experiences of war and internal exile, and communism was brought back to Orgosolo in 1943.

Writing for a communist-oriented cultural journal centered in Bologna, the well-known contemporary Orgosolo poet Peppino Marotto claimed he had his first lesson in "dialectical materialism" from a nineteenth-century shepherd poem in the Sardinian language called "The Divine Comedy," which satirized Dante to talk about exploitation by the rich, and the mystification of social injustice through Catholic religion. He said that he learned the poem by heart in 1946, as nearly all the herders memorized it and passed it on by singing. Marotto described in his mind's eye a time before there were paved streets and cars at Orgosolo, and pastoralists were able to come back to town only occasionally:

> They got together in a group and passed the evening visiting one another's own homes and the homes of relatives, eating, drinking and singing. All were concerned to learn the Sardinian songs by heart, to sing them in the chorus or in the solitude of the pastures to the rhythm of the bells of the herds. (1973, 332 [It])

Marotto believed there was a political education coded into the orally transmitted songs of the Nuorese pastoralists. According to Marotto, the traditional Sardinian male tenor quartet is the "characteristic chorus of Orgosolo, inherited from the forebears who perhaps imported it from the Saracens or else it was inspired [by] imitating the voices of animals" (ibid.).[8] Poems in dialect were sung at all sorts of occasions: during the religious festivals where formal poetry contests elaborated themes of opposition such as "the rich and the poor," at weddings, or in bars and private homes. During my fieldwork I still came across occasional impromptu tenor performances in bars and at gatherings of friendship groups.

Throughout the 1970s, professional tenor groups were formed at Orgosolo; several produced and recorded songs including critical content. Sardinian poetry competitions were held regularly in nearby towns, with a number of participants from Orgosolo, while "poets' wars" were occasionally held in association with festivals. Some of my young women friends noted that it was necessary to develop a special ear for the poets' language, and they did not always understand it themselves. Enthusiasts were almost always men. Sardinian poetry remains a recognized cultural form for male expression today. In tandem with other local transformations, including the development of tourism, the commodification of the signs of cultural authenticity might often draw attention from the content of the songs to the form and expertise of the cultural performance. Nevertheless, for those with the linguistic and cultural competence to decode the verses, the themes of pastoral work, of economic hardship and injustice, of the values of friendship and family, and of feeling for the landscape of the Supramonte continue to mediate an understanding of the past as well as the present.

Primordial Attachments?

The announcement that new Sardinian park legislation had been ratified in 1998 provoked a flurry of anxious questions in the towns whose lands were targeted for inclusion. In Orgosolo, the significant erosion of local control over the traditional territory of the Commons had sweeping implications, and town meetings were called several nights in a row. In the midst of this, the mayor of Orgosolo came into the local library one morning to use the phone, announcing her intention to call higher authorities and "get angry" over the liberties taken with centralized park planning. "What they're not counting on," she said, "is the primordial attachment of Orgolesi [born residents of Orgosolo] to the land." The link she presumed between common lands and collective action in rural highland Sardinia bears some reflection, because many authors have noted precedents for both social unrest and unified political initiative when control over the communal territory has been threatened. The idea of indigenous Sardinian "resistance" to colonization and "neocolonialism" has been affirmed as a mark of positive cultural distinction in many ethnonationalist narratives (Schweizer 1988).

A romantic presumption of local agency draws power from the historical examples of resistance against outsiders to protect corporately owned resources, so that recognized history shapes and gives force to collective endeavors in Orgosolo against the park. Orgosolo is, for example, particularly celebrated for its historical insubordination to the Piedmontese enclosure movement of the early nineteenth century.[9] Orgolese intellectual Giovanni Battista Salis claims that despite Piedmont's policies to eradicate free range herding on communal territories and institute private property, neither the Editto Sopra le Chiudende of 1820 nor subsequent laws to abolish feudal land-ownership structures had any effect in Orgosolo (1990, 100).[10] As Cagnetta summarized earlier, with fanciful appreciation,

> Not one enclosure was constructed at Orgosolo by virtue of the collective refusal by the herders, who saw themselves being despoiled of their most ancient communal pastures. (1954, 152)

Historical narratives have developed over time to attribute a nearly legendary status to the traces of collective action in Orgosolo. Spano's treatise on "the Sardinian question" says that after 1860, many communities in Sardinia were forced to sell their territories to speculators in order to pay high taxes to the demanding new Italian state, and only a few highland communities such as Orgosolo, isolated from the seats of administration in the urban centers, managed to preserve their forests (1922 in Del Piano 1979, 9). Cagnetta also noted that Sardinian communities during this period came under increasing fiscal pressure, the levying of troops, and a systematic despoiling of communal lands and forests which contributed to a growing phenomenon of endemic banditry (1954, 152).[11] Orgosolo was, according to him, the principal site of resistance to the penetration of the state at this time. In the late nineteenth century, however, Orgosolo was forced to cede over 4,500 hectares of its communal territory to the crown in payment of debt. Del Piano remarked that the pastoralists of Orgosolo felt themselves unjustly deprived of their lands by the crown forestry enterprise and this gave rise to "tumults and agitations" (1979, 16). That area nevertheless continued to be managed by the state, for the making of carbon and the harvesting of forest products, until 1956. It was then passed to the Region of Sardinia, constituted in 1949 as an autonomous region of the new, democratic Italy. The region carried on management of this domain and leased additional land from the community to carry on further operations, making a commitment to employ local laborers and to return 25 percent of the profits from harvested resources to the community.

Although government-managed forestry activities eventually became an important factor in the local economy, a plan in 1931 by the Azienda Foreste Demaniali, the State Forestry Enterprise, to take over more of Orgosolo's communal pastures met with determined opposition. Salis wrote that despite the risk involved in challenging the police during the fascist period, when people heard news of the decision, "the Orgolese population [did] not hesitate a moment to go out into the plaza to protest" (1990, 119). While Corda noted the centrality of the Commons to the herding-based local economy (1989, 209), Salis claimed that this action illuminates something fundamental about the enduring "character," "mentality," and "culture" of the residents of Orgosolo. Switching into the present tense, he told about the "uprising of 1931," but returned to the use of remote past verbs to describe how the authorities backed down from their decision to take over the communal territory, as though the act of protest were eternal and the successful outcome always already decided:

> One morning in April, when the women, as always, go to the nearby fountain to fill their water-jars, they read a written message: "Wake up, sleeping people, the Commons is sold!"[12] The same message appears on the walls of the churches of San Pietro and Santa Croce, and [by the cemetery], for those going to the early Mass. In less time than it takes to retell, the word spreads,

and hundreds of gathered women enter the town hall, chase out the administrators, and put the locks on the doors. They presided over the town hall for several days, in an apparently peaceful manner which however left no doubt about their firm determination, and that of their men, [who were] also wary. The alarm reached the Prefecture and the Ministry of the Interior with lightning swiftness, and there was a great explanation of the [potential police action], but the authorities refrained from a trial of strength with Orgosolo. It revoked the decision that had been made, and "the Commons," the whole territory, was not touched. (Salis 1990, 119-20 [It])

This instance in history exposes for the narrators a moment when the "true" nature of Orgosolo becomes apparent over the course of tense conflict with the state: residents are determined when it comes to protecting *su cumonale*. What gives them ultimate success in doing so (from the point of view constructed by these authors) is the mystical potency of community, of a culture implicitly connected to the Commons which seems to transcend, unify, and empower the individuals of Orgosolo.

The strongly imagined cultural protagonism of Orgosolo shepherds (Satta 2001) is attached to the symbolic potency of the Commons. This communal territory is a sine qua non of local narratives about both the past and the future in Orgosolo. Various individuals' visions of local development may diverge to emphasize herding over forestry, tourism over environmental protection, or new measures of ecological and cultural management as a means of transcending dependence on marginal pastoralism and uncertain agricultural subsidies. These multiple visions of possibility are nevertheless embedded in a sense of positive, inherited, communal tradition. Nostalgic futures are literally grounded in Orgosolo's Commons.

Modeling Culture and Environment

Many people in Orgosolo explained to me that the freedom to make use of their territory as they saw fit was profoundly important to them. In Orgosolo, *su cumonale* commanded the emotional resonance of the sacred. Even the most environmentally or progressively minded individuals found it alarming to imagine severing the ties of moral and legal ownership between the communities and their territories in order to create national parks. Why should this be so? There are three possible methods of modeling human, cultural relationships with the Sardinian landscape, each of which implies quite different approaches to the role of emotion and the senses. First, we can analyze ways in which the Sardinian commons constitutes a productive resource. This is the usual approach taken in the literature on environment and development. Rural Sardinians depend upon their communal territories for economic survival and success. The emotional charge of debates about a new park in central Sardinia does seem to be intimately connected to a widespread perception of vulnerability to the loss of economic possibilities associated with landownership. We could therefore try to explain emotional attachment to the commons in terms of basic subsistence needs and economic aspirations, particularly given Orgosolo's structural marginality in the context of nation and region. The problem of a park might then be resolved, according to the universal logic of sustainable development, by an exchange of socioeconomic programs in return for the concession of the traditional commons.

This was in fact a major thrust of negotiations for the new park throughout the 1990s, and these met with some limited success. It is clear, however, that many rural Sardinians remain unwilling to bargain over communal ownership of land, even though pastoral activities are declining and land development in the area of the proposed park is already prohibited by national legislation. A more nuanced materialist analysis could certainly help us to interpret the reluctance of many working-class Sardinians to commit support to a project with few guarantees for their own access to new jobs and funds. The economic crisis experienced in Italy since the 1980s (which cut down government investment in public works as well as new job openings in most arms of the public administration) has merely enhanced the role of the informal economy in places like Orgosolo, making communal assets a vital form of insurance against uncertainty, particularly for those without university degrees and political patrons.

We meet the limits of the materialist perspective on the Sardinian commons, however, in learning to take seriously the affective discourses of rural Sardinians, not only for the landscape and its productive possibilities, but also for its aesthetic qualities, its history, and its inherent relevance to social life. It should not be forgotten that economic possibilities are also personal and collective stories that have been, or are yet to be, inscribed upon the landscape. Is it possible, then, to explain the apparent sacredness of local connections to the commons in terms of symbolic resonance?

A cultural approach highlights the importance of the landscape and pastoral traditions in the politics and economics of regional and local identity, and in structuring social relations within and between towns. Shepherds and their work on the commons have been synonymous with highland Sardinia in the most positive cultural discourses about the area, including those devoted to tourism (see Schweizer 1988; Ayora-Diaz 1993; Satta 2001). While the land remains undivided and undeveloped common property, it validates a shared local past and many possible different futures. It symbolically defines and empowers the whole community in Orgosolo, notwithstanding growing fragmentation in occupation and cultural orientation. There is a romantic presumption of local agency that draws power from the historical examples of resistance against outsiders to protect the Commons, so that recognized history shapes and gives force to collective endeavors in Orgosolo against the park. This approach, however, still fails to understand the nature of affective ties, which entail more than economic calculations or intellectual, symbolic work. Talking with Sardinians made me realize that everyday practice, experience, and social memory shape political subjectivities that encompass both reason and emotion.

Senses of Belonging

Kay Milton (2002) suggested that people who choose to participate in environmentalist movements typically come to identify with and value the non-human beings, things, and relationships associated with the natural world when they are able to recognize them as "contributing sense, pattern and meaning to their lives as a whole" (105). This is precisely how we may also better understand rural Sardinian "love" for the Commons. Although it tends to converge only awkwardly with the global orientation preferred by some environmentalists (Milton 1996), who are more likely to define abstract "nature" as the proper object of care and devotion, this sense of sincere and encompassing intimacy with particular landscapes informed de facto local conservation practices (Meloni 1984) long before environmental values became fashionable to the discourses of governance in modern nation-states.

In the town of Orgosolo, an embodied attachment to the land is perceived as inherent to cultural identity, economic futures, and the persistence of community. Connections to the Commons pervade the sensual experiences of material culture—the flavors, smells, touches, and sounds of quotidian work and social life. Personal affection is expressed in the gift of a handmade cheese, or home-baked bread, with textures, tastes, and acts of sharing all redolent with histories of marginality, cooperation, hardship, devotion, celebration, and survival. Pastoral heritage remains relevant to the daily life of the Orgosolo law student boarding in Cagliari, whose brother drops off a parcel of meat or sweets that will be divided happily with her new friends at university. Similarly, pastoral pride remains relevant to the Orgosolo construction worker who ranges across the province to a job and invites acquaintances from another town to come and enjoy *carne arrosto*, "roast meat" with his friendship group at the foot of Monte San Giovanni, on the Orgosolo Commons. Pastoral skill remains relevant to the Orgosolo bartender who leads his tall horse through crowded streets of tourists for the celebration of the Madonna Assumption and takes part in the traditional horseback acrobatics held afterwards. Pastoral community remains relevant to the Orgosolo women who take charge of funeral processions and pilgrimages to the chapels on the Commons, walking to the cadence of the rosaries they sing in vernacular Sardinian (Heatherington 1999). Interdependence with—and belonging to—the town Commons is felt in the body and in the family. It is an object of ongoing "love," nostalgia, passion, worry, grief, and jealousy precisely because it is considered essential to the experience and agency associated with being both Sardinian and Orgolese.

Many Orgosolo residents were profoundly emotional about the politics of land management. Fiery ardor, expressed by raised voices, excited gestures, and occasional self-references to the speaker's own state of mind, marked many conversations about the park, forestry projects, and land improvement works at Orgosolo. Public debates themselves became objects of memory and feeling. One friend, for example, told me she actually avoided going to the public assemblies about the park because they made her upset. She did not want to listen, she said, but rather to speak out, and she feared others would not wish to hear what she had to say.

She explained to me in Italian, "*Per noi, queste cose sono brutte*," "For us, these things [the assemblies and topics of land development] are ugly."

Let me illustrate the depth and relevance of this comment by considering a conversation with a recently married couple, Monica and Salvatore. Late on an April evening in 1998, after I had been to the local auditorium for a public meeting about Gennargentu Park, Salvatore invited me to come back to the house and visit with him and Monica. All three of us were tired, but I had been friends with them for over a year, and the occasion was very informal. Monica brought out a tray of drinks as we talked. Salvatore informed his wife that the governmental accord to create Gennargentu Park had been signed in Rome the night before. It seemed that local efforts to stop the park were probably in vain, and there had been considerable tension at the public meeting. Monica was visibly upset.

A heartfelt debate about local politics and the park soon developed between the couple. Salvatore held a membership in the local *Partito Democratico di Sinistra* (PDS), and Monica irritably pointed out that the national and regional PDS had strongly supported Gennargentu Park as a regional development project. Both insisted that someone from outside Orgosolo could never understand the significance of the communal territory for the residents of Orgosolo, "because it did not belong to them and they [had] not grown up with it." I disagreed. I replied that the significance was obvious; the Commons represented economic possibilities beyond the activities currently taking place there, independent of outside public assistance. I suggested that it represented a guarantee of a minimum income, at least an informal one, in the event of crisis in the formal economy. Both of them accepted this point. Salvatore affirmed, "Yes, if you lose your job you know you won't go hungry because you can keep a couple of pigs on the territory." Monica changed her definition of outsiders, adding that I had stayed there long enough and interested myself in the matter "like a true Orgolese," but that "some ignorant person from [the city], for example, who had probably never been to Orgosolo," would have no idea how to read the ongoing events. My shared, firsthand experience of the community was taken to be key to my own comprehension of the role of the Commons.

It became evident, nevertheless, that I had so far grasped only part of the issue. There was far more at stake for Monica and Salvatore than economics. The two young people had salaried jobs with which to sustain themselves and help their families, and it was tacitly established that Orgosolo's territory meant far more to each of them than the baseline economic security of being able to keep "a couple of pigs" ranging on its pastures. We turned to talk about hunting, which was Salvatore's passion, and one of the chief ways that he was able to enjoy time with both friends and the natural environment. Hunting associations in central Sardinian towns are made up of formal, limited membership groups of men who coordinate hunting parties in season on specific areas of local territory, monitored by the regional forest ranger service. Although not all men practice hunting, for those who do, it can provide a chance to enact identities linked to pastoral traditions and masculinity. Despite the hardships entailed by rising as early as 3:00 a.m. to go stalking in the woods, those who hunt often prize the opportunity to appreciate healthy outdoor exercise, the aesthetics of the landscape, and the conviviality of celebration that follows a successful hunt. Salvatore claimed that local hunting companies had managed wildlife stocks with demonstrable success. The hunting associations, he said, were self-regulated and never in conflict with one another. He insisted that the merit for environmental conservation of the Commons belonged to the community.

Monica, who was exhausted from her work and little impressed by hunters, contradicted Salvatore irritably. Salvatore was still tense from the debate in the assembly. They began to argue. At last, Monica pretended to renounce the discussion, claiming sarcastically that she did not care if they created the park. Salvatore accused her a little angrily of never having been out to the territory; because she spent all her time in town, she would not know anything about the land. Monica looked annoyed, but responded to the implicit challenge that her personal tie to the Commons was weak by conceding that she might come to the next town meeting about the park.

This heated conversation demonstrated the role of emotion in the political subjectivities crafted by Orgosolo residents. The couple had quite different voting habits, jobs, and personal and gendered visions of that landscape, yet both recognized the priority of maintaining ties to the landscape, whether through direct interaction with nature or a political commitment to maintaining the Commons. The institution of a park would probably affect Monica and Salvatore, not only (or even primarily) at an economic level, but also at the levels of personal social life and community identity. The Orgosolo Commons were central not only to many local livelihoods, but also to family excursions, religious pilgrimages, school trips, and friendship group reunions. The symbolic and material products of the Commons were consumed with appreciation at every meal, work party, and special celebration, every exchange of hospitality and reciprocity. Emotions mediated these shared bonds, encompassing histories, bodies, and families. This defined the common ground of township, kinship, and friendship.

When they collaborated in affirming the authenticity of their emotions, residents like Monica and Salvatore transmuted their feelings of anger, mourning, vulnerability, and love for the Commons into the basis of a common political subjectivity. Narratives about moral authority to maintain control over key resources were rooted in local discourses of embodied history, and emotions both naturalized and legitimized intimate connections between people and landscapes. The role of social memory, condensed and embodied as sensation or feeling, cannot be overlooked in attempting to interpret political action (cf. Nazarea 2006). In an important comparative case, Aretxaga (1997) explored the role of emotionally potent personal memories, as well as expressions of pain and suffering, in constructing a new collective political subjectivity among working-class Catholic Republican women in Belfast. According to her, these women's preoccupation with the misery of sons, husbands, and fathers in prison led them to dramatize the physical conditions of the prison protests in public. From their perspective, political change must follow from wider public understanding of what was hidden from view, inside the prisons. They chose expressive and visual representations of prisoners to communicate their own direct, often shocking experiences of embodied suffering, humiliation, and loss. Through "the embodiment of emotion in social action" (Aretxaga 1997, 105), these women attempted to convey the experience of being Catholic Republican women in Northern Ireland.

Aretxaga's discussion is evocative in the context of Orgosolo, where women like Zia Maria have sometimes brought particularly gendered discourses of social suffering, physical hardship, and emotional anguish to bear on the matter of the park. Women undertake rituals of mourning on behalf of the community, as well as provide emotional and social support to those who have suffered the loss of family members. As key participants in Roman Catholic congregations, pilgrimages, and local associations, women like Zia Maria were instrumental in the maintenance of family ties and even in healing rifts between families. Even those women who were not actively involved with the church shared a common attention to the importance of family, community, and the intricate connections to the landscape that defined a distinctive way of life. Zia Maria's moving words, "I feel as if someone dear to me had died," therefore unified fragmentary personal experiences and mobilized a framework of sentiment to support community political action (see further discussion in chapter 7).[13] To grieve for the impending loss of the communal territory as though for the death of a person held dear is to grieve for the landscape with all the weight of rich social memory, faith, and experience in one's heart. It is to mourn a loss of community, commensality, and reciprocity that is part of that landscape and the property relations that have sustained it. For Zia Maria, the essential difference between welcome guests and uncomprehending strangers consisted in recognition of the ways that relations of reciprocity bound the community to the past and future and were rooted in the traditional commons. Nadia Seremetakis (1994b) has recalled attention to the role of commensality and material culture in constituting both historical consciousness and political subjectivity in rural Greece. My fieldwork pointed to emotions and the senses as modes of meaningful social and political exchange. It was not only by virtue of my study and interviews that Orgolesi expected me to earn comprehension. Rather, they obliged me to learn firsthand what the words and statistics meant to them, through the indeterminate medium of shared experience with its inherently fluid social, gendered, spiritual, economic, meaningful, power/resistance-laden, passionate, and sensual dimensions.

Meaning and Feeling in Rural Sardinia

How should we construe the role of emotion associated with both ardent "resistance" and the apparent cultural attachment to specific landscapes that paradoxically underlies opposition to the national park in Sardinia? The feminist scholars who first turned to the cultural study of emotion taught us to value and respect the emotive self-expressions of informants.[14] Their ethnographically informed insights emphasized that emotional subjectivity is never predetermined by biology, but is inherently engaged with a dynamic play of social and material, intrinsically meaningful relationships. By attending to real conversations, we can refute claims that devotion to the Commons, as well as "resistance" to a national park, is the outcome of an unreflexive, backward cultural psychology. Instead, we can examine the experiential basis of the meanings and emotions attached to the future of the Commons. Emotion is widely acknowledged to be a crucial aspect of political campaigns, and it is precisely the active and strategic interpretation of perceived biological states that grants meaning, force, and legitimacy to certain political practices. As politicians manipulate and use local models of the family, they bring into play the gendered, cultural, and developmental meanings commonly associated with emotions. The national media usually interpreted Sardinian political discourses of feeling and subjective experience according to established perceptions of southern Italian backwardness and criminality. Assumptions about the biology of gender, race, and culture structured how expressions of political sentiment came to be interpreted by the Italian public.

It is important to recognize that attempts at "objective" and "scientific" discourses about the nature of political emotion are themselves entangled with established regimes of power/knowledge, not only within the academy but also in the world at large. Sociocultural developmentalism is evident in Eric Hobsbawm's (1959) theory about Sardinian banditry as a primitive form of political resistance. Hobsbawm portrayed the "pre-modern" politics of rural Sardinians in opposition to the intellectually informed politics of a modern, European, civil society, making an implicit appeal to the Cartesian divide between feeling and thinking. Present-day Italian scholarly and public debates concerned with phenomena of mafia, patronage, and banditry in various parts of Southern Italy tend to reinforce notions of political practice—with a particular kind of "hot" emotional inflection—as the direct outcome of virtually innate Mediterranean-style cultural-psychological dispositions. Cartesian assumptions are imbricated in these debates.

The legacy of Begoña Aretxaga's (1997) post-structuralist feminist model of political subjectivity suggests how to understand local sentiments vis-à-vis certain environmental initiatives in Sardinia. According to Aretxaga, the articulation of marginal subject positions can draw force, meaning, and coherence from the evocation of embodied states. Here I have also drawn upon anthropological discussions of historical consciousness "embodied" through daily experience and social practices, whether strategic or habitual, which contribute to shared subjectivity.[15] In making sense of my fieldwork on Sardinian "resistance" to the park, I vigorously reject a false opposition between reason and emotion that demeans the intelligence of anyone whose stand is passionate. On the contrary, emotions can summarize and symbolically condense "rational" or literal thought.[16] When I report that people in Orgosolo felt deeply about communal landownership, I mean to highlight the extent to which self-conscious conceptual work conditioned this embodied experience and vice versa, so that a distasteful political debate became an aesthetically unpleasant experience, and an impending legal disempowerment provoked personal grief, or personal anger.

In Orgosolo, thinking, feeling, and social experience of the Commons were bound together in the problem of a park. Zia Maria's public comment that new legislation made her feel "as if someone dear to me had died" could be explained only by reflecting on local history encountered as embodied social experience. Political performances of cultural feeling for the traditional landscape remain salient for many townspeople in central Sardinia as they attempt to reappropriate spaces of action and discourse within the domain of environmental management. Disembodied, universalizing discourses of science currently define legitimate knowledge about "global nature." Yet local orientations and idioms of embodied history in Sardinia offer new ways of thinking critically about conservation and sustainable development. Social memory and emotion have been shown to contribute to ecological knowledge in cultures around the world (Nazarea 2006).

As in other areas of southern Europe, the communicative performances of everyday social practice are mobilized in central Sardinia as a means to creatively manage structural positions within sociopolitical spheres. This leads in particular to a dynamic play of historical consciousness, or "historicity," across different subject positionings and scales of identity construction. Rather than the coherent, linear, and expert narratives favored in conventional politics, then, rural Sardinians were apt to offer fragmented, personalized monologues and cultural interjections, all of which might shift the "global concerns" of environmentalists to be reframed within a moral sphere phenomenologically rooted in the Sardinians' own local world. Themes such as gender, hospitality, memory, and embodied identity are domains germane to social practice, knowledge, and experience in central Sardinia. They therefore represent necessary contexts to the environmental debates that have become embedded there. It is indeed only by straining to grasp multiple, locally rooted ways of "being-in-the-world" (Heidegger 1962; cf. Jackson 1998) that we can begin to understand how many different kinds of political—and ecological—subjectivity are possible.

In Orgosolo, metaphors of kinship, interdependence, and affection were extended by townspeople to the communal territory as they explained their own negative reactions to the planned Gennargentu Park. These metaphors affirmed that common lands are, in Orgosolo, an intrinsic part of the community and a basis for appropriate development. Meaning and feeling are blended both in the sense of intimate connection to the landscape and in the sense of how the embodied experience of environmental politics is enmeshed with local identity and the boundaries of social belonging. The social memory of marginality, scarcity, and hardship in the past is remembered in relation to the experience of transhumant herding and other forms of agricultural work. In this context, social agency is imagined as the product of intimate ties to both the community and the landscape of the town commons. Conversely, argument against the dismantling or appropriation of the commons—as in the case of the planned park—is explained as the outcome of a natural, historically rooted affinity for the land and is positively defined as a defense of traditional values. Contestation of a national park in Sardinia thus entailed not only a reappropriation of "ecology" and "the environment" as a sphere of political discourse, but also a fundamental reframing of environmental issues to take account of alternative frameworks of embodied moral authority.

PART III Alterity

Elder shepherds at the Pratobello demonstration (1998).

Chapter 4

Dark Frontier

Over to Uncle Petanu's

Like the landscape of the Commons, the bustling core of Orgosolo was
written over with signs of fluid, social time. The busy main street, the
Corso Repubblica, teemed with signs of inhabitation, memory, and
aspiration. From the crumbling walls of abandoned buildings with low
sloping ceilings, left over from years of hardship, to whitewashed houses
whose doorsteps were cleaned each morning and portions of naked
cement blocks that disclosed the intimacy of ongoing construction or
renovation, past, present, and future were dialogically engaged in built
spaces. People moved through the street on errands or business and
gathered in doorways and taverns to exchange news. Tourists passed
through daily to take pictures of Orgosolo's famous murals. The door
of the old town hall was pocked by shot marks; it was an image often
shown in newscasts related to Orgosolo's "black chronicle" of violence,
tragedy, and supposed cultural resistance to governing authority.

Perched on the yearning edge of a millennium, in 1999 the new town
hall building gleamed with deliberate innocence of history: no graffiti,
no gunshot, no murals, no advertising posters, no black-rimmed death
sympathies, no traces yet of disorderly habitation. Only bright, fresh
walls defined the new town hall complex on the lower periphery of
Orgosolo, strategically overlooked by the big square headquarters of
the police. Some elder women may need to ask their children to take
them there by car on errands, since it is now much farther to walk.
There is plenty of parking space now, and none of the bustle of the
Corso to hold up traffic. No bars, no shops, no daily masses nearby;

only the silent cemetery, and on Thursdays the market in the piazza on the other side of the police headquarters. There are big, unattached new homes, neat modern townhouses, and a preschool nearby. A quiet refuge for political administration, discretely removed from social life.

Here, perhaps, the click and whirr of a standardized bureaucracy might lead us toward a cosmopolitan future, where social memory is healed of ambivalence and violent tragedies are safely relegated to the past. Public structures were springing up here and there to carve out the conceptual spaces of a new era; a *belvedere*, a panoramic lookout, was constructed at the nether end of the Corso Repubblica, as well as a gracious stone terrace picnic area around the old fountain at the opposite edge of town. A new social complex was under construction adjacent to the library, near the plaza su Montilhu. There will be a recreation center for seniors and adolescents, and an outdoor amphitheatre for festival entertainments, perfectly nestled between the buildings in the hillside. New alternatives, then, to afternoons standing in the street beside the bars, to evenings sitting with neighbors on the street as motorcycles and cars roar by. Better public services, new areas of construction on the periphery, more streetlights in a charming, classic style, computers and a new audiovisual center in the library. Orgosolo glinted with the glamorous signs of progress.

Away from the richly haphazard inscriptions of the living past at the tangled core of town around the Corso, there were new architectures of forgetfulness. Public improvements swept visual and sensual elements into a unique collage of ahistorically "traditional" and "modern" qualities, an artistic appeal to transnational genres of socio-temporal order. Disparate cultural spaces were defined, divided, and enclosed: an old town was left at the core to authenticate folkish yesterdays according to the generic cravings of the tourist industry, but this was increasingly englobed and contained by the new Orgosolo. Glimpses of tradition were standardized and fixed in murals, catalogued books, and formal exhibitions. Still, inconstant memories tickled at the edges of structured certainty; social life ebbed and flowed through an insecure landscape of past, present, future.

On a July evening in 1999 we headed toward the belvedere, where the breeze seemed fresher. Zia Mariedda remembered when the area at the extreme end of the Corso Repubblica was covered with vineyards, before her own house was built there in the early seventies. She remembered, too, the family whose land was used to build the belvedere: she asked me sometimes if I wanted to walk *inte Tziu Petanu*, "over to Uncle Petanu's." For her, construction around the periphery of Orgosolo could never cancel out the vision of what had been before; rather, it merely laid one layer of reality on top of another, so that old stories were harvested from fresh brick and cement even as they had been from the grassy slopes now covered over.

We stopped to call on Zia Francesca and her mentally handicapped daughter Silvia, who fastened herself silently to my elbow. I asked Silvia what she had been doing that day and she smiled broadly as she proudly answered *pulinde*, "cleaning." Household life in Orgosolo continued to validate a time-honored role of *massaia*, or homemaker, and Silvia never failed to offer proof of her abilities in this field. On the days she was annoyed with me or jealous, she accused me of being *prithiosa*, that is, lazy, but this time she was content to simply list the achievements of her afternoon: she had washed the floor, done the dishes, and worked at her knitting. Silvia's memories of the day were bounded by a small world of family and neighbors and they were animated with a moral significance sustained by her simple knowledge of good traditions. Zia Mariedda and Zia Francesca, possessed of wider experience and subtler knowledge of life in Orgosolo, exchanged news of people in town and interpreted current events; the past was never absent from their accounts and expectations, there at the margin of the Corso Repubblica. Tides of memory set their stories in motion, catching us up in the familiar rhythms of local, gendered, and nostalgic meanings. They talked about an older woman from Orgosolo lately arrested in conjunction with a recent kidnapping. They considered her reputation and anecdotes about the history of the family, as well as the habits of police. "Anybody can end up in the hospital or the prison,"[1] as Zia Francesca once told me.

I listened to the tinkle of bells attached to the itinerant goats ranging below the belvedere, a present reminder of the town's pastoral heritage. Zia Mariedda said that the *ovile*, the animal shelter, below us would be moved away sometime soon, since young couples had bought the land to build new homes. Looking up, I saw magnificent *palazzi*, or multistory buildings, in various stages of construction; it is usual to take years to finish a single apartment, and some of the houses springing up in these new neighborhoods have been incomplete for a decade. Other signs of cultural hybridity were more immediate: both clapping hooves and fierce motors announced themselves as they rounded the tight curve before us, pursuing a continuous circuit of the Corso Repubblica and the Via Rinascita, which joined it at either end. The perceived decline of the evening *passeggiata*, "walk," in favor of (strongly male-gendered) practices of driving round and round was taken as evidence of a weakening social life. Even young adults (men and women) often complained that there were ever more vehicles in the Corso. They explained that up until a few years ago, people had strolled through the center of town in the evenings, but that now it was nearly impossible because there were too many young men racing in cars and on mopeds, and in certain periods over the summer, too many horsemen. These nostalgic stories defined a negative cultural transformation, signified, for example, by the increasing public disrespect on the part of certain *maleducaus*, ignorant persons, in the street: "These [wild idiots] break peoples' balls,"[2] as my friend Vittorio colorfully put it.

We left the belvedere and walked back along the Corso, saying good-night to Zia Francesca and Silvia. We neared a large group of neighbors —mostly women—clustered together on the sidewalk in front of a house. Zia Mariedda brought out a stool and joined them. The company represented a loose network of kinship and friendship ties; the women called each other to help with special tasks on occasion, and brought out ice cream or cake to share with one another on birthdays. When a man in the neighborhood turned one hundred years old, they organized a collection and bought him an expensive present. They chattered to one another in Sardinian, children gaily coming and going among them. They shook their heads when mopeds or cars went by too fast, but often returned greetings to the vehicles that drove by slowly and honked their horns. At this time of the year—presumed cultural transformations notwithstanding—they found occasion to see each other often; every evening after dinner they gathered *a su fris'u* "in the fresh air," *istoriande* "chitchatting."

Later in the night, the shatter of gunshot half-woke me. "*Che stronzi*," "what turds," said the university-educated young Ananiu the next day, looking at the bullet holes in the door of the unfinished recreation center as we drove by; the lovely structure was marred even before it could be opened to public use. "Here one could live with tranquility, there are sources of potential in this town. But no: here there are always jealousies, it will never change."[3] Ananiu struggled to find the rightful significance in terms of community that material signs conveyed. And so, amid inventions of modernization, decline, solidarity, authenticity, and stagnation, the built spaces of Orgosolo resounded with the plural echoes of imagination, enchanting both culture and the sense of time itself.

Culture of Violence, Culture of Resistance

Journalists, tourists, and scholars came often to Orgosolo. They were usually fascinated by a dark vision of the Sardinian interior: a vision of shepherd-bandits in the mountains and dark-clad women in the towns who keep silence for their men, a vision of dangerous youths and hardened kidnappers. These stereotypical images—crafted for the most part by outsiders to the community—have taken on lives of their own in literature, film, and the daily news, drawing reference from selected personalities, events, and scenes of Orgosolo and a few nearby towns. The stories and images contribute to the imagination of cultural alterity. The ongoing presence in Orgosolo's public spaces of potential storytellers from the outside and, above all, of journalists implicated in the reproduction of Orgosolo's *cronaca nera*, the "black chronicle" of criminal violence and tragedy, has also reinforced the boundaries of cultural intimacy (Herzfeld 1997) at the community level and contributed to the intensification of the cultural performances which narrate a positive version of local identity.[4] In this crucible of identity/alterity, individual and communal practices of self-making have been pitted against the machine of mass media representations.

This chapter explores how processes of cultural production similar to those supporting "orientalism" (Said 1978) have affected Orgosolo from the birth of the nation-state and beyond, shaping not only environmental politics but also the formation of subjective identity as a whole. Nelson Moe (2002) points out that the whole of Italy took on a particular marginality in the European imagination during the mid-nineteenth century. Divides of cultural otherness came to be nested, so that Italy and the Mediterranean were to Europe as Sardinia and the Mezzogiorno were to the rest of Italy. Jane Schneider's (1998) work on the "orientalization" of Southern Italy also supports this approach. Cultural differences between the industrial north of Italy and the agricultural south were essentialized through the interpretation of postwar economic statistics, demographic patterns, and evidence of sociopolitical organization (Gibson 1998; Patriarca 1998). This contributed to the racialization of cultural distinctions that still persist today. While the first section of the book traced out the distinctions between different viewpoints with respect to the landscape and ecological relations, the focus of this section shifts to the problem of cultural representations. It is important to recognize here that Sardinia, too, internalizes orientalism in perceived divides between city and country, lowlands and mountains, coasts and internal zones. This chapter documents how perceptions of cultural alterity in central Sardinia have informed economic and environmental policy in Italy, and how stereotypes of backwardness continue to be reified in media narratives and visual discourses.

Only the Nuoro-based Sardinian news channel, dedicated to a local, Sardinian-speaking audience and the promotion of a positive Sardinian identity, appeared willing to balance a chronicle of the misfortunes occurring at Orgosolo with a "white chronicle" of felicitous events, and to portray some of the subtleties associated with local-level debates. The national news channels and regional papers devoted brief attention to just a few of the positive occasions; moments of tragic violence, on the other hand, inspired repeated coverage and even special editions and talk shows. The lack of fit between the general news media's conception of "events" and the local conception of "events" is of course a matter of conventional mass marketing by the press, that is, the manipulation of preconceived cultural archetypes in a repetitive pattern which information consumers throughout Italy can easily grasp and identify as interesting and probable. Italian national channel television (RAI) cameras customarily sought out the exotic images of traditionally dressed men and women, of the entrance to the town hall pockmarked with the ostentatious traces of gunshot, or of the murals depicting a junked stolen car and a teenage boy squealing by on a motorcycle. Existing cultural stereotypes strongly influenced the selection of persons for on-the-street interviews and also the editing of clips, so that every story told tended to bear a heavy-handed resemblance to stories heard before.[5]

Academic, artistic, and media discourses about Orgosolo have contextualized and tempered residents' efforts at self-presentation to the outside world as well as to one another. Residents of Orgosolo are constantly engaged in an implicit dialogue with outsiders' representations of local life. Ironically, the meaningful narratives that suffuse cultural and political practice are often legible only through the lens of local knowledge, language, and experience. Outsiders' and insiders' representations converged to reify and essentialize local culture, so that the history, territory, and economy of Orgosolo appeared to demarcate and unify the town as the bearer of apparently "natural" sociocultural attributes. This has had a profound impact, as I go on to discuss, upon the cultural politics of environmentalism. The stereotypes of banditry and backwardness associated with many towns in central Sardinia have been compounded with stereotypes of ecological ignorance and destructiveness (cf. Argyrou 1997; Krauss 2005; Theodossopoulos 2003; Sivaramakrishnan and Vaccaro 2006).

Songs from a Mountaintop

In the spring of 1997, a young woman from a well-to-do family on the Nuorese coast was kidnapped. Because the victim of the kidnapping was a woman and a mother, the crime was generally considered to violate "traditional" codes of honor native to central Sardinia, as well as the core teachings of the Roman Catholic Church. Public campaigns by her friends and family pleaded for the release of the woman, enlisting the vocal support of figures of religious and civil authority.[6] Posters appeared in Orgosolo and throughout the province advocating her release, with a collage of the woman's photographs shaped as a map of Sardinia. These suggested an urge to "clean up" regional identity by dissociating it from kidnapping criminals. Such efforts scrutinized Nuorese mountain communities in particular. Ironically, these same communities were used to authenticate Sardinian cultural identity portrayed in tourism advertising narratives and in regionalist (ethnonationalist) discourses of historical identity. Orgosolo, home of the famous bandit Graziano Mesina and of convicted criminals associated with earlier kidnappings, was implicitly targeted for suspicion as a possible source of the plot.

The Nuorese bishopric radio station sponsored a special outdoor concert on Italy's May first labor day in support of the anti-kidnapping campaign, to be held on the slopes of Monte San Giovanni, a celebrated and strikingly beautiful natural landmark at the heart of Orgosolo's communal territory. Some of my friends in town explained to me angrily that the organizers presumed the woman was being held on the territory of Orgosolo, and would hear the concert from where she was. They tried to point out that a large concert was inappropriate for the environment, because the noise disturbed the animals and the people trampled on the plants and would leave garbage behind. Except for the representatives of the municipal government and some people active in the local church, the concert was largely boycotted by Orgosolo residents, although many groups of friends planned day excursions of one kind or another for the holiday. Martino, a student active in the Catholic youth group and against the kidnapping, was offended by what he saw as an unsubstantiated presumption that the guilty parties were part of the Orgosolo community. He said that the Nuorese artist performing at the concert was a good singer, "*ma non avrebbe dovuto farlo,*" "but he shouldn't have done it."

Italian-style kidnappings are lengthy affairs, and the concert was eventually followed by an official demonstration of sympathy with the anti-kidnapping campaign. This consisted of a procession of cars carrying the mayors of all the towns in the region near the victim's home, taking a route which included stops to meet officials in the provincial capital as well as in several towns in the Barbagia, including Orgosolo. The procession attracted several curious onlookers, but few participants, leaving the mayor and the priests to cope with officials and the journalists who followed them. Only one person was interviewed. This formidable woman dressed as a widow in black pleated skirt, black blouse, and black shawl, with her hair in a characteristic traditional bun, pleaded with the kidnappers to release the young victim, speaking of the suffering of the family and the forgiveness of God and community. She was one among several senior women *priorissas*, strongly active in the Roman Catholic Church, who believed it important to show their support for the victim's release.

The campaign continued, and the newscasts often showed the victim's picture, but the victim remained in the custody of her kidnappers throughout the summer. At the end of September, the young woman made a miraculous "escape" from her latest campsite prison, apparently in the valley below Orgosolo. The event excited an immediate frenzy of press coverage, with repeated statements by the victim and by protagonists of the campaign for her release, as well as by the police authorities responsible for the investigation. Within days there were doubts cast upon the authenticity of the kidnapping story, and the young woman's father came under suspicion for the payment of a ransom. A Cagliari businessman and friend of the family finally stepped forward to announce that he had volunteered to pay the ransom on the family's behalf, since the bank accounts owned by family members of the victim were frozen by a national law which aimed to prevent kidnapping attempts. This, together with two new kidnapping cases on the Italian mainland roughly coinciding with the woman's release, sparked a national media debate on the viability of the anti-kidnapping measure. Her imprisonment at Orgosolo was later confirmed by authorities, who eventually arrested individuals from Orgosolo (and another town) in relation to the kidnapping, including an older woman who was said to have cooked for the victim. This last detail was important, for just as the choice of a woman and mother as a victim of kidnapping was presumed to be a manifestation of declining morality, so too was the deliberate involvement of a woman and a mother in the kidnapping plot understood by many as a further testament to negative cultural transformations in the community of Orgosolo.

The Black Chronicle

In autumn of the same year, both the media and the town council of Orgosolo received a letter from an entrepreneur in the thriving coastal town of Tortolì who claimed to have uncovered a plot by Orgolesi to kidnap a member of his family. The man's father had also been the object of a sequestration plot and had died in the custody of his kidnappers years ago; individuals from Orgosolo were allegedly involved in this plot as well. He challenged the town to affirm its solidarity against kidnappers by having citizens sign a civil petition. The challenge drew on notions about the existence of Sicilian style *omertà* in rural communities—that is, a cultural code of silence about criminal activity. By calling on citizens of Orgosolo to confirm their opposition to kidnappings publicly, the Tortolì entrepreneur implied that those who refused were complicit in the acts themselves.

Since the letter openly cast aspersions on the community identity, the mayor of Orgosolo convened a general assembly at the town auditorium on October 15th, 1997, to read and discuss the letter and to make an official response. Journalists were called in, and there were several television cameras and a number of correspondents. The audience filled in quickly with a mix of women and men of all ages. Inevitably the photographers targeted the shepherd's caps and kerchiefs of the mature and senior individuals, now emblematic of the rural mountain towns. The mayor opened the meeting in Italian, read the letter, and offered her sympathies to the author, but insisted that the town council should not hold *un processo in piazza*, "a judgment in the public square [kangaroo court]." She said the community needed economic initiatives. Then the microphone was passed to other councilors.

Micheli, a young man in a black turtleneck and jeans, interrupted from the back right-hand corner, making an animated comment in Sardinian. He demanded that *il popolo*, "the people," be allowed to speak, and denounced the continual accusations of criminality aimed at Orgosolo. An older man wearing a cap stood up from the back center of the auditorium, where he sat with other older men, and called out "It's always Orgosolo, Orgosolo, Orgosolo!" He was agitated and repeated his statement several times. The tense audience murmured, shifted with embarrassment, irony, and mutters of amusement and agreement. The mayor called the meeting to order a couple of times.

A well-known Orgosolo politician for the *Partito Sardo d'Azione* (PS d'Az), the Sardinian Action Party, began to speak in measured Italian about the failures of the region and the need to support the school system; Micheli again leapt into the fray with an explosive Sardinian-language comment. He addressed the mayor and several other individuals, including an undercover policeman, by first name, personalizing and localizing the dialogue. He expressed anger about the letter, and this provoked spontaneous applause from the audience. Another older man broke in, standing up to call out his assent. This generated multiple conversations amidst the audience. The meeting continued with a regional councilor from Orgosolo who lived and taught school at Nuoro; in Italian, he called for long-term cultural and economic modification of the agro-pastoral system. Another teacher, a member of the *Partito Democratico di Sinistra* (PDS), the Democratic Party of the Left, and past mayor, spoke (in Italian) about the need for development and infrastructural investment in the area, and the valorization of the Sardinian language in the school system.[7]

By this time the RAI television cameras had retreated, and only the director of the *Telesardegna* (Sardinian language) news, an intellectual whose wife comes from Orgosolo, and one or two other journalists remained to listen to the end of the meeting. The new parish priest (who took over after the former head priest was promoted to bishop and moved to another Sardinian diocese) was welcomed by the mayor and made a brief speech to denounce sequestrations but also to point out that no journalists had shown up to attend the Christian youth convention held at Orgosolo the spring before. Another PDS party member and past communal councilor spoke about the socioeconomic unease at Orgosolo. Two hours after the meeting had opened, the mayor closed the discussion on kidnappings and opened a discussion on the park. Most of the audience stayed, but the last journalists disappeared.

This meeting highlights the contrast between local ways of constructing events and the genre of narrative habitually employed by journalists to explain events in central Sardinia. The RAI television cameras focused only on three things: first, the formal response (in Italian) of the local mayor to the accusatory letter; second, the brashly spontaneous, angry response (in Sardinian) of the young man who interrupted her, implicitly claiming to speak on behalf of "the people"; and third, the response (applause and mostly Sardinian interjections) of the local audience in support of the angry young man. This was a time-efficient strategy to capture key images on film and array them in a very conventional narrative: the incongruous young woman mayor of a rough town speaks in civilized Italian but refuses to draw up a formal petition against kidnapping; a male youth speaking backwardly in Sardinian shows how tenuous is the mayor's control over the local situation, while the general population—stereotypically rural, uneducated, and exotically traditional shepherds and widows—apparently supports the cause of criminality and disorder. For most journalists it was probably unimportant that this young man, Micheli, was politically engaged and eloquent in his first language. For them he was indistinguishable from other "dangerous" Sardinian youth simply because he was angry to be accused of solidarity with alleged kidnappers.

Since many of the RAI employees come from city backgrounds, they may not have been able to understand much of what was happening in the local dialect of Sardinian, and far less the overwhelming reception given by Orgosolo audiences to the language switch itself. Code-switching from Italian to Sardinian implied for the local audience an enhanced capacity for their participation, since most Orgosolo residents use Sardinian on a daily basis and tend to remain uncomfortable framing their opinions in Italian. For the average Italian-speaking listener watching regional editions of the news on the RAI channels, on the other hand, the shift to Sardinian-Orgolese would make local discourses unintelligible, and translations were not provided. The use of Sardinian highlighted the intimate knowledge shared by Orgosolo residents that remained impenetrable to the outside world, evoking images of *omertà*. The general association of Italian with cities, education, high culture, and authoritative political discourses would also tend to mark Sardinian interpolations as intellectually inferior, at least from a non-local point of view.

The RAI people engaged in additional on-the-spot selectivity by dismissing the future comments and responses of local intellectuals in Italian and leaving early. Most journalists opted not, therefore, to make important to television audiences the complex debate on socioeconomic issues related to the origin of criminal phenomena. In contrast, this was pressingly relevant to local residents. The discussion of Gennargentu Park, which followed up the local controversy over the infamous letter, was actually an extension of this socioeconomic debate. While the Orgosolo audience continued to listen and participate, none of the journalists perceived the rest of the meeting to be part of the main event. Their constructed reports of the public meeting reduced a sophisticated political-cultural exchange to a flat cultural caricature, fit for the preconceptions of a broader Italian public. They were therefore unlikely to inspire real reflection upon local problems. The news media had unreflexively reconfirmed the prejudice that Orgosolo residents were criminally inclined, if not by direct action, then by their choice of silence. It was, however, the media itself that created the appearance of *omertà*, through a process of highly selective representation.

The same cultural tradition of journalistic representation was demonstrated again one month later, at a special television debate in which Orgosolo was invited to participate. Following the release of the woman kidnapping victim in the valley of Locoe and the furor over the letter to the Town of Orgosolo, a well-known talk show organized a feature on sequestrations. A remote crew was set up in the Orgosolo auditorium, with the permission of the town council. In the meantime, on the continent, other kidnappings were ongoing. A second remote service was set up to allow the schoolmates of a boy who had died recently as a victim of kidnapping to participate. Naturally, the author of the letter to the Town of Orgosolo and a famous kidnapping victim were invited to the central studio as special guests. The Santoro talk show debate on kidnapping phenomena was broadcast on Thursday, November 18, 1997.

The Orgosolo auditorium was full to the brim for the occasion, but mostly with school-age youths, attracted by the idea of being on television. There were very few of the active citizens and councilors who regularly attended other public meetings. The two town priests were there, together with some members of the local church associations and the parish council. There was an overabundance of brightly uniformed state police arranged in shiny straight rows of four or five together. I counted seventeen inside the auditorium, but other policemen were also stationed in the atrium and outside the building.

The journalists scouted for possible speakers before the beginning of the broadcast and deliberately sculpted the crowd. They arrayed a few chosen individuals near the front of the room to one side and simultaneously isolated most of the local intellectuals and experienced speakers farther away from where the microphones would be. The members of the crew had placed two television sets at the front of the auditorium so that the audience at Orgosolo could ostensibly hear and watch the broadcast in which they were participating, but the audio quality was very poor and the arrangement was inadequate for such a large venue. In fact it was difficult to catch even the speeches made within the room, since the microphones fed into the recording lines and not into the auditorium speakers.

The show opened with the host's commentary on recent kidnappings in Italy and then cut to an interview with the kidnapping victim's mother. After a retelling of the story of the kidnapping and release, the mayor of Orgosolo was given an opportunity to speak. She said that the town was tired of discussions about kidnappings and did not deserve the totalizing stereotype with which it was apt to be condemned. The broadcast cut to scenes of the ostensible kidnapper's "hideout" in the valley below Orgosolo where many people have vineyards and gardens. The host of the show argued that the picturesque view was misleading, in contrast to the awful experience of the kidnapping victim. Mature people in the auditorium, including some individuals with university educations, chuckled with distaste at the host's sarcastic turn of phrase, "this gentle hill of Orgosolo."

The television program played back spontaneous street interviews taped that day with school children from Orgosolo and older people at the local market. The children made offhanded replies to questions about kidnapping, discomfited by the attention. An older widow said that not everyone in Orgosolo was bad, and people were afraid to speak. The audience at Orgosolo began to show signs of nervousness, recognizing that the town was taking on a too-familiar provincial image in the story being crafted on television. On the viewscreen we saw that they were broadcasting images of Orgosolo and its environs, while the journalists continued romantic monologues. The editing was insidious in its reification of cultural stereotypes. Murmurs took wing around me because the broadcast reproduced what we had been hearing on the television news for two days straight. Audience participation in the televised dialogue was minimal at this point. Far more lively were the private exchanges of conversation taking root in every part of the auditorium at Orgosolo.

Having pointed out that the valley of Locoe was full of houses, the journalists narrating the clips on the television posed the question of why nobody in Orgosolo knew about the tent in which the kidnapping victim was ostensibly kept for several weeks. They turned again to the mayor of Orgosolo, who began to explain what was obvious to anyone from the area, that the "houses" found in the countryside outside the town were cottages adapted to occasional use rather than residences, and that gardens and vineyards were tended by day, sometimes irregularly. A young man in his early twenties, wearing a bright yellow sweater, stood up to say that Italy's politicians rob people worse than kidnappers, and should be punished first. The large number of very young people in the audience at Orgosolo burst out in nervous cheers and applause, while older heads shook back and forth, because they realized that such outbursts would be used against them.

Members of the town council began to chafe at the bonds of backstage silence and demand that adult speakers be given a chance. The efforts of a former mayor to take the microphone were denied by the journalists, and he walked out. His action met with applause from the older people seated in one corner of the room. One town councilor got up to follow, but sat down again. At last the inimitable Zia Pasqua, a *priorissa* garbed in her traditional widow's attire, succeeded in appropriating the microphone. She held on to the microphone (still in the hand of the journalist, powerless to escape her formidable grip with public grace) while explaining that Orgolese were against kidnappings, and that it was not right to blame an entire community for the actions of a minority. The local audience applauded.

The television show cut to images of Orgosolo's Corso Repubblica, underscored by sinister music. There were familiar shots of the town hall door filled with buckshot, and then a map of Orgosolo marked with yellow highlighter to show the streets where accused or convicted kidnappers and perpetrators of homicides lived. The whole town was therefore portrayed as complicit in the project of kidnappings, whether by direct activity or silent consent. The mayor of Orgosolo responded with growing irritation at the continued offensiveness of this program, and the older crowd applauded, showing solidarity. In the background of the studio on the continent, there were posters with slogans about how silence before the law—*omertà*—kills. A sense of doom prevailed among the mature members of the audience, who began to whisper about the uselessness of being involved with the media. It seemed that the broadcast had been staged long before any Orgosolo residents came out to participate that night. The journalists returned to profit from the ingenuous rage of the young man in the yellow sweater, then the camera cut to show a group of high school students on the continent, full of grief for the loss of a companion who had died recently as a victim of kidnapping. The last scenes of the show degenerated into a moral battle between the youth of Orgosolo, angered by renewed accusations of complicity with kidnappings and expectations of criminality imposed upon the town as a whole, and the young companions of the dead boy, full of pained, self-righteous wrath.

As the broadcast finished, there was a tremendous stir in the auditorium at Orgosolo. The parish priest, who had not been allowed to speak to the cameras, commented ironically to upset parishioners that the journalists should be proud of themselves, for inspiring a fight between two adolescent boys. One older woman nodded to me and said in Italian, "We've played the clowns and now we'll go home." As they prepared to leave, the journalists were immediately besieged by small turbulent seas of Orgosolo's most upstanding and now most offended citizens, a group of pious older women. The short, formidable figures in dark pleated skirts washed up around the tall, thin young man who had held the microphone, pointing at him and remonstrating with him as though he were a child. It was difficult for me to imagine that such women feared to break a code of silence with their own children or neighbors, much less condone an act of kidnapping. These women were forceful protagonists of the church; almost militantly prayerful, they were accustomed to a fair share of power and respect in the public spheres of Orgosolo. After the journalist team managed to pack up, it fled far and fast, disdaining the dinner offer extended dutifully by the town council, despite its members' own bitter disappointment at how Orgosolo's image had been exoticized, defamed, and exploited.

Objectifying Orgosolo

The impasse of cultural stereotypes evident in the live television debate about Sardinian kidnappings was not the outcome of spontaneous exchange, but of a history that goes back to the forging of the nation-state in 1860, and even earlier. In John Dickie's recent discussion about post-unification representations defining essential differences between Southern Italy and the north, he writes that the Mezzogiorno has been represented as "a place of illiteracy, superstition, and magic; of corruption, brigandage, and cannibalism; of pastoral beauty admixed with dirt and disease; a cradle of Italian and European civilization that is vaguely, dangerously, alluringly African or Oriental" (1999, 1).[8] Dickie is particularly concerned with how attempts to define Italian nationalism and modernity depended upon strategic contrasts to the Italian Mezzogiorno and the imagination of "the Southern Problem" as a metaphor for the country's problems as a whole. He suggests,

> Still today, Italian culture is dense with stereotypes of the South and with the anxieties about national identity that those images often signal. Fascination, disgust, exoticism, and fondness are still on the palette of responses to the South's difference. (1999, 144)

What Johannes Fabian (1983) has described as "discourses of alterity," a set of narratives that actively inscribe cultural distance between the reader or audience and the objects of discussion, can be discovered at work in central Sardinia, past and present. The objectification of Orgosolo as a criminal culture has many precedents in Italian scholarship and political-bureaucratic discourses. These in turn find roots in earlier romantic and colonialist discourses about Sardinia.

The whole area of mountainous central Sardinia was historically notorious for its fierce resistance to the Romans and Carthaginians, earning the name Barbagia, "Barbaria," and various characterizations of incivility in the records kept by Roman administrators (Mastino 1995).[9] By the second century A.D., Christianization was well underway in Sardinian cities along the coast, but central Sardinia was brought under the sway of the church only much later; Orgosolo's first missionaries were martyred at the hands of the local population toward the end of the third century (Sanna 1997, 17). Orgosolo belonged to the *giudicato*, or jurisdiction, of Arborea during the brief moment of independence Sardinia enjoyed through the medieval period: Arborea was the last of the Sardinian territories to fall again to outsiders in 1358. Sardinia then came under the feudal rule of Christian Spain. The first Roman Catholic chapels were erected in Orgosolo during the seventeenth century. There are references in the nineteenth-century records of the Church to the bandits of Orgosolo, the spirit of vendetta, and how other Sardinians feared the people of Orgosolo (Cagnetta 1954, 87).

Elettrio Corda (1989, 9) documents that the phenomenon of Sardinian banditry began to escalate slowly around the end of the eighteenth century. In the first half of the nineteenth century, Piedmont's enclosure movement and anti-feudalism laws exacerbated economic pressures on herder-peasants and resistance to the formal authorities took many forms. Organized bands of outlaws took shape (ibid.) while a discourse about the criminal tendencies of Sardinian shepherds began to flower just at the time the nation-state of Italy was founded. A bishop visiting before 1847 exhorted the population of Orgosolo to stop robbing animals from lowland communities, otherwise they could not be Christians. People answered, as the story goes, that God would surely have pity on them because the shepherds of the plains had many sheep and they had only a few (Cagnetta 1954, 89). In 1869, Mantegazza said that "the errant herder, a perfect character for the anthropologist and the novelist, is the ruin of Sardinia" (in Niceforo 1897, 52). A parliamentary inquest into Sardinian banditry was made. During the last two decades of the nineteenth century, Orgosolo was riven by a blood feud and an intense period of banditry (Cagnetta 1954, 89; Zizi 1994, 140). A second parliamentary inquest was commissioned, and it was presented in 1896. As the turn of the century approached, physical anthropologists in the Italian tradition of positivist anthropology began to theorize "scientific" explanations for the high rate of state-defined crimes which occurred in the province of Nuoro.

Given the theories of social evolutionism prevalent in Europe at that time, the criminal activity in central Sardinia was considered evidence of bio-social inferiority vis-à-vis the national culture of continental Italy. A state inquest found that "the Sardinian herder of the Delinquent Zone is the incarnation of a disappeared morality and society" (S. de Francesco 1895 in Niceforo 1897). Two protagonists of positivist anthropology in Italy, Alfredo Niceforo and Paolo Orano, traveled through central Sardinia and came to Orgosolo in 1895. Gino Satta (n.d.) characterizes Paolo Orano's 1896 treatise on the psychology of Sardinia as a theory of "born delinquents" and suggests that the diffuse perception that central Sardinia had been physically isolated from outside contact throughout history made it an attractive object of interest for scholars committed to assumptions of biological determinism. Satta suggests that Orano was fascinated by the proverbial "resistance" of central Sardinia:

Orano does nothing else but repeat the identifying myth of the indigenous resistance to invaders, cultivated by Sardinian intellectuals as an imagined liberation from an actual subalternity and then propagated by travelers in their [written] works, reversing their [symbolic] value. The resistance is not a spirit of liberty and independence, but inadaptability; the conservation of one's own cultural characteristics is not fidelity to oneself, but simply an indication of lagging behind in the development of civilization. (n.d., 6)

Niceforo, in comparison, was scientifically ambitious and measured the heads of residents in each town, whom he thought representatives of an "atavistic" race. For him, central Sardinians were part of a society which was "not completely evolved" and therefore manifested "the criminal acts proper to a primitive society, that is to say homicide, theft, robbery, violence, encroachment, vandalism, fire" (Niceforo 1897, 4; my translation). Niceforo argued that cranial forms varied from zone to zone in Sardinia in proportion to the contact of indigenous Sardinians with foreign populations, and therefore with the degree of penetration by colonial forces; these cranial forms corresponded to observed ethnographic differences and "psychological dispositions" (31–35). He saw racial physiology as the conditioning factor for "passions, tendencies and impulses," determining the form of the crimes practiced (36). Niceforo, too, associated the problem of criminality with the culture of transhumant herders, and saw the so-called Barbagia as

that zone, stopped on the path of evolution, still saturated with old superstitions, with antique and strange ideas, [which] has same the brutal concept of morality that primitive nations, primitive tribes, had. (43)

Niceforo went so far as to identify the town which fostered the archetype of delinquency in central Sardinia, and this town was Orgosolo. According to him, Orgosolo itself was "the criminal nodal point of a criminal zone" (21).

Within a short time of the racist scientific publications by Niceforo and Orano, Italy intensified its police campaign to repress criminality in Sardinia. In May of 1899, for example, 368 individuals were arrested in the environs of Nuoro in one night; after two years without a trial, 362 of these people, mostly working-class shepherds, were released. The state's crackdown on criminality also resulted in a shoot-out on the territory of Orgosolo. One night in July of 1899, over 200 police and soldiers were sent into position in the territory between Orgosolo and Oliena to find a notorious band of five outlaws, some of whom were from Orgosolo (Corda 1989, 48–49). They located the camp and killed three of the bandits on the spot, with one policeman killed and one wounded. They pursued the other two and killed the fourth, though another soldier lost his life. The sister of two of the bandits, who were from an Orgosolo family, was later charged with aiding and abetting the criminal acts of her brothers, and sentenced to eighteen years in prison. Two years later, the fifth and last member of the band was hunted down on Orgosolo territory and killed in the area called Morgogliai by a patrol group of six, who then had a picture of themselves taken as they posed with their guns around the dead man. This picture became famous because of its similarity to images of boar-hunting parties; from a local perspective, it became symbolic of police attitudes toward the people of Orgosolo. Decades later, the artist Francesco del Casino painted this scene as a mural on the Corso Repubblica, with the caption *Caccia Grossa ad Orgosolo*, "Big Game Hunt at Orgosolo." A little way down the street he also painted a mural ironizing the work of Niceforo.

A high level of internal violence, illegal activity, and police repression was more or less a constant for people in Orgosolo throughout the first half of the twentieth century. By 1954, when Franco Cagnetta wrote his famous monograph, *Inchiesta su Orgosolo*, "Inquest on Orgosolo," he commented:

> The criminal situation in Orgosolo in truth is not normal. . . . If there existed a statistic of homicides, woundings, conflicts, blackmailings, kidnappings, robberies, and criminal acts such as sheep theft, cutting the hocks of animals, land theft, vandalism of crops, setting of forest fires, etc., probably Orgosolo . . . would be at the head of all the towns in Sardinia each year. From a study of all the Sardinian newspapers from 1901 to 1954 (with the approximation possible), I have revealed that in Orgosolo (and especially during the hot months that coincide with the presence of the herding population) there occurs about one homicide every two months (six each year) . . . for an annual percentage of one killed for every 600 inhabitants. [As for] the aggressive acts committed by people from Orgosolo (and especially during the cold months on the plains to which [the shepherds] go down), there takes place about one each week. (1954, 42–43)

Working within a modernist paradigm of social anthropology, Cagnetta was deeply critical of police action and public policy in central Sardinia. He contributed a Marxist deconstruction of class and state structures at the time and urged investment in local development. He was particularly fervent in his scholarly reproach of the use of police tribunals (with special powers to condemn "banditry" on the basis of anonymous accusations) to exile communist party members and repress a politics of anti-colonialism; he collected life histories to illustrate the links between violent phenomena and lack of economic development. Yet because he confirmed abnormally high criminal activity at Orgosolo and located the source in economic and social structures tied to shepherding, many of the nuances of his ethnographic work were overlooked.

> The town of Orgosolo has a singular destiny, unique, probably, among all the towns of Europe: for three thousand years it has been under permanent military and police siege. Facing its radical internal turbulence, Carthaginians, Romans, Byzantines, Spanish, Piedmontese, Italians, have never been able to conquer it decisively, to penetrate it: they have been limited from the first to attacking it, constrained to keep it at bay surrounded by troops; to contain it then, once occupied, with a continuous police regime. For centuries the relations between Orgosolo and the State have been fundamentally the same: conflicts, wars, tensions, hostilities. (Cagnetta 1954, 145)

When this acclaimed and controversial ethnography was transformed into a movie, *Banditi a Orgosolo*, filmed in the town itself by Vittorio De Seta during the 1960s, its analytical focus was dimmed and simplified. The textual script of the film was minimal; rather, the producer relied on images of harsh life in the Mediterranean brush to convey the notion of how shepherds were transformed, by dint of circumstance and socialization, into brigands. The shepherds themselves had few words to describe their own stories or criticize the structures that impinged upon them, and they spoke in Sardinian that the audience can understand only through the subtitles. The images are images of "others," the people of Sardinia who are distinct from Italy, whose speech is unintelligible, whose lives are circumscribed by unimaginably austere conditions. The irony and suffering portrayed in these stories was the outcome of both economic and cultural constraints on individuals. Like the film *Padre Padrone*,[10] the film *Banditi a Orgosolo*[11] represented the shepherds' world as a landscape of isolation and aggression, and that landscape was distinctively Sardinian. The metaphorical equation of shepherds with bandits and Sardinia with violence and backwardness has powerfully framed even these artistic discourses on local life. These famous films disseminated images of Sardinian alterity in Italian popular culture.

The Greening of Backwardness

During the 1970s, further outlaw activity and general strikes occurred in central Sardinia, and were seen by intellectuals of the left as an incipient liberation movement. Their reading of history emphasized highland Sardinian traditions of local autonomy and resistance to foreign intruders and foreign cultural influences. Shepherds were romanticized as the carriers of a subaltern culture, a distinctive and untainted Sardinian culture with its basis in egalitarian communities (Schweizer 1988). Throughout the 1970s and 1980s, highland Sardinia was vulnerable to both negative stereotypes of backwardness and romantic stereotypes of traditionalism. Expert discourses about banditry and criminality continued to shape the Sardinian frontier.

Although postwar development discourses dispensed with outright racism and accusations of moral or mental primitiveness, evolutionism remained implicit in notions about the stages of economic growth and modernization. In 1962, the first Piano di Rinascita (Plan of [Economic] Rebirth) for Sardinia aimed at modernizing agricultural production and encouraging industrialization. Sardinia, and highland Sardinia in particular, continued to be defined by tropes of backwardness (Ayora-Diaz 1993). Between 1966 and 1969, a wave of violence affected the island.[12] Sardinian politicians in Cagliari lobbied for another parliamentary inquiry into the alarming increase in "banditry," including homicide, extortion, theft, and kidnapping (Clark 1989, 448). The resulting Medici Inquiry linked the high incidence of criminal activity to the continuing archaism of the socioeconomic organization of highland, central Sardinia, since the Sardinian "psychology" and culture as a whole were strongly influenced by the shepherd communities of the interior (Pirastu 1973: 97–99). The study concluded that bandits had, since the seventeenth century, come out of shepherd societies (ibid., 95), and that the solution to the problem of banditry must involve the abandonment of transhumant pastoralism as well as the modernization of herding practices, including the use of communal lands and unimproved pastures (ibid., 157). The Regional Law for the Reform of Agro-Pastoral Production of 1974, together with the second "Plan of Rebirth" of 1976, aimed to attain these goals (Vargas-Cetina 1993b, 346–47).

The socioeconomic transformations undergone by highland Sardinian communities since World War II were thought to have produced a partial displacement of "archaic" traditions, values, and practices by modern capitalist society, provoking an "imbalance" or "incompatibility" between shepherd societies and the structures of the modern state.[13] Violence and poverty were seen to be the scourges of a culture that remained dependent upon an outdated pastoralism. Propositions to create a national park were consistent with other development plans for the area. In this way, the shepherd-other became the object of environmental discipline in the postwar Region of Sardinia.

Looking back, we find that discourses about Sardinian alterity suggested an ecological dimension from the outset. During the nineteenth century, the prototypical Sardinian shepherd was deemed thoughtlessly harmful to environmental resources, apt to destroy "an ancient woodland by caprice or for vendetta, to make room for his goats or [to gratify] innate sentiments of destruction" (Cettolini 1895 in Niceforo 1897, 53). He was believed to both shed blood freely and set fires indiscriminately. The media still portrays Sardinian shepherds as somewhat savage and ignorant, and this image permeates even the discourses of forestry and agricultural science. Anthropologist Giulio Angioni notes that the Sardinian shepherd has often been characterized, for example, as "the prototype of the pyromaniac" (1989, 25). As concerns about environmental conservation gained prominence, the heritage of agro-pastoral culture in highland Sardinia was increasingly blamed not only for criminality but also for ecological deterioration. In particular, the rising problem of anthropogenic forest fires was explained by tropes of culturally embedded violence and ignorance. Sardinian "troubles with wilderness" were not merely a matter of talk; as in Northern Ireland during the peace process, the ambiguous signs of "resistance" were sometimes embodied in real conflagrations.

Official discourses about criminality and ecology in Sardinia strongly converge because each tends to reify and homogenize local culture. Both emphasize planned resource management and economic development, controlled by the state in ways that recall Foucault's idea of "discipline" (1977, 1978). Central Sardinia is riddled with police roadblocks on a daily basis and subject to aerial vigilance by police helicopter. Professional surveillance of the landscape and the deployment of scientific knowledge to manage it has been long institutionalized in the form of the forest ranger corps, but the number of rangers was expanded tenfold during the 1980s. Even today, forest rangers in the Sardinian Corps for the Defense of the Environment carry guns, and in their ongoing patrols across the open territories of the highlands, they have often been tacitly expected to watch for signs of kidnapping rings and other illicit activities. The methods of environmental concern—to know the environment, to define normal and authentic ecologies, to institutionalize ecological expertise, to elicit public and individual participation in environmental projects, and to disseminate environmental values—are all methods of exerting authority, discipline, and control over the Sardinian Supramonte, seen as a dark frontier.

The alterity long associated with Sardinia's "criminal zone" continues to be reaffirmed as an ecological alterity. The images of danger and violence that have become intertwined with images of nature and culture in Sardinia resonate with similar processes of cultural representation in other frontier zones around the world. They recall, for example, the ambivalent imaginaries conjured around Amazonian rainforests (Slater 2000; Raffles 2002). Such imaginaries suggest far more than an accumulation of romantic adventure stories and images; they have had real, material effects in shaping political platforms, development policies, and the social interactions between government agencies and individuals in the areas in question. As global movements and interactions "speed up" (Harvey 1989) and cosmopolitan identities become a constitutive aspect of social and political life in the urban metropoles, these frontier imaginaries only gather force. Paradoxically, they grow more powerful in proportion to the perceived dwindling of wilderness and biological wealth.

Neoracisms and Environmental Justice

In the first chapter of this book, I discussed the problem of ecological alterity in relation to discourses of indigeneity. Drawing on evidence from cases in different parts of the world, I discussed how double-binds of authenticity are produced by naïve forms of multiculturalism embedded in the global dreamtimes of environmentalism. Visions of autochthonous ecological tradition in Sardinia are tenuous, because Sardinians do not fit stereotypes of indigenous people as childlike, inherently good, passive victims, or "natural ecologists." First, central Sardinia has long been viewed as a "criminal zone" (cf. Niceforo 1897; Corda 1989), and continues to garner notoriety for its association with famous kidnappings and political intimidations. Frequent media reports about homicides and other criminal phenomena are referred to as Sardinia's "black chronicle." From an environmentalist perspective, the occasional evidence of hunting out of season, mistreatment of animals, or setting forest fires is damaging. Central Sardinians are therefore often represented as dangerous rather than innocent, both in social and ecological terms. Second, central Sardinia is represented as a landscape of vehement "resistance" to government and external authority. The defense of pastoral traditions and village commons was an important focus for grassroots action going back to the Piedmontese era. Over the course of the twentieth century, residents in some rural towns like Orgosolo sustained opposition to plans for a centralized national park. Neither passive nor inarticulate, central Sardinians have been active in all the major political parties and the voluntary sector. Many of them are university educated and participate in government institutions. Nevertheless, where objections to a national park are concerned, they are commonly represented as an emotional, ignorant, and culturally backward minority (see chapter 2). Rural Sardinians have not endeared themselves to environmentalist lobbies, and their pastoral traditions are widely considered to be troublesome "cultural" blocks to wilderness and wildlife conservation.

Faye Harrison (1995, 2002) argues that the kinds of cultural essentialisms at play in today's ethnic identity politics are often de facto forms of racism. The island of Sardinia is considered part of the troublesome southern "Mezzogiorno" region, and has a peculiar history in Italian discourses of governance. As we have seen, nineteenth-century physical anthropologists made explicit connections between race, culture, and criminality in the shepherd towns of highland Sardinia. In the early twentieth century, the perceived cultural-economic backwardness and ongoing criminality of central Sardinian shepherds was one of the factors legitimating the move to take control over large areas of traditional commons by creating Gennargentu Park. This is a form of embedded cultural racism that implicitly shapes new policies and campaigns in environmental governance.

The rise of global environmentalism, with the recent synthesis of efforts toward protecting biological and cultural diversity, constitutes one aspect of what Michael Herzfeld has described as "a global hierarchy of value." According to him, the "increasingly homogeneous language of culture and ethics" (2004, 2) practiced across transnational spheres of government, interest groups, and business constitutes the rhetoric of universal morality. This indicates one of the subtler, but most nefarious, forms of globalization. The global hierarchy of value is "a logic that has seeped in everywhere but is everywhere disguised as difference, heritage, local tradition" (ibid.). Those who come to embody resistance to such logic often acquire modest amounts of cultural distinction within a limited sphere of social action, only to support the larger system of hegemony that objectifies such resistance as just another form of backwardness, by turns heroic and dangerous. The culture of resistance becomes commodified and held up to generic standards, kept in its place because its value is always brokered by more powerful outsiders. In Sardinia, it excites mild desire on the part of tourists bored by mundane hedonism, and modest investments on the part of governments for its appeasement and transformation. In return for their own investments in authenticity, however, central Sardinians bear the cost of ongoing prejudice and marginalization.

Chapter 5

Seeing Like a State, Seeing Like an ENGO

A Death and a Donkey

During the winter of 1997, a man about thirty years old was found shot dead near the main street of Orgosolo, late on a Saturday night. Orgosolo was his home town, but he lived in Siena, where he was well-known as a jockey at the famous *palio*. He was visiting with his family and friends. That night, he had been out riding a donkey from bar to bar, as young men in central Sardinia occasionally do to entertain themselves during the Carnival season. People were careful to explain to me that taking the donkey out for a ride was a manifestation of the victim's love of animals. The cause of the murder was not immediately apparent, but there had been an exchange of insults in a bar and people inferred that an argument had escalated until a fight occurred in the street. When another young man from the town was found missing, it was surmised that he had killed the jockey, panicked, and fled into the Mediterranean *macchia*. That is, people suspected that he had gone up into the mountain brush to hide out, in the tradition of outlaws. It is not unusual, unfortunately, for young men to go out armed, and there are sometimes one or even two homicides in a year in the small town. In this case, however, the jockey's donkey was also wounded, and the media coverage was even more animated than usual.

The morning after the homicide, I accompanied my friend Sonia to the mid-morning Catholic mass, where the officiating priest suggested that the congregation "pray for the sins of the community." Sonia said that these tragedies often happened around festival times; there was soon talk among the church congregation of cancelling the Carnival parade as a sign of mourning. The extension of moral responsibility for the criminal action to the town as a whole was consistent with cultural discourses—both inside and outside rural towns like Orgosolo—that represent violence as rooted tradition in central Sardinia.

My acquaintances in Orgosolo listened avidly to the newscasts throughout the next days, and circulated newspapers and informal accounts as details came to light and narratives about the incident took shape. Many of them were bothered by the attention that the outside world paid to the issue of the donkey. The WWF had offered to pay for the animal's emergency care, and its representatives were interviewed several times regarding their concern for the donkey's well-being. The funeral was attended by hundreds of local residents who recognized with sympathy the human tragedy that had befallen the families of both the victim and the perpetrator. On the same day, the channel RAI Due broadcast live from Orgosolo. A newscaster stood close to a large cluster of state policemen on duty, as he told the story to the camera. He attempted to draw local mourners into conversation, unsuccessfully. The cameraman had to make do with shots of men entering a bar, and of women dressed in quasi-traditional dark costumes with headkerchiefs and shawls, walking rapidly away. These furtive attempts to capture local people on film tended to reinforce their images as uncomplicated ciphers of tradition and backwardness, and as stereotypical bearers of the ominous values of silence and resistance vis-à-vis the state, reminiscent of Sicilian mafia-style *omertà*.

The newscast then turned to a discussion with veterinarians and environmentalists, who had discovered that the wounded donkey was pregnant. She was dramatically airlifted out of Orgosolo by helicopter on the very afternoon of the funeral, and this too was shown on the news. The donkey's prognosis was discussed at length, while she was removed from the perceived cultural locus of violence in rural Sardinia to the expert care available in the lowland cities.

One Orgosolo woman was angry at the television news report she saw upon her return from the funeral and a visit of condolence to the jockey's family. She told me, "Look at this, Teresa, it seems like a joke."[1] From her viewpoint, the local tragedy of the jockey's death had been dehumanized by the media and the WWF, while the donkey had been treated like a person. For her and others with whom I spoke that day, this dramatized the gap between outsiders and insiders to Orgosolo, and especially, a fundamental gap in perspective between "environmentalists" and "Sardinians."

A year later, in 1998, when it looked as though the new legislation to create Gennargentu Park might succeed, the WWF asked Orgosolo to host an international group affiliated with the organization. A local cooperative agreed to coordinate the visitors' itinerary, including tours and hikes on the communal territory, a short walk through the historic town, a meal of authentic local foods, and space to conduct a meeting. Although members of the cooperative hoped for opportunities to engage the WWF visitors in a respectful, open, and challenging discussion of Gennargentu Park, they were limited to providing menial services. These individuals from the cooperative were well educated, relatively open-minded, and strongly engaged in auto-critiques of their own cultural heritage, and they suffered criticism from other residents for their willingness to do business with the WWF. WWF organizers neither sought nor welcomed dialogues beyond their membership on this occasion, and they excluded local residents entirely from their meeting.

In June 1999, however, when the Gennargentu Park initiative was again faltering, elements of the WWF's Orgosolo ecotourism itinerary appeared on the English-language international website "Panda P@ssport." The old-growth oak forest designated to be at the core of the protected area was named as the WWF's "forest of the month," as part of the group's promotion to establish the national park in central Sardinia. Identifying the area among the European forest "hotspots," the website document argued that the zone was distinctive for its geological age, its indigenous fauna, and its large area of wildlands, habitat diversity, and archaeological sites. Supposedly, a low population density together with the historical isolation of the island had provided for the survival of these ecological riches. Over-grazing, fires, agriculture, urbanization, and poor environmental management were indicted on the public website as escalating threats to this forest. The site urged internet visitors to send messages in support of the park because the political process had been blocked, in part by a "cultural heritage" that inculcated resistance to state initiatives.[2]

Transnational NGOs now have increasing authority in the interpretation and administration of environmental governance worldwide

(Chapin 2004; Campbell 2005; Goldman 2005; West et al. 2006). The World Wide Fund for Nature has become a principle partner mediating the environmentalist visions and policies of the European Union. Involved in a series of projects associated with parks and conservation across Italy and Sardinia, the WWF produces visual narratives of environmentalism on the web, for example, which profoundly affect how nature and culture come to be viewed in a global dreamtime of environmental futures. More importantly, they have taken on a role in mediating the cultural identities of Sardinians and others who are seen as obstacles to the realization of environmentalist goals. These cultures are often seen as too rooted in the local to perceive the promise of an ecologically minded global village.[3] These negative stereotypes provide the justification for attempts at the "public education" of local residents who stand opposed to the conservation frameworks championed by powerful outsiders. Changing visions of environmental governance are therefore as much about "seeing like an ENGO," for example, as they are about "seeing like a state."[4]

I have already discussed a history of cultural imagination embedded in projects of social, economic, and environmental governance by the nation-state in central Sardinia. The region remains a dark frontier to the eyes of governing authorities and many others. The narratives of the WWF about Sardinia in the late 1990s bore striking similarities to the earlier narratives about criminality, banditry, and "backwardness" in Sardinia found in Italian scholarship and government discourses since the late nineteenth century. This suggests that, like the Italian state, big environmental NGOs are focused on managing not only nature, but also culture. In this chapter, I consider the ongoing role of cultural alterity in the projects of political identity formation, and ask, what is at stake in the stories being told about science, culture, and environment in Sardinia? How are cultural translations deployed to frame local issues and events in an out-of-the-way part of the Mediterranean as relevant to broader European and even global concerns? How are these stories linked to the global dreamtimes of environmentalism, and in what ways are these acts of imagination creatively reframed from the bottom up?

Like a story that refuses a plot, the hesitant tale of Gennargentu Park in Sardinia, Italy, has troubled its would-be authors and protagonists since the early days of European cooperation. First proposed in 1958, it was surely intended to follow a modernist narrative from conception to felicitous birth, as a microcosm of regional and national progress affirming the larger imagined history of European civilization. Yet the proposition to transform municipally owned territories devoted to traditional rights of usufruct into a unified and expertly managed conservation area proved to be extraordinarily controversial. What has kept the plan to create this park alive for four decades, in the face of significant local opposition? Does it merely testify to the sincere commitment of political leaders and environmental lobbies to noble visions of conservation? What forms of capital have been attached to projects of ecological modernization in Europe, and how are rural, marginal areas implicated in the generation of this capital?

After two world wars in the early twentieth century, the reconstruction of Western Europe meant a massive effort to inscribe disrupted national landscapes with the legitimate and coherent storylines of prosperous modernity. Both the countryside and the city were to be governed by rational planning; industrial growth and technological improvements to agriculture were high priorities. Environmental protection as yet received little attention, except inasmuch as it might be thought important both as a token gesture and for the development of tourism (Judge 1993). Members of the newly formed European Economic Community agreed to increase the proportion of lands dedicated to national parks within their boundaries. Italy designated several areas for integrated conservation, including the area that became the famous Abruzzo National Park as well as the lands in Sardinia's Nuoro province that were selected to become part of Gennargentu Park.

The two "Plans for Rebirth" in central Sardinia sought a way to impose a modern sense of order, meaning, and discipline upon the too-social landscape of troublesome shepherd-bandits.[5] What James C. Scott (1998, 80) identifies as a state "project of legibility" is evident here. Scott suggests that states are motivated to pursue a God's-eye view of resources, landscapes, and populations for the purposes of administration, producing stylized facts that reduce complex natural and social systems to "thin simplifications" (76–83, 309–11). In postwar Italy, elaborate statistical data were defined and collected in attempts to explain the development disparities that marked a "miracle" boom of industrialization in the north versus continued "backwardness" and agricultural dependence in the south.[6] Efforts to spur economic growth in Sardinia entailed the differentiation of landscapes for the purposes of administrative governance, according to types of resource exploitation to be pursued. Industrial investments were focused on "poles of development" around some of the larger rural towns. The "Category One" nature protection planned for a significant area of highland Sardinia fit into the same modernist vision. Unsurprisingly, existing systems of communal land tenure were deemed inefficient by government authorities and blamed for the declining quality of ecological resources.[7] The creation of a national park would go beyond existing provisions for forestry and hydro-geological management and circumvent local politics and institutions, moving toward a more totalizing project of nature protection.

"Seeing like a state" (Scott 1998) in postwar Sardinia was never simply a matter of governing resources efficiently; rather, it was also a means of furthering control over a troublesome, ethnically and socioeconomically marked population. The first legislation to create a national park in central Sardinia coincided with efforts to establish a permanent NATO base with an artillery practice range on the communal pastures of Orgosolo, efforts that might easily have been considered antithetical to the project of conserving wildlife and wilderness. The long-term military occupation of Orgosolo's territory would, however, have supported attempts to modernize agricultural practices and promote sedentary ranching by reducing the area of communal lands available to pastoral herders. According to the results of the study commissioned by the state in 1969, as I explained in the previous chapter, this would counteract the root source of Sardinian criminality by working to transform the perceived culture of violence based on transhumant pastoralism.

Michael Herzfeld (1985, 1987a) has established that European nationalist discourses have tended to reify cultures in their own rural peripheries as embodiments of official history, and these also provide foils for visions of progress assumed to inhere in contemporary urban civilization. The inscription of linear historicity on the material landscapes of architecture (Herzfeld 1991) and environment is instrumental to legitimizing the nation-state's accounts about both its past and its future. Nothing could be further from the visions of Rome's classical heritage or Milan's fashionable modernism than the representations of mafia-ridden cities like Naples and Palermo, or the rural Sardinian towns that are assumed to shelter post-peasant herders and kidnappers alike. Paradoxically, Sardinia's apparent "backwardness" and banditry have also been important to establishing the authenticity of the "natural" rural environment, while serving as an essential point of contrast to cosmopolitan culture. The transformation of the Sardinian Supramonte into a museum-like nature park would therefore serve an additional purpose, attesting to the natural authority of the governing structures that succeed in restraining endemic violence and protecting vulnerable ecological resources. A national park would naturalize, commemorate, and control Sardinian landscapes of alterity. As an instrument of "ecological nationalism" (Cederlöf and Sivaramakrishnan 2006), the policy initiative to create Gennargentu Park promotes centralized projects of landscape and social engineering as a testament to the modernity of the nation-state. In this, it serves "[to bring] wilderness and wild people . . . into the fold of progressive possibilities" (ibid., 3). It simultaneously rehabilitates Sardinian national identity for the Autonomous Region, opening the path to cosmopolitan identity formations and better marketing strategies.

From a European perspective, rural, "less developed" areas like highland Sardinia were recognized to hold value not only as untapped economic resources, but also as symbolic assets.[8] In the 1970s, highland Sardinia and other ecologically sensitive, marginal areas of Europe were targeted for special supports to traditional agriculture and herding activities. Later classified by the European Community as an "Objective 1" region that was "lagging behind" the rest of Europe in terms of economic development, the region of Sardinia has also been the recipient of European structural investment.[9] During the 1980s and 1990s, the "greening" of European Community policies in agricultural, structural, and regional development dramatized the importance of the environment as a domain within which the architects of the "new Europe" constructed both European cooperation and European identity.[10] The

Special Programme of Action for the Mediterranean region sponsored from 1986 to 1991 illustrates this. With the rise of international dialogues on the conservation of biological diversity, efforts to improve economic growth in Objective 1 regions incorporated nature protection and ecodevelopment. Environmental issues entailed increasingly strategic claims to new kinds of post-national identity in the turbulent process of Europeanization. We might see this as a new form of "ecological nationalism," since we can identify "abiding concerns of sovereignty, self-determination, and place-based collective identities played out in the entanglement of nature devotion and [post-] nationalist aspirations" (Cederlöf and Sivaramakrishnan 2006, 3).

By the time the Maastricht Treaty was signed to create the new European Union, several European initiatives for species and habitat conservation had already been put in place. In 1992, the European Commission laid the policy framework for "Natura 2000," proposed as a coherent network of special areas for the conservation of species and habitats "of European importance." Under this initiative, another "project of legibility" (Scott 1998) can be identified: all "natural" habitat types found within European Union member states were defined and coded under the auspices of a scientific working group established by the Habitats Committee of the European Commission. Demographic statistics on the populations of various wild species were compiled, and habitats were classified according to the level of priority for conservation of particularly threatened or endangered species and high biodiversity zones. The quality of "Europeanness" now defined natural monuments, habitats, species, and ecosystems valued for their exemplarity. This constituted a means of fostering "European" subjectivities by making the existence of the European Union real, natural, and immediate to citizens' experience (Borneman and Fowler 1997; Shore 2000). The national parks and other protected areas incorporated into the Natura 2000 system made the "margins" of the European Union central to the process of Europeanization, as they inscribed traditional landscapes with new meanings.

National parks have come to be a significant "technology of nationhood" (Harvey 1996). Because they are predicated on fictions of wilderness, national parks enable ecological science and modern bureaucracy to mediate experiences of authentic nature that substantiate official narratives of history. As we saw in chapter 2, the stories embodied by

Map of the Natura 2000 system of parks and reserves of the European Union as of 2006. Reprinted by permission of the European Environmental Agency. Retrieved May 2008 from Natura 2000 Web Portal, http://ec.europa.eu/ environment/nature/natura2000/

"natural" landscapes commemorate folk culture and celebrate the absence of industry, machines, and other signs associated with the human modification of landscapes, all the while providing an aesthetic contrast and balance to the cultural achievements of the city. The human agency by means of which such wilderness must be carefully styled out of rural landscapes is effaced from perception. Environmental historian William Cronon reminds us that the most powerful irony of the nineteenth-century wilderness movement in the United States was the way it coincided with the last wars against aboriginal Americans and their removal to reservations.[11] He writes,

> The myth of wilderness as "virgin" uninhabited land had always been especially cruel when seen from the perspective of the Indians who had once called that land home. Now they were forced to move elsewhere, with the result that tourists could safely enjoy the illusion that they were seeing their nation in its pristine, original state. (Cronon 1995, 79)

Cronon has argued that the famous national parks of the United States are landscapes that embody the American frontier myth, supporting the legitimacy of American nationhood.[12] Narratives of American national identity that are told through the material landscapes of Yellowstone National Park and the Grand Canyon have been shaped by particular, privileged perspectives. Such narratives have the effect of obscuring their own craftedness, leading visitors to forget the history of human inhabitation and violent expropriation upon which the parks themselves were founded. If, as many contemporary parks advocates hope, times have changed and the disenfranchisements suffered in the past by resident peoples such as native North Americans need no longer be the sine qua non of environmental conservation, national parks nevertheless continue to tell stories of nationhood from privileged but self-effacing perspectives. Moreover, these stories tell us not only about imagined histories, but also about imagined futures.

Official discourses about the European Union have been characterized by an almost nostalgic relationship to an envisaged age of globalization. Abélès (2000) described European officials' efforts to identify the political object of their own visions as a "quest for the future," the dimensions of which were only provisionally imagined. Where a diversity of languages and cultures failed to provide the customary signs of commonality so vital in the era of the modern nation-state, and while issues of national membership and the nature of individual citizenship remain indeterminate and passionately contested, it is the symbolic terrain of the future itself that marks the legitimate bounds of the European Union. The Habitats Directive (Council Directive 92/43/EEC) confirmed the participation of European member states in a shared future, where global concerns would transcend the needs of individual nation-states. National parks today act to confirm the attainment of newly enlightened, post-industrial values that, as Kay Milton (1996) points out, are now attached to nature. In a national park, the symbolic and aesthetic commodities associated with "nature" are experienced by ecotourists as the visible and sensual effects of prosperous development. This "nature" is the product of cultural enlightenment and of ecological management technologies so sophisticated that they can actually hide themselves from the nature lover/consumer.[13] European member states, therefore, demonstrate a particular kind of universal scientific expertise and global awareness by means of their "forward thinking" conservation policies and programs.

Transforming Citizenship

Visions of environmental governance were dominated by nation-states throughout most of the twentieth century. Although the concept of "seeing like a state" (Scott 1998) offers one provocative way to think about national parks, in terms of modernist visions of development and governance, it fails to complicate the authorship of state policies, or explore the tensions and open-endedness of state narratives. It does not recognize the intrinsic complicities of power and resistance, or seek comprehension of the political economic transformations attending globalization and emergent technosciences.[14] As James Ferguson argues, the structures of governance are increasingly transnationalized, so that we find a "hydra-headed transnational apparatus of banks, international agencies, and market institutions through which contemporary capitalist domination functions" (2006, 107). This is no less the case for the Objective 1 areas of Europe than it is for the debt-ridden countries of Africa; governance projects in rural Sardinia may include various forms of participation from the European Union, state agencies, the Region of Sardinia, provincial governments, municipal authorities, the WWF, corporate enterprises, local cooperatives, universities, UNESCO, and so forth. These heterogeneous, flexible partnerships transform both the ideologies and practices of power in ways that James C. Scott failed to anticipate. The instrumentalist focus of Scott's approach further misapprehends the fundamental importance and systemic embeddedness of a symbolic economy (Bourdieu 1977, 1991) of political discourses. The ability to legitimize and naturalize the power-knowledge systems adopted by administrative bureaucracies is at least as crucial to the success of governance as the practical orientation of the knowledge systems themselves; nation-states (and their bureaucracies) are actually interdependent in their strategies to assure this. Arturo Escobar suggests that concerns with biodiversity conservation indicate a "postmodern" guise of ecological capital (1995, 203) that now privileges global concerns, but nevertheless recreates the essential production conditions, power hierarchies, and discourses of legitimacy associated with earlier, "modern" visions of development.[15] Global environmentalism is necessarily articulated with the transforming political spaces of national discourses, at a time when "an emerging set of institutions and practices . . . make up, in Foucauldian terms, a new technology of government" (Gupta 1998, 293).

Environmentalism has become both a rich site of cultural production and a new discursive regime that mediates "relationships between and among nature, nations, movements, individuals, and institutions" (Brosius 1999c, 277). If the stories associated with global environmentalism have created a space for the invention and contestation of new forms of political agency, how do these stories come together with visions of a "new" Europe that members of the European Commission have attempted to foster? "Global" approaches to the environment have clearly reinforced the legitimacy of European integration, particularly by highlighting the need to collaborate across national boundaries. The environmental subjectivities (cf. Agrawal 2005) fostered by new cooperative frameworks in the European Union were intrinsically associated with political subjectivities that were hoped to transcend identification with the nation-state and embrace new forms of citizenship. Ecological capital continues to support nation-building projects, but also new forms of post-national governance that emphasize flexible partnerships between neoliberal states, international organizations, non-governmental organizations, and private enterprises.

In the margins of the new Europe, projects to streamline and enhance governance of landscapes, populations, and resources abound. These do not constitute coherent or unified expressions of social agency. Under the conditions of late capitalism, these projects may be less important as administrative tools than for their capacity to generate powerful cultural representations that naturalize new articulations of authority, capital, and expertise. The real source of power rests in the hegemony of a global, neoliberal, technoscientific future, and in the simulacra of ultramodernity that consolidate what we might call the "re-imagined community" (cf. Anderson 1983) of the European Union. The fiction of wilderness in Sardinia implied first national, and then regional possession of symbolic capital in the form of "natural" landscapes, as well as the modern scientific knowledge and technology required to preserve them. In many ways, the political stakes involved in the creation of Gennargentu Park were merely amplified by efforts at identity construction associated with European unification in the 1990s. Multiple forms of "ecological nationalism" (Cederlöf and Sivaramakrishnan 2006) entailing projects of vertical encompassment and hierarchy have largely supported one another. Yet existing networks of power-knowledge have been qualitatively transformed by emerging models of environmental partnership. The paradoxes of sovereignty in the age of neoliberal governance (Ferguson 2006) must direct our attention beyond "seeing like a state" (Scott 1998). This is not to suggest that the state is "withering away" in an age of globalization. Rather, it is being reconfigured in ways that both co-opt and recognize the critical discourses generated by civil society "partners." Paradoxically, the ideological legitimacy and material power of nation-states may be bolstered by this realignment (Sivaramakrishnan and Agrawal 2003).

European unification introduced a dedicated budget for environmental funding in the member states and consolidated a new model for public-private partnerships in conservation management. The "LIFE" fund launched in 1992 coincided with the signing of the international Convention on Biological Diversity in Rio De Janeiro, and the enactment of the European Habitats Directive. About 45 percent of LIFE spending in the first two phases of the program went to support nature conservation, and the LIFE-NATURE program remains a staple of European investment in the environment.[16] In Italy, the World Wide Fund for Nature has managed, either directly or under the auspices of public administrations, fifteen projects financed by the LIFE fund. One of these was a program that ran from January 1999 to December 2001, called "A Community Contribution to the Adoption in the Gennargentu of the Idea of a Park." The project outlined a range of human impacts on the area designated for Gennargentu Park, especially as a result of pastoralist activities. The plan entailed a component of guardianship aimed at the protection of threatened indigenous species;[17] assistance in fire-fighting and anti-poaching, normally the responsibility of Sardinian forest rangers; and the monitoring of rare bird species. Finally, it entailed a program for what it called "environmental sensitization" in the Sardinian province of Nuoro.

The WWF section in Sardinia was established in 1976, focusing mainly on the protection of bird and animal species and educational initiatives. In 1985 it bought 3,000 hectares and opened a park in the forest of Monte Arcosu, a habitat of the Sardinian deer, an endangered species. It has consistently worked toward the institution of Gennargentu Park and other protected areas in Sardinia, and it published a series of coffee-table books on Sardinian flora, fauna, and landscapes during the late 1980s, in anticipation and support of the new regional parks system. Since 1998, it has focused on the preservation of Sardinian coasts and marine habitats. Environmental subjectivities (Agrawal 2005) have been fostered in highland Sardinia through forestry management projects that employ a portion of the rural labor force, and general environmental management that involves a small number of educated forest rangers drawn from rural areas. Participants in big ENGOS (Legambiente, WWF), however, are drawn mostly from lowland urban areas. Typically, WWF organizers remained aloof from the people in central Sardinia whose attitudes vis-à-vis protected areas they hoped to change.[18] Although I met people in central Sardinia who considered themselves to cherish a love of nature and who sought better environmental management, very few thought a national park would be a good idea, and all my acquaintances in Orgosolo found the actions and statements of the WWF in Sardinia to be virulently disrespectful. In the remainder of this chapter, I consider how the WWF has represented Sardinia's "troubles" with wilderness through a series of cultural translations, and how other cultural translations have been brought to bear by Sardinians who wished to subvert and complicate their typecast roles in the dreamtime of environmentalism.

The uncomfortable exchanges between rural Sardinians and urban-based WWF representatives, concerned with global environmentalism and cosmopolitan connections, produced particular kinds of stories. National media coverage of the story of the jockey's wounded donkey, as well as the WWF website's narrative about "the forest of the month," illustrates the transformation of local events and debates into global concerns. The impacts of such cultural translations across such projects of "scale-making"[19] have been highlighted by a number of authors. Anna Tsing (1997) reflects on globalization not merely as a set of objective effects, but also as a creative process of imagination that undergirds new translocal and transcultural alliances.[20] Tsing considers how "strategic universalisms" enable the negotiation of cultural alterity, so that local concerns come to stand in for larger inclusive fields (259). The example of the jockey's wounded donkey, however, shows instead a reverse impact of cultural translation: how "local" ecological alterity can be reconfirmed through storytelling for an audience only dimly aware of the cultural-historical context, and certainly uncomprehending of local perspectives. In this case, the WWF's acts of cultural translation undermine potential for rural Sardinians to make strategic alliances across national and cultural divides. They are isolated, and even estranged, from movements that feature indigenous cultures as the guardians of nature.

In the modern nation-state of the twentieth century, everyday bureaucratic practices associated with state agencies once tended to generate taken-for-granted effects of spatial and scalar hierarchy (Ferguson and Gupta 2002). As transnational agencies and non-governmental organizations come to participate in "mechanisms of governmentality that take place outside of, and alongside, the state" (ibid., 122), the imagination of space and scale is more fluid, contested, and mischievous. Tsing's (2005) recent discussion of global "frictions" highlights the indeterminacy and possibility inherent in heterogeneous projects of scale-making. In an Indonesian example, the miscommunications between young environmentalists from the city and the tribal people whose interests they endeavored to champion paradoxically enabled a productive alliance between them. In Sardinia, however, we see hegemony in the making instead. Events in Orgosolo were translated by WWF advocates and the news media for the national and global stage, so that they were given meaning for a predominantly urban television audience across Italy and a larger audience of environmentalists across Europe. Global orientations and postmodern moralities were naturalized and legitimized in these stories about the vulnerability of non-human species to capricious forms of ecological backwardness. The problems imagined in interactions between Sardinian culture and environment, by all appearances, could only be resolved through the intervention of environmentally educated outsiders.[21] In Sardinia, outsiders' perceptions of ecological alterity shattered all hope of forging alliances based on fortunate misunderstandings. Rather, I witnessed the transcription of cultural racisms into the domain of environmental discourse, and the recreation of rebellious frustrations associated with marginalized local voices and perspectives.

Global Dreamtime of Environmentalism

At the "Global Network" website of the WWF, "environmental activism online" has become a prominent aspect of the organization's bid to attract support for its work to protect non-human species and habitats. Fundamentally, this is a fundraising effort that shows off the work of the organization around the world. It also entails an effort to raise political awareness about the campaigns and participation in political lobbies. The "Panda P@ssport" offered the armchair environmentalist access in twelve languages to participation in online lobbies, unfettered by national sovereignties or borders. The website featured a selection of well over a hundred active campaigns around the world. According to the WWF website, "P@ssport is your licence to campaign for the environment, no matter where you are in the world, all over the world. It is for people who care about our planet, who are short on time, but who want to have a real impact!"[22]

Since the campaign to institute Gennargentu Park was featured on the English-language Panda P@ssport site from 1999 to 2001, the peaks of the Supramonte have become not only attractive images for tourist brochures and coffee-table books, but also a vibrant virtual landscape in the vast frontiers of the internet that mediate the global vision of wilderness and its relation to civil society. Technologically sophisticated websites managed by the WWF, Greenpeace, Parks Italy, the International Union for the Conservation of Nature (IUCN), and the European Green Parties are crowded with voluptuous images, colored texts, and animations that invoke the simultaneity and immediacy of a shared experience of environmental degradation across the planet. The transnational nature of increasingly urgent environmental problems, such as the accumulation of greenhouse gases causing worldwide climate changes, has augmented (despite setbacks) the political will to cooperate across borders, continents, and economic zones (Yearley 1996; see also Jasanoff 2004). Problems of deforestation and industrial pollution have therefore received increasing attention in international settings, as environmental advocates work to offset the ecologically destructive aspects of late capitalism.

Environmental movements have developed and grown since the 1980s, just as environment and development issues have gained recognition in the international sphere. In tandem with the professionalization of certain prominent ENGOs operating transnationally (Diani and Donati 1999), electronic media have become both instruments and symbolic staples of global environmentalism.[23] Mario Diani notes that organizations such as Greenpeace, Friends of the Earth, and the World Wide Fund for Nature depend on the World Wide Web and other media to raise resources for the support of campaigns managed by professional staff. Membership is broad but not necessarily active, and most of the constituency remains dispersed, with little influence on the definition or presentation of a collective identity (Diani 1995; 1999, 8-9).[24] Access to cyberspace[25] as a medium of environmental networking is important not only for instrumental utility, however, but also because it supports a distinctive sense of history, knowledge, and agency that is invaluable to the vision of global environmentalism crafted by big transnational ENGOs.

Morley and Robins (1995) argued that during the 1990s there was a growing "mythology of global media" as an instrument of "progress toward freedom and democracy on a world scale" (11–12). Global commercial networks promoted the idea that "communication is a good thing and the more freely it flows, the better it is; experiences shared on a global scale, through the new communications media, will help us transcend the differences between different cultures and societies" (12).[26] Popular cultural constructions of what it means to be "connected" to the World Wide Web help to reify transnational, or post-national, visions of civil society and environmental action. Like images of the blue planet Earth as seen from space, or pictures of DNA as the building blocks of life (Lury et al. 2000), the everywhere and nowhere of the World Wide Web condenses and literally reconfigures our vision of the global. Accordingly, it alters our capacity to imagine human agency on a new scale. The Internet has acquired panache among the computer literate as an unprecedented means of research, reputed to deliver access to both the universal knowledge of leading-edge science and the immediate, local knowledge of current events. Possession and use of Internet technologies symbolically condenses the power of knowledge at one's fingertips.

The World Wide Web continues to embody popular images of globalization, famously described by David Harvey (1989) as a process of "time-space compression" where human experience and interaction accelerate and transcend the traditional limitations imposed by geography.[27] Electronic communications confer the power to "be present," and to act and interact across borders, to be truly cosmopolitan. While environmentalists are often among the most persuasive critics of modernity and globalization, they have adopted "advanced" or "high" technologies with ingenuity and success. New forms of political subjectivity entailed in environmentalist visions of post-national citizenship are linked to technologies that have themselves become symbols of the future.[28] This has much to do with the recent popularity of ideas that concerned and responsible individuals must transform not only national but also global politics and practices. Ecological citizenship demands skepticism vis-à-vis the capacity of nation-states to manage environments effectively, together with a broad sense of global biotic allegiance.[29] The World Wide Web itself is therefore an agent of cultural translation in the scale-making projects of transnational ENGOs. Websites like the "Panda P@ssport" offer a convenient means to fulfill this call to arms on behalf of non-human species. Such websites foster and mediate cyborg forms of environmental activism that naturalize the primacy of technoscience, expert management, and private action on a global scale.

Educating the Gennargentu

Let us return once again to the alternate landscape of virtual Sardinia, where new moralities, technologies, and regimes of governance reconfigure our perception of nature according to the perspective of a transnational ENGO. Vassos Argyrou (2005) has argued that dominant streams of environmental philosophy, and even the most radically biocentric wings of the environmentalist movement, all remain trapped in the cultural logic of European modernity.[30] Mainstream varieties of global environmentalism therefore invite participation in a shared sense of progress. Nostalgia for an imagined time of relative innocence and harmony in human-environmental relations is always implied. Paradoxically, to be an environmentalist today is not usually conceived as a retreat into the past, but rather, as a move forward through time, into the global, post-industrial world that should recreate human harmony with biological support systems. In the global dreamtimes of environmentalism, this future is already real, and you can enter it with a touch on your keyboard.

On the WWF–Sardegna website, there is a graphic story called "Gennargentu Adventure" by Gian Marco Ibba.[31] Four young companions named Gavino, Paolo, Anna, and Mirko are hiking on an excursion in the Gennargentu. Gavino, wearing jeans with the cap and vest stereotypical of Sardinian shepherds, guides the other three through the countryside without aid of a map. Paolo, Anna, and Mirko are carrying backpacks and appear to be less familiar with the territory. When Paolo, who appears to be a student, consults a map and discovers that they appear to be lost, Gavino swiftly becomes aggressive and begins to argue with Mirko. Paolo continues to look at the map placidly, commenting, "I really don't understand where we are," while Anna looks around thoughtfully at the landscape and responds half to herself, "perhaps in a magical place!"

Paolo and Anna walk a little further apart, where they see a mouflon in the distance. This is a rare and privileged sight to which Gavino and Mirko, still taunting one another, are oblivious. It is the mouflon, an endangered species of indigenous wild sheep, that has often been the poster animal for Gennargentu Park. Some rural Sardinians protested—both in the 1960s and in the 1990s—that environmentalists were more thoughtful about the fate of mouflons than about the poverty and underdevelopment experienced by most people in rural Sardinia. Despite high levels of vigilance and exorbitant fines levied against poachers, a few residents continue to hunt and "cull" older animals in secret. In the environmentalist dreamtime of our website comic strip, Gavino and Mirko finally hear Paolo's calls to look up and see the mouflon. "*Forte!*" says Gavino, an archetype of the anthropocentric shepherd, "if only I had my father's gun!"

Paolo, in contrast, believes the mouflon is trying to communicate that the young people should follow him. Their non-human guide eventually leads the hikers to a sign that says "Gennargentu Park." They are all surprised to find that the park already exists, and discover how many people are there. Soon they see a crowd of tourists near an agrotourism center, and a great bird flying overhead. They see people working, and a woman silhouetted in the distance, collecting spring water in the traditional way. To one side there is a modern tractor with a plot of earth being plowed, and other people working the land. In the foreground, cheerfully surrounded by sheep, is a man wearing jeans and a sheepskin vest, but carrying a cell phone. Paolo, Anna, and Mirko find that the park has created new jobs for their own family members. Mirko stops beside a great oak tree to talk to his father, who is wearing the green uniform of the forestry service and has a pair of binoculars in his hand.

"By some strange magic we've ended up in the future," says Paolo. Anna is ecstatic. Soon Mirko, Anna, and Paolo are running along happily. Only Gavino, the young shepherd, has been left behind, still frowning at the mouflon that poses graciously on a rocky outcrop.

Mirko, his argument with the shepherd forgotten, pauses to say, "Hey Gavino, what's wrong with you? We're having a lot of fun! Come and join us!" Now, at last, Gavino gets the idea and leaps after his friends, still subject to the serene, benevolent (but faintly patronizing, it appeared to me) gaze of the mouflon. He turns his head to look back at the stately, enigmatic beast, and begins to run toward it. His shepherd's cap rises away from his head, and a smile spreads over his face. Gavino has at last accepted the promise of a national park.

Gianmarco Ibba's online graphic story, "Gennargentu Adventure," manipulates stereotypical orientations to "tradition" and "modernity" associated with central Sardinia. The character of Gavino illustrates the "ignorance" and "backwardness" often imputed to be at the base of herders' opposition to Gennargentu Park. He is stubborn, defensive, and quick to anger, and he immediately threatens violence when Mirko stands opposed to him. He views the landscape as a set of resources for material benefit, and sees in the mouflon only the possibility of material consumption. Little of his expression is in fact verbalized, as though he himself hardly understands or articulates the reasons for his actions. In contrast, the more literate (map-reading and bespectacled), soft-spoken Paolo and gentle Anna are the first to grasp the majesty of the natural landscape and value the wonder of the experience. They literally run ahead into the future, following the mouflon, which embodies environmentalist values. Meanwhile, Gavino, bitterly recalcitrant, hangs back in the past until the last moment.

In the environmental dreamtime of a high-tech website, the cultural re-education of Gavino is the fulfillment of the goal identified by the WWF LIFE-NATURE project. In real-life central Sardinia, WWF organizers still perceive a culture of alterity as a block to species and habitat conservation. Priscilla Weeks's (1999) discussion of a similar WWF online campaign, to save tigers in India, acknowledges a set of rhetorical devices brought into play in website narratives. These were used to provoke emotional sympathy for tigers, while distancing readers from Indian villagers, whose material interests and homes in designated forest preserves are affected by environmental initiatives. In both Sardinian and Indian campaigns promoting nature preserves, iconic stereotypes and scientific discourses were evoked to construct environmental blame as the result of the cultural backwardness of rural peasants.[32] Both entailed moral and spiritual orientations that naturalized cosmopolitan perceptions of place. This suggests that "seeing like the WWF" entails a pattern of cultural translation that transcribes local events and debates into stories and visual discourses of global concern, defining a distance between civilization and backwardness, between areas of culture and wilderness, and between universal ecological science and local ways of knowing and being in the landscape. Far from engendering the kind of positive and creative international connections that might empower the participation of rural Sardinians in environmental management, the WWF's cultural translations both uphold the hegemony of global concerns and legitimize the increasingly powerful role of the organization in partnerships of neoliberal governance.

Incongruous Translations

Both governmental authorities and the large international ENGOs produce preservationist discourses with regard to "natural" landscapes and habitats that should be examined in terms of "allochronism." Johannes Fabian introduced the term "allochronism" to name practices of representation prevalent in anthropological writing, where the "denial of coevalness" was a device used systematically in a given discourse to define the distance between observer and observed (1983, 32). Claims to legitimate knowledge were accomplished by rendering contrasts between the dynamic, present time of the researcher's own culture and the timeless past in which other cultures were situated as objects of the ethnographic gaze. Cultural alterity was mapped onto both history and geography. Taken in broader perspective, allochronism is not a technique unique to colonial anthropology, but has inflected many kinds of Western discourses on modernization, development, and globalization. It can naturalize the authority of the text as a cultural distance between the author and the object of discourses, creating not only "primitive" others from indigenous peoples, but also "backward" others from the inhabitants of local peripheries. As a result, some people and places in Sardinia today are perceived as only partway "here" to the European, globally savvy present/future.

Environmental nostalgia is the doppelganger of Western industrial progress. As Fabian's model suggests, techniques of allochronism have been used to map this nostalgia onto the cultural and natural margins of Europe. For example, the argument is often made that traditional knowledge and institutions for communal land management in Sardinia have ceased to be a viable means of ecological management (cf. IASM 1983). The highland "wilderness" is now a scarce resource, particularly valuable because it appears to reflect nature back in time: a truly pre-modern, pre-industrial space.[33] According to the WWF's narrative, the land itself has remained a "relatively intact" exemplar of Mediterranean environments of the past. The rural people who own it today, however, are depicted as caught up in both an outmoded economy of pastoral herding—grazing on natural pastures and sometimes using fire to clear land—and a capitalist culture of exploitation that values material wealth and therefore places increasing demands upon available resources. Opposition to the park project was interpreted as another example of cultural anachronism: fear of losing traditional rights of usufruct to common lands was treated as a product of unreasoning backwardness. For the WWF, only the creation of a national park—entailing the dispossession of local communities—would enable the cultural and economic transformations necessary to protect Sardinian habitats, by institutionalizing ecological expertise and disseminating environmental values.

When Zio Luigino, a local herder, invited me to attend the workparties that he was gathering for veterinary checks in the summer of 1997, I discovered that Sardinian herders and other residents worked symbolic mischief on this logic with a different kind of cultural translation. Luigino kept large flocks of cattle, both imported and indigenous species. These were put out to graze within sight of Monte San Giovanni, free ranging on the natural pastures of Orgosolo's communal territory. For the occasion of the checks they all had to be gathered within an enclosure, then lassoed one by one and kept still for testing and inoculations, and finally released into a separate fenced area. Luigino had sons, but needed to call upon a larger circle of friends for assistance. The work was hard, but spirits were high and there was a picnic roast to look forward to. Since women are rarely present on these occasions and I had a camera, I was treated to a certain amount of showing-off; these roundups required some impressive athletics.

"Oh, Teresa! We're the cowboys of America,"[34] called out my friend Luciano, cheerfully. Some people would say that Luciano was nothing of the sort; he was one of several young colleagues associated with Luigino's second, informal employment, assisting with an ecotourism enterprise. In fact, only one or two of the men present were full-time herders, but most already had some skills working with animals, since workparties for sheep shearing, veterinary checks, and other labor-intensive operations routinely draw in flexible networks of family, neighbors, and friendship groups. Many men, too, spend a few months or a year or two helping out with one of the herding enterprises in the extended family at one time or another, to fill in gaps of unemployment or underemployment. The sense of connection to pastoral heritage is generalized; men are proud of horsemanship and other skills related to animal husbandry, skills they recognize that their counterparts in other, less "authentic" or "traditional" Sardinian towns and cities have lost. Even women may feel themselves a part of this heritage, as a result of their family connections and helpmate roles. "We are all herders at Orgosolo," said my friend Laura during a late evening *passeggiata*, as we amused ourselves driving round and round the town. So perhaps Luciano really was an authentic cowboy.

The Old West of colonial America is a favorite theme of the popular imagination in Italy, from "spaghetti Western" gunfights to the cowboy-and-Indian adventures of comic strips. In Orgosolo, young men made enthusiastic references to the comic book characters Tex Willer and Capitano Mark, adventurous heroes in an imagined frontier of undomesticated, dangerous wilderness. The Old West evokes archetypes of wild spaces, wild men, tragic violence, and spirited resistance. It presupposes temporal anteriority: a place removed in time. It also implies open landscapes populated by a colonial Other: the indigenous people of America. Given the decades-old debate over Gennargentu Park and the role of colonial experience in local historicity, it is probably not accidental that my Sardinian friends were often proud of their comic book heroes for showing a stronger affinity to the Indians than to the governing authorities, settlers, and cowboys. In fact, left-leaning local critics of the park project were apt to announce, "We are the Indians of America: they are about to steal our land."[35] This romantic affinity for indigenous Americans was always tinged with regret and ambivalence. On the one hand, it spoke to the issue of cultural authenticity, implying deep connections to precontact wild landscapes. On the other hand, it evoked a colonial experience of cultural and material loss. Cowboys, after all, were far more fortunate than Indians in New World land claims.

The very incongruity of a wild Old West so near the heart of European colonial power made occasional comments like "we live in the Old

West"[36] both poignant and mischievous. In light of tragic events like the tavern argument that apparently led to the homicide of the young jockey in 1997, and the criminal status of the even younger renegade who had shot him, such comparisons to the Old West suggested a distressed melancholy. Life in Orgosolo sometimes embodied the metaphor too closely. The Italian romanticization of the American West became an object of irony in Orgosolo because some people recognized the way in which they themselves, not entirely without their own complicity, had become the locus of a frontier fantasy. If a frontier zone is not a place or a process, but an imaginative project that is at once a site of cultural transformations and a space of desire (Tsing 2005, 32), then central Sardinia remains a dark frontier. It continues to embody a shifting terrain of cultural contradictions that facilitate encounters across the perceived timescapes of past, present, and future. Tourists still go to Orgosolo looking for glimpses of bandits and wilderness. Forces of authority still scour both town and countryside for outlaws, while journalists follow icons of tradition, danger, and backwardness along the Corso Repubblica. Residents themselves celebrate, and occasionally re-enact, histories of "resistance."

Yet, in the ambivalent local appropriation of the Old West legend, there is a strategic reorganization of European and global environmental discourses about history, modernity, and time. Spaces are opened for the disarticulation of hegemonic discourses about governance and global concerns in central Sardinia. The convergent allochronisms of environmental nostalgia, development dreams, and studies of criminality are playfully exposed by direct comparison to popular icons of alterity. The metaphor itself remains quixotic and unfixed, undoing linear interpretations. Do central Sardinians think of themselves as cowboys, or Indians? In the present context of international discourses about indigeneity and environmentalism, new storylines could emerge from some of the incongruities inherent in the Sardinian frontier fantasy. The next two chapters in this book explore some of those that unfolded in 1968 and 1998.

The arid highlands of Sardinia have become a fertile landscape for narratives about science, culture, and environment, with significance to global debates as well as visions of a new Europe. This is truly a neverending story, in which characters identified as Sardinians, politicians, and environmentalists—categories often less distinct and more hybrid than usually explained—no sooner offer their own readings of this landscape than they become the heroes and villains in other tales, often incomplete and told in snatches. Not only governments and scientific institutions, but also elements of "civil society," including the news media and private organizations, have played important roles in mediating these cultural translations. The dreamtime of environmentalism has inscribed Sardinian landscapes with the global concerns of transnational ENGOs. Of course, not all ENGOs "see" eye to eye. The cultural production associated with global environmentalism has, however, been dominated by certain of the largest organizations, like the WWF. With their powerful advertising campaigns and partnerships with public agencies, such organizations have contributed to the legitimating discourses of governance. "Seeing" like a big ENGO has reconfirmed visions of Otherness—visions of ecological alterity—that reduce the multidimensional and heterogenous subjectivities of central Sardinians to seemingly childlike, fundamentally anachronistic, forms. This has undermined goals of conservation as well as the heritage and future aspirations of residents in central Sardinia. The challenge of provoking government bureaucracies, ENGOs, or global corporations to think beyond "thin simplifications" (Scott 1998) of culture and environment is a test that goes to the heart of anthropological writing. As Vargas-Cetina asks, "How can we enter a candid dialogue with local and translocal advocates?" (2003). The point is not to indict projects of global imagination, or environmental groups themselves, but rather to bear witness to complexity with open-ended stories and uncomfortable questions (Tsing 2005, 267). To support hopeful collaborations of advocacy, ethnographers must learn to speak to a new generation of environmentalists, as they seek better forms of cultural translation empowered by perspectives from the bottom up.

PART IV **Resistance**

Mural by Francesco del Casino on the old town hall on the Corso Repubblica
of Orgosolo, depicting the first demonstration at Pratobello in 1969 (1998).

Chapter 6

Walking in Via Gramsci

The Time of Ferment

I first met Tina in 1997 at the library of Orgosolo, where she worked for a time to assist in creating a new local history resource section. She soon pulled me into one of the library archives to show me a set of photographs depicting the famous murals of Orgosolo. Many of these, she pointed out, commemorated scenes from Orgosolo's famous demonstration at Pratobello on the town Commons in 1969. The lively, often tense, four-day occupation was led by a left-wing youth group to protest NATO exercises on the town commons. Tina compared it to the gathering at Woodstock, New York, the same year. She was two years old at the time.

"*E c'ero io!*" she exclaimed, smiling, "And I was there! They took me!"

This chapter begins the work of exploring political "resistance" in central Sardinia from an ethnographic perspective. In contrast to visions of cultural alterity that define local objections to a national park as a form of mere backwardness, as I discussed in chapter 3, this perspective reveals the practices of "resistance" to be the outcome of reasoning political subjectivities grounded in the self-reflexive embodiment of history, identity, and experience. Considering the cultural embeddedness of Gramsci's thought in Orgosolo, I describe the social memory of "resistance" and political action that took place around the time that the first initiative to create a national park was launched by government authorities. Tina often spoke to me with animation about the social and political ferment that Orgosolo enjoyed during the 1960s and 1970s.

She said she remembered all sorts of meetings in the central piazza during political races when she was a child, and many famous politicians visiting because Orgosolo was acknowledged as a symbol of Sardinian resistance. Her love of music by the Beatles, Branduardi, and particularly, Fabrizio de André reflected her nostalgia for the period. She sometimes lamented she had not been born earlier, so she might have enjoyed those days as a young adult.

Later, I learned that Tina lived on Via Gramsci. Her father was a shepherd and one of the founding members of the town's communist party. He served a period of internal exile to a prison camp during the height of anti-communist policy.[1] Years after his return to Sardinia, he played a prominent role in Vittorio de Seta's famous film, *Banditi a Orgosolo* (1969). Tina said the film was very authentic in showing how life used to be, because the directors hired real shepherds rather than actors to play the parts. She was proud of her father's contribution to the historical record. His model clearly plays an important role in her own sense of identity, and her political leanings to the left. Although Tina was critical of religious organization, her mother is a devout Catholic. She had worked as an agricultural laborer before her marriage, and continued to play a central role in family subsistence strategies throughout her life. Both parents were in their seventies when I met them. Tina's older brother runs a successful honey production business, with beehives on the town Commons and at the family gardens in the countryside. He is one of the few local residents of his generation, people noted, to be successful at earning a living in agriculture without depending on outside subsidies. Tina herself had found work in a number of cultural initiatives like the one in the library. She had helped to run a "living history" museum for one summer. Without a formal university degree, many of the administrative roles in which she might have succeeded were closed to her, but her diploma gave her a higher level of schooling than many of her peers. For a few years, she belonged to a cooperative of young people that launched several entrepreneurial projects, drawing on a variety of soft funding schemes related to cultural tourism.[2]

In 1997, Tina took on an important part in the organization of the traditional two-week summer festival of the Madonna Assumption. A group of friends decided to revitalize the festival by drawing volunteers from the entire age-group of those born at Orgosolo thirty years earlier.

When Tina discovered that I was her age-mate too, I was invited to join in. It was the first time the leadership of the festival had been opened up beyond the scope of a small friendship group, to include individuals with exceedingly diverse backgrounds, occupations, political preferences, and orientations to the Roman Catholic Church. Tina herself went to the church to coordinate festival activities with the priests. As a non-practicing Catholic, she herself usually avoided the church, although she donned the traditional costume of Orgosolo annually for the ritual procession of *ferragosto*, Assumption Day. In this case, she recognized a need to transcend political and religious differences to make a statement about community spirit. Tina saw Catholic ritual as an inherent part of local history, one of the riches of the past, which should be commemorated.

What Tina wanted most was to witness a revitalization of cultural heritage and political engagement, twin aspects of positive community life for Orgosolo residents. She remembered in her early teenage years, at the end of the '70s and beginning of the '80s, the ongoing exchanges between groups of close friends, known as *criccas*. Many groups of young people took over abandoned houses and transformed them into "clubs," where they gathered almost nightly to talk, eat, and play music. The *criccas* would visit one another, she said, generating an atmosphere of intense social connections amid townspeople. Sports leagues, voluntary associations, and cooperatives were started as a result of these active connections and the concern to improve the quality of life in the town.

This was also wrapped up in the political ferment that had taken place over the preceding decade, as communist, socialist, and ethnonationalist political parties gained footholds of opposition against the Democrazia Cristiana (DC), the Christian Democrats, in Orgosolo. By the end of the 1960s, several political parties were active and two youth groups led demonstrations and lobbies concerning a variety of issues. Labor migrants were traveling out to continental Europe, and people were beginning to see some relief from prior economic hardship. Standards of public education and the level of local literacy were already rising. The increasing popularity of the Partito Comunista Italiano (PCI), the Communist Party of Italy, was reflected in the 1970 election of eight town councilors for the left, while the majority party of

Orgosolo remained the Christian Democrats, with twelve councilors. In 1975, Orgosolo elected its first local administration with a strong majority from the left-leaning political parties.[3] This coincided with the height of PCI success at the national level, when the party contributed an essential minority to the governing coalitions. From the beginning of the 1970s until the mid-1990s, the political balance between left-leaning and center-right political coalitions in Orgosolo could be described by the alternating motion of a pendulum swing. After each five-year term, the local elections inverted the relations between the majority and minority coalitions.

Another friend, Anna, was a young woman in the 1970s, and she recalled,

> They held demonstrations and assemblies for everything . . . at [piazza] su ponte or at piazza Gramsci . . . they used to have more meetings, you were always hearing an announcement on the loudspeakers, or [a car going round to make announcements] advertising a meeting for one party or another, and if the Christian Democrats had a meeting, the Communist Party had to have one too, they vied with one another to see who had more meetings. (July 1998)

This time of political ferment supported a number of important transformations in the community. Town councils were able to foster infrastructural development; services were improved, new neighborhoods built, and the water supply stabilized. New taxes were levied for urban works, new buildings constructed to government codes, schools and public housing erected. The occupational structure became more diversified, with a gradual decline in the numbers of men involved in herding. More women joined the formal labor force. Cooperatives were created for shepherds, construction enterprises, agricultural and forestry activities, eldercare, and nursery care. The town was able to take advantage of a development assistance fund available in Southern Italy, the Cassa per il Mezzogiorno, the Mezzogiorno Fund, to launch its own reforestation projects on the communal territory. Positive cultural and economic transformations were visible everywhere. Even the streets of the Corso Repubblica reflected a celebration of political action and change, as a local teacher and artist began to commemorate political demonstrations and debates with colorful wall murals.

Anna believed that since that time, the political leadership of the town had changed and become complacent. "They all settled down [with salaried jobs],"[4] she told me.

Intellectuals and politicians claimed, instead, that it was the citizenship that had become complacent. According to a former mayor, Orgosolo residents, like many other Italians, had become politically indifferent and distrustful of politicians. He noted that "political life today is less intense than that of yesterday: probably one believes less than before, one has less faith, one is tired of the behavior of the political world or of the government."

Apparent disaffections from political life were contextualized by larger socioeconomic and political shifts affecting not only Sardinia, but also Italy as a whole. With the creation of the Republic of Italy after World War II, the nation's complicated multiparty system was motored by extensive patronage networks. Throughout Southern Italy in particular, the Christian Democrat Party distributed favors such as jobs and pensions.[5] Other major parties did the same, as much as their power base permitted. With a large part of the Italian economy located in state enterprises, party membership became vital to social and economic networks, and was often connected to religious choices as well as social identity (Kertzer 1980; Shore 1990, 1993; see also Bull 2000). During the 1980s, this political system based on patron-client ties was increasingly linked with scandal and economic decline. Widespread dissatisfaction with the state rose (Ginsborg 1990, 1996). Patronage and corruption stories provoked a political crisis, and the early 1990s saw the breakdown and reorganization of both the Christian Democrat Party and the Communist Party of Italy, formerly the two most important sections in Orgosolo politics.[6] David Kertzer (1996, 15) notes that when the communist movement reinvented itself as the Democratic Party of the Left (PDS) in 1991, this process was fundamentally upsetting to party members whose sense of personal identity was often deeply enmeshed with that of the party. Despite the efforts of party leaders to revitalize communist projects in Italy after the fall of the Berlin Wall, the PDS suffered a decline in membership following the change of name and political program. Political affiliations had long shaped personal identities and social networks throughout Italy.

In Orgosolo, partisan lines once deeply divided the community.[7]

The Roman Catholic Church, with its ties to the Christian Democrat Party of Italy, promoted a severely anti-communist discourse in Orgosolo right up through the 1970s. One elderly woman I met said that the priest had told her all the bad things communists would do if they were elected; she was told they had storage rooms ready to take poor people's food provisions right out of their larders and canteens. When I asked her for whom she had voted, she confirmed that her family had always favored the Christian Democrats. "We always remained [just so]," she said in Sardinian,[8] making a gesture with her hands that denoted correctness. Zia Mariedda, who had brought me to visit the old woman, explained that the priests used to say it was a mortal sin to vote communist. She recalled that from the mid-1950s through the late 1970s, the head priest in town refused to allow communist party members to become godparents or get married within the church building. If they wanted to marry, communists had to perform the ritual in the courtyard of his parochial house.

The political vision of left-wing organizers nevertheless acquired great resonance at Orgosolo. Both Franco Cagnetta (1954) and Peppino Marotto (1978) once argued that the historical experience of Sardinian shepherds was exceptionally suited to the development of class consciousness.[9] Whether or not these claims are considered objectively true, they have commanded rhetorical force. The rise of the political left in Sardinia can be linked in particular to the example of two key historical figures in the early twentieth century: Emilio Lussu and Antonio Gramsci. Lussu was a military hero of the First World War, who went on to a long and active political career. He supported Sardinian nationalism, played key roles in three different left-leaning political parties, and was renowned for his participation in the anti-fascist resistance movement.[10] Gramsci was an even more celebrated Sardinian, despite his shorter lifespan. He inspired pride as a world-famous intellectual and founding member of the Italian Communist Party. Gramsci's provocative discussion of hegemony and class set a challenge that was taken up by a generation of left-leaning students and other young people in the 1960s. It is the legacy of this generation in Orgosolo that always inspired my friend Tina.

Hegemony, Class, and Political Action

Su Pensamentu de Gramsci, "The Thought of Gramsci"
When all, convinced,
United, go to battle,
Sardinians will no longer
Be constrained to emigrate,
Abolishing the chains
Of avaricious exploitation. . . .
(Peppino Marotto 1996 [1989], 147; excerpt translated from Sardinian)

By the 1950s, Antonio Gramsci figured as a "party martyr" and a "patron saint" of the Communist Party of Italy; he has remained an important role model for the new Democratic Party of the Left (Kertzer 1996, 15). Gramsci's life, 1891-1937, reflected an early experience of poor health, physical disability, and very harsh poverty in rural Sardinia, and continuing economic hardship as a student and political activist, first in the Sardinian capital of Cagliari, and then in the mainland city of Turin. This culminated in a struggle against fascism that resulted in his criminalization and long imprisonment, leading to an early death.[11] There is much in this example to inspire a sense of resonance with the larger history of central Sardinia, and certainly with social memories of misfortune, suffering, criminalization, and "resistance" in Orgosolo. Nairn (1982) contended that Gramsci's intellectual contributions could not be disentangled from his direct knowledge of abjection as a poor Sardinian hunchback. Both the severe economic distress of central Sardinia and the racialized ethnic prejudice suffered by Sardinians on the mainland must have conditioned Gramsci's perceptions of historical reality. His critical engagement with revolutionary Marxism informed reflections on the structural circumstances of his own life and a deep commitment to political activism. He is best known for his attempts to transcend crude materialism and restore attention to the role of cultural praxis inherent in articulations of power and resistance.[12]

Gramsci's models for political analysis and action sowed many seeds of provocation for later generations.[13] Although Gramsci demonstrated firm conviction in a radical revolutionary mandate, from which cold-war cohorts of Western intellectuals were apt to distance themselves, the idea of "hegemony" has remained a captivating problematic, even in the age of globalization and neoliberal governance (Morton 2007). Hegemony is an unkempt concept, initially conceived to explain how subordinate classes become complicit in their own domination, and therefore can fail to generate a class consciousness sufficient to organize and activate the envisaged transition to communism. For Gramsci, however, hegemony was not a predetermined mechanism but rather a process indicative of both social agency and possibilities for change. Anne Showstack Sassoon's working definition suggests: "Probably Gramsci's key concept and the one which is most controversial, hegemony is used in the sense of influence, leadership, consent rather than the alternative and opposite meaning of domination" (1987, 13). It is helpful to keep in mind that in Gramsci's Italy, the pragmatics of embedded patron-client relationships, filtered through the loyalties and mutual regard associated with kinship, friendship, and community, are implicit to social life.[14] Acceptance of a system of hegemony does not imply a complete failure of perception and understanding; rather it is the outcome of specific circumstances, in which persuasive legitimating narratives, threats of force, structural limitations, and tacit trade-offs converge to reaffirm that system (Gramsci 1971, 12-13). Gavin Smith explains,

> Hegemony is about the mastering of history. That is to say, it is about praxis: the use of people's will and agency to drive their own history into the future; and it is about the weight (or lightness) of the past, carried on the shoulders of the present. Fundamental to the concept is a rejection of the idea of the social person as object, passive recipient, or cultural dope. Thus, while it is possible that a person's or a group's ideas about the world might be partial (in both senses: one-sided and incomplete), the notion of false consciousness is not consistent with Gramsci's understanding of hegemony. (2004, 217)

Gramsci's writing about hegemony is intimately connected to two issues of special relevance here: his assessment of regional relationships across Italy, and his discussions about the role of intellectuals as the social agents of change. In his "notes on Italian history," Gramsci outlines a theory of internal colonialism that affected Sardinia and other parts of Southern Italy.

The poverty of the Mezzogiorno was historically "inexplicable" for the popular masses in the North; they did not understand that unity had not taken place on a basis of equality, but as hegemony of the North over the Mezzogiorno in a territorial version of the town-country relationship—in other words, that the North concretely was an "octopus" which enriched itself at the expense of the South, and that its economic-industrial increment was in direct proportion to the impoverishment of the economy and the agriculture of the South. (Gramsci 1971, 70–71)

Gramsci was scornful of essentialist explanations often given for the ambiguous outcome of national unification. The remainder of this passage demonstrates an outspoken critique of racist approaches to problems of political economy in the South:

The ordinary man from Northern Italy thought rather that, if the Mezzogiorno made no progress . . . in the way of modern development, this meant that the causes of the poverty were not external, to be sought in objective economic and political conditions, but internal, innate in the population of the South. . . . There remained one explanation—the organic incapacity of the inhabitants, their barbarity, their biological inferiority. (Ibid., 71)

This indictment shines out in contrast to the biological essentialism embedded in studies of Southern Italy published by the Lombroso school of criminology, including the work of Alfredo Niceforo in Sardinia (Gibson 1998). In Orgosolo, some people came to see the communist movement as a possible antidote to both racist and conservative nationalism. Gramsci's provocative discussion of "the southern question" took on particular significance given northern Italy's remarkable economic development during the postwar period, as many Sardinians began to migrate away for industrial and agricultural jobs on the continent.[15] Across Sardinia, patterns of left-wing political critique became established. They thrived in particular during the 1960s and 1970s (Schweizer 1988), as postcolonial and dependency theories gained acceptance around the world, and political parties of the left gained strength across Italy.

Gramsci was interested in various groups of intellectuals whose activities in the cultural sphere might contribute to the hegemonies of exploitation, or promote the counter-hegemonies of the working class. The challenge was to understand how political consciousness and activism could be inspired among the peasant classes of rural Italy, particularly since the South was dominated by agricultural interests. The South, he said, typically produced a large share of "traditional" intellectuals, that is, scholars and educated bureaucrats who mediated contacts between peasants and the state, as well as priests who mediated contact with the Church (Gramsci 1971, 14–16).[16] Gramsci was concerned that the rural classes could not produce what he called "organic intellectuals," individuals with particular intellectual skills and the organizational capacity to forge political alliances, who remained integrally embedded within the peasant mode of production (ibid., 6, 12). Gramsci spent most of his adult life away from Sardinia, and there is evidence of doubt on his part about the ability of rural peasants to transcend fascinations with magic, superstition, and religion to develop class consciousness. Had he lived to see it, however, Gramsci might have recognized opportunities for cultural transformation afforded by changing socioeconomic patterns across rural Sardinia in the postwar period.

In the late 1960s, the phenomenon of "youth circles" (politically active youth groups involving university students and others, influenced by political dialogues of the left) appeared in highland Sardinian towns (see Madau 2005). In Orgosolo, the chronicle of the left-wing youths' struggle to act as "organic intellectuals," to grasp political economic connections with the broader world and lead an anti-hegemonic initiative, was commemorated with journalism, pamphlets, poetry, memoirs, photography, and even street murals. Coinciding with student activism across Europe, the youth circle's political activities were most vigorous in 1968–1969. In November of 1968, it occupied the Orgosolo town hall to speak out on issues of both local and regional relevance, such as the school curricula, the reduction of communal pastures through privatization, the lack of resources available for agriculture and job creation, and new legislation anticipated to create the Gennargentu National Park[17] (*Orgosolo Novembre 1968*, 16–17). In February of 1969, it hosted a convention at Orgosolo on the question of Gennargentu Park, now working together with a counterpart youth group coalescing in support of the Christian Democrats. The organizers calculated that over 130 Orgosolo shepherds were likely to be displaced from communal lands earmarked for integral nature protection, and they denounced government authorities for the adoption of an "imperialistic" American parks model, designed by a team of scientific ecology consultants from the Massachusetts Institute of Technology.

A month after the convention that rallied critical opposition to the park plan, government plans were announced for the construction of a NATO base on the communal territory. People conjectured that both projects to occupy the Orgosolo Commons supported a hidden agenda to quell banditry and subdue local opposition to the state (Muggianu 1998, 216). The left-wing youth circle circulated a pamphlet in Orgosolo, announcing that "the herders are not cannon fodder," and giving information about upcoming military exercises across a large area of the Commons (ibid., 220). The youth circle called on all the social categories they recognized—students, herders, women, and wage workers—to unite and assist in a demonstration against the base. For the left-leaning youth circle, the defense of communal tradition was an affirmation of progressive class consciousness.

Remembering Pratobello

Pratobello
Until yesterday, Orgosolo you were known
By everyone as the land of bandits:
But today at Pratobello, all united
Your sons have descended in battle
Against the military invasion
That they were planning down there.
Instead of tractors to plow
There arrived tanks and cannons
And troops of slaughter to train
Sent by the same buffoons
Who wanted the Barbagia to develop
With parks for wild pigs and mouflons.
   . . .
Of Orgosolo proud and courageous
All the population sings
All this it has understood and, threatening

It goes out armed with sticks to send away
This fascist and hateful troop
That is then constrained to turn around
And leave the mountains and plains
Crossing the sea again.
Not bandits but partisans
They showed themselves to the capitalists
That armed only with sticks and bare hands,
Orgosolo sends away the fascists.
(From the album *Su lamentu de su pastore*, Gruppo Rubanu,
    1980; excerpts translated from Sardinian)

As the tale was retold in Orgosolo in the late 1990s, the demonstration of 1969 happened "spontaneously" and boasted the solidarity of the entire town, including rival political factions of the DC and the PCI, priests themselves, and ordinary folk, men and women, "everyone," from the very old to the very young. The events were often remembered for me over the course of my years at Orgosolo, told by the authoritative voices of the participants, or else by the alternately fond and irritable voices of their sons and daughters, who have heard the anecdotes and private chronicles of the "Battle of Pratobello" ad nauseum.

The youth circle's account estimated that over 3,000 people went out to the field of Pratobello, on the Orgosolo Commons, to join the first day of the demonstration against the NATO base on June 19, 1969 (Haensch n.d.). According to the organizers, there was a mood of festival as people occupied the area designated for military exercises. They listened to speeches, sang, danced, picnicked, played traditional (illegal) gambling games, and even offered food to and sought out personal debates with the soldiers standing guard. On the second day of the demonstration, the state police set up heavily manned roadblocks to prevent people from attending, and tensions mounted. Many of the demonstrators found their way around the roadblocks on foot and arrived at the military camp to confront a line of "blue berets," armed with machine guns. Youth circle members used a megaphone to persuade the troops of their common class interests, while women targeted Sardinian policemen individually to shame them by telling them that their families would not approve of taking land away from its rightful owners. More military troops arrived, as well as representatives from the major political parties. Violent confrontations were narrowly avoided, but the demonstration was disbanded in the afternoon, when military commanders promised delegates that military exercises would be temporarily suspended. People returned to town, where "demonstrators saluted one another with clenched fists" (ibid.). An assembly was held at the plaza Su Ponte, close to the offices of the PCI (the party founded by Gramsci) and the PSIUP (the party founded by Emilio Lussu), to discuss further strategies.

Minor dissensions emerged between the politicians, who wanted to take control over the negotiations with authorities, and the youth circle organizers, who decided to use nonviolent protest strategies to interrupt military exercises that were reinitiated on June 22. Together with some young shepherds, they spent the night on the Commons to keep watch over military activities, and sent word to town in the early hours of the morning that the demonstration should resume. Men and women, students, forestry workers and herders, Catholics and Marxists arrived. They attempted to disarm the soldiers on the range and destroy firing targets. A real-life game of cat and mouse ensued, with groups of protestors reportedly dashing around the designated firing range and then hiding themselves while the soldiers attempted to pursue and remove them. When captured, individual protesters were put inside a circle of armed guards in a nearby field, which they named a "ghetto" and a "concentration camp." They called the soldiers "fascists" and "nazis" (Haensch n.d.). The "prisoners" sought to engage their guards in conversations and win over their sympathies. Over 600 protesters were detained and interrogated that day, but no one was wounded. This pattern continued for another three days, with protesters from Orgosolo going up to the Commons early each morning, albeit in declining numbers. As the soldiers pursued them, people scattered leaflets on the ground that taunted the Blue Berets. In another area, groups of protesters goaded a reconnaissance helicopter, then scattered to hide amid trees and underbrush when the squadrons arrived. The youth circle reported that one shepherd "kept thick groups of police in checkmate, roving about on horseback at his pleasure" (ibid.).

In town, more political assemblies were held; party leaders gave speeches and communications of support arrived from various associations and politicians elsewhere in Sardinia. Emilio Lussu sent a telegram of solidarity with Orgosolo protesters to the president of the Regional Assembly. He called the NATO base a "colonial provocation" whose like had not been seen since fascist times (Haensch n.d., 97). Intellectuals in the regional capital, Cagliari, published a pamphlet against the military exercises, which were said to have a hidden agenda, "to strike down the fight against colonization which has risen up in Barbagia and which has had until now the principal but not sole theme of rejecting the Park" (ibid., 107). The grand scale of participation in the Pratobello demonstration was a victory of the youth circle organizers, for whom the "total solidarity of the people" was symbolically important. Local consensus against the NATO base was also key to the ultimate success of their efforts, although the youth circle and parties of the left ultimately lost control over the protest and negotiations.

After June 26, 1969, an agreement was reached that limited the duration of military presence to that summer. Shepherds were compensated for inaccessible pastures, forestry workers were compensated for lost work days, and military supplies were purchased from local businesses. No permanent military base was constructed at Orgosolo, although permanent NATO bases were built in other areas of the island. A number of the youth circle voted against ceasing tactics of protest against the military presence on the Commons, but could not rally support. Several protesters faced charges related to resisting public officers and entering a prohibited military area; a handful spent a few months in prison. Members of the youth circle were interrogated, and organizers of the demonstration were charged with sedition (related to the protest) and defamation (related to political pamphlets). None of these charges were upheld, but they may have curtailed enthusiasm for political activism (Muggianu 1998). Later, the leaders of the youth circle went on to establish successful careers in education, politics, public bureaucracy, and the agricultural cooperative. Although the DC claimed a share in the success of the demonstration, the local PCI was able to capitalize on political support for the left in the aftermath of Pratobello.

Events at Pratobello became a touchstone for memories of collective action and resistance, in Orgosolo and for Sardinia as a whole. Local poets (notably N. Rubanu, translated above, as well as Peppino Marotto and A. Sini) performed famous pieces in commemoration. In 1976 and

1984, a striking mural of the Pratobello demonstration was painted and repainted across the entire face of the old town hall. The artist was Francesco del Casino, former member of the left-wing youth circle. Del Casino had come to Sardinia from Siena to work as a teacher, and married into a local family. He lived in Orgosolo from 1965 to 1984. During this period, he executed several murals around town to memorialize protest placards from Pratobello, quote Sardinian poetry about it, and honor the herders who worked the land. His many other murals highlighted Marxist and regional debates on a variety of subjects.

The Work of Nostalgia

Inexorably, however, the tenor of political life began to shift away from the popular activism that characterized the 1960s and 1970s. During the 1980s and 1990s, phenomena of political intimidation grew serious in many communities of Sardinia. Orgosolo councilors also began to receive threats at various times, in the form of letters and telephone calls. One retired mayor described the situation as one of increasing "barbarization," although he noted that a small number of individuals were at fault. "A few delinquents," he said, "have shot at their houses and filled the families of administrators with fear." By 1995, not many people were willing to take on the unpopular job of local governance.

"They had to go looking for people on the street [to join the election list] because nobody wanted to do it," my friend Gianni told me. "You've seen what they've done to them," he said, "they slashed X's tires, they destroyed Y's garden cottage." Accordingly, only one coalition was presented for the Orgosolo election that year, and the local administration presiding when I went to do fieldwork was made up of individuals from across the political spectrum.[18] Gianni was a former student of del Casino and part of a group of young people (men and women) in the 1980s who called themselves Gli Api, "The Bees," who were concerned about declining political participation in Orgosolo. They began to paint political murals themselves, and even spraypainted graffiti below del Casino's mural on the town hall to criticize the political passivity that had succeeded the earlier era of ferment. It said, "Sweet dreams on the mattresses of Pratobello." When the town council commissioned the mural to be refreshed, the graffiti was erased.

Diminishing political activism was matched by the commodification of cultural assets and a folklore boom. In this context, the heirs of Gramsci sought the means to revitalize political dialogues, and use cultural forms of expression to inspire political reflection. The poet Peppino Marotto, a herder and one of the founding members of the communist party in Orgosolo, dedicated several new poems to Gramsci, the labor movement, and emigration issues. These poems were first performed in various local public contexts, and later collected in a published volume (Marotto 1996) with the support of Sardinian language advocacy organizations. Meanwhile, the artist Francesco del Casino painted murals that read like a manual for Gramsci's vision of political practice.[19] In 1989, del Casino—now living in Siena—painted four more murals of Pratobello at the plaza Su Ponte, sometimes nicknamed "Piazza del Popolo," where political assemblies had once been held outside the headquarters of the PCI and the PSIUP. These were modeled on sepia pictures taken at the demonstration by the famous photographer Franco Pinna, and depicted the protagonism of ordinary residents, even old shepherds and women with children, as they confronted armed soldiers. Peppino Marotto's famous Sardinian poem, "The Battle of Pratobello,"[20] provided captions.

Del Casino later explained the purpose of his murals as a form of political communication, inspired by the social ferment of the sixties. "I believe that the party sections were not only the seats of political imbroglio," he said, "but places of debate and cultural growth, where one also challenged everyday habits and problems, and the discussions went out from there and continued in the bar, in the plaza, in the council meetings, even in the houses" (interview by B. Madau, 1997).[21] In a town where the excessive rate of school failures and dropouts was a notable problem (Ligas 1990), del Casino's mentorship of students in Orgosolo also suggests an appreciation for Gramsci's approach to education as a means for deep cultural transformation. "At the base of everything," he said to Madau, "there is a precise goal from an educational-didactic point of view: break down the wall that divides the school from the society" (B. Madau, 1997).

The murals of Orgosolo became famous over time, not only as material memories of Pratobello, but also as a source of cultural distinction in themselves.[22] In late March of 1998, the town council awarded Francesco del Casino an honorary citizenship in recognition of his contribution as the primary muralist of the town. His example had drawn other groups and individuals, including local artists Pasquale Buesca, Vincenzo Floris, and "The Bees," to paint murals. Tourists came to Orgosolo to visit the murals on a regular basis, energizing the local economy. The honorary citizenship ceremony itself presented festive traditional culture, folklore, and the best face of community. According to my friend Tina, the event was laden with nostalgia for the period between 1965 and 1975. As we sat in the bar afterward to talk with friends, she was upset that the generation of youth today seemed to have so much less imagination and initiative, and lamented that it would not be possible to work with high school students the way del Casino had in the 1970s. She said she had wanted to interrupt the congratulatory speeches and ask why new initiatives were not taken on the basis of these role models, but refrained from casting gloom on the event.

Both del Casino and Don Sanguinetti,[23] the other person awarded honorary citizenship that year, were leaders of nonviolent social ferment, which stood out in contrast to the tactics of political intimidation and destructive vandalism that often jeopardized the local council's initiatives. They were each commended at the ceremony for their willingness to transcend partisan divides and seek positive modes of cultural expression. "I have never asked anyone to show their party membership," Sanguinetti volunteered. It was a relief to many left-leaning families when Sanguinetti took over the parish during the 1980s. After years of partisan tensions, local communists could return to practice in the Church. Don Sanguinetti had been the beloved head priest in Orgosolo for many years, and had been elevated to a bishopric the year before receiving honorary citizenship. He was given credit for his part in petitioning the Church to elevate an Orgosolo girl, Antonia Mesina, to beatified status. Del Casino, on the other hand, received appreciation for his active protagonism in events at Pratobello.

In 1999, del Casino's work, and the artist himself, featured in a seasonal re-opening of a "living museum" in an abandoned house along the Corso Repubblica. Tina, Gianni, and several former members of "The Bees" were instrumental in organizing and running the displays. Tina was passionate about showing visitors what the town was really like earlier that century. The little house with its low, sloping roof and dirt floors was furnished and decorated with a number of borrowed antiques.[24] Del Casino painted a new mural on the front of the house, depicting a man reading a newspaper, and his artwork was displayed in an upstairs room. Like the photographer Franco Pinna, the artist himself had found a place in local narratives about Orgosolo's "real" social history. In 1997, the Orgosolo public library also inaugurated a new local history section with a display of Pinna's photography.

The ongoing work of nostalgia contributes to the reification of Orgosolo as having a culture of resistance. For local residents, the romance of Pratobello is linked to an embodiment of total unity: a sacred moment when internal tensions and strife were put aside, and the power of community was revealed. For left-leaning activists, it signified the possibility of fulfilling the dreams of organic intellectuals, on their own terms. For Sardinian ethnonationalists, it was an occasion when the most authentic spirit of independence became manifest. For everyone, it was a time when politics itself seemed more genuine. As late as 2005, the demonstration at Pratobello was commemorated with a touring display of Pinna's photography and accounts of the protest presented at a convention sponsored by the Association of Sardinian Emigrants.[25] In light of recent debates about creating nuclear waste disposal sites on the island, as well as enlarging the NATO presence, the model of Orgosolo's grassroots political activism at Pratobello remains resonant in a wider context.

Return to Resistance

PRATOBELLO '98

TO SAY NO
To the State's Park of the Gennargentu
Of Law 394

TO SAY YES
To a Project of Self-Managed Development
In the Territory

April 26 beginning at 10 a.m.

HUGE POPULAR FESTIVAL
One day you will be able to say:

I too was at Pratobello

You are all invited to participate

The Base Committees of: Arzana—Baunei—Dorgali—Gairo— Oliena—
Orgosolo—Talana—Urzulei—Villagrande—Villanova
The Movement for the Rights to the Territory

(Text of official poster advertising the 1998 demonstration at Pratobello)

By April 1998, there was full consensus in the bars, in the streets, and in political assemblies at Orgosolo: "no to law 394," the law that institutionalized Gennargentu Park in ways that minimized the town's control over traditional common lands. As panic arose about the imminent confirmation of the law, rural working-class "base committees" from several towns planned to orchestrate an inter-community demonstration to be held on the Commons of Orgosolo. One might say they planned to build a kind of time machine, able to align one iconic event with another remembered and empowering moment, wresting agency from the patterns of social time.

Could a whole town be transported back three decades, to a time of social ferment? Back to a fleeting period in the late 1960s when it still seemed possible to believe that the people decided, and the politicians signed papers accordingly? Was it possible to erase internal social boundaries arising from the diversification in economic strategies, transcend the threat of violence, and engender cohesive local action? If so, one might reason that it could only happen beyond the shadows of corruption that had come to taint the party politics of communists and Christians alike. This could only be imagined in the sensual site of hopeful nostalgia, on the Commons, at Pratobello. The collaborative public performance of protest would be framed by performances of local authenticity, and promote the moral authority of municipal governance over communally owned territories. And so they built the time machine at Pratobello: A symbolic re-enactment that would take the town back to the late 1960s, giving form to their own fluid historicity, replenishing the political sphere with the signifying power of the local, and recovering the pure resonances of the past for a needy present.

Ironically for the heirs of Gramsci, the political consciousness mobilized by rural working-class intellectuals in late twentieth-century Sardinia shifted the domain of activism outside of party politics entirely. Given the bitter memory of Italy's scandalous "Clean Hands" political corruption trials of the 1990s, people were largely convinced of the inclination of political classes to participate in corrupt systems of negotiation. Elected politicians were displaced from leading the campaign against the park, and cultural identity replaced class analysis as the motivating narrative of resistance. The vast literature on new social movements and identity-based politics suggests that this shift coincided with a defining new wave of political organization around the world. Briefly put, authors such as Alain Touraine (1988) and his student Alberto Melucci (1989) argued that orientations to culture and identity defined transnational movements such as environmentalism, feminism, and gender-rights advocacy in the late twentieth century, in contrast to what they saw as an earlier wave of class-based mobilizations (see also Laclau and Mouffe 2001). Anthropological commentaries on the burgeoning literature that succeeded have urged attention to historical continuities such as the ongoing role of class, to the wider social fields within which these movements operate, to the complexities of social experience, the production of subjective identity, and fragmentation within the movements themselves, and to the central importance of reflexivity in the ethnography of power relations (Gledhill 2000; Edelman 2001). The Orgosolo case suggests how ongoing consciousness of class, locally embedded senses of history, and changing national constructions of partisan identity have come together in this process. Cultural politics "from the bottom up" in central Sardinia emerged in tension with the cultural orientations advocated by global environmentalism. Dynamic engagements with other cultural minority movements and projects for postcolonial "decolonization" have helped to shape this local identity-based mobilization. The complexities and tensions inherent within this mobilization are discussed in the next chapter.

While the shadows of a partisan divide linger on, today the deepest social rifts in Orgosolo follow the lines of occupation (and unemployment). These class divides are somewhat distinct from political party loyalties and affiliations, which tend to follow familial and social networks. Gramsci's vision for a transformative politics appears dimmed before the sense of political betrayal and disaffection articulated by community members in the 1990s. Few young people in Orgosolo maintained formal membership in political parties, and attendance at most political events had dropped. Near Tina's house, however, in the same neighborhood as the town's first communist mayor, the late poet-balladeer Peppino Marotto, and the former home of the muralist Francesco del Casino, there is a small plaza dedicated to Gramsci. People in Orgosolo remembered how left-wing activists used to gather there in the open air. Murals on the wall paid tribute to Gramsci's thought, and Tina looked to the days of her earliest childhood for a model of what Orgosolo could be.

Chapter 7

Sin, Shame, and Sheep

Blessedness and Disgrace

Each year, on May 17, Orgosolo celebrates a festival in honor of its very own Blessed Antonia Mesina. The Orgosolo girl was beatified in 1987 as a "martyr to purity." Her reliquary is now displayed in a special chapel beneath the main church. Bone fragments are contained within a full-size figure dressed in the well-known women's folk costume of Orgosolo and laid out in a glass coffin that serves as an altar for masses during the nine days of prayer dedicated to Mesina's memory. She is without doubt the most powerful icon of traditional female identity at Orgosolo, admired not only for her model piety but also for her contribution to her family's survival of hardship during the fascist period. Because she helped care for younger siblings and participated in the many necessary chores associated with household production strategies, her example validates the self-sacrifice and hard agricultural work of women as the historical means of surviving poverty, marginality, and misfortune. The irony is that Mesina coped with structural violence, only to fall victim to a local sexual predator. The girl was collecting firewood outside of town in 1935 when she was attacked, and died defending herself from a brutal rape. In Orgosolo this martyrdom is celebrated not only for Mesina's religious attachment to virginity, but also for her will to resist domination. As a feminine metaphor for Sardinian identity, Mesina's story of "resistance" strongly evokes her historic and cultural context. Antonia Mesina lived and died with a direct, authentic connection to the local land and the community.

For the festival of Antonia Mesina in 1998, the local parish organized an outdoor mass and picnic on the Orgosolo Commons, near the area where she was killed. Over a hundred animals were donated to prepare the famous local meat dishes that would be distributed in a massive show of local hospitality to the pilgrims, tourists, and townspeople who gather for the event. It was an important occasion. Orgosolo has often drawn negative outside attention in connection with homicides, forest fires, and kidnappings. On this day, the town should have celebrated a virtuous moment in its troubled history. But this morning another *disgrazia*, another "disgrace," marred the positive vision of local identity and highlighted the local violence implicit in the story of Antonia Mesina. At the same time, it referenced but disengendered her spirit of resistance to illegitimate encroachment.

A mouflon, one of the endangered wild sheep indigenous to Sardinia, was found slaughtered and hanging at the crossroads leading to the festival on the Orgosolo Commons. Red spray-paint covered the road, spelling out new threats to local, regional, and national politicians if the recently ratified government plan to institute a new Gennargentu park were carried through. Residents interpreted this as an attempt by a violent minority to affirm the authority of "traditional" herders over the land. An anonymous group calling itself the "Armed Anti-Park Front" had already taken responsibility for several acts of vandalism against the forestry service, as well as for threatening local administrators. Many Orgolesi had been offended and frustrated in preceding months by the failure of the national, regional, and provincial governments to acknowledge their protests against a new parks law. Most residents, nevertheless, were demonstrably outraged and affronted by the slaughter of the mouflon. Practicing Catholics were shocked by the timing; those with "love" of local fauna and environment were appalled by the disregard for wildlife; those with interests in tourism and development were upset by the bad publicity; and many innocent herders resented the implication of their own complicity in the violence.

The slaughter of the mouflon, a well-known totem for the Sardinian parks movement and the wildlife protection campaigns of the World Wide Fund for Nature (wwf), caused almost as much scandal and indignation within Orgosolo as it did within the ranks of environmentalists and the wider Italian audience. How can we understand the multilayered and contested significance of the action? Some critics were quick to attribute it to either a fundamental cultural indifference toward ecology, or a historically rooted culture of resistance to the state. Yet the symbolic charges of this ecological terrorism go well beyond opposition to a park, to evoke religious faith, gender models, and cultural identity. More than a simple "weapon of the weak" (Scott 1985), the action constituted a contentious element in a local debate about political practice itself.

This chapter continues the ethnographic study of "resistance" in Orgosolo by looking at grassroots protest against a second initiative to create a centralized Gennargentu Park, approved in 1998. This movement mobilized significant support through references to the historic local protests of 1968-69, and particularly the events of Pratobello described in the previous chapter. The movement comprised, however, a number of rather incongruent understandings and expectations that can be seen to be in tension with one another as one examines closely the events and public debates of 1998 in Orgosolo. The slaughter of the mouflon, for example, can be contextualized within the range of identity discourses and practices that shape profoundly the cultural politics of environment in Orgosolo. There is evidence of a widespread ideology of the shepherd as the most vital component of local identity (Satta 2001). The social construction of masculinity in central Sardinia therefore bears on the interpretation of this event, and the responses to it. The violence perpetrated by the anonymous Armed Anti-Park Front might have been perceived by some rural Sardinians as legitimate political strategies in the tradition of male *balentia* (see Berger 1986, 226–32); that is, the ability to protect oneself, one's family, and one's economic interests in the face of threats from other individuals or from the state. Yet in the 1990s, many Sardinians passionately disavowed such violence in private and in public. In fact, they sought to transcend the blocks it regenerated to their own more moderate political lobbies against the national park.

In contrast to the dramatic gestures of the Armed Anti-Park Front, residents involved in Orgosolo's grassroots "Base Committee" in a broader grassroots movement, Regional Movement for the Defense of Rights to the Territory, promoted nostalgic, idealized visions of community to make space for political voices outside established party politics. What I call their "politics of the weak" was rooted in a moral discourse of embodied connections to land and landscape not only as actual herders, but through broadly shared ties of work, food, and history linked to the Commons. By referencing a range of positively esteemed daily practices in central Sardinia with their own cultural performances and narratives, they sought to affirm the unity of local cultural values as a foundation for empowerment. Their visions of cultural authenticity as a source of authority over the landscape included different social classes and categories among local residents.

The entangled stories of two martyrs, Mesina and the mouflon, highlight tensions and disruptions embedded in local constructions of cultural authenticity in 1998. A double narrative of blessedness and disgrace was mediated by archetypes of "traditional" Sardinian women and Sardinian shepherds. Particular kinds of ecological and gendered relationships were evoked in the celebration, subversion, reappropriation, and ongoing negotiation of these embodied identities through political practice. The stories of Antonia Mesina and the mouflon are interwoven with the larger, unfinished account of Gennargentu Park, where wild sheep and other such undomesticated "natural" species would be cherished on precisely those lands once thought too marginal to be developed for purposes other than herding. Studying the process of contestation ethnographically complicates notions of "resistance" (cf. Ortner 1995), by recognizing how social agency "from the bottom up" is inflected with ironies, inconsistencies, and double-binds that are implicated in reinscribing relations of power. Ethnography reveals the play of strategy, morality, and transgression embedded in so-called "resistance" to a national park in rural Sardinia.

Environmentalism and the Social Life of "Resistance"

Tania Li (2005) notes that James C. Scott's (1998) representation of the state and its exercise of power is highly stylized for the purposes of his argument. Because development schemes "work in and through the practices and desires of their target populations," they incorporate multiple spatial scales and complex arrays of bureaucratic authorities, including non-governmental organizations (Li 2005, 383). Li highlights the kinds of situated, hybrid knowledge and practice that are imbricated with bureaucratic power relationships. Recent ethnographies regarding parks and biodiversity conservation also emphasize the institutional complexity involved in "governing nature" today.[1] The Italian context highlights problems in Scott's representation of the state. We cannot talk about a single, small group of technocrats in Rome who have wished to redesign the nation's periphery. The Region of Sardinia and the Province of Nuoro have been involved in the national park initiative from the outset. Support for "green politics" has ripened across Italy, Europe, and the international sphere, while the rhetoric of stakeholder participation has reorganized aspects of ecodevelopment design and implementation. Modernist visions of governance and development have supported somewhat convergent rhetorics across these different scales of organization, but it is important to reflect on the kinds of ambiguity and dissonance generated by bureaucracies themselves, let alone institutions operating with different goals and cultural logics.[2]

The Sardinian case also invites us to critically revisit Scott's (1985) ideas about "everyday forms of resistance." Scott's attention to perspectives "from the bottom up" provoked scholars to consider the capacity for hidden resistance in everyday strategies for survival, moral recognition, and identity-making. Once such "weapons of the weak" could be distinguished, forms of collective consciousness and agency could be identified that were disregarded in earlier studies of peasant movements for rebellion and revolution. In Orgosolo, this consciousness and agency can be discerned in the way that residents continue to speak about their embodied authority over the land, on the basis of the community's living pastoral heritage.[3] Since pastoralism is a recognized marker of tradition, the related stereotypes of central Sardinia as a "culture of violence" vs. a "culture of resistance" tend to condition how outsiders perceive the popular opposition to the Gennargentu Park project. Yet "resistance" in Sardinia cannot be taken at face value as a way to describe past events or cultural inclinations because it has acquired so much strategic significance in political discourses. By the time Italy achieved unification in 1860, its southern regions were already perceived as loci of brigandage and resistance. This was viewed positively in the context of Sardinian ethnonationalism and anti-fascist movements after the turn of the century. The legacies of Italian anthropologist Franco Cagnetta (1954) and later, historian Eric Hobsbawm (1959) highlighted—and even celebrated—the links between pastoral experience, banditry, and "resistance" in central Sardinia, and in Orgosolo in particular. In fact, Hobsbawm's treatise on the "social bandit" actually included a letter from a famous Orgosolo bandit, Pasquale Tandeddu, in illustration. Years later, in the 1990s, Orgosolo's Graziano Mesina, casting himself as a modern-day version of the social bandit, published his own memoirs. It is easy to see that "resistance" in Orgosolo, and in Sardinia writ large, is not an objective category, but an object of ideology and cultural imagination that continues to shape social practice and political life. In this way, it is implicated in an ongoing process of hegemony.

An intimate look at the dynamic tensions inherent in the cultural politics of popular opposition to the park in Orgosolo can help us shun the temptation to reify central Sardinia as a location that produces, fixes, and contains "resistance" as the embodiment of alterity. As Donald S. Moore (1998, 1999) points out, post-structuralist approaches to power and resistance in the 1990s tended to reproduce a "culture-as-text" metaphor that poorly represented how the individuals and groups who participate in popular opposition movements are caught up in multiple overlapping fields of power and signification. In contrast,

> An emphasis on the cultural politics of place underscores the simultaneity of symbolic and material struggles over territory. These struggles are highly localized, laying claim to specific terrain, yet are never simply local, sealed off from an outside beyond. My ethnographic grounding for remapping resistance suggests a move from hermetically sealed sites of autonomy to relation spaces of connection and articulation. (Moore 1998, 347–48)

Moore's approach highlights the role of historicity and complex, negotiated subjectivities in open-ended practices of resistance. He suggests how to look at everyday resistance in a way that reclaims Gramsci's vision of social agency on the part of marginal actors, through close attention to processes associated with "the crucible of cultural politics."[4] I draw upon Moore's insights from Zimbabwe to consider how residents in Orgosolo have variously reframed visions of identity, authority, and authenticity in response to ongoing events and contexts. Their evolving dialogues about the park and the Commons invoked memories of resistance that were linked to place and to social experience. As in Moore's study, a populist understanding in Orgosolo confirms that historical resistance to "colonial" or "neocolonial" initiatives for land and resource appropriation constitutes an innate connection to the Sardinian landscape. A discourse about this resistance as embodied tradition continually highlights and "remaps" the relation between culture and the Sardinian Supramonte. Yet even as heterogeneous, gendered, and contested practices of place inscribe politically fraught local meanings onto the landscape, they also raise important questions about the translocal connections that support, transform, and constrain them.

The Animals of Gennargentu Park

"If they make the park, they will bring the wolves," said a young man in Orgosolo in April 1998, at a town meeting to discuss the park. The wolves, in this case, were understood to be powerful strangers with ravenous appetites for any valuable resources belonging to the people of Orgosolo. The reference strategically highlighted a background of structural inequality in which politicians are assumed to be inherently complicit in capitalist interests. Since a national park would have meant generous funding for the administration of a new park agency and associated ecodevelopment projects along the border of the park, the project of wilderness conservation was often talked about as a variety of neocolonialism in the Italian periphery.

It is the specter of dissimulation associated with government initiatives and the political party system itself that has nurtured the fears of Orgosolo residents that ecodevelopment was merely another form of communal dispossession. In 1993, the town council agreed to concede another 1,800 hectares of its territory to the state forestry enterprise for a thirty-year period, in exchange for local job creation. The area would continue, under this contract, to be subject to residents' legal use-rights for pasture and other resources, except where areas might be temporarily closed for young plants to take root. The town would receive a portion of profits deriving from land management, while the remainder would be reinvested in land improvement and resource management. This plan was met with such heated debate and popular discontent that it required years to achieve a local consensus, and the new forestry camp at Iseri was opened only in 1997, after a long polemic between shepherds and unemployed laborers in the town. Despite the dire need for the 240 seasonal and 15 permanent work posts created (a portion of which was allocated to the herders barred from using their customary pastures), many people continued to worry that the initiative was merely a prelude to the wholesale annexation of the area for a national park.

When the question of Gennargentu Park returned to the fore later in 1997, the fences that had been erected in the areas of Iseri were systematically vandalized one night, and parts of the older forestry outpost at "Montes" were set on fire. The symbolism of the fence is prominent in ethnonationalist historical narratives about the Piedmontese enclosure movement of the nineteenth century, which credit the towns of central Sardinia for broad-based resistance. The forestry service at Orgosolo later opted to erect fences around individual trees rather than whole pastures, and local herders were generally much more supportive of such measures. By 1998, the Iseri forestry camp was operating more or less smoothly. Significant investments in forestry and land improvements made by the Sardinian forestry service and the Sardinian agricultural service contributed to Orgosolo's economy.

The diffidence of many residents with regard to the government's future intentions was perhaps merited, for the government did indeed later include the areas leased by the forestry service at both Montes and Iseri on its map of the intended Gennargentu Park. In late March of 1998, town councilors announced that local representatives had been misled in their negotiations with the government prior to the final approval of the park perimeter. The central levels of government had circulated only a small-scale map of the park in the meetings, and had refused requests to provide local representatives with high-resolution maps of the areas to be transformed to parkland. They were accused of acting in secrecy to enlarge the park perimeters without the explicit consent of local councils.

Dangerous Hosts and Wayward Guests

In 1998, Orgosolo's Base Committee organized a protest against the national park. Organizers collaborated with committees from other towns in attempting to legitimize and re-empower a culture of resistance that drew authority from regionalist discourses of Sardinian identity and its pastoral roots. They did this by subverting the customary structure of party-organized political campaigns and planning a demonstration that celebrated folk culture, language, and social practice. Not only was Sardinian privileged over Italian in this event, but discursive access to a public audience was given first to the most local and informal tiers of representation, and only second to higher-ranking political figures. Shepherds and other "ordinary" people were encouraged to speak, and party politics was meant to be formally excluded from this event by the organizers. Instead, it was conceptualized in the form of a local festival, complete with a country picnic, musical performances, Sardinian poetry, and traditional round dancing. The explicit performance of authenticity has some precedent in the rhetoric and symbolic practice of the Sardigna Natzione party as well as the more established Partito Sardo d'Azione, and it was by appropriating a regional "politics of recognition" (see Honneth 1995; Taylor 1994) that anti-park activists sought to make their voices heard. The 1998 demonstration was distinctive, however, in making continual reference to the experiential domain of everyday life in central Sardinia.

Throughout central Sardinia today, regionally and locally specific hospitality practices constitute a means of negotiating social ties and social distinctions. Models of hospitality were evoked in the organization of the demonstration to affirm the moral superiority of local residents as hosts in opposition to politicians, tourists, and environmentalists from outside. This "politics of hospitality" resonates with the ascendance of reciprocal "invitations" as a moral imperative of daily social life in Orgosolo. Such hospitality constitutes an important sphere of political engagement, where the host-guest relationship can both highlight and invert structural relations of exploitation (Herzfeld 1987b).[5]

The politics of hospitality put into play during the 1998 demonstration enacted a fluid but predominantly masculinized vision of local identity. This vision resembles the gendered visions of Sardinian pastoral culture projected through the evolving tourism tradition of "lunch with the shepherds" at Orgosolo. Tourism entrepreneurs went to some lengths to represent an "authentic" experience—not only in terms of the food served, the open-air setting, and the entertainments animating the gathering, but also to the extent that the helpers participating should embody the visible signs of the traditional male herder (Satta 2001).

In one enterprise, only men were allowed to undertake this work, and those who did so had to present themselves with appropriate clothing, haircuts, and demeanor.

The Misadventures of Goatface

Animal metaphors commanded a particular resonance in the local discourses contesting the park project, and these were applied in mischievous ways to characterize the politicians closely identified with environmentalist initiatives. One example is the nickname "Goatface," invented for the president of the Region of Sardinia by a young male forestry worker at Orgosolo. These animal metaphors can only be understood in terms of cultural negotiations over the "nature" of local identity, especially through the medium of the politics of hospitality. Orgolese conversations about the park issue negotiated identities and visions of authority through an idiom of embodiment and authenticity.

The grassroots Base Committee was headed not by members of a political party, but by a small network of male herders and forestry workers. Participants in the grassroots committee meetings and the organization of the demonstration in 1998 were mainly forestry workers and a number of women from families associated with herding and forestry. Yet the campaign against the park emphasized the agency of traditional Sardinian herders, hunters, and horsemen as the real heroes and protagonists of wildlife management. Animal metaphors reversed and ironized power relations between politicians as personifications of the state and ordinary residents. Politicians were caricatured in posters, for example, as passive animals in need of herders or threatened by extinction. The president of the region at the time was featured with his head attached to a number of indigenous species such as the mouflon and the vulture. The nickname "Goatface" inspired an older shepherd to compose a satirical poem about the various politicians who were "The Animals of the Gennargentu Park."[6] In a banner from another town, local protagonists were portrayed as various kinds of indigenous animals who actively resisted the illegitimate and unskilled husbandry of politicians and environmentalists, kicking them off the land. Here, the essential collaborative bond between pastoralists and nature was apparent in the fusion of the male shepherd persona with both wild and husbanded animals. Such authentic Sardinians exposed the inner essence of politicians and representatives of the WWF as less than human, wayward semi-domesticates in need of a firm hand. These ironic satires on human-animal relations of mastery tended to evoke both ethnonationalist models of Sardinian identity and the local norms regarding proper roles of hosts and guests. Where outsiders do not enact appropriately respectful roles, they lose their claim to the social status of guests and become less than human. Rural Sardinians attempted to reorder a symbolic universe of local residents, politicians, environmentalists, and wildlife according to local moral standards.

Both the self-selection of participants in the Base Committee at Orgosolo and the debates about the park in the context of town meetings and informal gatherings revealed a strong reference to popular ideas about the authenticity of embodied social identities in the context of "resistance" against the state. Male forestry workers and herders were symbolically linked to the Commons through their work.[7] Although women rarely worked on the Commons (with the exception of two or three young forestry workers), traditional gender roles were strongly tied to pastoralism. Women were recognized as wives, sisters, and mothers in working collaboration with active shepherds in household production, and often as intermediaries between the shepherds and local bureaucracies. Many women maintained gardens privately owned by the family and collected a variety of useful items from the Commons themselves, including herbs, firewood, and spring water. In local stories remembering past events of resistance in defense of the Commons, particularly the demonstration at Pratobello in 1969, the agencies of "shepherds" and "women" were seen as complementary. The common denominators of embodied cultural authority over the land were extended to women on the basis of their involvement in locally valued domestic processing of "authentic" foods and crafts, their use of the Sardinian language, their practices of "traditional" hospitality in the home, and their roles in the family and the church.

The Gender of "Resistance"

Some narrative inconsistencies emerged as grassroots activists in Orgosolo mobilized opposition to the park. These related to gendered discourses of embodied authority emphasized by working-class men and women in Orgosolo. Women adopted a fluid set of expressions of marginality in dynamic tension with pastoral-based visions of embodied resistance. An elderly shepherd's wife, who joined a Base Committee organizational meeting by chance when her granddaughter brought everyone to the house to make posters, suggested a slogan that read: "We don't want the park because we have known hunger, because we have carried firewood on our heads from the Commons."

The idea of "hunger" is connected to metaphors of marginality frequent in many areas of southern Europe (Herzfeld 1985), but it is also an important marker of Sardinian women's efforts to feed their families during times of scarcity such as the fascist occupation. The reference to firewood is especially potent in gender terms because it was traditionally a woman's chore to bring wood down from the Commons. Orgosolo's Blessed Antonia Mesina was attacked and killed as she was collecting a load of firewood for the oven. One local priest referred to Antonia Mesina as "the daughter of the fields," claiming an important place for both women and the church on a landscape otherwise symbolically dominated by male herders. By invoking the memory of carrying firewood on her own head, the shepherd's wife suggested a gendered vision of embodied authority that linked women directly to the Commons, the experience of marginality, and a source of symbolic agency. It implicitly linked women to Antonia Mesina, an exemplar of Sardinian feminine virtue, and through her to the institutionally, politically, and morally powerful Roman Catholic Church.

The old woman suggested another poster slogan: "We don't want the park, because we want our territory green, not black."

In terms of mobilizing support, this was a risky choice because it acknowledged the fear of many who participated in the Base Committee that if they failed in their efforts to block the park project, an "ignorant" minority would take over the project of resistance and set fire to wooded areas. The local mayor had already received threats of violence from the Armed Anti-Park Front, which claimed responsibility for extensive vandalism of the forestry camp. The Base Committee (directed by male, non-practicing Catholics) avoided highlighting in public the threat posed by the Armed Anti-Park Front. In other contexts, women and priests have taken the leading roles in publicly addressing the impacts of local violence at Orgosolo, while the perpetrators have almost always been male. Working-class women who put themselves forward to speak during town meetings about the park as well as the anti-park demonstration were recognizable as *priorissas*. The *priorissas* of Orgosolo are members of active women's companies comparable to confraternities within the Catholic Church. They mediate between the community and the church by singing the rosary for the dead, leading religious processions, and working informally to offer aid and consolation to women in mourning, particularly after homicides when there is danger of a blood feud between families. These women have in the past shown active solidarity with the mothers of kidnapping victims, and have articulated discourses of sacrifice, atonement, and forgiveness for "the sins of the community." Zia Maria, a woman I introduced in chapter 3, was also a *priorissa*. During an extremely emotional town meeting in 1998, immediately after the region and state signed the agreement to create the park, it was Zia Maria who spoke out to explain that the imminent loss of the local territory meant a very personal grief for her: "I feel as if someone dear to me had died," she said.

This sense of mourning expressed on behalf of the community frames a gendered discourse of political subjectivity in which women have a pivotal role to play in representing the community.[8] This effectively reconfigures the politics of place-based identity to support female agency.[9] Women in central Sardinia have been somewhat distanced from the "culture of violence" by virtue of their gender, and are able to draw on visions of folk culture and embodied identity in positive ways. Yet attempts to narrate issues from an implicitly woman-centered perspective never succeeded in becoming part of the programmed rhetoric of the Base Committee. Despite the enthusiasm, numbers, and supporting roles of women involved in the grassroots movement, their gendered voices were relatively marginal in the formal presentation of an imagined collective position. Nobody listened to the old woman's poster suggestions. Although posters for the demonstration were drawn up by women, much of the content was transcribed from clips of famous Sardinian poems, written by men, selected by a male organizer who had once been active in the ethnonationalist movement. In trying to project a nonviolent, nonpartisan, grassroots voice against the park project, members of the Base Committee worked to dissociate the movement from institutional affiliations, including both formal politics and the church. The secular emphasis undermined an important element in many women's idioms of political subjectivity.

Embodied Authority

The mayor of Orgosolo at the time of the second Pratobello demonstration in 1998 was a woman who articulated a very different kind of gendered voice. She came under considerable suspicion during the Gennargentu Park debates in 1998, alongside other town councilors and all those thought to have privileged connections with government. She had tried to negotiate an acceptable deal with the Region, and some residents believed she had made valiant efforts to protect the interests of the community. She later protested that local mayors had been deceived, while government had conducted its real negotiations with environmental groups, behind closed doors. An intimidation letter received from the anonymous Armed Anti-Park Front was written directly and personally to her, associating her with "friends" at higher levels of government, including the Italian minister of environment and the president of the Region. During a Base Committee meeting she was invited to attend in 1998, organizers asked her how she had represented the town's position on the park, because "the people are against it."

When the mayor wanted to know other people's opinions, some women called to her, "The position is no, that's it—not even a [square] meter." This conversation took place entirely in Sardinian-Orgolese.

What happened over the course of this meeting was that the mayor was asked repeatedly to assure the group of her status as an insider, an Orgolese. The mayor was a university-trained white-collar worker who enjoyed the security of a government salary. She was active in the Partito Democratico di Sinistra. She spoke elegant Italian more frequently and comfortably than Sardinian. Although she was born and raised in Orgosolo, her speech patterns in local dialect were Italianized, and she followed a model of gendered social identity associated more closely with "modern" Italian society than with local and traditional social practice. All of these things made her social identity difficult to place: somewhere on the margins between Orgosolo and the outside world.

While this improved her reception as speaker for the community in formal political spheres, it undermined her ability to embody the authority of "authentic" local tradition in the eyes of her constituents.[10] Apart from the mayor and one of her female colleagues on the town council, both in their forties, all the women whom I witnessed making public speeches over the course of the spring of 1998 were in their fifties and sixties and bore the formal markers of traditionally modelled female seniority, including relatively traditional dress and the status of motherhood. The mayor, on the other hand, belonged to the first generation of women (currently in their forties) to have given up the modified costume of Orgosolo in favor of modern designer clothes. Women her age or younger are rarely seen to speak publicly in the town. Like most young women, she entered certain bars—considered male-only spaces until recently—upon occasion with friends and colleagues. More unusually, she had remained single and childless and even lived by herself in the city, away from her family. She was not a regular participant in the parish. She travelled in the predominantly male domain of formal politics. She was clearly a "boundary-crosser" (Haraway 1991) according to dominant local constructions of both gender and cultural identity.

This made people uncomfortable. While her hybrid cultural experience and forthright character made the mayor an able negotiator, she was often perceived as riding the political fence, perhaps well-intended but inclined to collaborate with higher levels of government and so betray the community. In very private and informal contexts, where men criticized her politics, her portrayal of modern, perhaps dangerously feminist, womanhood might also occasionally earn her the label of "*putana*," a prostitute. In public settings, she was repeatedly asked by townspeople to reject all dealings with the government and proclaim a position against the national park. If she failed to declare unequivocal opposition, she was greeted with disgruntled murmurings and outspoken, personalized, contradictory comments. In the case noted above, two senior women chastised her for a general failure of resistance to the state, telling her that the position of Orgosolo with regard to the park was simply "no," that Orgosolo would not begrudge even a square meter of its communal territory to the government.

Other women's attempts to participate in the grassroots Base Committee, in political parties, and as public speakers voicing grassroots perspectives indicated an important gendered dynamic in the negotiation of political subjectivity in Orgosolo. When Sardinian women voiced their concerns about the Commons on behalf of the community, they engaged with discourses of local resistance in inconsistent and sometimes subversive ways, often privileging the master narratives of the Catholic Church as a reference point for moral authority. Rejecting violence as a source of communal sin and shame, they emphasized the autochthonous traditions of both men and women's hard agricultural work, Christian suffering, and self-sacrifice in the face of historical poverty and structural disinheritance. While women's roles in political actions to defend the Commons have been represented as pivotal in the past, their strategies to narrate the embodied authority of an explicitly feminine cultural experience of the landscape have remained disjointed and secondary.

Strategy, Morality, and Transgression

Orgosolo women's narratives of "resistance" to the park in the late 1990s illustrate the marginalization of "modern" identities and highlight the desire for cultural authenticity reflected in local strategies of political practice. This reproduces important shifts in the nature of political engagement within the larger community as well as the Sardinian-Italian context. In Italy during the 1990s, political dissent was the norm in party politics, yet the democratic process itself could be seen as a mechanism of disenfranchisement for those falling outside patronage networks and educational entitlements, more or less as Bourdieu's model of political "distinction" (Bourdieu 1984, 1991) predicted.[11] In Orgosolo, however, those who remained outside political parties used cultural tactics based on the social ideals of "community" and "tradition" to make space for their voices in the context of special town assemblies. When the issue of the Commons came up, and the economic stakes were raised high for many households in Orgosolo deriving income from herding or forestry, their fragmented political action gathered force to organize collective political action in defense of communal lands. During these events, many individuals from diverse occupational categories and socioeconomic positions participated. Audience members intent upon expressing their political opinions disrupted the pre-constructed order of the assembly to open access to discursive spaces. Then, over the course of repeated meetings, they reorganized those spaces in a radical way by provoking shifts in language use from Italian to Sardinian-Orgolese,[12] by personalizing discourses, and by requiring the authentication of the local identity of speakers. These participants appropriated the space of political dialogue and refashioned it within a clearly bounded, common social sphere: a space strategically marked by the signs of the local.

Everyday forms of cultural performance linked to the authentication of local identities were deployed within political arenas.[13] This strategy represented a critical, if transitory, challenge to the cultural form of party politics in Italy, by implicitly transfiguring the nature of the "symbolic capital" (Bourdieu 1977, 1984, 1991) authorizing political voices. The festival-like demonstration at Pratobello provided further opportunity to focus the symbolic power of local identity. This event became the key "moralizing moment" (Moore 1993) for the grassroots movement against the park. With the politicians cast in the role of guests, Base Committee organizers asserted the authority of hosts. Through the politics of hospitality, the moral world of rural Sardinians and the legitimacy of embodied relationships to a traditional landscape were asserted as superior to Italian moral discourses of environmental and social governmentality.

Adapting James C. Scott's (1985) analytical framework in a spirit of heuristic play, we might call this *the politics of the weak* at Orgosolo. According to Scott, increasingly marginalized agricultural workers at the time of the green revolution in post–World War II Malaysia brought locally based standards of tradition to bear against the local landowners pursuing mechanization, and acutely discerned the socioeconomic interests underlying their discourses of modernization. In Scott's example, "the weapons of the weak" were a set of tactics that manipulated everyday practices associated with work and social life strategically, so as to constitute a form of class resistance to domination and exploitation. These were mobilized on an individual basis (Thompson 1966, 1975), yet these tactics, he suggests, cumulatively empowered the economic survival of the peasants. This stimulates provocative questions about the relationship between rooted cultural practices and political systems in changing "post-peasant" contexts such as Sardinia (Weingrod and Morin 1971), suggesting that everyday forms of resistance can also shape political life in the margins of the modern nation-state. Although residents of Orgosolo could not lastingly alter the structure of political decision-making with their cultural tactics in 1998, they did temper the processes and effects of environmental governance in modestly important ways.

The inherent ambiguity of traditional and modern subjectivities and the nature of multiplex translocal connections that are part of everyday social life both constitute fault lines exposing the limits of these practices as a form of agency, since consensus was the evanescent product of an urgent political moment.[14] The slaughter of the mouflon, one month after the demonstration at Pratobello, illustrates these fault lines. The violent transgression by the Armed Anti-Park Front signified and reinscribed an enduring political marginality. As a "weapon of the weak," it strategically appropriated the ideology of resistance and supported it with the threat of material sanctions against politicians and state institutions. Yet it simultaneously undermined the moral authority of benign collective action by the Base Committee and relegitimized the "everyday exercise of power" (Sivaramakrishnan 2005) by governing authorities. The violent action challenged the mode of political practice legitimized by the Base Committee, just as the grassroots initiative challenged the institutional frameworks sanctioned by formal party politics.

What are the limits of structural subversion in the Sardinian case? Scott's understanding of resistance fails to assess the disruptive ironies embedded in social practice.[15] It is important not to mistake Gramsci's notion of "hegemony" for false consciousness (Smith 2004). The latter assumes that subordinate classes are liable to crudely misconstrue the nature of exploitative systems, while the former implies a much more subtle dialectic of coercion, persuasion, and consent. Paradoxically, cultural practices of resistance can be part of this dialectic. The very tactics of resistance may uphold the ideologies of modernity and national identity that legitimize structural violence against marginalized groups and classes. Hegemonies are an aspect not of naïve misrecognition, but of the mundanely encompassing world of everyday embodiment, practice, and even resistance (Herzfeld 2004). The Sardinian politics of the weak draws creatively upon the material experience and sensually saturated memories of local life to reconfigure and mobilize resistance. This "resistance" is nevertheless dubious, ambiguous, and constrained. The social production of Sardinian resistance as a form of cultural authenticity is rooted in a local sphere of hospitality practices and moral expectations that are not shared by the wider Italian or European public. The ambivalent results of the politics of the weak highlight the gap in cultural frames of meaning and experience between the local and the national or the European, a gap that is especially evident in the projects of cultural representation mediated by mass communications technologies. In general, it is the environmental martyrdom of the wild mouflon that commands global attention to Sardinia, and not the cultural, feminine sufferings of the Blessed Antonia Mesina.

Frictions

The gendered construction of discourses against Gennargentu Park highlights the paradox of a politics that seeks to affirm the authority of embodied traditional identities, yet actually perpetuates the ambiguity of a culture of violence/culture of resistance. The grassroots movement attempted to cleanse the signs of violence from visions of tradition; however, by focusing on the pastoral heritage of local towns, it invoked the ambivalent stereotype of the shepherd-bandit. The political power of folk-style auto-representations was clearly undermined by the symbolic attack on a mouflon by the Armed Anti-Park Front a month after the demonstration. Women were caught up in a similar double-bind when they attempted to affirm the authority of tradition. Because of their ritual roles in funerals and festivals as protagonists of the Catholic Church, their vigorously traditional dress, and their legitimate roles within the domestic sphere, the priorissas in particular were able to manipulate discourses of cultural authenticity very effectively. Their cultural narratives, however, were constantly fragmented and displaced from the focus of attention by ongoing homicides, kidnappings, and bombs. The timing of the attack on the mouflon, moreover, insulted the festival in honor of Antonia Mesina and ridiculed the cultural authority of her (predominantly female and practicing Catholic) devotees over the landscape.

Although people say that feminism flourished alongside communist political action in the 1960s and 1970s, and women's actions to protect local authority over common lands are remembered as complementary to the roles of shepherds, workers, and youth leaders, the feminized and Catholicized narratives of embodied local identity were marginalized during the local protests against Gennargentu Park, just as "modern" women's identities were.[16] The articulation of political subjectivity by women in Orgosolo was implicitly isolated from feminist alliances and mediated by master narratives of Sardinian history that portray the landscape of the Commons as innately connected to both masculine and pastoral identity. Gender identity, socioeconomic class, and cultural orientations to tradition or modernity were conventionally assumed to tie together in ways that predicted a simple position for or against Gennargentu Park, a theory that belied not only the complexity of the mayor's commitment to conservation as a strategy for local development, but also the real range of political subjectivities present in Orgosolo. The women—modern as well as traditional, Orgolese as well as outsiders, or perhaps the inveterate boundary crossers (Haraway 1991) of whom we've heard tell—who attempted to voice their concerns with regard to the future of the Commons in Orgosolo were simultaneously empowered and limited by the story of Antonia Mesina, whose sacrifice defined appropriate relationships between local culture and Catholicism, men and women, humans and animals.

Meanwhile, the president of Sardinia, or "Goatface," as one came to know him in Orgosolo, had a difficult time reforming Sardinian landscapes according to global visions of wilderness conservation. After the combination of grassroots protests, ongoing political lobbies, and the violent threats of the Armed Anti-Park Front in response to the ratification of the Gennargentu Park proposal in spring of 1998, the plan proceeded with marked slowness. Even today, there is more evidence of a centralized Gennargentu Park on the Internet's virtual landscapes than in the mountains themselves. The misadventures of "Goatface" on the Commons of Orgosolo confirmed the centrality of reified shepherd identities as well as hospitality practices in local techniques for comprehending and managing not only local social relations, but also the marginal role of rural communities in the political economy of Sardinia, Italy, and Europe. "Frictions" (Tsing 2005) were inherent in encounters among the grassroots committees of the Sardinian Movement for the Defense of the Territory, environmental lobbies for Gennargentu Park, and the various levels of governmental authority. These frictions opened the possibility of social agency from below, and reconfirmed the hegemonies associated with nation-state politics and global science.

Although Sardinian nationalists celebrate a culture of "resistance," the results of this political praxis are as irrepressibly uncertain as the existence of the park itself.

The institutional structures of conservation management were not greatly altered through the 1990s or the early years of the new millennium. Standards of environmental governance continued to privilege scientific authority as mediated by the Sardinian forestry service, the armed corps of regional forest rangers, the WWF lobbyists, and the imagined new park service. Despite the adoption of "parks and people" rhetoric by today's conservation proponents (including some local advocates), most efforts to address local concerns have fallen under the category of "public education" and involve unilateral attempts to teach local townspeople some of the principles of scientific ecology. Although occasionally a Sardinian poet like Peppino Marotto achieves literary and cultural acclaim for his elegant portrayal of nature, such acknowledgements fail to translate into park planning.[17] The importance of indigenous language and social idioms is generally overlooked with respect to the environment. Little effort is expended in learning the "traditional ecological knowledge" of Sardinian shepherds, let alone that of women who share in agricultural and pastoral work, collect herbs, wood, and water on the Commons, and walk annually in pilgrimage to the place where the Blessed Antonia Mesina died in the Sardinian forest.

This story of wild sheep and semi-domesticates, the story of Gennargentu Park, shows few signs yet of resolution. Tangled up as they were with gendered narratives of sin, shame, and saints, explanations of local "resistance" to the park in rural Sardinia reproduced familiar but ambiguous plotlines of both blessedness and disgrace. Ambivalent cultural essentialisms have been re-naturalized in relation to landscape and biodiversity. In an area the Romans once called "Barbagia," relations of power are reconstituted through the very play of strategic political and cultural practices, moralizing discourses, and violent transgressions associated with the romance of resistance.

PART V Post-Environmentalisms

Town councilors from Orgosolo survey the Commons (1997).

Chapter 8

Beyond Ethnographic Refusal

The Ambivalent Ethnographer

With my research, I have hoped to challenge the legacies of earlier scholarship about banditry and backwardness in Sardinia. I once imagined that my role would be to interpret local feelings for the landscape across linguistic and cultural divides, affirm local ecological knowledge, and expose the problems and injustices of "top-down" conservation. My sense of anthropological advocacy verged on the romantic. The difficulty with this became apparent during my very first trip to Sardinia in 1990, when I visited several other highland towns. Invited by a friend into the privacy of one relatively poor herder's home, I was offered a roasted meat dish that I later learned was made from one of Sardinia's most famous endangered species, the mouflon. These animals had not been legal to hunt since before protection was legislated in the 1970s. The family, however, had followed a different logic and morality in choosing to cull an older animal from the herd.

"Better to eat [it] and say nothing," I was quietly admonished by my hostess, with a challenging wink. Her warning was redoubled with a keen look when an unsuspecting forest ranger arrived on a personal errand as we sat at the table.

Forced to confront the limits of my own cultural relativism, I wondered what I should write. For me as an ethnographer, the ironies and ambiguities of Sardinian cultural ecology represented a series of ethical quandaries. In my earliest writing I instinctively accepted many of the boundaries marked by Sardinian demonstrations of "cultural intimacy" (Herzfeld 1997). At first, I wished to avoid talking about "poaching" to outsiders, for example, because it might only highlight images of criminality and backwardness in highland Sardinia. While I knew many Sardinians to be openly critical of local politics, society, and culture with regard to environment and development issues, I could not imagine how to support these critiques without undermining the efforts of others to represent their own cultural identity in a positive light and so sustain important land claims.

I shared with Sardinian interlocutors a critical standpoint on the kinds of global discourses articulated by wilderness movements, including the WWF. Yet along with a quiet minority of residents in central Sardinia, I was also critical of the changing land management practices that might seriously compromise local ecologies over the long term. I believed that it was important to address the inequalities associated with emerging differences in structural access to various kinds of resources, including land, funding, and "symbolic capital" (Bourdieu 1984, 1991), and to seek out environmental partnerships that might provide alternatives to the highly centralized national park model. The bipolar debates that have dominated the Sardinian politics of environmentalism tend to preclude such options. Both strategic essentialisms adopted by Sardinians and negative stereotypes circulated in the Italian media and bureaucratic discourses tend to heighten and reify this bipolarity.

The moral discourses of environmental governmentality treat local culture as a black box that should fit within highly conventionalized categories of "tradition." Representations of rainforest tribes as historically and culturally diverse as the Penan and the Kayapo are made to fit the mold of "noble ecological Indians" (see Vargas-Cetina 2003; Slater 2003), a strategy that belies the real roots of their sophisticated ecological practices.[1] The heirs of rural peasant-herding cultures fit into postmodern visions of landscape and biodiversity management with greater awkwardness, as I have discussed for the Sardinian case. My concern is that, in a period when huge and prosperous environmental NGOs have begun to mediate environmental politics and governance internationally, anthropological advocacy has become too vulnerable to the clamorous expectations of a generic brand of global environmentalism. When strategic cultural essentialisms are undermined by embedded cultural prejudices, they may poorly support environmental justice.

In this chapter, I return to the paradoxes of advocacy examined in the introduction and explore how my Sardinian research empowers us to reflect upon them. The use of both self-reflection and deep attention to the personal voices of several Sardinians are effective analytical tools to disrupt and unsettle the conflicting assumptions that still encumber environmental anthropology today. Here I consider the critical efforts of Sardinians themselves to draw creatively upon historical subjectivities to meet the challenges of urgent environmental management issues. The politics of cultural representation are vital to how forest rangers, resource management bureaucrats, ENGO advocates, and other environmental experts interpret the guidelines for valuing local knowledge and local participation in environmental management in places like central Sardinia. Is there a means of purging ecological alterities, including stereotypes of local resistance, from the global dreamtimes of environmentalism? Anthropology has a role to play here in making visible the ways that current systems of environmental power/knowledge are negotiated, and what effects they ultimately produce. Yet ethnographers themselves, true to Gramscian warnings, may be implicated in a hegemonic value system associated with cosmopolitan projects everywhere.

So-called "traditional" and "modern" local and extra-local knowledges and institutions have become intrinsically engaged with one another on the Sardinian landscape, while the gaps and incongruities of each contribute to environmental problems today. The Sardinian case was particularly fraught for me as a young ethnographer because I wished to both support grassroots initiatives to resist new embodiments of environmental racism, and retain a degree of integrity in my own visions of appropriate social and ecological models. The task of supporting and respecting local knowledges on their own terms while engaging in productive critical discourses represented a deep paradox. I was not prepared for the ambivalence I would feel as I came to recognize how ongoing homicides, vandalism, violent threats to politicians, forest fires, and public tensions undermined the vision of community by which my hosts struggled to live. From the bomb exploded to intimidate the leadership of the local agricultural cooperative in 1996, to the threats from the Armed Anti-Park Front and the crucifixion of a mouflon in spring of 1998, violence was imbricated with the cultural politics of environmentalism in Orgosolo.

Of all my experiences in central Sardinia, it has been hardest for me to know how to write about the violence that shaped the lives of people every day. Given North American traditions of anthropological advocacy that emphasized the cultural critique of nation-states, government institutions, and dominant social groups, I had always considered the local voices joining critiques of a supposed "culture of violence" in Sardinia as the outcome of class tensions associated with education, occupation, and the rural-urban divide. Only when I began to think of myself as truly interdependent with other local residents over the long term, did I realize that I could not contribute to breaking cycles of political economic marginality, cultural racism, and institutional disempowerment without also addressing the problem of violence in central Sardinia. Until I knew the sound of police helicopters often roaming overhead and encountered the habitual police roadblocks on the main streets and the roads connecting Orgosolo to other towns, I did not understand what it meant to live under constant observation for threats of criminality. Until I met men who knew what it was to be drawn into the cultural logic of barroom aggressions, to become the unpremeditated perpetrators of grave violence, to endure the continued shame and anxiety of prison paroles and the power of institutional prejudice, I could not have comprehended the depth of tragedy, inequality, bitterness, or indeed forgiveness, intelligence, and courage that marks Orgosolo. Only then did I begin to take seriously the obligations of internal cultural critique from an ethnographic perspective. Yet there were always others, such as media journalists and urban bureaucrats, whose efforts to portray the genesis and effects of violence in central Sardinia were less self-reflexive, less receptive to complexity, and less informed by genuine human engagements than my own.

What should I write? If I ignored the ways my fieldsite failed to sustain the positive stereotypes of tradition that Sardinian residents themselves presented to outsiders in support of their claims to authority over the landscape, then my own cultural representations would reify the secondary status of local knowledge vis-à-vis science by promoting static, homogenized, and standardized visions of "local" cultural practice. Minority initiatives to revitalize cultural knowledge and manage important community resources could be undermined by my own effort to support representations of cultural authenticity. There was also the danger of reinforcing insidious cultural racisms now transposed to the plane of discourses about environmental governance. How could I take into account processes of structural violence without condoning kidnapping and arson, or negating the existence of creative political subjectivities? In finding a way past my earlier "ethnographic refusal" (Ortner 1995; cf. Dove 2006) to examine the dark side of Sardinian "resistance," I have discovered unexpected seeds of optimism.

Fire and Ice

> *Su ballu 'e su fogu,* "The Ballad of the Fire"
> They have covered the mountains of my town with fire.
> They have reduced the whole place to charcoal and in the winter the ice
>   has destroyed it all. . . .
> The unpunished reckless ones are killing nature and reducing great pieces
>   of land and great forests to desert. These stinking crows want to poison
>   everything; we must isolate them like chained dogs in jail.
> They have covered the mountains of my town with fire. . . .
>   (Tonino Cau 1983, excerpts translated from Sardinian
>   by Ciriaco Fronteddu)

This excerpt comes from a popular folk-style song written in Sardinian for a neo-traditional tenores quartet. The writer, Tonino Cau, was influenced by the thriving folk traditions in the Sardinian "Barbagia" and inspired by the poetry of Peppino Marotto, a well-known Sardinian balladeer from Orgosolo. He was also impassioned to speak out against the terrible forest fires that devastated areas of the territory, and the threat of new fires that hung over the landscape whenever tensions over environmental governance and the use of the territory flared. In Sardinia, the incidence of forest fires rose rapidly between 1950 and 1970 (Meloni 1984), and these continue to be the cause of great concern.[2] Intensifying patterns of summer drought and heat waves associated with global climate change in the Mediterranean are likely to exacerbate the risk of fires in the future.

During the 1990s, Cau's traditional tenor quartet produced two music videos related to landscape and environment in Sardinia. As examples of cultural authenticity, Sardinian tenor and folklore troupes became popular tourist attractions during the 1970s and continue to tour abroad. As a critical genre, however, Sardinian poetry has particular resonance and popularity on the island itself, and especially throughout central Sardinia. The medium of a culturally and linguistically "authentic" music tradition created a somewhat intimate space for the tenor singers to engage other Sardinians in their concerns about abuses to the landscape undertaken in the name of political and economic "resistance." Peppino Marotto, the Orgosolo poet, was a role model in this form of cultural reflexivity.

This illustrates a thread of cultural auto-critique that mobilizes social sanctions against those who practice forest arson to protect or avenge their own perceived interests. In Orgosolo, informal social mechanisms helped to protect the Commons against fire. During the mid-1990s, I met a number of young men—working-class herders, construction laborers, forestry personnel, and others—who outspokenly denounced arsonists and threatened angry repercussions if they found out who was responsible for certain attempts. Others worked calmly behind the scenes, to dissuade fiery tempers, so to speak. Pyromaniacs were typically disdained as deviant and ignorant—the real examples of criminality, immorality, and backwardness who tainted the living cultural heritage of the town. The town's forest fire problem had diminished markedly during the 1990s. On those isolated occasions when fires were discovered, many volunteers from the community arrived to assist forest rangers and professional firemen in putting out the flames.

It was my quiet friend Carlo who brought my attention to "The Ballad of the Fire" in 1991. Carlo had strong family ties to the pastoral community in Orgosolo. He himself had studied agriculture at university and gone on to join the Sardinian forest ranger corps when it expanded in the late 1980s. As a ranger, he helped to monitor for signs of fire throughout the dangerous summer season around the territory of the town where he was posted. He loved the long walks in the countryside associated with his jobs on patrol. Carlo was one of those who took "ecological learning" (Neves-Graca 2004) seriously, and sought to promote an environmental consciousness that was crafted from a dynamic exchange of pastoral history and global discourses. Carlo's personal career choices reflected not only economic and political transformations in Sardinia, but also a new way of articulating local knowledge and cultural attachments to traditional Sardinian landscapes with the formal, expert knowledge of forestry and environmental science.

Auto-Criticism in Action

When Beth Conklin (2003) reminded anthropologists of our responsibility to "speak truth to power," she called upon us to find ways of communicating contemporary models of dynamic cultural process to the wider world, and acknowledge the complexity of social and ecological critiques internal to indigenous communities. In highland Sardinia, such auto-critiques were intrinsically part of wider community efforts to define environmental justice. People were critical not only of the policies, governments, and broader economic structures they perceived to shape their lives, but also of their own actions and decisions as a community. Often muted, for fear that the self-recognition of faults, tensions, and problems in central Sardinia might reinforce negative cultural essentialisms in media representations and policy discourses,[3] the voices of internal cultural critique were powerful instruments of social change and ecological improvement. I listened to a number of friends like Carlo as they struggled to reflect upon current events. I witnessed some of them launch new social and economic initiatives with the possibility to transform the invidious and arbitrary symbolic boundaries that distinguished "modernity" and "tradition" as polar opposites. I hope to guide my own efforts at cultural representation by their initiatives to engage in critical debates and public dialogues. More than this, I hope to open more legitimate space for these voices of "productive discomfort" (Herzfeld 1997) in Sardinia.

When I arrived in Sardinia in 1996 prepared for dissertation work in Orgosolo, I was sent to Dr. M., a local intellectual, retired teacher, and former mayor, with an old-fashioned letter of introduction from a gracious and well-regarded lawyer in Lanusei. By the time I heard the chronicle transcribed below, of his time in public office between 1975 and 1980, I was already aware that the town had undergone tremendous socioeconomic transformations during the late 1960s and the 1970s. Dr. M.'s communist-led administration was the first coalition of the left to be elected at the local level. At the same time, both demographics and cultural ecology were changing across Sardinia as patterns of outward labor migration became established. Gradually, cereal cultivation was abandoned and herding practices were transformed to use more land, fewer men, and more inputs, and the herds themselves became larger (Meloni 1984). Eventually, motor vehicles were introduced, although many herders in the town continued to milk by hand and produce their own cheeses. Traditional grazing areas on the Commons remained important.

Of land associated with the town, about one third remained under town management, subject to the exercise of civic-use rights permitting access to firewood, fodder, and pastures. According to current law, this land cannot be alienated, although it can be leased out for particular extraction and improvement activities. Historically, a balance of agricultural and pastoral activities were rotated on this area of the Commons, and a fallow period of two months was mandated annually during the spring transhumance, when herders would move their animals out to privately contracted pastures. This excerpt from our interview documents a decline of *su vardau*, the system of fallows regulation, in the town.

[Dr. M.:] After seventeen years, I express an [overall] positive judgment of [our] experience [in office]. . . . We were convinced that . . . that which is public must prevail over that which is private. And so, to some extent, the ambitions, the goals, the interests of private individuals must be subjected to the interests of the collectivity. That is what we did. . . . [We pursued] the acquisition of building lots from private property to public property so that it was possible to build public works, roads, schools, plazas, the nursery, and many other things. . . .

That which leaves a bitter taste in my mouth, which leaves me unsatisfied, is the question relative to the management of the communal patrimony. . . . Up until my administration the communal resource-use norms were generally observed by everyone and particularly by the herders. . . . *Su vardau* was the best part of the communal territory [each year], where the grass was allowed to grow . . . generally, from March 20 until May 19–20, pasturing was not allowed. Every year, in particular to allow the shepherds to be able to leave their late autumn/winter pastures, pastures that were often outside [the town's] territory, [privately owned] expensive pastures [for which] very often the shepherd [was obliged to pay] a great part of the product—milk, lambs, and wool—therefore in the pastoral economy, the return to protected communal pastures that had been rested for two months represented a relief, a lightening of the burden. Naturally this was all relative because not everything depended on [simply] protecting the territory [from grazing], it also depended on the year, the climate, the rain, and so all these [factors were taken into account each year] in the communal resource-use norms.

During my administration what happened? A small group of herders did not want to obey this rule, a rule respected for perhaps 100, 150 years. These herders said that they could not transfer their herds from the prohibited areas because there was *ferula*[4] in the area where pasture was allowed. [But] we have always had *ferula* . . . for twenty years previous . . . and the herders made sure their animals stayed away from lethal plants or removed the pernicious weeds from the area of pasture, but this required more labor. It was a pretext, a means of saying that they didn't care about the rule. It was perhaps [only] ten herders, and naturally the other herders said that the administration must intervene, and [so it did]. It intervened in several ways, warning these herders, threatening that we would apply sanctions and provisions. But they pretended not to hear, and if they heard, they did not obey. We had two or three guards, and they couldn't very well capture 200 sheep at a time [for] there was no place to put them. The others complained; we turned to the state police but what could they do, poor things, they captured the sheep and then the animals wandered here and there. In the end, we applied the administrative sanctions and won the court case, but the damage was done, the rule was disrespected, the pasture degraded.

And so, the other herders, the herders obedient to the rules, [nevertheless] did nothing to help us. They did not lift a finger; they only came to protest against the administration that it did nothing against the disobedient herders. However, they just stood there looking on and complaining about the administration.

[T. H.:] If something like this had happened twenty years earlier, what would have happened?

[Dr. M.:] Twenty years earlier no one would have hazarded to disobey.

[T. H.:] Why?

[Dr. M.:] Because the control of [social sanctions] was greater. Usually it was the herders themselves who would go to the disobedient herder and say [for example], "Take note that your pigs have got in here." And they came together [to the administration] to say, "Look here, the animals of so-and-so have entered into the area prohibited from pasture, so undertake to make him pay the fine." And the herder at fault paid the fine, he paid the penalty.

Today, [or rather] from that time on, the herders no longer paid the fine.

They rebelled [saying], "Look here, I am not paying, I was within my [civic use] rights, the territory is mine, the territory doesn't belong to the town, the territory belongs to everybody. I can't let my family die of hunger. If the animals die, I have nothing to eat" . . . [and so on with] various pretexts. . . . If twenty years earlier the rules were almost sacred, it was because the town economy was prevalently pastoral.

[T. H.:] And so what happened?

[Dr. M.:] The [economic] interests of everyone were concentrated on the communal territory, but in 1975 the animals and the numbers of herders were fewer than before and [so] the interest in regulating the territory was diminished. Also, because this herder had put this herd on private territory, [while] that one's son had found some other [kind of] work, [or] had taken care of his animals in some other way, or else made up for the lack of [pasture] by buying feed, through funding from the European Community. It was a loss for everybody, for the town, for the herders themselves. However, it must be said that since that time, the communal territory has not been regulated.

Today I don't know whether it can be said that the herders are better contented that the [communal] territory is free from almost any prohibition, of any impediment, of any regulation, or not. It does not seem that the herders ask the town to intervene to revitalize the old customs, the old ways of benefiting from the communal territory. But today the relations between the herders and the town have become very tense, [and] obedience to the rules of law . . . has diminished also in other regards. (personal interview, 1997)

Dr. M.'s administration made several attempts to find new ways to stem the degradation of the commons. Efforts to achieve better use of the land by dividing areas of the Commons between pigs, cows, and sheep, for example, fell prey to a similar lack of community support. The town had fencing built, only to find it systematically vandalized, dismantled, and carried off. On a larger scale, efforts to eradicate the African swine pest across Sardinia during the same period failed because a number of local herders hid their pigs rather than accepting the indemnities.

Evidence from Orgosolo supports the importance of co-management solutions (environmental partnerships with a strong element of local participation) to environmental concerns (see McCay and Jentoft

1998).⁵ Clearly, Orgosolo had changed as a community and as a cultural ecology since the 1950s and 1960s. The community was certainly undergoing rapid socioeconomic change owing to the adoption of new technology and the rise of alternatives to pastoralism. Cereal agriculture was abandoned, herding began to be practiced in a very different way than it once had been and gradually, fewer families were directly involved in pastoral production. Older herders were concerned that important cultural knowledge about their own environment was being lost. Meanwhile, government forestry, cooperative arboriculture, and independent ecotourism have all fostered new hybrids of local and scientific knowledge about the environment, and new interpretations of cultural history and authentic tradition. Yet these transformations cannot be reduced to the straightforward "falling apart" of a system of cultural ecology.⁶ Rather, they represent a more complex pattern of ecological change coupled with the ongoing reinvention of relevant but inherently contested communal identity. The dynamic reality of cultural bricolage suggests that neither ecological practices nor their degree of embeddedness within "communities" are reducible to neatly defined, evolutionary categories.⁷

As other ethnographers have highlighted, the signs of modernity and tradition—particularly in relation to the urban-rural divide—have become elements of symbolic capital used to negotiate authority and privilege in Mediterranean Europe (Ayora-Diaz 1993; Argyrou 1996). As Charles Zerner (2000) has suggested, learning to evaluate environmental justice in relative cultural terms requires consideration of a range of subjectivities attached to visions of citizenship and nature. He suggests that changing social and natural landscapes are not so easily defined and divided as the organizing visions of modernity once promised. Rather,

> We are situated, inexorably, in a landscape of shifting configurations of nature/culture, a landscape traveling within and across genomic, individual, communitarian, national, and international boundaries, confounding the social and environmental world watchers, monitors, and surveillance/information specialists attempting to keep people, things and nature in their place. We need to imagine and to create more radically pluralist, democratic

visions of nature and societal interconnections: visions in which the Creole and the hybrid, the mobile as well as the sedentary community, the provisional design as well as the ancient species are valued citizens of the changing state(s) of nature. (Ibid., 17)

How do folk models of justice with regard to the distribution of local resources coincide with particular embodied histories of community and its relationship to land? Fluid and fragmentary visions of history emanate from the margins. In Orgosolo, transforming uses of Orgosolo's territory are interpreted, contested, and defended with reference to local models of the communitarian past. The embodied landscape is integral to positively valued social relationships of community, and to the ability to respond effectively to the structural experience of marginality. Land claims are considered the foundation of social and environmental justice. The commons is a living metaphor of cultural survival, the capacity to change and adapt as a community.

Although it suggests a number of ways that local ecological knowledge and institutions for regulation of the Commons have declined, Dr. M.'s account witnesses critical internal engagement with such problems. Dr. M. searched for the roots of declining sustainability in changing occupational patterns and socioeconomic strategies. His administration improvised a series of measures in the face of changing times. Although these measures failed at the time, they nevertheless nourished discourses of communal self-reflection about the problem of the Commons. By the 1990s, the decline of the fallows was widely recognized by local residents as symbolic of cultural transformations gone wrong. Although the "question of the Commons" in the town remains complex and contentious, local efforts at understanding and solving the problem have multiplied.

The town's elected officials have played important roles in finding effective ways to support positive transformations in cultural ecology. Dr. M.'s government supported the formation of an agricultural cooperative that was highly innovative in rehabilitating and improving areas of the communal territory, managing wood extraction, and seeking out international partnerships for the development of clean energy solutions. Public works have been carried out to promote aesthetic uses of the landscape and assist tourism operators. A second forestry camp was eventually leased to the state forestry service. Finally, local officials have sought to establish a positive but critical working relationship with higher government, in order to redefine efforts at conservation.

Revitalizing Local Ecological Knowledge

Luigino, an active middle-aged herder who kept cattle on Orgosolo's Commons, was concerned about the effects of occupational fragmentation over recent decades. He saw that the divergence of economic and political interests within the town had provoked misunderstandings and antagonisms between members of different occupational groups. Herders had been blamed for both public discord and environmental deterioration on the Commons, although the entire community was at fault. Ultimately, he suggested, the herders were the only ones who paid the municipality for their use of the land, but the Commons was there for everyone to benefit from, use, and enjoy. "There's room for everyone," he said, "herders, forestry workers, tourist guides, everyone."

When I asked if the herders envisioned any kind of environmental improvements, he said, "Yes! Instead of reforesting, we want to clear, plow and plant [return to agricultural rotations to improve the pastures]."

Older and retired herders were sometimes very critical of the way herding practices had changed over the years. While they themselves remembered vividly the hardships of remaining with their animals away from town for months at a time, now young herders all had vehicles and simply visited their flocks once or twice a day to carry out necessary tasks. Strategies of dividing flocks and monitoring pastures carefully had been simplified to minimize labor inputs.

Luigino, too, had left school as a boy to take on duties as a herder. Like others of his own age and older, Luigino appreciated the positive efforts of some younger shepherds to care for their flocks conscientiously and utilize elements of traditional ecological knowledge. He respected that some young herders had also developed guide businesses and "lunch with the shepherds" excursions to supplement their incomes, and he assisted with two of these. He hoped to see more collaboration between herders, forestry laborers, and ecodevelopment entrepreneurs in caring for the Commons. For him, revitalizing forgotten skills associated with mixed herding and agriculture promised a better economy and a better ecology.

Luigino's commitment to the Commons was also political. He became one of the local organizers of the grassroots "Base Committee" of the "Regional Movement for the Defense of Rights to the [Communal] Territories," discussed in the previous chapter. This was a loose-knit group of people collaborating from across several highland Sardinian towns to mobilize opposition to the ratification of Law 394, which pertained to parks and protected areas in Sardinia, and particularly, the creation of Gennargentu National Park. The group claimed non-partisan, grassroots status, and maintained a critical stance toward municipal governments, which were run by the educated, salaried class employed in the public sector. I knew many women and men from the families of herders and forestry laborers, who, like Luigino, participated in hosting the demonstration at Pratobello in 1998, organized by this network. Paradoxically, opposing a national park was also considered a means of protecting the forest itself from the corruption deemed to be rampant in modern Italian bureaucracies. The park, they reasoned, might prove to be yet another form of over-centralized "development" that was harmful to the environment as well as the community.

Luigino's vision of a return to pastoral heritage incorporated hybrid elements of forestry and ecotourism. It privileged self-critical discourses operating within the networks of local shepherds, mobilizing a commitment to pursue positive ecological relationships. Above all, it envisioned the revitalization of community, entailing the reinstatement of relations of trust, collaboration, mutual respect, and reciprocity across different occupational groups in the town.

Voicing Common Concerns

One of my favorite photographs posted in the office shows Zia Annedda, a *priorissa*, at the political demonstration hosted on Orgosolo's Commons in April 1998. In front of her old-fashioned dark blouse and skirt, she holds up a modern-looking T-shirt that says, "NO TO THE PARK!" in Sardinian. She sits among a few older men and women, while a handful of children move around them. Despite misgivings that social tensions might erupt over controversial issues, or that there could be conflicts with the state police that would undermine efforts to voice local concerns, there was a festive atmosphere to the gathering and a sense of determined optimism. Sardinian music played over the loud-speaker. People were smiling and talking with excitement among themselves, mostly in Nuorese dialects of Sardinian, as they waited for the demonstration to begin.

To some Italian technocrats and international advocates of nature conservation, this picture might symbolize the backwardness of Sardinian environmental psychology—an example of ingrained resistance to the state and clinging to an apparently outdated agro-pastoral system of communal land use. After a decade of conversations with many Sardinians, I see it quite differently. Zia Annedda's family still lived on herding. Her sister had taken me to her gardens and spoken to me of agricultural work in earlier times of poverty. Annedda's colleagues among the *priorissas* had urged me to join them in Catholic processions to pilgrimage sites in the countryside. For them, the loss of the Commons implied truncating ties to a pastoral heritage with deep roots in history, land, religion, family, and language. To me, the picture in my office captures a moment of poetic and sincere attachment to the land and the community, as well as the nuances of sophisticated cultural auto-critique. As I discussed in the previous chapter, one element of this was that the organizers and participants hoped to prevent violent reactions that they thought might be undertaken by unruly men in their own towns as forms of resistance to a park that seemed created deliberately to strip them of their sole economic security and birthright. The tacit fear that this dispossession might inspire forest arson and eco-vandalism was widespread.

The demonstration of April 1998 was accomplished peacefully despite grave social tensions across the town. This was due in part to the social subtlety of grassroots organizers, men and women who were able to negotiate a contingent consensus among residents. This event indicated the vitality of an initiative that in fact entailed strong currents of auto-critique acknowledging an ongoing local problem of a violent minority that could target people, institutions, and landscapes. There emerged important dialogues across the increasingly heterogeneous occupational groups, such as herders, construction workers, forestry workers, agricultural workers, salaried officials, teachers, shop owners, tourism entrepreneurs, and the unemployed. What most compromised these efforts were the indications of political marginality that emerged over the course of planning and presenting the event. In particular, legitimate political action was undermined by the decision of government officials to ignore the authority of local mayors in representing the interests and voices of townspeople against the park plan.

Marginality in a Global Context

Strategic auto-essentialisms in rural highland Sardinia are informed by global discourses of modernity and tradition that compromise claims of authenticity from the outset. Most of my Sardinian acquaintances essentialized culture and community in an uncomplicated, positive manner when they presented themselves to tourists, journalists, and other outsiders. In contrast to the drugs, prostitution, poverty, and homelessness that were thought to characterize "modern" life in the cities, they sought to show how central Sardinia was more wholesome and egalitarian. They demonstrated the generous hospitality of traditional herding towns, the piety of local Catholic rituals, the continuity of Sardinian language practice, and the healthful, flavorful qualities of authentic local foods. They also claimed a special guardianship over the landscape based on their deep history of cultural inhabitation. Though by no means unfounded, this vision of tradition is ultimately too narrow and categorical to endure the fray of contemporary Sardinian reality. Representations of indigenous ecological tradition in Sardinia will probably continue to fall prey to brutish deconstructions, unless communities effectively re-establish enduring, outwardly visible commitments to ecological self-regulation.

I have come to believe that my anthropological interventions should celebrate not an essential cultural unity or authentic "tradition" in towns like Orgosolo, but rather the intelligent attempts of many rural Sardinians to transcend social differences, curb violence, and pursue collective organization. The question of the Commons is genuinely important to rural people themselves, and for this reason I owe my friends and hosts in Sardinia, as well as my colleagues and other activists, the support of another honest critical voice. Clearly, it remains crucial to recognize larger economic and cultural processes that impinge upon these efforts. Cultural racisms, for example, can contribute to the processes of political and structural marginalization, allowing some isolated members of the community to feel justified in the recourse to violence that only brings tragedy and undermines further the political position of local residents. The ongoing effect of cultural racisms embedded in the institutions and the politics of Sardinian conservation is part and parcel of international discourses about environment and development. As anthropologists, we can challenge the cultural categories at the source of environmental racisms and champion the ingenious possibilities of cultural hybridity and heterogeneity.

The Sardinian voices in this chapter reflected explicitly upon the complex and fluid class formations in which they themselves were embedded, from rather different subject positions in the forestry administration, in local government, and in herding and tourism enterprises and grassroots activism. What I have begun to appreciate in the course of trying to write about Carlo's love of landscape, Dr. M.'s political disillusionment, and Luigino's hopes for ecological revitalization, for example, is that their individual sentiments, their critical contributions, and their distinctive cultural visions hold real productive value for a transformative political ecology. There is so much more to Orgosolo than the "black chronicle" of violence featured in Italian newscasts can tell us. There is more, too, than conventional evaluations of reified cultural ecology tend to give credit for. Despite the appearance of fractiousness, the efforts of some residents to revitalize local knowledge and explore the larger implications of institutional transformations—expected to affect them all in different ways—were deeply provocative. By questioning the role and nature of tradition in the community today, these efforts grapple with broader hegemonies in the world system. They breathe reflexivity into projects of cultural recognition, so that Gramscian struggles are truly repatriated and refashioned anew. By creatively addressing questions of contemporary land use, acknowledging failures of environmental governance at the community level, exploring structural disparities, and seeking nonviolent alternatives to resist marginalization in political debates, rural Sardinians revitalize worthy cultural resources in a context of dynamic change. And here lies the potential for them also to help decolonize the global dreamtimes of environmentalism, by challenging and complicating visions of indigenous nature on their own terms.

Chapter 9

Hope and Mischief
in the Global Dreamtimes

Changing Projects of Landscape

It is June of 2006, and I have returned to Sardinia to set up a new research project in the Ogliastra. A few things have changed since I began research on the island, over fifteen years ago. I finished school and obtained a faculty position; many of my friends and acquaintances here, also students or else junior in their jobs when I first met them, are likewise settled with careers, homes, and families. My contemporaries are now active in political life and in the leadership of organizations, enterprises, and professional activities. I have grown more critical, but also more pragmatic, in my approach to fieldwork. In 2004 I married a linguistic anthropologist, Bernard Perley, who has accompanied me on recent ethnographic trips. Both my perspective and my interlocutors are transformed. I am writing now not only for teachers, colleagues, and hosts, but also for my students, who are almost entirely unfamiliar with European contexts and still learning what might be done with both anthropology and environmentalism in North America and the wider world.

Sardinia remains striking as always, with its towering heights, rich scents, sun, and wind reviving old memories. The road system is improving, though, and computer access is growing. Mobile phones are ubiquitous, carried by most working adults, university students, many teenagers, and even by some grandmothers. Even I have been able to acquire one now. Along the coast, towns have grown up considerably; some Germans and other regular tourists have acquired second homes here. Some knowledge of English grows more prevalent. Although the quality and availability of emergency medical care in rural areas is still considered inadequate, various services are improving. Recycling programs are being introduced. Photovoltaic panels are growing desirable in private residences, for those who can afford the initial investment. The system of provinces on the island has been reorganized and broken down so that the administrative system is more decentralized.

The projects of landscape mediated by governmental and non-governmental organizations are now transforming. The question of Gennargentu Park remains in the background, having come to a head again recently in the autumn of 2005, when the regional Law 394 was to have been implemented. The grassroots "Base Committee" associated with the "Defense of Rights to the Territory" once again mobilized to hold a demonstration in Cagliari, the capital city of Sardinia. Several towns, including Orgosolo, sent busloads to join in. People of each town were identified by T-shirts or hats specially designed for the occasion. They carried posters and banners with slogans against the park. The issue weighed into regional electoral politics. The creation of the new park authority was blocked indefinitely, yet the debate on the national park continues. Some argue that it should still be implemented, based on the principle of "free adhesion" on the part of the communities. It has been suggested that instead of a park authority composed of a minority of community representatives together with technical staff and advisors from environmental associations, a park committee should be formed, including representatives from every one of the communities involved. Others counter that at this point, given the fundamental unpopularity of the initiative in many of the towns whose territories would be most critical to conserve, it is useless to go on with the provisions specified in Law 394. Centralized legislative controls on land development and habitat conservation are already in place, managed under the auspices of the Sardinian Forest Authority. For the moment, the ambiguous promises and threats associated with the national park are forestalled once more.

The problem of the park is now overshadowed for many Sardinians by the so-called Soru Law, which was passed by the regional government elected in 2004 to 2009. This is a regional landscape planning initiative that blocks construction within 3 to 5 kilometers of the coastline all around Sardinia, aiming to protect marine resources from rampant tourism development and encourage rejuvenation in the towns of the interior. It has just come into effect.[1] The Soru Law is a welcome initiative for WWF–Sardinia, which recently refocused its lobbying efforts on the preservation of marine and coastal areas. People in Orgosolo and other areas of the "Barbagia" are largely unaffected, except insomuch as the measure may be intended to support the eventual implementation of the park plan. Others, in the Ogliastra region of central Sardinia, for example, are already feeling the impacts of the new law. If the initiative to create a national park once signaled the contingent convergence of ecological nationalisms (Cederlöf and Sivaramakrishnan 2006) across several scales of political identity discourse, from the regional to the Italian and European levels, then the Soru Law confirms the growing importance of transnational discourses and economic exchanges in the projects of imagining and governing landscapes. With the dominance of neoliberal governance strategies comes the surging prepotence of the global dreamtime of environmentalism. This is not lost on Sardinia's president, Renato Soru, a graduate of the famous Università Commerciale Luigi Bocconi in Milan. Soru is also the founder of the burgeoning internet company Tiscali-Net, and has been called Italy's "Bill Gates" (d'Acquino 2000). It is said that he worked closely with technocratic experts and WWF representatives in designing the Soru Law.

In the meantime, thanks to the independent efforts of the previous regional government in collaboration with authorities in the provinces of Nuoro and Ogliastra, the oral traditions and intangible cultural patrimony of central Sardinia have been declared one of UNESCO's new World Masterpieces of Intangible Cultural Heritage in 2005. This is exciting news for me, and I wonder how it will come to bear on stories being told about culture and environment here.

On a sunny Sunday morning, our friends escort us to a special exhibit and public presentation organized by the Ogliastra provincial government in a small town nearby. Inside a tent put up for the occasion, glossy posters introduce *Il Pastoralismo*, "Pastoralism," which is the theme that inspired Sardinia's successful bid to be recognized by UNESCO. It is also the name of the new book written by a senior Sardinian anthropologist, Bachisio Bandinu (2006), who brought his own work to bear in support of the effort to collaborate with UNESCO. This poetic, beautifully illustrated tome is destined to grace libraries and coffee tables all over the island, and this morning I am offered one of the prized advance copies in time to request an autograph from my elder counterpart, who is a guest of honor. Local elections were concluded just as we arrived last week, and we are meeting some of the new mayors this morning, as well as a variety of other officials and curious spectators. Also there for the occasion are several experts in the *canto a tenores*, the traditional Sardinian tenor quartet, who are the recognized protagonists of Sardinia's "Masterpiece" in the narrative articulated for UNESCO. The unusual vocalizations, indigenous language, and oral traditions associated with the Sardinian tenor quartets are seen as indicative of a unique and indigenous cultural patrimony on the island. In this representation, (male) herders are synonymous with the unique history, culture, and landscape in Sardinia. They are considered exemplary of a distinctive autochthonous culture and a way of life now fading out across Europe in the days of modernity and globalization.

Once the exhibition is set up, the event gets underway with brief presentations from politicians, the anthropologist Bandinu, and the president of the Sardinian Tenor Association. They alternate between Italian and Sardinian in their speeches. Then the tenor quartet invited for the occasion takes position in front of the microphone and performs. The local audience is sparse, but we are introduced to Mario, a part-time shepherd and the cousin of a close friend who accompanies us. Mario is dubious about the effort to promote Pastoralism; he says it seems *finta*, "put on." He invites us for a drink and asks us what we think of it. I translate for my husband Bernie, who, as it happens, is a member of the Maliseet Nation in eastern Canada. The dialogue is therefore nuanced with hidden irony, as the two men tacitly evaluate their relative senses of "indigenousness" and find common ground in their own marginality to the exhibition at hand. Bernie answers that it reminds him of the public performances of drumming and chanting on the reserve; he still appreciates the beauty of the cultural form, but this kind of "culture on display" is qualitatively different from the spontaneous performances that are more embedded in community life. Mario agrees that it is a different thing to listen to the tenor groups sing informally. For my part, I suggest that perhaps the Pastoralism initiative is an optimistic one, because it is certainly more open to local participation than a national park. I will keep an open mind until we see what comes of it. Mario agrees that without a doubt, this initiative is better than that of the park. He values the cautious optimism, but he is not convinced that local herders and other residents will get as much out of it as the politicians. He says he is happier to have met Bernie than to have witnessed the event itself. The trans-local trade of "indigenous" perspectives yields better optimism for mutual empowerment than the cultural performances enacted for a wider audience.

In the background of the presentations, a Sardegna Uno television crew is shooting a segment on Pastoralism. They interview several of the guests of honor, and by surprise I am ensnared by an old acquaintance, now a cabinet member in the provincial government, to accept to be interviewed myself. So I sit on the steps of the small piazza with a woman my own age named Daniela, who is intrigued to know why a foreign researcher without family ties to the island would come here. "What strikes you most about Sardinia?" she asks simply.

I struggle for words, since my Italian is now rusty, and I hardly know how to address such a big question, after all this time. Although I have reservations about the discourse of pastoralism and the way it homogenizes Sardinian culture, I find myself unwilling to cast doubt upon the collaboration with UNESCO, which is after all the fruit of considerable efforts by local politicians and intellectuals. These include some extraordinary people who searched for a way to grant value to the traditions of rural communities, and seek fresh possibilities for appropriate development. I settle upon a heartfelt response.

"Friendship," I say, trying to express gratitude to all those who had taken me in over the years, who were so generous in helping a stranger whose goals must appear inscrutable. I keep returning to Sardinia now, because it is part of me, because my friendships here have come to be an important part of my life, and because the questions that originally brought me here only grow more complex as I learn more about the place. "And courage," I add, "the courage of people to tell their own stories, their own history, a history that is not static, but that moves, that is dynamic, that is alive."

I have not seen the television transmission, and I wonder what contexts my stumbling words might have fallen into. *Pastoralismo* adds a new theme to the polyphonic play of ecological nationalisms in Sardinia. Is it ironic that my voice, as a foreign academic, may have been drawn into a story intended to create another global vision for Sardinia? Will it be taken to legitimate the idea of pastoralism, or offer an inconsequential counterpoint to the emerging discourse? I cannot escape my own place in the ambiguous debate, which brings Mediterranean-style authenticity at last within the framework of international discourses on indigeneity.

In Critique of the Global Dreamtimes

As I reflect on my journeys to Sardinia spanning more than eighteen years so far, I am still struck by the problem announced to me by my Sardinian acquaintances in 1991: "You cannot be an environmentalist and an anthropologist at the same time!"

If one is convinced that to be an environmentalist means to give absolute privilege to the needs of "ecosystems" or "biodiversity," while to be an anthropologist means to give absolute privilege to the needs of local people, this statement may sometimes be true, although I believe that other definitions are both possible and preferable. Yet tensions in worldview cannot be ignored, and must not be erased by naïve multiculturalisms, lest the potential to acknowledge and criticize existing structural inequalities be lost. In her nuanced ethnography of conservation in Papua New Guinea, Paige West (2006) explored the divergent worldviews and lived experiences around the Crater Mountain Wildlife Management Area; this tension led to many disappointments on all sides. Her local Gimi "family" understood conservation and development as a system of ongoing social exchanges that should bring them access to the benefits of medicine and technology, for example. The projects of conservationists did not necessarily engage their indigenous knowledge or sense of participation and profoundly social engagement with the landscape and wildlife. The biologists and conservation workers from elsewhere who arrived at the conservation area were often frustrated by local fights and by the apparent failure of the Gimi to appreciate the importance of biodiversity. They were deflated by the refusal of Gimi people to conform to their expectations of what indigenous people should be like. West explores how the imagination of place is socially produced, so that conservation workers and Gimi people saw the lush forests of New Guinea through very different eyes. The cultural disconnect that she describes is rooted, in part, in what I understand to be visions of ecological alterity. These come to be applied to local and indigenous cultures through works of imagination associated with global environmentalism. It is the ongoing cultural production associated with this imaginary that reifies and regenerates apparent conflicts between people and environments, precisely by failing to treat the people affected by conservation initiatives as competent and valuable interlocutors, anytime they appear to reject the prevailing models of scientific conservation.

Environmentalism as a transnational social movement is both fragmented and quixotic. Since the mid-twentieth century, it has encompassed vastly disparate and incongruous cultural locations. Participants in the social ecology movement in India (Guha 1989a) and Caribbean environmentalists (Lynch 1996) are each historically and philosophically quite different from British birders (Milton 2002), or Canadian wilderness enthusiasts (Braun 2002). Whether they agree or not on the appropriate methods and goals to be adopted, people who undertake forms of environmental advocacy today usually consider themselves to share some fundamental values with others around the world who are also involved in the movement. They generally accept implications for both the critique of Western culture and for political action. "Environmentalism" is often idealized as a philosophy transcending class, culture, and nation, connected to both a universal science and globally shared concerns about the Earth's future.

Because of this, "environmentalism" has become an important way of imagining a shared experience of, and response to, processes of globalization (Vertovec 2001). Images of the Earth seen in the distance from space reference a global level of awareness that is increasingly vital to the successful articulation of environmental issues.[2] Appeals to this global vision of environmentalism can mobilize support for local campaigns. Yet the processes of cultural translation that must operate to make local issues comprehensible in terms of global concerns necessarily both obscure differences between varieties of environmentalism, and at the same time imply their mutual transformation (Garb 1997; Tsing 1997). Although environmentalism may appear to be a transcultural discourse, that is, a discourse that transcends the contexts of place (Milton 1996), its manifestations in practice are embedded in multiple and distinctive historical experiences. What many disparate elements of environmentalism actually have in common is the attempt to appeal to the global imagination and seek support beyond the boundaries of conventional nation-states.

What I have called the "global dreamtimes" of environmentalism consists of a jumbled set of narratives and visual images associated with environmental issues. They are systematically decontextualized from specific geopolitical contexts and tethered instead to markers of universal human experience and global citizenship. This fosters a sense of shared values, goals, and experiences that work to naturalize a postnational kind of "imagined community" (Anderson 1991). Despite an intensely plurivocal authorship, the outcome of this is a sense of unified progress through history. Because the very idea of the global itself constitutes a sacred landscape and evokes a pattern of ritual journeys through time, I have borrowed the metaphor of the Australian Aboriginal Dreamtime to describe it. This is somewhat different from thinking about environmentalism as a "master narrative" (Harper 2001), a "transcultural discourse" (Milton 1996; cf. Mühlhäusler and Peace 2006), or even a system of power/knowledge (Escobar 1995), for example, because it implies richer dimensions to the agency, experience, and open-ended practices associated with global environmentalism. As "nature lovers," many environmentalists consider an element of spirituality to be inherent in their approach to human-environment relations (Milton 2002; Sponsel 2001), an element that has seemed to give them something in common with indigenous peoples.

Vassos Argyrou (2005) argues that paradoxically, Western streams of environmentalism maintain the universalistic pretensions of modernism. A totalizing approach to history as the progressive human/technological exploitation and degradation of the natural environment has inflected mainstream narratives of environmentalism. The dominant model of sustainable development supports what Michael Herzfeld (2004) has called a "global hierarchy of value" that makes all indigenous cultures and local heritages appear commensurate and interchangeable. The moral discourses of the global always subordinate the needs, aspirations, and sovereignties of smaller groups to apparently transcendent universal values. Yet Herzfeld also recognizes the mischief embedded in social action. The narratives of global environmentalism are always open to irony, disruption, and play, as we have seen in Sardinia. As

K. Sivaramakrishnan and Arun Agrawal have recalled, "In the every-day world of livelihood and identity, social struggles and state-making, signifiers of modernity are drawn very quickly into contentious debates and contested practices" (2003, 48). These mischiefs make space for indigenous life projects amid the trials of authenticity associated with global concerns about the environment.

Trials of Authenticity

The international Convention on Biological Diversity, or CBD (UNCED 1992), portrayed cultural advocacy and environmental advocacy as having uncomplicated common goals. Some indigenous nations have successfully collaborated with ENGOs like the WWF to resist losses of biodiversity resulting from government policies and corporate activities. Environmental anthropologists have sometimes played important roles in these projects. Darrell Posey's well-known advocacy of indigenous peoples' resource rights, for example, presented a kind of global ethno-biology.[3] His scholarship both supported the collective resource rights of Kayapo communities where he undertook ethnography, and advanced a goal of Western cultural critique acknowledged by anthropologists to be valuable and important (see Marcus and Fisher 1987). Anthropological work on traditional environmental knowledge in tribal and peasant societies has made significant contributions to cultural recognition on a global scale.[4] Yet cultural advocacy has routinely promoted strategic cultural essentialisms, even to the point of making indigenous groups with very different histories and traditions sound *essentially* the same. As we move toward more nuanced assessments of political ecology in a changing world, the representation of authenticity and local knowledge with regard to culture and environment becomes fraught.[5]

Although indigeneity has attained a degree of respect and value in global environmental discourses, it remains problematic for local groups to lay claim to cultural authority over landscapes and biodiversity resources without conforming to gross stereotypes of the "noble ecological Indian." Simplistic assumptions about natural alliances between environmentalists and indigenous peoples can no longer be supported. Such alliances are often dominated by the objectives and media strategies of the environmental groups (Harries-Jones 1993; Brosius 1997, 1999a; Bending and Rosendo 2006). A community's right to voice and authority in environmental governance is usually concomitant with the authenticity of indigenous cultural identity, as perceived by powerful outsiders. The allochronistic narratives of environmentalism—stories that reify a divide between sophisticated, modern, globally-oriented conservationists, and anachronistic, backward, or parochial local communities—restrict participation.

In a globalizing world, the boundaries between cultural advocacy and cultural critique are ephemeral and contentious. They depend, in fact, upon the very discourses of alterity that we are motivated to challenge. Marginal communities, including indigenous groups, can no longer be imagined as cultural isolates existing apart from nation-states and global processes. Some traditions are impaled by structural violence, others are reborn, renegotiated, re-engendered, revitalized, modernized, gentrified, or even cyber-spatialized. Communities change, technologies transform, identities shift. What is the ethical role of environmental anthropology in contexts of increasing cultural hybridity and fluidity? The politics of representation in environmental anthropology has high stakes for cultural survival (Conklin 2003; Dove 2006). What should ethnographers do when positive cultural essentialisms are routinely turned upside down in policy, ENGO, or media discourses, and apparent failures of sustainable resource use are attributed to the dubious or maladaptive legacies of compromised indigeneity? Do we simply shore up the leaks in visions of cultural authenticity? Do we take it upon ourselves to deconstruct and expose illusions of authenticity? Or can we find other ways to shape and direct anthropological knowledge in support of marginal communities and their environments?

Sardinia is clearly a surprising sort of place to be talking about indigeneity. Situated on the periphery of one of the cradles of European civilization, rural Sardinians live in towns, wear familiar European clothes, drive motor vehicles, watch television, practice labor migration throughout the European Union, and cultivate the global consumption patterns of "First World" citizens, to the extent they can afford. Three decades ago, Weingrod and Morin (1971) dubbed them "post-peasants." Most households still practice some form of subsistence agricultural production in combination with other income-generating strategies. Today, the signs of modernity are juxtaposed everywhere with signs of tradition. Yet Sardinians share a distinctive historical experience as an agro-pastoral people of autochthonous origin, who have encountered—and, according to ethnonational celebrations, "resisted"—waves of colonial occupation culminating in incorporation within the nation-state of Italy. Indigenous dialects of Sardinian, a direct derivative of Latin, are still spoken as a first language in many towns in the highland area; Sardinians are a recognizable cultural and linguistic minority among Italians. Unlike the Penan or the Kayapo, however, the iconic "indigenousness" of rural highland Sardinians is not definitively established. It is in fact this lack of fit that serves to highlight the extent to which the strategic essentialisms made to sustain Sardinian claims to environmental stewardship are caught in a double-bind.

The romanticization of pure tradition on the one hand, and of resistance as a cultural disposition on the other, has undermined the recognition of complexity in relations between culture and environment in Sardinia. The richness of biodiversity itself has often overshadowed the cultural history upon which its existence is predicated. This history is anything but generic. It is marked by a peasant pastoralism with deep ecological roots, by waves of colonialism in the Mediterranean, by idiosyncratic cultural and linguistic formations, by the legacy of Roman Catholic missionization, and by peculiar kinds of marginality within Italy and the new Europe. The real distinctiveness of local traditions, however, suggests new possible modes of cultural revitalization in the context of environment and development planning. Although cultural transformations may sometimes entail processes of "forgetting" aspects of traditional ecological practice, they may equally empower creative dialogues of science and traditional knowledge. Innovative forms of ecological learning and memory can recombine elements of traditional, local knowledge with elements of global environmentalism, science, and even deep ecology (Neves-Graca 2004). The resulting knowledges resist stereotypical and static visions of culture and cultural boundaries. Likewise, they resist Cartesian divides that naturalize the authority of Western science in opposition to "other," indigenous knowledge systems (see Nasdady 2005; Ranco 2006). Experimental forms of environmentalism can sometimes follow from the dynamic engagements of indigenous traditions with both science and activism.

As local communities engage with new classes of environmental science experts, ecotourists in search of authentic nature, and social movements that champion global concerns about the environment, they have become direct participants in the cultural production of environmentalism. They may find themselves in collaboration with transnational environmental NGOs, such as the International Union for the Conservation of Nature (IUCN) and the WWF, or in situations of apparent antagonism toward them. New genres of identity practice and political subjectivity emerge as a result. Some residents become anchored in networks of environmental bureaucracy and governance. Arun Agrawal (2005) uses the idea of "intimate government" to describe the contingent impacts of community partnerships in environmental management, for example. In this case, "Practice and sociality rather than expertise form the basis of intimate government to regulate villagers' actions. The ability of regulation to make itself felt in the realm of everyday practice is dependent on channeling existing flows of power within village communities toward new ends related to the environment" (Agrawal 2005, 195). Such nuanced relationships cannot be apprehended with the bald, uncompromising concepts of "domination" and "resistance." Rather, the techniques of environmental governmentality come to shape local ways of knowing and being in extremely subtle ways, as a result of the very collaboration that seems to empower grassroots participation. The alternative epistemologies available to local actors in turn dialectically transform the stories and practices attached to environmental management.

Agrawal's discussion emphasizes that the logic and motives of the various actors engaged, implicated, or targeted in environmental governance initiatives cannot be easily predicted. This is precisely the point Tania Li (2005) also made in her attempt to problematize the role of "métis" knowledge in biodiversity management. For example, rural farmers may well choose "modern" technologies and short-term economic gains over "traditional" methods whose long-term benefits they well understand. Officials may seek not to eradicate or efface local knowledge, but merely to co-opt it, deploying "underground practices" to fill in the gaps between the plans on the books and the facts on the ground. In such instances, Li says, the exercise of power depends upon "an uneasy set of compromises" (2005, 390). A reader of Antonio Gramsci might explain this as an emerging process of hegemony.

Gramsci's particular focus on the role of intellectuals in new arrays of political and economic power goads us to consider the problem of agency here. New classes of intellectuals step up to mediate the messy engagements of biodiversity conservation, participating in global dream-times of environmentalism that naturalize new ways of conceptualizing citizenship and ordering governance. The important function of an edu-cated, nationally oriented elite as economic and political "mediators" in small-town Southern Italy has been noted since the work of Sydel Silver-man (1975) and Jane and Peter Schneider (1976). In the shifting insti-tutional ecologies of Italy and the new Europe, and especially with the rising interest in environmental partnerships, such mediators have come to play a critical part in sustainable development initiatives like Gen-nargentu Park. They often share common goals with self-educated and politically engaged shepherds, tourism operators, agriculturalists, and others in rural Sardinia, among the local actors whose orientations to identity and practice are increasingly marked by complex associations with environmental science discourses and central institutions for envi-ronmental management.

Where such actors are self-critical of their own positions within networks of power and privilege, where they remain fundamentally in touch with the culturally situated epistemologies and daily lives of marginalized local groups, and where they are committed to princi-ples of environmental justice, their collaborations support truly creative ways of thinking about culture and ecology. What I call "post-environ-mentalisms" include the creolized and heterogeneous ways of know-ing that inform the most resourceful of their approaches to imagining and practicing conservation, in particular and often eccentric contexts. Such diverse post-environmentalisms are distinguished from their famil-iar cousins by their ability to transcend a dichotomy between global and local orientations, and resist assumptions associated with a pre-dominant "global hierarchy of value" (Herzfeld 2004). They actively disrupt cultural racisms and constraining cultural essentialisms, map-ping out dynamic cultural critiques and possibilities. They recognize human communities as extremely complex sites of meaning and practice that are deeply embedded in historical landscapes, but never entirely contained by place (cf. Moore 1998). Intrinsic to their form is a vivid energy for dialogue that challenges the predispositions and assumptions associated with science, culture, and environment. They demonstrate a fundamental capacity for self-critique. Hope and mischief go hand in hand in the healing of the global dreamtimes.

These approaches do not exclude middle-class, urban activists or even outsiders who seek to support environmental initiatives from a distance. Anna Tsing (2005, 245–68) directs us to appreciate, for example, the efforts of young activists in Indonesian universities, who have responded to the devastation of upland forests by foreign logging companies, seeking out alliances with rural villagers who depend upon the trees for their livelihoods. People need not think alike, she says, in order to help each other. Despite the naïve idealism and romantic cultural misperception that undergird much of the effort to work across these communities, and despite the profound miscommunications that occur, the conversations taking place are both important and empowering. What matters is the way that the nature of political dialogue about environmental issues is fundamentally transformed by the commitment to listen to voices from the margins. When it is possible for these voices to reach an audience prepared to put aside stereotypes of indigenousness and recognize local perspectives on their own terms, then conservation has a chance of succeeding.

Just as the self-critical contributions of local Sardinians can enable grassroots efforts at environmental management, so too can the self-critical reflections of conservation practitioners empower real collaborations. Like the phoenix arising from its own ashes, new visions of environmentalism may even be born from the institutional and philosophical failures of modernist schemes for conservation, from the failures of participatory or traditional models for ecological management, and from the disillusionment of apparent cultural loss. Because such failures disrupt the "just so" stories that naturalize structures of authority, they can inform reflexive action. When Anna Tsing describes the hope for environmentalism as "a Gramscian optimism of the will" (2005, 267), I believe she champions not only the possibility of agency for both marginal subjects and privileged activists, but also the potential and necessity for self-examination.

Post-environmentalisms are not exclusive to the margins, but they do engender a reflexive awareness of how the efforts of cosmopolitan activists and experts are articulated in relation to the marginalization or empowerment of local groups. ENGOs and individual environmentalists today are often drawn into the hegemonies of nation-states and multi-national corporations. This implies a set of quandaries not so different from those faced by local intellectuals concerned with problems of governance, or from those I face myself, as an anthropologist concerned with the impacts of my cultural representations. I believe it must be possible to be both an anthropologist and an environmentalist at the same time. But to do this, we must understand aspirations for human development to be profoundly interdependent with the projects of stemming biodiversity loss. None of us can escape the structural circumstances that mediate our passionate understandings. We can, however, recognize them for what they are, and strive to inhabit the contingent spaces of self-critique.

APPENDIX: LIST OF ACRONYMS

Environmental Organizations

BINGO   big international non-governmental organization

CBD   Convention on Biological Diversity (United Nations)

CI   Conservation International

ENGO   environmental non-governmental organization

IUCN   International Union for the Conservation of Nature

TNC   The Nature Conservancy

WCU   World Conservation Union

WWF   World Wide Fund for Nature/World Wildlife Fund

Political Parties

DC	Democrazia Cristiana (1942–1994)	Christian Democrat
PCI	Partito Comunista Italiano (1921–1991)	Italian Communist Party
PDS	Partito Democratico di Sinistra (1991–current)	Democratic Party of the Left (splinter of PCI + PSI)
PPI	Partito Popolare Italiano (1994–2002)	Italian Popular Party (formerly DC)
PS d'Az	Partito Sardo d'Azione (1920–current)	Sardinian Action Party
PSI	Partito Socialista Italiano (1892–1994)	Italian Socialist Party
PSIUP	Partito Socialista Italiano d'Unita Proletariano (1964–1972)	Italian Socialist Party of Proletarian Unity
PRC	Partito della Rifondazione Comunista (1991–current)	Communist Refoundation Party (formerly the PCI)

NOTES

Preface and Acknowledgments

1. Methods elaborated by pioneering fieldworkers in the early twentieth century emphasized the scholarly discipline inherent in long-term research in the field, acquisition of local languages, participation in daily routines and special events, and rigorous attempts to document aspects of daily life, cultural beliefs, and social relationships. However, epistemological models of ethnography as science underwent some critical challenges and transformations during the late twentieth century. Accordingly, projects like mine no longer take "culture" for granted as the transcendent object of ethnography. Many cultural anthropologists accepted new mandates for critical self-reflection and attention to writing choices (Clifford 1988). They more often disdained claims to universal objective knowledge in favor of modest, positioned perspectives (Haraway 1991; Harding 1986). Yet, in the exuberant aftermath of anthropology's "experimental moment" (Marcus and Fischer 1986), many key principles of methodological discipline remained relevant. Most ethnographers continued to rely on first-hand fieldwork of some kind, including interviews, ongoing social interaction, and participant observation, but the shape and focus of these methods became more playful and adaptive.

2. On honor and shame in the Mediterranean, see for example Schneider (1971); Herzfeld (1980, 1984); Blok (1981); Gilmore (1987); Pina-Cabral (1989); Goddard (1994).

3. Sardinian dialects are considered direct derivatives of Latin, with various Italian and Catalan influences. See Ferrer (2002), Mensching (2000), and Ligia (2002) on Sardinian language genealogy and maintenance.

4. Alexandra Jaffe's (1996) work on dual language practices and code-switching in nearby Corsica illustrates similar patterns of language use, marking spheres of bureaucracy and urban centers apart from spheres of informal social

life and rural areas. With EU support of minority languages, Sardinian language advocates have made new headway in their efforts to standardize and promote a common indigenous language. A regional law of 1997 recognized Sardinian as an official language, and within ten years, popular support for language revitalization has mushroomed (Oppo 2008).

5. The late 1980s and early 1990s are often identified as the "postmodern moment" in anthropology, when a thriving experimentation with ethnographic writing styles and formats began. Feminist theory (with its attention to subjectivity, gender, and emotion), anti-colonialist theory, and various strains of post-structuralism were all brought to bear in critique of dominant models of knowledge construction and representation in anthropology. At this time, the emerging importance of first-person narratives and searching reflections upon our own role as ethnographers, as well as our relationships with the living subjects of ethnography, became widely recognized, but also provoked rifts within the discipline.

Introduction

1. Communal use rights, called *usi civici*, are based on town residence and customary practice. The right of pasture, the right to gather acorns for fodder, and the right to collect firewood on village-owned commons were legalized at the national level in 1927.

2. He turned to me and exclaimed in Italian, "*Non puoi fare l'antropologa e l'ambientalista alla stessa volta!*"

3. Darrell Posey's work is particularly salient, given his championship of indigenous ecological knowledge and sovereignty over resources (see, for example, Posey 2004). "Indigenous" groups have apparently now attained a degree of respect and value in global environmental discourses, reflected, for example, in the Convention on Biological Diversity (CBD) and subsequent United Nations Development Programme (UNDP) programs. Nevertheless, easy alliances between environmental groups and indigenous peoples can no longer be assumed (Harries-Jones 1993, Brosius 1999a, Doane 2007).

4. See in particular *The Limits to Growth* (Meadows et al. 2004), commissioned by the Club of Rome, which attempted to model the impacts of population growth on finite world resources.

5. For discussion, note Smith (1990), Harvey (1996), McCarthy and Prudham (2004), and Heynen and Robbins (2005).

6. For example, Peet and Watts (2004) reframed global environment and development issues within the context of Marxist political ecology. Research on feminist political ecologies (Rocheleau et al. 1996) took this project further

by mandating engagements with feminist epistemologies. Contributions across social and cultural anthropology (see, for example, Escobar 1995, 1998), sociology, international development studies, and human geography (see also Bryant and Bailey 1997, Braun and Castree 1998, and Castree and Braun 2001) during the 1990s have enlarged the critical discourses on environmental justice in the United States to engage the problematics of culture, race, gender, and marginality on a global scale.

7. This is not to say that environmental science or environmental social science constitute mere "social fabrications." On the contrary, disciplined efforts to account for physical and social phenomena produce important criteria for decision-making. To assume that such efforts are "objective" in absolute terms, however, can be systematically misleading. It is a premise of political ecology studies that the concepts and analyses associated with key features of environmental governance should be measured against their social, cultural, political, and economic contexts.

8. Statistics provided by ISTAT, Ufficio Regionale per la Sardegna ("Gli indici di deprivazione per l'analisi delle disuguaglianze tra i comuni di Sardegna," downloaded January 15, 2007, from http://www.istat.it/istat/attivita/sediregionali/sardegna/postercagliari.pdf).

9. See Pungetti (1999: 117–22), Casu et al. (1984), Capitta and Gaias (1990-91), and Camarda et al. (1986) for detailed discussion of Sardinian ecology and conservation.

10. Information drawn from the Sardinian Forest Service website (http://www.forestesarde.it/), consulted January 17, 2007; website moved to http://www.sardegnaambiente.it in 2008.

11. Roy Rappaport (2000) and Darrell Posey (2004), for example, were among the leading scholars in this tradition. See also Biersack (1999) and Kottak (1999).

12. See, for example, Escobar (1995), Ferguson (1990), Sachs (1991), and Scott (1998).

13. See Brockington (2002) for discussion of "fortress conservation" in Africa; see also Hardison (2004), Igoe (2004), and West et al. (2006) for comparative notes on parks and people.

14. Examples have been discussed by Peter Harries-Jones (1993), Peter J. Brosius (1999), Priscilla Weeks (1999), and Luis Vivanco (2002).

15. See, among others, Beth Conklin (1997, 2002), Nora Haenn (2005), Celia Lowe (2006), Hugh Raffles (2002), Suzana Sawyer (2004), Candace Slater (2003), Anna Tsing (2005), Christine Walley (2004), and Paige West (2006) for excellent models.

16. See Ionta (2006, 2008) for discussion of regional media and identity in Sardinia.

17. Use of the singular "dreamtime" vs. plural "dreamtimes" is inconsistent across anthropological literature. Attempts to recognize distinctions in cosmological models associated with different groups generally mandate the plural when discussing these models collectively. When using this metaphor to discuss the Sardinian case or a particular ENGO, I use the singular "dreamtime." I adopt the plural form, "dreamtimes," to emphasize the fragmentary nature of the larger field of environmental imaginaries.

18. For detailed discussion of Aboriginal religions and their links to landscape in Australia, consult Swain (1993), Morphy (1995), and Strang (1997), among others. See also Myers (1986) for an exploration of Aboriginal subjectivity in relation to place, and Hume (1999) for provocative debate on the interpretation of Aboriginal Dreaming as a form of alternative consciousness.

19. See, for example, Strehlow's (1970) functionalist account of the "totemic landscape" of central Australia.

20. The term "totemism" is used to describe systems of belief that revolve around sacred bonds between human communities and particular non-human species or objects. In some cases, this includes the belief that particular groups of people are descended from non-human ancestors—an understanding that contributes to the social organization of kinship groups and their relationships to one another. See Andrew Lang's (1994 [1912]) early discussion of totemism in relation to Western Australia. The cross-cultural study of totemic religious forms was popularized by Emile Durkheim (1915).

21. Jasanoff's interest in the songlines is inspired by Bruce Chatwin's (1988) popular novel narrating his own travels in Australia set against a rich background of Aboriginal stories, landscapes, and cultural encounters. Although Chatwin's account is textured enough to be appreciated by many ethnographers, Jasanoff's reading of it is arguably thin, since it considers human experience and belief only in terms of the symbolic domain. Anthropologists look for greater complexity in the study of the songlines.

1. Ecology, Alterity, and Resistance

Some themes of this chapter were developed from "Ecology, Alterity and Resistance" published by the author in *Social Anthropology* 9, no. 3 (2001), 285–302, and "How to Challenge a Green Giant" published by the author in *Identities: Global Studies in Culture and Power* 12, no. 3 (2005): 439–50.

1. Said (1978) explored how the colonial projects of Western nations were supported and shaped by efforts of imagination taking place in fields as diverse as history, biology, economic and political theory, and literature, for example. According to Said, discussions emerging across multiple domains of aesthetic,

humanistic, and scientific production all defined and reified cultural distinctions between the West and the East. By force of common reference, these discussions about "the Orient" naturalized the emerging hierarchies of power entailed in the imperial contexts to which the agents of such discourses owed much of their own legitimacy. Said has, of course, been criticized for his over-reliance on discourse analysis, and for his tendency to both undervalue and undercomplicate social agency. His example, nevertheless, compels us to continue exploring links between the cultural imagination and the practices of power. This work remains as crucial to environmental studies as it is to other projects across the social sciences. For a thorough, critical discussion of Edward Said's legacy in anthropology and the relevance of his work to contemporary political debates, consult El-Haj (2005).

2. The sexualizing gaze in the following passage, describing the clothing of women in the streets of Cagliari, is unmistakable:

> But a fair number of peasants in the streets, and peasant women in rather ordinary costume: tight-bodiced, volume-skirted dresses of hand-woven linen or thickish cotton. The prettiest is of dark-blue-and-red, intermingled, so made that the dark-blue gathers round the waist into one colour, the myriad pleats hiding all the rosy red. But when she walks, the full-petticoated peasant woman, then the red goes flash-flash-flash, like a bird showing its colours. She has a plain, light bodice with a peak: sometimes a little vest, and great full white sleeves, and usually a handkerchief or shawl loose knotted. It is charming the way they walk. With quick, short steps. When all is said and done, the most attractive costume for women in my eye, is the tight little bodice and the many-pleated skirt, full and vibrating with movement. It has a charm which modern elegance lacks completely—a bird-like play in movement. (D. H. Lawrence 2002: 66)

Lawrence thought that "in these women there is something shy and defiant and un-get-at-able" (67), and mused that in contrast to "modern" sentiments, courtships in Sardinia were marked by a "certain wild, salty savour" (67). In rural Sardinia, he was again smitten by "wonderful little girl-children, perfect and demure in the stiffish, brilliant costume [of Tonara]" (119) and described in detail the sight of "the beauty of the shuffling woman-host" making a Catholic procession through the countryside (120).

3. As Horden and Purcell (2000) note, the idea of "the corrupting sea" was historically significant to perceptions of the Mediterranean as far back as ancient Greece. Insomuch as these authors attempt the broad historiography of the Mediterranean with a spirit of lively doubt, their ambitious work assists the project of critical engagement. Following Braudel (1972), they are principally interested in reaffirming the unity of the Mediterranean as an appropriate object of analysis, in contradiction to challenges from social theorists such

as Herzfeld (1980, 1984) and Piña-Cabral (1989). Horden and Purcell recognize the survival of ecological determinism and interactionism in conventional understandings of Mediterranean unity, yet despite their efforts to nuance and update an historical ecological approach, they fail to apply a post-Kuhnian critical sociology of knowledge. In particular, the contention that continental European ethnographers and folk study scholars are exempt from intrusive cultural presuppositions in their analyses of "pan-Mediterranean" cultural phenomena seems problematic. Recent commentaries on this debate (Peressini and Hadj-Moussa 2005; Chambers 2008 and some contributions in Harris 2005) insist that cultural-political contexts have conditioned writing about "the Mediterranean," and that these contexts are not innocent.

4. According to Edward Said (1978), with regard to the East, the effect of such parallel, mutually reinforcing visions was to elevate a more or less unified cultural imaginary of "orientalism" to hegemonic status. The racist tropes and cultural stereotypes—incorporating both repulsion and desire—produced by the orientalist imagination proved so durable that they persisted into the postcolonial era, and could be seen to linger on late in the twentieth century. Schneider (1998) has recently traced a very similar discursive process regarding the southern regions of Italy, including Sardinia. I discuss this further in chapter 4.

5. Conservation International tracks species diversity worldwide and posts information on its interpretation of "hotspot science" online. For more information, see "Biodiversity Hotspots—Mediterranean Basin" (Conservation International website, http://www.biodiversityhotspots.org/xp/Hotspots/mediterranean, consulted July 7, 2008). The World Wide Fund for Nature (WWF) has also recently initiated a set of campaigns organized around "ecoregions" (WWF website, "About Global Ecoregions," http://www.panda.org/about_wwf/where_we_work/ecoregions/about/what_is_an_ecoregion/index.cfm, consulted Jan. 17, 2007).

6. Information cited from WWF website, "Forest Conservation in the Mediterranean," http://www.panda.org/about_wwf/where_we_work/europe/what_we_do/mediterranean/about/forests/index.cfm, posted Jan. 31, 2006. Downloaded Jan. 17, 2006.

7. Information cited from WWF website, "Mediterranean Forests, Woodlands and Scrub—A Global Ecoregion," http://www.panda.org/about_wwf/where_we_work/ecoregions/mediterranean_forests_scrub.ctm, posted July 7, 2006. Downloaded Jan. 15, 2007.

8. Information cited from WWF website, "Mediterranean Sea—A Global Ecoregion," http://www.panda.org/about_wwf/where_we_work/ecoregions/mediterranean_sea.cfm, posted July 18, 2006. Downloaded Jan. 17, 2007.

9. The Euro-Mediterranean Partnership was first signed in 1995 by the fif-

teen European Union member states and the European Commission, together with twelve other countries around the periphery of the Mediterranean Sea, for the promotion of free trade and cooperation across the larger Euro-Mediterranean area. Subsequent five-year plans in 2000 and 2005 expanded and revised financial instruments to support less developed, non-European Mediterranean countries in such areas as sustainable development and the environment (Europa portal of the EU, Summaries of Legislation, "Euro-Mediterranean Association Agreements," http://europa.eu/scadplus/leg/lvb/r14104.htm, consulted July 12, 2008.

10. Their idea constitutes one approach to global phenomena that gets beyond reified dichotomies of global and local, and beyond generalizations about the abstract structures of globalization, to focus attention on "the actual configurations through which global forms of techno-science, economic rationalism, and other expert systems gain significance" (Collier 2006, 400). The heterogeneity, flexibility, and contingency of such configurations suggest new insights into the instabilities and conflicts associated with political ecology. Much like Anna Tsing's (2005) idea of global "frictions," in which the author challenges tendencies to naturalize global forms that originate in particular "scale-making" projects linking local events and experiences with narratives that encompass a global vision, the notion of global assemblages implies the critical importance of situated perspectives on particular actors, structures, and moments. According to Collier, "The relationship among the elements in an assemblage is not stable; nor is their configuration reducible to a single logic. Rather, an assemblage is structured through critical reflection, debate and contest" (2006, 400).

11. Strategic practices of identity construction are implicitly guided by the standards and expectations negotiated at the level of transnational discourses about culture, environment, and development. Michael Herzfeld (2004) argues that these moralizing discourses constitute a form of globalization that forces indigenous cultures to conform to expectations about what local heritage and tradition should look like. Such expectations privilege the values of urban, global, and cosmopolitan-oriented individuals.

12. Studying historical and contemporary land evictions associated with Arusha National Park (Neumann 1998) and the Mkomazi Game Reserve (Brockington 2002), political ecologists have argued that the protection of wilderness and wildlife in Tanzania is a project that reinscribes the inequalities of colonial power and privilege in a neocolonial context. This sets up the terms by which indigenous tribal communities can only pursue their own livelihoods and cultural survival by resisting conservation. Igoe attempts to complicate this further, by looking at Maasai NGOs and emerging models for participatory co-management of protected areas. Noting that indigenous communities in many different

parts of the world have been "displaced by national parks and the global conservation agenda" (2004, 167), Igoe suggests that possibilities for implementing socially progressive models for conservation are largely limited by power contexts, including lack of sovereignty.

13. The problematic nature of James C. Scott's vision of state power has been well critiqued in recent work by Gupta (1998), Agrawal (2005), Ferguson (2005), and Li (2005). See also discussions of Scott's approach to resistance in Ortner (1995) and Sivaramakrishnan (2005a, 2005b). I explore the implications of such critical readings of Scott in later chapters.

14. Pira (1978), Pirastu (1993), and Brigaglia et al. (1995) provide a range of discussions engaging the issue of Sardinia as a historical and contemporary "periphery." See also ethnographies by Cagnetta (1954), Bodemann (1979), Meloni (1984), Berger (1986), Ayora-Diaz (1993), and Vargas-Cetina (1993b). The discursive production of Sardinia as a marginal area has been powerfully relevant to varied interpretations of development issues.

15. See Schweizer (1988) and Satta (2001) for discussion of Sardinian nationalist discourses.

16. For analysis of historic and recent criminal statistics, see Lilliu (2002).

17. This builds on the work of Johannes Fabian (1983), as I discuss in chapter 5. Fabian's famous interrogation of ethnographic writing as a way of distancing and primitivizing anthropology's chosen objects of analysis transformed Said's (1978) method of discourse analysis, taking the focus from the structure of cultural categories to the process of cultural production. Later anthropologists viewed the cultural construction of identity and difference as the active, ongoing, often self-conscious work of social memory and nostalgia (see Lowenthal 1988). Similarly, we can highlight the dynamic agency embedded in the "social poetics" of marginality, as well as the irony and ambivalence that may pervade the performance of identity (Herzfeld 1985, 1991, 1997).

18. See, for example, Agyeman et al. (2003) as well as ethnographic works (Checker 2005; Brower and Johnston 2007). Giovanna di Chiro's (2004) critical review of the implications of pan-racial political activism in environmental justice movements is also insightful.

19. See Candace Slater's (2002) commentary on the IMAX film about the Ecuadorian Amazon, and Luis Vivanco's (2006) analysis of several rainforest documentaries.

20. Herzfeld's important critical work on the anthropological framing of Greek identity suggests that present-day Greeks themselves have been made to embody an essential contradiction between West and East, European and exotic stereotypes. As "aboriginal Europeans" credited with a key role in the development of Western civilization, contemporary Greeks "seriously and frequently

ask themselves if perhaps they now belong politically, economically, and culturally to the Third World" (Herzfeld 1987a, 3). The marginality of modern Greece in Europe has stood in contrast to the ideological importance of classical Greece within the framing discourses of European history, according to him. Herzfeld effectively draws into question how "the Mediterranean" has been configured as a marginal and backward culture area through studies in European and national folklore, history, and ethnography.

21. According to Povinelli (2002), the "politics of cultural recognition" (Taylor 1994) tends to fall short of its humanistic goals, even as it gains ground. Yet it is often problematic to deny the cultural essentialisms chosen by minorities for themselves. Unlike moves to simply deconstruct the authenticity of indigenous self-representations (see, for example, Krech 1999), Povinelli's approach is rooted in the way the politics of indigenous representation is framed by ongoing processes of marginalization and disempowerment. Thus without undermining indigenous movements, she problematizes the double-bind associated with liberal discourses of indigeneity. This is also a theme explored in Niezen (2004, 144–67). For a comparative discussion on indigenous essentialisms and resource rights, see Dove (2006).

22. Shepard Krech's (1999) claim to debunk myths of the "ecological Indian," for example, failed to problematize the complex postcolonial contexts with which Native American and indigenous self-representation and economic strategies are necessarily engaged. See Doxtater (2004) and Ranco (2005, 2006) for critical discussion. A similar critique could be made of Kay Milton's (1996) attempt to outline the problems with idealizing "primitive" cultural ecologies. Bengt Karlsson's (2006) critique of Roy Ellen (1986) and Tim Ingold (2000) provides a similar perspective, drawing on a case study from India. Paul Nasdady's (2005) contribution to the debate suggests that by expecting indigenous peoples to "live up" to the stereotype of the "ecological Indian," we assert the privilege of Western cultural paradigms associated with environmentalism and conservation, which are equally problematic. As Moore et al. (2003, 13) have pointed out, Rousseau's original vision of the Noble Savage was shot through with an "ambivalent primitivism" that cast doubt upon the environmental values of indigenous cultures from the outset.

23. Larry Lohmann (1993) has used the term "green Orientalism" to describe the ethnocentric discourses associated with environmentalism.

24. See Langton et al. (2005) for further comparative analysis and problematization of indigenous co-management systems in Australian parks and protected areas. Timothy Doyle (2005) has also discussed the problematic engagement of Aboriginal Australians with the environmental movement focused on wilderness preservation.

25. Since the different nomenclatures chosen by indigenous peoples for themselves are relevant and important to their life projects within different national contexts, I try, as much as possible—given my limited knowledge and the need to preserve clarity—to use them appropriately. In the U.S. context, for example, many call themselves "Native Americans" or "American Indians." In Canada, indigenous communities have coordinated their political voices as an Assembly of First Nations. The term "First Nations" supports recognition of distinct cultural, historical, and linguistic differences across these communities, as well as their status as sovereign peoples within the Canadian nation-state. Although Canada subscribes to a vision of multiculturalism and has engaged the politics of indigenous sovereignty more directly than many other postcolonial nation-states, it still enshrines the dominant privileges of two European "founding" cultures, French and English (for discussion, see, for example, Perley 2006). Depending on the context, citizens of First Nations may call themselves Aboriginals, Natives, or Indians.

26. See Cronon (1995) and Spence (2000) for treatment of the North American case and Moore et al. (2003) for excellent comparative discussion of the cultural politics of landscape and environment.

27. See also Peter Harries-Jones (1993).

28. The idea that First Nation histories and perspectives are often subject to systematic processes of erasure has been central to critical writings by indigenous scholars (see, for example, Ranco 2006, Perley 2006) and other advocates. In future chapters, I return to develop the idea of cultural or epistemic erasure further, in relation to the global dreamtimes of environmentalism.

29. Kay Milton (1996) has argued that we can distinguish between "local" and "global" visions of the environment. Although this definition becomes problematic as we recognize complex "translocal" connections (e.g., Tsing 2005), it should be recognized that global orientations still organize much of the cultural production associated with environmental initiatives. For further discussion, see Escobar (1998) as well as Mühlhäusler and Peace (2006).

30. This erasure of complexity leads to the "thin simplifications" that James C. Scott (1998) has associated with modernist regimes of governance and development.

31. Consult Schneider (1998) and Dickie (1999) for details on state discourses of "otherness" in Southern Italy. I discuss this theme further in chapter 3.

32. In general, international organizations follow the precedent established by the 1993 UN Declaration of the Rights of Indigenous Peoples. This recognized a definition provided by the Martinéz Cobo Report to the UN Sub-Commission on the Prevention of Discrimination of Minorities in 1986:

Indigenous communities, peoples and nations are those which, having a historical continuity with pre-invasion and pre-colonial societies that developed on their territories, consider themselves distinct from other sectors of the societies now prevailing in those territories, or parts of them. They form at present non-dominant sectors of society and are determined to preserve, develop and transmit to future generations their ancestral territories, and their ethnic identity, as the basis of their continued existence as peoples, in accordance with their own cultural patterns, social institutions and legal systems.

33. I follow Paul Farmer (2004) in my use of the term "structural violence." Farmer draws on the work of Johan Galtung (1969) to analyze diverse forms of human suffering generated as a result of structural inequalities associated, for example, with poverty, gender, race, or minority status, in addition to inequities organized at the international level.

34. Several African cases are salient here. In addition to Christine Walley (2004), geographer Roderick Neumann (1998) and anthropologists Dan Brockington (2002) and Jim Igoe (2004) have all documented the racist legacies of colonialism in Tanzanian protected areas. See also Igoe and Kelsall (2005) on the NGO movement and indigeneity in Africa.

35. Consider, for example, the representation of "eco-goodies and baddies" in relation to wildlife management in the Congo (Köhler 2005). Here, Western stereotypes of Baka (Pygmy) hunter-gatherers living in tune with nature contrast with stereotypes of Bantu farmers who exploit nature without any "natural" conservation ethic. Colonial histories of racial prejudice are embedded here in the management of species protected under the UN Convention on International Trade of Endangered Species (CITES).

36. On the links between scientific ecology and the "misreading" of African landscapes, see also the volume edited by Fairhead and Leach (1996). Recent debates about the land claims of ≠Khomani San within national park territories in southern Africa have highlighted the ways in which "cultural" features of indigeneity have been essentialized and primordialized in relation to landscape (see Sylvain 2002).

37. David McDermott Hughes's (2006) recent study of environmentalism in southern Africa offers further perspective on the ways that liberal multiculturalism, biodiversity protection, and ecodevelopment have been used to legitimize new waves of land dispossession along the Zimbabwe-Mozambique border zone. Ostensibly to promote racial integration between white investors and black peasants, as well as sustainable development, some ancestral communal lands in this region were privatized and offered for sale to tourism firms, owned and operated by whites. This is another case in which "participatory development" schemes failed to live up to their promise.

38. Anthropologists studying practices of identity formation struggle against the objectification of cultural identity and "alterity" as mere binary oppositions. Using empirical evidence to trace shifting relational and contextual notions of selves and others, we can critique notions of identity as "sameness" and pursue "a multidimensional and fluid approach to identity/alterity" (Gingrich 2006, 16). Efforts to understand the interplay of identity and alterity at an ethnographic level necessarily problematize wider, transdisciplinary theories of identity as the natural outcome of essential human/cultural similarities and differences (Baumann and Gingrich 2006). This move opens a path to transcend the dangerous politics of essentialism and recognize the legitimacy of hybrid or creolized identities. For example, Baumann (2006) suggests that it is possible to explore "different modalities of selfing/othering," including orientalization, segmentary fusions and fissions of identity and alterity according to context, and the co-optation of minorities by hierarchized encompassment. Gingrich argues that "othering and belonging are mutually constitutive components of identity" (2006, 4).

2. Envisioning the Supramonte

This chapter revises and extends an essay by the author that appeared in *Magic, Science and Religion: The Museum as a Ritual Site*, edited by Mary Bouquet and Nuno Porto (New York: Berghahn Books, 2005), 141-60.

1. "Sar Vaddes" is a linguistic variation of "Sas Vaddes."
2. Gino said, "*Il parco già c'è'. . . . Il parco, l'abbiamo fatto noi.*"
3. For details, see Diana (1998), Chironi (1998), and Scroccu (1998).
4. From WWF-Italia website, "Parco del Gennargentu, riparliamone," posted Oct. 17, 2005. (www.wwf-it/sardegna/news, consulted November 2005; page now discontinued.)
5. For additional analysis of the role of parks and the ideological production of "nature" in relation to American identity, see, for example, Alexander Wilson (1991), as well as William Cronon (2003). Mark David Spence (2000), Philip Burnham (2000), and Karl Jacoby (2003) have recently explored the expulsion of Native Americans from parks in colonial North America.
6. The famous case of Taos Pueblo's conflict with the U.S. Forest Service, over possession of Blue Lake in the state of New Mexico, serves as an example. See Gordon-McCutchan (1991) for extensive discussion of this case.
7. Schwartz's (2006) insightful discussion of how a national park in Latvia reconfigured the "homeland narratives" of the communist era suggests an important comparison. See also Cederlöf and Sivaramakrishnan (2006).

8. For discussion, consult West and Brechin (1991); Wright and Mattson (1996); Brosius et al. (1998); Fortwangler (2003); and West et al. (2006).

9. See, for example, Tassi (1998).

10. This bodily and sensory engagement is inherent to a ritual orientation (Bell 1992, 98).

11. Lund (2005) suggests that senses of place are not only determined by historical "rootedness" in particular geographic areas, but also by an enduring connection to other residents, and an appreciation of one's own relation to places over time. In her study of the construction of social identity in relation to "local" and "outsider" perspectives on the making of a natural park in Spain, she highlights the role of socialization and travelling in the orientation of residents to "nature."

12. This artwork is signed by Gianmarco Ibba, the same artist who designed the cartoon, *l'Avventura del Gennargentu*, discussed in chapter 4.

13. From Parco Nazionale del Golfo di Orosei e del Gennargentu Internet Portal, maintained by WWF Sardegna (http://www.parcogennargentu.it, updated January 11, 2000, consulted May 2002).

14. From Il Portale dei Parchi Italiani, maintained by FEDERPARCHI— Federazione Italiana Parchi e Riserve Naturali (http://www.parks.it, accessed May 2002).

15. From WWF Italia Internet Portal, "The environment from restriction to opportunity: Train and support the parks local communities" (http://www.parcogennargentu.it/adapt/style/home.htm, consulted May 2002).

16. From Parco Nazionale del Golfo di Orosei e del Gennargentu Internet Portal, maintained by WWF Sardegna, "Area Protetta" (http://www.parcogennargentu.it/AreaProtetta.htm, updated January 11, 2000, accessed May 2002; page moved to http://www.parcogennargentu.it/ParcoGennargentu4.htm).

17. From Parco Nazionale del Golfo di Orosei e del Gennargentu Internet Portal, maintained by WWF Sardegna (http://www.parcogennargentu.it/ViverellParco.htm, updated January 11, 2000, accessed May 2002; page moved to http://www.parcogennargentu.it/ParcoGennargentu4.htm).

18. Mamuthone is an indigenous traditional clown or trickster figure associated with the area of "the Barbagia" and in particular, with the town of Mamoiada, which borders Orgosolo. A closely related clown figure is the Maimòne traditional in Orgosolo. In both cases, the character represents a kind of simpleton, madman, or drunk whose masked costume and sombre antics are still popular in Nuorese Carnival processions. Dolores Turchi (1990, 21-22) suggests that these Nuorese trickster figures are related to the Cretan Dionysian cults.

19. There is surely tremendous cultural and linguistic diversity in the ways

that people engage with computers and the internet. While McLuhan (1994) imagined how technology-mediated communications might create an experience that "abolishes" time and space to create a "global village," and recent writers (McLuhan and Powers 1992; Barnes 2003) have suggested interesting ways in which this idea applies to an evolving range of computer-mediated communications, the agency in this process should not be invested in technology itself. I do not review or suggest evidence for cognitive transformations associated with virtual worlds. Instead, I explore how participation in activities on the internet might shape the popular imagination of globalization as it is broadly grounded in Western and cosmopolitan experience.

20. Sources representing the park project as a neocolonialist enterprise include Circolo Giovanile di Orgosolo (1973), Mereu (1992), Zucca (1989, 1992), and Pintore (1993). Discussions cautiously favoring the park project include Camboni (1991), Liori (1993), Colombano (1993), Mastroni (1993), and Fancello (1992).

21. Note the relevance of Pierre Bourdieu's (1977, 1984, 1991) studies of symbolic capital here. I discuss the problem further in chapter 6.

22. See Berglund (1998), Harries-Jones (1993), Yearley (1993).

23. See Herzfeld (1985), Tsing (1993), Steedly (1993), Stewart (1996).

3. Intimate Landscapes

An earlier version of this chapter appeared in *Mixed Emotions: Anthropological Studies of Feeling*, edited by Kay Milton and Maruska Svasek (New York: Berg, 2005), 145–62.

1. She spoke in Sardinian, "*Eo appo sa sensatzione omente si fit morta una pessone cara.*"

2. For further discussion of historicity as a heuristic device in social analysis, consult Herzfeld (1985, 1991); Faubion (1993); Sutton (2000); Malaby (2003); Mitchell (2002).

3. Following Csordas (1990, 1993, 1994), I approach "embodied" experience as "the starting point for analyzing human participation in a cultural world" (Csordas 1993, 135). Therefore, "embodied identities" are not merely aspects of political discourse and representation, but are caught up in intersubjective modes of both meaning and feeling, informed by human senses of perception.

4. See Steedly (1993) on stories from the margins that "ride the gaps" of dominant narratives. Anna Tsing (1993) and Kathleen Stewart (1996) have also addressed issues of subjectivity and storytelling from marginal positions.

5. This story may refer to the famous murder of the Beata Antonia Mesina, but it is not made explicit by the author.

6. Sio is an Orgosolo-born student of commercial economics who undertook an excellent oral history study of changing contractual relations between herd owners and servant-shepherds in his home town. Sio's work is exceptionally good because it reflects the highest possible linguistic sensibility and his own familiarity with the social context of the town. His work was carried out in Sardinian and translated by him into Italian for the purpose of submission for the *laurea*. Quotes here are my translations from parallel Sardinian and Italian texts to English.

7. Reverse transhumance is the seasonal movement of herds down from mountain pastures to lower altitudes over the cold winter months. Consult Le Lannou (1971), Angioni (1989), Berger (1986), or Vargas-Cetina (1993b) for an extensive explanation of the practice in Sardinia. This seasonal migration has been associated with Sardinian banditry in the policy discourses, and many of the initiatives to modernize herding in central Sardinia have aimed to sedentarize shepherds.

8. See Andrea Deplano (1997) for a discussion of the *tenores* tradition as social communication. Tenor-singing is a specifically male institution in Orgosolo. In contrast, women "traditionally" sing the Catholic rosary or poetic laments upon the occasion of a death. While men's songs are tuned to civil festivity, women's are tuned to serious and religious occasions.

9. Ortu perceives the Piedmontese enclosure movement as contributing to a process of proletarianization of the shepherd class in highland Sardinia (1981).

10. For an excellent English-language source on the uneven impacts of the enclosure movement and anti-feudalism in highland central Sardinia, see Berger's (1986) dissertation in the political economy tradition of anthropology.

11. Areas of oak trees in particular were sold off by many communities; these were valued for the production of railway ties and coal (Bodemann 1979, 35, 130). Orgosolo's mature oak forest, conserved not by the forestry service but by the town on its communal territory, has become a rare environmental resource in central Sardinia.

12. Corda reports that one message simply read, "*Svegliati, popolo, venduto il Comunale!*" while at the churches, the message was "*Santi, aiutateci, venduto il Comunale!*" (Saints, help us, the Commons is sold!) (1989, 209). Note that the language of the graffiti was Italian; Sardinian was not generally written. The form of the sentences, however, followed the grammar pattern of local dialect, especially in the use of "il comunale" which corresponds to the Sardinian *su cumonale*, instead of the more formal Italian *terreni comunali, territorio comunale,* or *pascolo comunale.*

13. The focus of this book leaves limited space to explore the intricacies of women's roles in development, but it is clear that in Orgosolo, women of faith have often stepped into public debates about local land use and the maintenance of local authority over the Commons. Their sense of intimacy with the landscape is generally shared with other men and women across the community, but takes on a particular quality as a result of their deep engagement with the Roman Catholic Church. While many men were more apt to see the Church as an apparatus of state intrusion, fundamentally compromised by the self-interest of priests or by political connections, many women—particularly mothers and elders, but also a fair share of younger women—recognized the Church as an intrinsic part of their Sardinian heritage. On important saints' days and festivals, four local companies of women *priorissas* lead religious processions through the streets of Orgosolo, and sometimes into the countryside, where special chapels and sacred sites are located. Their paths commemorate and recreate a particular gendered experience of belonging to the landscape, which cannot be dissociated from their general sense of being the guardians of families and of the community as a whole.

14. See, for example, Rosaldo (1984); Abu-Lughod (1986); Lutz (1988). Although the cultural models of emotion proposed in the 1980s were limited by their conventional interpretative focus and the clinging assumptions of bounded, stable symbolic systems, a key methodological contribution remains. Political-emotional subjectivities must still be encountered through exactly the kind of conscientious interpersonal engagement that feminist traditions in ethnography have championed.

15. See Merleau-Ponty (1964); Bourdieu (1977); Jackson (1983); de Certeau (1984); Csordas (1990); Herzfeld (2004); Svasek (2005).

16. See, for example, Leavitt (1996); Strathern (1996); Stoller (1997).

4. Dark Frontier

1. She said, in Sardinian, "*S'ospedale e sa galera tzirana pro tottus.*"

2. Using colloquial Italian, he said, "*Rompano le palle alla gente questi ballallui.*"

3. Ananiu spoke to me in Italian, "*Qui si poteva vivere tranquilli, le potenzialità ce ne sono in questo paese. Invece no: qui hanno sempre gelosie, non cambierà mai.*"

4. Shifts in my own status back and forth between "insider" and "outsider" to the community indicated the intensity of code-switching linked to language and hospitality, for instance. Most people in Orgosolo, hearing that I was an

anthropologist, presumed that I would be interested in traditions and customs. They were eager to show me this positive side of local life, as much as they were anxious to make sure I understood how the community itself interpreted evidence of criminality and sought not to condone it, but to atone for it.

5. Lutz and Collins's (1993) discussion of exotic representations of "otherness" in *National Geographic* offers a comparative perspective.

6. Another kidnapping in the early 1990s of a child from the area of the Emerald Coast was also considered a violation of "traditional" codes of honor thought to apply even to criminal acts; joking discourses occasionally treat kidnapping as a kind of dark hospitality in which "guests" get fat on authentic local foods and fall in love with the beauty of Sardinia and sometimes even the kidnappers themselves. Increasing evidence of violence associated with kidnappings, however, has demonstrated in the eyes of the moral majority of Orgolese that kidnappers absolutely fail to follow the model of benevolent hospitality. In this case, the child's mother was brought to speak in Orgosolo's church, and many women of the community hung white linens from their windows to show solidarity with her.

7. In fall of 1998, a law was passed at the regional level to add Sardinian to the school curriculum; it was to be implemented for the school year of fall 1999. A local teacher told me in August of 1999 that the faculty had yet to decide upon a spelling system for Orgosolo's dialect, particularly for the annotation of glottal stops. My own decision to use the "h" as a glottal stop reflects the prevalent choice in Orgosolo before this time.

8. Dickie (1999) draws upon Edward Said's (1978, 1994) work to frame his approach. He argues that the so-called southern question should not be taken at face value as reflecting objective analyses of differential political, economic, and social patterns across the regions of Italy, but should instead be evaluated as rhetorical strategies associated with the invention of the nation-state.

9. There is considerable archaeological evidence of Sardinia's indigenous Nuragic culture at Orgosolo, but scant traces of Roman presence in the archaeological record (Cagnetta 1954, 81).

10. *Padre Padrone* (1977), directed by Vittorio Taviani, based on the 1975 novel by Sardinian-born Gavino Ledda, translated in English as *My Father, My Master*.

11. *Banditi a Orgosolo* (1961), directed by Vittorio de Seta.

12. See also Moss (1979) for discussion.

13. Carta (1980, 205); Corona (1980: 76); Raggio (1980: 191).

1. She said in Italian, "*Guarda, Tere, sembra una barzaletta!*"

2. This explanation is revealing in several ways. First, a history of cultural inhabitation, as well as colonial exploitation, has been erased. The forest referred to in the website was called Sar Vaddes, the forest still managed as part of Orgosolo's communal territory, as I explained previously. Sar Vaddes was conserved by the municipality despite the enclosure laws and heavy taxation introduced during the nineteenth century. Second, the political context is reduced to a contrast between civil society and backward rural culture. A complex range of political voices in central Sardinia is collapsed into monolithic "resistance," while the tacit agendas of governments and NGOs are obscured from view. The uniquely Italian struggles of Catholic-based and Marxist-based party politics, and the ways in which these have been seated in families, neighborhoods, and networks of privilege (see, for example, Kertzer 1980, 1996), are likewise effaced. Finally, the ugly influence of cultural racisms present in bureaucratic discourses, which naturalize relative poverty and marginality in Southern Italy as the effect of corruption and innate cultural psychology, is rendered invisible.

3. Such models are, in some sense, an insidious resurrection of Edward Banfield's (1958) notion of amoral familism in Southern Italy, in which a moral orientation to the welfare of the family created a basis, as he saw it, for ongoing political and economic backwardness.

4. James Ferguson (2005) suggests that James C. Scott's (1998) approach fails to acknowledge important contextual shifts attendant to globalization that make oil companies and other corporate actors important partners in neoliberal governance. NGOs, similarly, have come to mediate visions and strategies of governance in a global world.

5. Escobar (1995) has suggested that the vision of such policies originated in the "development dreams" of the postwar period. Moore (1999), however, suggests that much deeper colonial histories are implicated. For critical anthropological discussions of development projects in the province of Nuoro, Sardinia, from 1950 to 1980, consult Bodemann (1979), Berger (1986), Vargas-Cetina (1993a), and Ayora-Diaz (1993). For a historical perspective see also Clark (1996).

6. See Schneider and Schneider (2003) for a discussion of Sicilian mafia and anti-mafia. See Schneider's (1998) volume on orientalism in Italy, and particularly chapters by Gibson, for discussion of race and southern Italian "deviancy," and Patriarca, for discussion of statistics in the Italian Mezzogiorno.

7. Garrett Hardin's (1968) famous essay on "the tragedy of the commons"

was published just at the time that Italy, with encouragement from the new European Community, was first attempting to establish Gennargentu Park in Sardinia. The essay summed up the perspective of liberal economic theory at that time toward common property regimes, supporting arguments to reform land tenure systems in favor of private or state-owned property. Hardin predicted that common property resources would inevitably be depleted by over-exploitation because individual "free-riders" would derive greater immediate economic gain from overusing that resource than they would suffer loss due to the degradation and declining "carrying capacity" of that resource over time. With respect to environmental conservation, the tragedy of the commons theory was powerfully suggestive. The modernizing states of postwar Europe were necessarily concerned with their economies and the role that different categories of natural resources would play in national development. Common lands, legislators believed, could neither be efficiently exploited nor efficiently conserved for the future.

8. Sarah Green's (2005) study of conservation programs in Greece also questions the role of "re-branding" marginal or peripheral regions in Europe to highlight biodiversity and nature.

9. Since the mid-1980s, European cooperation has focused upon regional-based programs of structural investment in lieu of older national-level incentive-based development initiatives. Refer, for example, to the *Programma Integrato Mediterraneo* on Sardinia (EC 1988), in which environment and development figured as a prominent theme. Reforms to the Common Agricultural Policy have also had particularly important impacts in Sardinia (see Eckelmans and Smeets 1990; Fennell 1987; Joyce and Schneider 1988; Rosenblatt et al. 1988; Navarru 1989).

10. Anthropologists have been interested in the domains of practice within which European national identities are reinvented in the context of the European Union. Bellier 2000; Borneman and Fowler (1997); Bellier and Wilson (2000); Wilson and Smith (1993); Macdonald (1993). According to Cris Shore (2000), the European Commission's efforts to foster pan-European identities were focused on the invention of symbolic attributes common to modern nation-states, including new government buildings, a new flag, common currency, passports, and narratives of common history.

11. This precedent for the expulsion of indigenous peoples from conservation areas is, unfortunately, anything but isolated. The quite recent removal of tribal people from a Tanzanian wilderness park is the subject of Brockington's (2002) monograph on "fortress conservation."

12. Cronon (1995) reminds us that the wilderness "preserved" in the American West, the wilderness that provided a model for the export of nature conser-

vation to Europe and its colonies, was the wilderness of urban, white, Western, and post-enlightenment fantasies of modernity. Roderick Neumann (1998) and Jim Igoe (2004), for example, develop related arguments with respect to the colonial legacies of wilderness conservation in East Africa. This might be understood as a form of cultural erasure (cf. Braun 2002; Perley 2006).

13. Penelope Harvey's (1996) account of national exhibits at the World Fair of 1992 suggests an important comparison. According to Harvey, many prosperous nation-states sought to portray advanced national culture as the effect of cutting-edge "high" technology. By employing dramatic technologies such as IMAX film, simulating hyper-real, immediate, and intimate experiences for the audiences, these nations affirmed their participation in the universal "culture of no culture" (Haraway 1997) associated with science and technology. This constituted a claim to both cultural and temporal location in a global world of progress. National parks, I suggest, can be understood as a similar "technology of nationhood" (Harvey 1996).

14. See critical reflections on James C. Scott by Ferguson (2005), Li (2005), and Sivaramakrishnan (2005a).

15. Arturo Escobar's (1995) discussion of "ecological capital" suggests one of the critical weaknesses in Scott's approach to the problem of resource governance. Adopting a post-structuralist paradigm for the analysis of "regimes" of international development, Escobar has highlighted the discursive construction of objects of intervention, concepts and theories, and the system of power mediating development practices, as well as the forms of subjectivity fostered through the experience of development projects (ibid., 10). From this perspective, "sustainable development" models widespread during the 1980s and 1990s constituted a form of "ecological capital" that reasserted the primary role of science and technology in defining and implementing ecologically friendly initiatives for economic growth; at the same time, "sustainable development" models reaffirmed the role of expertise and planning in the mediation of human-environment relations (ibid., 202). Like Scott, Escobar recognizes the Enlightenment heritage of ideas about modernity and development. Yet Scott is limited in his ability to appreciate the social and cultural dimensions of political subjectivity. Escobar, in contrast, is able to engage both the nuances and the ambiguities of development programs as a dynamic play of scales engaging diverse cultural practices and imaginations.

16. Between 1992 and 2004, the LIFE fund spent approximately 1.36 billion euros to support projects costing an estimated total of 3.6 billion euros; an additional budget of 317 million euros extended the program through 2006. The next phase of the program, 2007-2013, corresponds to Europe's Sixth Environmental Action Programme.

17. The plan called for the fencing off of areas used by threatened birds for nesting (accipiter *Gentiles arrigoni*) and to protect a species of bush (*Ribes sardum*).

18. To my knowledge, the only WWF office in central Sardinia, located in the capital of Nuoro province, was never actually open while I was in the field for two years. I had no success contacting WWF representatives for an interview.

19. David Harvey (1989) discussed globalization as increasing the scale and speed of interactions across defined geographic spaces; see also Smith (1998) and Brenner (1997) for discussion of globalization as an effect of scale-making. In my use of the term "scale-making," I follow Tsing (1997, 2005) rather than these debates in geography, since I highlight the crafts of cultural imagination and not the objective processes of globalization. A parallel approach is demonstrated in Paige West's (2006) beautiful examination of conservation as development in Papua New Guinea, in which the author discusses visions of place as an effect of imagination.

20. Yaakov Garb (1997), for example, examines how cultural translations of the story of the Chipko movement (famous rural Indian women of the 1980s who hugged trees to prevent the clear-cutting of communal forests) became connected to larger narratives in international discourses about women's role in development and environmental sustainability. The story has travelled and been retold in many versions, serving as a metaphor for other "local" events to become linked to global narratives as well. But if the Chipko movement is celebrated as a positive example of how "local" peasant women protect with their lives the "global" environmental resources that their families depend upon from the predations of "global" capitalism, not all "local" events are so felicitous to the eyes of cosmopolitan outsiders. Both Chipko women and Orgosolo women have enacted political protests to defend communal resources from outside exploitation because the well-being of their families depended upon them. Yet the latter are trapped in webs of signification, not of their own making, that facilitate ungenerous perceptions of their actions as the self-interested and unreflexive outcome of backward social and cultural orientations.

21. Luis Vivanco points out that environmental films also deploy stories about science, culture, and environment to reify "normative visions of the causes and consequences of environmental degradation" (2002, 1195). According to him, the objectivist, realist pretensions of documentaries about the rainforest of Costa Rica, for example, tend to invoke iconic images of cultural groups, and portray morality tales involving third-world peoples and heroic environmental activists. An important contrast between Vivanco's South American case and the present study of marginal Europe is found in the different ways that resident peoples fit into the stereotypical categories of indigeneity.

22. From WWF Panda Passport Website, "Panda Passport—How It Works" (http://passport.panda.org/explanations/index.cfm?fuseaction+howitworks&lang=13, consulted May 2002; page revised and moved to http://passport.panda.org/about).

23. Anthropologists, sociologists, and cultural studies scholars have been increasingly interested in the possibility of distinctive "cybercultures," "virtual communities," and virtual social movements that are made possible by new electronic communications technologies. Escobar's (1994) exploration of "cyberculture," for example, builds on themes related to the impact of science and technology in society (cf. Hess and Layne 1991; Hess 1995), particularly at the confluence of exciting developments in computer engineering and genetics. Certainly the websites such as those I reflect upon here hardly reveal much in ethnographic terms, since despite the romance of "interactive" sites, communication is predominantly one-way.

24. Sydney Tarrow claims that such "computer-mediated communications" have become important to transnational social movements but qualifies that to organize collective action effectively, they must be "both rooted in domestic social networks and connected to one another through common ways of seeing the world, or through informal or organizational ties" (Tarrow 1994 cited in Diani 1999, 10). Diani argues that the use of websites, e-mail, discussion groups, bulletin boards, and other means of electronic communication mainly facilitates and strengthens pre-existing ties within face-to-face communities and social or organizational networks (1999, 12). The point that virtual social movements tend to be embedded in "real-life" social ties and practices does not, however, diminish the significance invested by many people in their very use of the "World Wide Web." Here McLuhan's (1994) famous insight "the medium is the message" is relevant, as the marketing campaigns for Macintosh, Vaio, and other Internet-ready personal computers were quick to establish. It is not only introduction of new scales and means of social interaction that are at stake, but also the very idea of these novelties that enhanced new framings for "imagined communities" (Anderson 1983).

25. William Gibson coined the idea of "cyberspace" in his well-known cyberpunk novel about "the Net," Neuromancer. The term quickly gained favor among science fiction fans and hackers themselves, and has entered the vocabulary of anthropology as a gloss for all spheres of sociocultural interaction associated with computer-based communications (Hakken 1999). In theory, on the Net, one can learn anything instantly and speak directly to anyone, anywhere, anytime. Christopher Pound mischievously suggests that the term "cyberspace" highlights a paradox of "amnesiac subjectivity," in which the establishment of a grid of telecommunications that creates the geography of cyberspace occurs

at the same time as an operation to efface all evidence of distance (1995, 535–36). For Pound, then, cyberspace is not the embodiment of time-space compression associated with late modernity, but rather the experiential dissolution of space itself. My own concern is with the symbolic implications of somewhat less sophisticated folk models of cyberspace evident in the daily public discourses of news media and commercial advertising, and particularly in the discourses of transnational ENGOs themselves. Cyberspaces are predicated upon new technology that became simple to use and widely available in the Western world during the 1990s (Askew and Wilk 2002, xi). Since the technology itself has been rapidly improving, users are able to perceive and present themselves as riding the crest of progress in a swiftly changing world.

26. These authors question how transformations in the "new media order" have affected Europe. They argue, for example, that the shift away from nationally based broadcasting networks to commercial broadcasting services delivered by global corporations like Time Warner, Sony, and the Walt Disney Company has contributed to the re-imagining of identity in the new Europe as fundamentally shaped by globalization (Morley and Robins 1995).

27. Hakken's (1999) experiences with computer technology networks in Norway, Sheffield, and New York indicate that especially among the architects of cyberspace, the folk model of a "computer revolution" that marks a fundamental transformation in the nature of culture and society is widespread. The technological optimism usually associated with perceived progress toward "computopia" tends to ignore that even in Western nations, access to cyberspace is often limited by class and education. The term often used to describe this is "the digital divide" (Compaine 2001).

28. If the envisioned emergence of an "ecological democracy" entails the blurring of distinctions between public and private and the ultimate absorption of the state by civil society (Beck 1995), then computer-mediated communications are usually assumed to be an important means to this goal. In comparison with ecologically dubious forms of motor transport, electronic communications media confer the advantage of low environmental impact in addition to relatively low cost, flexibility, and ease of adoption.

29. For example, Mark Smith's vision of "ecological citizenship" compatible with the values of "deep ecology" (cf. Naess 1989) attempts to reformulate Beck's model of civil society so that "relations of entitlement and obligation break through the species barrier and beyond . . . human beings have obligations to animals, trees, mountains, oceans, and other members of the biotic community" (Smith 1998, 99). Smith insists that the complete merging of public and private spheres is necessary to support a reassessment of human obligations to the non-human world. Smith's radical formulation strongly personalizes and

individualizes human responsibility and invests doubt in the capacity of state institutions to deal with the complexity, uncertainty, and interconnectedness of ecosystems.

30. Argyrou's (2005) historical approach tempts an oversimplification of a social movement that is certainly fragmented and hybridized across a diverse range of cultural spaces and intellectual histories. His overview of the epistemological underpinnings of Western and "global" environmental movements is nevertheless persuasive.

31. See "L'Avventura del Gennargentu," copyright GianMarco Ibba 2000, http://www.parcogennargentu.it/ParcoGennargentu6.htm, accessed March 15, 2009.

32. In another comparative case from nearby Greece, Theodossopoulos (2003) describes how rural farmers' attitudes to turtle preservation are systematically misunderstood by a Greek conservation NGO, which similarly constructed discourses of blame.

33. Another example of WWF discourses of allochronism in Sardinia can be found in the series of coffee-table books co-produced by the ENGO at the end of the 1980s. In the first volume, *Sardinia to be saved: A system of national parks and reserves for the great wild expanses of our island* (Colomo and Ticca 1987), hardly a person was pictured amid the hundreds of illustrations celebrating the exemplary geological, faunal, and floral assets of the Gennargentu mountains. Like the Gennargentu Park website created later under the auspices of the WWF, this colorful tome accomplished the work of "forgetting" that central Sardinia has been continuously inhabited since prehistoric times. Positive influence on the environment was virtually reduced to the ancient production of archaeological sites.

34. He said in Italian, "*O Tere'! Noi siamo i cowboy di America!*"

35. In Italian this was, "*Noi siamo gli Indiani di America: stanno per rubarci la terra!*"

36. "*Noi viviamo nel Old West*," I was told in Italian.

6. Walking in Via Gramsci

Sections of this chapter were developed from "In the Rustic Kitchen: Real Talk and Reciprocity," published by the author in *Ethnology* 40, no. 4 (2001): 329–45, and "Murals and the Memory of Resistance in Sardinia," published by the author in *Irish Journal of Anthropology* 4 (2002): 7–25.

1. By the time of Italian fascism, individuals suspected of criminal activity in Sardinia could be sent to the *confini*, internment camps on the continent, for up

to five years (Cagnetta 1954, 167–68). Trials were held before police tribunals that possessed the power to condemn without proof. As communism gained strength, anti-banditry policies were used to persecute left-wing activists (ibid., 267–68). Emilio Lussu, a key figure in the left-wing Sardinian ethnonationalist movement and later, the Italian Socialist Party in Sardinia, experienced the *confini* himself. In Orgosolo, a number of young communist organizers were targeted in the same way, particularly during the late 1940s and early 1950s. The subjects of exile returned to Orgosolo after a few years, and generally maintained left-wing political loyalties. See also the account of Luigi Podda (1976).

2. This was the cooperative that was criticized in town for its work in providing services for a WWF conference held in Orgosolo.

3. There were then sixteen councilors in Orgosolo from the PCI and Partito Socialista Italiano (PSI) coalition, as well as four councilors from the "progressive" wing of the DC.

4. "*Si sono tutti sistemati, Tere,*" she told me in colloquial Italian.

5. Consult Spotts and Wieser (1986) on Italy's "difficult democracy"; see also Pasquino (1995); Piattoni (1998).

6. See Caferra (1995); della Porta (1996) on the issue of "*tangentopoli,*" the corruption scandals; see also Mammarella (1995); Scoppola (1995); Furlong (1996); and Hellman (1996) on transformations of the major parties.

7. David Kertzer's (1996) discussion of the history of the Italian Communist Party documents the existence of such Catholic vs. Communist partisan divides elsewhere in Italy, notably Bologna. Consult Kertzer (1980) for an extended discussion of Vatican policy vis-à-vis the Italian Communist Party during the 1960s and 1970s.

8. She said, "*Nois semus sempere abbarau [gasi].*"

9. See discussion in chapter 2.

10. Lussu helped to found the ethnonationalist-oriented Sardinian Action Party (Partito Sardo D'Azione, PS d'Az), took a stand against fascism, and was criminalized and sent into internal exile on the island of Lipari. He escaped to France and Spain until the armistice of 1943, when he returned to Italy and resumed a key role in the Italian Action Party. As a result of ideological conflicts, he left to join the Italian Socialist Party, serving as a member of Italian parliament. In 1964 he broke away again to help establish a splinter party, the Italian Socialist Party of Proletarian Unity (PSIUP).

11. Cammett's (1967) biography of Gramsci is useful for its detailed account of Gramsci's early life in Sardinia, as well as its rich account of the context of Gramsci's work. There is so much to be said about Antonio Gramsci in relation to the Sardinian context and the question of power that it far exceeds the scope of this discussion. For further debate, see, for example, Convegno Internazionale

di Studi Gramsciani (1967), Laclau and Mouffe (2001), Anne Showstack Sassoon (1982, 1987), and resources on the website of the International Gramsci Society (http://www.internationalgramcisociety.org, consulted July 12, 2008).

12. A number of anthropologists (Comaroff and Comaroff 1991; Crehan 2002; Smith 2004) insist that despite widespread interpretations of "hegemony" as thinly cultural, Gramsci was concerned with the whole mesh of cultural, economic, and social processes that enabled the production and reproduction of power relations and their legitimacy.

13. Gramsci's complicated discussions anticipated some important themes later explored in post-structuralist theories. His writing on hegemony indicated an early concern with discourses and the role of institutions in naturalizing relations of power, issues that returned to prominence again in the guise of Foucauldian analyses of authoritative discourse. For example, his interest in the balance between physical coercive force, as exercised by the state, and the mechanisms of civil society that produce ideological persuasion hints at the search for a complex vision of power, approaching that articulated by Foucault (1978) in his critique of the repressive hypothesis. Similarly, Gramsci's devotion to exploring the hegemonic role of intellectuals foresees some of the work carried on by Pierre Bourdieu (1984, 1991) on the microdynamics of social class and its political dimensions.

14. It is worth noting that the historical agro-pastoral context of highland Sardinia is perhaps a little different from other well-known cases in Sicily and Southern Italy, where latifundia played a significant role in the development of political patronage systems (clientelism). Political patronage and clientelist relations are certainly important in Sardinia, but they are configured rather differently, in part because of the strength of collective property systems there.

15. Prior to his (1971) *Prison Notebooks*, Gramsci outlined an approach to the Southern Question in 1926. See translation and commentary by Pasquale Verdicchio (Gramsci 1995). Urbinati's (1998) excellent essay on the body of Gramsci's work regarding Italian nationalism, political consciousness, and the problem of the South is also useful.

16. These individuals might be persuaded in favor of the communist movement, but their class position was inherently alienated from their peasant origins, and peasants themselves felt ambivalent about their leadership. Only by "feeling" a part of these classes as an outcome of ongoing participation in agricultural production could these organic intellectuals begin to articulate effective counter-hegemonies that would resonate with rural life experiences in the aftermath of recent historical shifts (Gramsci 1971, 418).

17. *Orgosolo Novembre 1968* (pamphlet), 16–17.

18. The governing local coalition of 1995–2000 was an unusual collabora-

tion of the PDS, the Partito della Rifondazione Comunista (formerly the PCI), PSd'Az, the Partito Popolare Italiano (formerly the DC), and an independent.

19. In 1993 and 1997, in response to invitations from the town council to paint new murals, del Casino depicted role models such as Gramsci, Gandhi, Che Guevara, Rosa Luxemburg, Pablo Neruda, Massimo Troisi, Vittorio de Seta, and Franco Pinna.

20. See "Sa lota de Pratobello" (1969) in Marotto (1996, 46–49). The poet emphasizes the experience of land-poor herders returning to Orgosolo after the spring transhumance, only to find that communal pastures were closed to them.

21. Originally published in *La Nuova Sardegna*, August 21, 1997, p. 22; reprinted in Rubanu and Fistrale (1998). My translation.

22. Rubanu and Fistrale (1998, 19) suggest that murals have declined as a form of popular political dialogue, even though more and more have been painted throughout several Sardinian towns, because town councils have begun to invite professional artists to visit their towns and paint in order to beautify the area and attract tourists. Mural painting has, accordingly, become professionalized.

23. Sanguinetti, too, was instrumental in cultural revitalization efforts. Some of these were focused upon religious processions and companies. In Orgosolo, he was able to re-establish a company of male *priori*, who accompanied statues on procession through the streets and into the countryside. Given the tendency for religious practice to be divided along lines of gender, this brought some prestige back to male participation in the Roman Catholic Church.

24. Practicing Catholics in the parish also maintain a similar museum in the house once occupied by the Beata Antonia Mesina. It is visited by pilgrims accompanied by a member of the parish.

25. See the Sardigna Ruja website maintained by the Sotziu de Sos Emigrantes Sardos ("Pratobello 1969," http://sardignaruja.altervista.org/content/view/27/2/, consulted July 12, 2008), which presents both the transcripts of the conference (Sardigna Ruja 2005) and its efforts to campaign against nuclear waste disposal and NATO activities in Sardinia.

7. Sin, Shame, and Sheep

An earlier version of this chapter appeared as "Sin, Saints and Sheep in Sardinia" in *Identities: Global Studies in Culture and Power* 13 (2006): 533–56.

1. See, for example, Walley (2004), Brechin et al. (2003), Goldman (2005), and Agrawal (2005).

2. At the level of the EU, various and often mutually impinging initiatives convey multiple visions, concerns, and aspirations with regard to sustainable development. These have been directed, for example, toward species and biotope conservation; support to agricultural enterprises, forestry, and ecotourism; and structural funding in economically marginal areas.

3. While many pastoral towns suffered serious demographic decline in the postwar period, in Orgosolo this was less pronounced, perhaps because of access to an exceptionally large commons. The population remained steady, around 5,000 people, through the 1990s. Despite significant economic transformation and occupational diversification in Orgosolo since the 1960s, the Commons is a crucial resource for herders whose production strategies are central to the formal and informal economy of the town. Herding still supplies "authentic" meats and cheeses to both local consumers and tourist enterprises. With over 8,000 hectares of municipally managed common lands, Orgosolo has maintained a vital element of pastoralism in addition to tourism and agroforestry.

4. One of the problematic elements in Scott's (1985, 1990) reading of Antonio Gramsci (1971) is his apparent willingness to conflate "hegemony" with "false consciousness." Moore (1998) suggests that Gramsci's formulation of subalternity actually resists the strict bifurcation of power and resistance, political consciousness and false consciousness, onstage and offstage, upon which Scott predicates his critique. According to Moore, Gramsci's vision implies that the spaces of power and performance are always entangled with those of resistance, so that domination is inherently prone to disruption, while resistance can never be relegated to an autonomous sphere. This contradicts many of the spatial metaphors commonly applied in studies of resistance, and highlights the social construction of resistance itself as part of an ongoing process of hegemony. See also Moore (2005) for further discussion.

5. For further discussion of links between hospitality and politics at Orgosolo, see Heatherington (2001).

6. It is important to recognize that all "older shepherds" do not necessarily share the same viewpoints or symbolic strategies. Marotto commented (personal communication) that he did not like the "Animals of the Gennargentu Park" poem because it implicitly restricted the capacity of townspeople to change their minds in favor of a national park, if the structure of the plan were altered to suit the needs of local people.

7. Where their political interests might conflict, as for example in a debate on leasing more areas of traditional pasture to the state forestry enterprise to provide more jobs in forestry, some herders argued that other residents were selling out the values of the community. The two successful local cooperatives

were severely criticized for their distance from "traditional" occupations and the state support they enjoyed.

8. For more discussion, see Heatherington (1999).

9. This recalls Donald S. Moore's (1998, 1999) notes on popular opposition movements in Zimbabwe. There, women's roles in the struggles over territory that occurred during the 1970s confirmed the connections of women to the broader nationalist movement, and supported the later land claims even of women not originally native to the area, because they had "suffered for the land." The role of Orgosolo women in the Pratobello demonstration served a similar function in the place-based practices of resistance that would later incorporate links to the iconic Antonia Mesina.

10. One other councilor suggested that it was better to have a female mayor, because as a woman she had a "purer" identity than a man.

11. Bourdieu predicted that those socioeconomic classes relatively disempowered with respect to state institutions would commonly exhibit apathy to politics and restrict themselves to dispositions of indifference (1984, 406; 1991, 175). In Orgosolo, this was frequently the case for regular council meetings, party meetings, and many demonstrations and political assemblies with a component of provincial-level representatives (that is, non-local, career politicians) participating. It was not the case, however, for town assemblies dealing with topics related to the management of Orgosolo's communal territory.

12. Such language shifts have been acknowledged as meaningful and patterned "code-switching" since the 1970s (Woolard 2004). Specific patterns in code-switching are now recognized as important indicators of how communities of speakers are engaged with macro-processes, and how they understand and negotiate their own relationship to social structure (Gal 1987). See also Jaffe (1999) for comparative insights on the role of language shifting in relation to identity politics and "resistance" in Corsica.

13. See Heatherington (2001).

14. K. Sivaramakrishnan points out that "at times social structures, roles, statuses and contingent factors modify agency and its consequences" (2005b, 351), so that internal contradictions are inherent in the riddle of how power and resistance are enmeshed. As Timothy Mitchell (1991, 573) discussed in his formidable critique of James C. Scott, the very language of "power" and "resistance" implies a binary world where ideologies and intentions can exist separately from material reality. The reproduction of this two-dimensional vision is itself an effect of power.

15. Following contributions in Fernandez and Huber (2001), I see irony not as a mere literary device, but as an element of political subjectivity. In this sense,

the ironic metaphors embedded in the politics of the weak are not a matter of passive reflection, but rather, of strategic action. At the same time, self-irony suffuses political practice with the recognition of limits to subversive play.

16. While people often told me with pride about participating in the large demonstration at Pratobello in 1969, only a few women spoke of feminist demonstration in Orgosolo during the seventies. They mentioned, with some embarrassment and chagrin, that they had marched with a group of "hardened feminists" from the city of Nuoro, shouting "the vagina is ours, and we'll keep it to ourselves" while a group of men followed behind, heckling raucously that "the penis is ours, and we'll put it where we want to." Their efforts were not rewarded with reverent memories, and the category of "feminist" is not a popular one in Orgosolo today.

17. Orgolese shepherd Peppino Marotto (1996), for example, published an important collection of his Sardinian poems as part of a language initiative. Figuring prominently in his work was the theme of the nature of the Supramonte, the high plain where shepherds often resided with their animals for months at a time until it became more common for shepherds to be able to afford motor vehicles. His work has been widely acclaimed and appreciated in Sardinia, yet mainly in a spirit of cultural, linguistic, and literary celebration.

8. Beyond Ethnographic Refusal

1. As Michael Dove has pointed out, "The study of indigenous movements and violence, indigenous resource rights and knowledge and the deployment of indigenous status and identity all raise questions about the politics and ethics of research" (2006, 201–2).

2. In 1990, for example, between July and August there were 1,500 fires on the island, with the province of Nuoro (the highland region) suffering the greatest losses: 5,383 hectares of pastureland, 1,359 hectares of forest, and 113 hectares of other land-use areas (*L'Unione Sarda*, October 2, 1990, p. 7). Up to 90 percent of these fires were attributed to agro-pastoral activities, particularly the clearing of pastures by shepherds (*L'Unione Sarda*, October 4, 1990, p. 24). Real-time and recent satellite data on forest fires in Sardinia can be accessed at the Incendi di Sardegna website, maintained by Centro di Ricerca Progetto San Marco, Università la Sapienza di Roma (http://www.incendi.sardegna.it/, accessed July 12, 2008). For more information on the history of fire prevention and current measures in place for fighting fires in Sardinia, see "Il problema degli incendi," Sardegna Foreste web portal maintained by the Ente Foreste Sardegna (http://www.sardegnaambiente.it/foreste/foreste_parchi/incendi.htm, accessed July 12, 2008).

3. Michael Herzfeld's (1997) concept of "cultural intimacy" might be adopted to explain the cautiousness with which Sardinians habitually approached public discussion of "faults" or "sins" that might be attributed to their community or to their culture as a whole.

4. *Ferula communis*; an herb that makes animals sick when eaten.

5. In his essay on two experiments with environmental partnerships in rural Samoa, Paul Alan Cox (2000) emphasizes that strong elements of local control over partnership projects are critical in order to ensure that culturally constructed perceptions of environmental justice and privilege are taken into account. This, he suggests, is a prerequisite to successful conservation. Anthropological approaches to environmental justice developed in Zerner (2000) strongly support this contention with a range of complementary case studies.

6. Ciriacy-Wantrup and Bishop (1975) criticized Garrett Hardin's (1968) "tragedy of the commons" theory as having conflated common property regimes with conditions of unregulated open access, and pointed out that corporate institutions (such as small towns) were able to limit and supervise the use of some natural resources owned in common. Anthropologists working on issues of cultural ecology and cooperation were able to support this challenge to the tragedy of the commons theory (Netting 1977); McCay and Acheson 1987; Ostrom 1990). Scholars have confirmed that both success and failure of sustainable management could be associated with communal property, private property, and government property alike (Feeny et al. 1990, 12). In some cases, commons users have been empirically observed to react to declining yields, define a community, allocate use-rights, and sustainably manage communal property. Communal property arrangements can be a valid means of resource management, yet where important socioeconomic transformations have occurred, co-management solutions may prove more effective than autonomous local management of ecosystems. The role of "disembedding processes" (Giddens 1979) in the apparent failure of local Commons management techniques in Orgosolo during the 1970s is, however, ambiguous, for reasons I describe in the text.

7. Orgosolo illustrates how unsatisfactorily the shifting and multidimensional representations of community can be understood in terms of "the existence of cultural values" or "the strength of community ties." Networks of residents in Orgosolo are differently positioned with regard to occupation, education, gender, religion, and political orientation. Nevertheless, virtually all attempted to affirm and express a holistic community identity and direct its implications for political issues and local development.

The more public and open the occasion, the more forcefully encompassing become the assertions of overarching communal identity.

1. Whereas the plan for a national park in Sardinia mainly affected the provinces of Nuoro and Ogliastra in the most famously "backward" and "undeveloped" areas of the island, one local intellectual commented that the new law levels the playing ground among coastal towns. According to her, many of the landowners in the cities and the thriving tourist areas can no longer distance themselves from the residents in less prosperous zones, whose aspirations to build or expand living quarters on their properties near the beach have been similarly thwarted. Demonstrations are being held in some towns to protest the new law; political opposition would surely have been overwhelming had the Soru government not employed strategic measures to ensure that it passed.

2. See discussions of global visions of the "blue planet" by Ingold (1993); Lury et al. (2000); Tsing (1997); Jasanoff (2004).

3. Highlighting the spiritual aspects of ecological philosophies practiced by small-scale subsistence hunter-gatherers in different parts of the world, Posey naturalized the contributions of tribal groups to sustainable environments. He argued, for example, that "indigenous peoples frequently view themselves as guardians and stewards of nature. Harmony and equilibrium are central concepts in most cosmologies" (Posey 2003, 125).

4. See, for example, recent contributions by Menzies (2006) and Sillitoe (2006).

5. Posey himself indicted the signatories of the Convention on Biological Diversity, for example, for failing to go far enough in protecting intellectual property rights over local knowledge and indigenous sovereignty over natural resources (Posey 2003, 131–32). Ultimately, the international guidelines of the CBD leave it in the hands of government elites to arbitrate which local communities truly embody "traditional lifestyles relevant for the conservation and sustainable use of biological diversity" (UNCED 1992).

GLOSSARY OF ITALIAN AND SARDINIAN WORDS

Italian Words

api.   Bees; name chosen by members of a mural group

Barbagia.   Roman name for region of highland central Sardinia

caccia.   Hunt

canto a tenores. Tenor singing; traditional Sardinian male a capella
                 quartet

corso.   Avenue

cronaca nera.   Black chronicle of tragic and violent events found in
                 news

disgrazia.   Disgrace; misfortune

ferragosto.   Assumption Day; festival of the Madonna Assumption

finta.   Fake; put on

giudicato.   Jurisdiction; a medieval Sardinian political unit

inchiesta.   Inquest

macchia.   Macquis; Mediterranean scrub; hiding place for outlaws

malessere.   State of suffering; poor quality of life

muflone.   Mouflon; *Ovis musimon*; indigenous species of wild
                 sheep

nuraghe.   A prehistoric structure unique to Sardinia

omertà.   Silence before the authorities

passegiata.   Stroll; walk

pastoralismo.   Herding; when capitalized, a Sardinian cultural system
                 related to pastoral traditions

pastore.	Herder; usually a shepherd, goatherd, or cowherd
piazza.	Plaza
putana.	Prostitute
sistemato.	Settled down [with jobs, homes, families]
Supramonte.	Area of high plains in central Sardinia
via.	Street
Zia.	Aunt; respectful term of address for female elder
Zio.	Uncle; respectful term of address for male elder

Sardinian Words

a su fris'u.	In the fresh/cool air
arrostu.	Roast (meat)
balentia.	Courage; manliness; ability to protect ones' interests
cricca.	Friendship group; a "gang" or circle of friends
cumonale.	Commons; communal territory; common lands
ferula.	*Ferula communis*; an herb that makes animals sick
galera.	Prison
istoriande.	Chit-chatting; telling stories
maleducau.	Ignorant; rude; poorly socialized
massaia.	Homemaker
priore.	Participant in male confraternity in the Roman Catholic Church
priorissa.	Participant in female company associated with the Roman Catholic Church, usually an elder woman
prithiosa.	Lazy
pulinde.	Cleaning
Tzia.	Aunt; respectful term of address for female elder
Tziu.	Uncle; respectful term of address for male elder
vardau.	Fallows system
velutu.	Modified traditional costume worn by elder men
vestedda.	Modified traditional costume worn by elder women

REFERENCES

Abélès, Marc. 2000. Virtual Europe. In *An anthropology of the European Union: Building, imagining and experiencing the new Europe*, ed. Irene Bellier and Thomas M. Wilson, 31–52. Oxford: Berg.

Abu-Lughod, Lila. 1986. *Veiled sentiments: Honor and poetry in a Bedouin society*. Berkeley: University of California Press.

aco (Amministrazione Comunale di Orgosolo) et al. 1997. *Orgosolo: Omaggio a Franco Pinna*. Rome: Frigidaire.

Agrawal, Arun. 2005. *Environmentality: Technologies of government and the making of subjects*. Durham, NC: Duke University Press.

Agyeman, Julian, Robert Bullard, and Bob Evans, eds. 2003. *Just sustainabilities: Development in an unequal world*. Cambridge, MA: MIT Press.

Alpers, Svetlana. 1990. The museum as a way of seeing. In *The poetics and politics of museum display*, ed. S. Lavine and I. Karp. Washington, D.C.: Smithsonian Institution.

Anderson, Benedict. 1991 [1983]. *Imagined communities: Reflections on the origin and spread of nationalism*. London and New York: Verso.

Angioni, Giulio. 1983. *A fuoco dentro/A fogu aintru*. Cagliari: EDES.

———. 1989. *I pascoli erranti. Antropologia del pastore in Sardegna*. Naples: Liguori.

APN (Amministrazione Provinciale di Nuoro). 1999. *Cos'è il Parco del Gennargentu?* Official information pamphlet.

Appadurai, Arjun, ed. 1988. *The social life of things*. Cambridge: Cambridge University Press.

———. 1996. *Modernity at large: Cultural dimensions of globalization*. Minneapolis: University of Minnesota Press.

Aretxaga, Begoña. 1997. *Shattering silence: Women, nationalism, and political subjectivity in Northern Ireland*. Princeton, NJ: Princeton University Press.

Argyrou, Vassos. 1996. *Tradition and modernity in the Mediterranean: The wedding as symbolic struggle*. Cambridge: Cambridge University Press.

———. 1997. Keep Cyprus clean: Littering, pollution and otherness. *Cultural Anthropology* 12(2): 159–78

———. 2005. *The logic of environmentalism*. Oxford: Berghahn Press.

Asch, Michael, and Colin Sampson. 2004. On "the return of the native." *Current Anthropology* 45 (2): 261–62.

Askew, Kelly, and Richard Wilk, eds. 2002. *The Anthropology of media: A reader*. Malden, MA: Blackwell.

Assembly of First Nations. 2006. Assembly of First Nations chiefs express concern and strong opposition regarding prime minister's comments on "race-based" fisheries. Press release.

Assmuth, Laura. 1997. *Women's work, women's worth: Changing lifecourses in highland Sardinia*. Helsinki: Finnish Anthropological Society.

Ayora-Diaz, Steffan Igor. 1993. Representations and occupations: Shepherds' choices in Sardinia. Ph.D. diss., McGill University.

Bandinu, Bachisio. 2006. *Il Pastoralismo*. Milano: Zonza Editore.

Banfield, Edward. 1958. *The Moral Basis of a Backward Society*. Glencoe, IL: The Free Press.

Barnes, Susan B. 2003. *Computer-mediated communication: Human-to-human communication across the Internet*. Boston: Pearson Education.

Baudrillard, Jean. 1983. *Simulations*. Trans. P. Foss, P. Patton, and P. Beitchman. New York: Semiotext(e).

Baumann, Gerd. 2006. Grammars of identity/alterity. In *Grammars of identity/ alterity*, ed. G. Baumann and A. Gingrich, 18–50. Oxford: Berghahn Books.

Baumann, Gerd, and Andre Gingrich, eds. 2006. *Grammars of identity/alterity: A structural approach*. Oxford: Berghahn Boooks.

Beck, Ulrich. 1995. *Ecological politics in an age of risk*. Malden, MA: Polity.

Bell, Catherine. 1992. *Ritual theory, ritual practice*. Oxford: Oxford University Press.

Bellier, Irène. 2000. A Europeanized elite? An anthropology of European Commission officials. In *Europeanization: Institutions, identities and citizenship*, ed. R. Harmsen and T. M. Wilson. Yearbook of European Studies 14. Amsterdam: Rodopi.

Bellier, Irène, and Thomas Wilson, eds. 2000. *An anthropology of the European Union: Building, imagining and experiencing the new Europe*. New York: Berg.

Bending, Tim, and Sergio Rosendo. 2006. Rethinking the mechanics of the "anti-politics machine." In *Development brokers and translators: The ethnography of aid and agencies*, ed. D. Lewis and D. Mosse, 217–38. Bloomfield, CT: Kumarian Press.

Berger, Allen H. 1986. Cooperation, conflict and production environment in highland Sardinia: A study of the associational life of transhumant shepherds. Ph.D. diss., Columbia University.

———. 1990. Cos'è la Barbagia? I problemi della definizione e della delimitazione di una zona culturale. *Quaderni Bolotanesi* 16:71–82.

Berglund, Eeva. 1998. *Knowing nature, knowing science: An ethnography of environmental activism.* Cambridge: White Horse.

Biersack, Aletta. 1999. The Mount Kare python and his gold: Totemism and ecology in Papua New Guinea highlands. *American Anthropologist* 101 (1): 68–87.

Blok, Anton. 1972. The Peasant and the brigand: Social banditry reconsidered. *Comparative Studies of Society and History* 14:494–503.

———. 1981. Rams and billy-goats: A key to the Mediterranean code of honour. *Man* 16 (3): 427–40.

Bodemann, Yark Michal. 1979. Telemula: Aspects of the micro-organisation of backwardness in central Sardinia. Ph.D. diss., Brandeis University.

Borneman, John, and Nick Fowler. 1997. Europeanization. *Annual Review of Anthropology* 26:487–514.

Bourdieu, Pierre. 1977. *Outline of a theory of practice.* Cambridge: Cambridge University Press.

———. 1984. *Distinction: A social critique of the judgement of taste.* Cambridge, MA: Harvard University Press.

———. 1991. *Language and symbolic power.* Cambridge, MA: Harvard University Press.

Brandes, Stanley. 1992. Sex roles and anthropological research in rural Andalusia. In *Europe observed*, ed. J. Pina-Cabral and J. Campbell. Basingstoke: Macmillan.

Braudel, Fernand. 1972. The Mediterranean and the Mediterranean world in the age of Philip II. Trans. Siân Reynolds. New York: Harper & Row.

Braun, Bruce. 2002. *The intemperate rainforest: Culture and power on Canada's west coast.* Minneapolis: University of Minnesota Press.

———. 2006. Environmental issues: Global natures in the space of assemblage. *Progress in Human Geography* 30 (5): 644–54.

Braun, Bruce, and Noel Castree, eds. 1998. *Remaking reality: Nature at the millenium.* London: Routledge.

Brechin, Steven R., Meyer R. Wilshusen, Crystal L. Fortwangler, and Patrick C. West, eds. 2003. *Contested nature: Promoting international biodiversity and social justice in the twenty-first century.* Albany, NY: SUNY Press.

Brenner, Neil. 1997. Global, fragmented, hierarchical: Henri Lefebvre's geographies of globalization. *Public Culture* 10 (1): 137–69.

Brigaglia, Manlio, Alberto Boscolo, and Lorenzo Del Piano. 1995. *La Sardegna contemporanea*. Cagliari: Della Torre.

Brockington, Dan. 2002. *Fortress conservation*. Bloomington: University of Indiana Press.

Brosius, J. Peter. 1997. Endangered forest, endangered people: Environmentalist representations of indigenous knowledge. *Human Ecology* 25 (1): 47–69.

———. 1999a. Green dots, pink hearts: Displacing politics from the Malaysian rain forest. *American Anthropologist* 101 (1): 36–57.

———. 1999b. On the practice of transnational cultural critique. In Special issue on ethnographic presence: Environmentalism, indigenous rights and transnational cultural critique, ed. J. P. Brosius, *IDENTITIES: Global Studies in Culture and Power* 6 (2-3): 179–200.

———. 1999c. Analyses and interventions: Anthropological engagements with environmentalism. *Current Anthropology* 40 (3): 277–309.

Brosius, Peter, Anna Tsing, and Charles Zerner. 1998. Representing communities: Histories and politics of community-based natural resource management, *Society and Natural Resources* 11:157–68.

Brower, Barbara, and Barbara Rose Johnston, eds. 2007. *Disappearing peoples? Indigenous groups and ethnic minorities in south and central Asia*. Walnut Creek, CA: Left Coast Press.

Bryant, Raymond, and Sinead Bailey. 1997. *Third world political ecology*. London: Routledge.

Bull, Anna Cento. 2000. *Social identities and political cultures in Italy: Catholic, Communist and "Leghist' communities between civicness and localism*. Oxford: Berghahn Books.

Burnham, Philip. 2000. *Indian country, God's country: Native Americans and the national parks*. Washington, D.C.: Island Press.

Caferra, Vito Marino. 1995. La corruzione. In *La politica Italiana: Dizionario critico 1945-95*, ed. G. Pasquino, 405–16. Rome: Laterza.

Cagnetta, Franco. 1954. *Banditi a Orgosolo*. Reprinted 1975. Rimini: Guaraldi.

Camarda, Ignazio, Sabina Falchi, and Graziano Nudda. 1986. *L'ambiente naturale in Sardegna*. Sassari: Carlo Delfino.

Camboni, Gino, ed. 1991. *Il Gennargentu*. Cagliari: EdiSar.

Cammett, John M. 1967. *Antonio Gramsci and the origins of Italian communism*. Stanford, CA: Stanford University Press.

Campbell, Ben. 2005. Introduction: Changing policies and ethnographies of environmental engagement. *Conservation and Society* 3 (2): 280–322.

Campisi, Jack. 1992. *The Mashpee Indians: Tribe on Trial.* Syracuse, NY: Syracuse University Press.

Capitta, Gian Carlo, and Marisa Porcu Gaias, eds. 1990–91. *Lo stato dell'ambiente in Sardegna.* Sassari: Editrice Finopen.

Castree, Noel, and Bruce Braun. 2001. *Social nature: Theory, practice and politics.* Oxford and Malden, MA: Blackwell.

Casu, T., G. Lai, and G. L. Pinna, eds. 1984. *Guida all flora e alla fauna della Sardegna.* Editrice Archivio Fotografico Sardo, Nuoro.

CEC (Commission of the European Communities). 2006. *Establishing an environmental strategy for the Mediterranean.* Communication from the Commission to the Council and the European Parliament. Brussels, May 9, 2006.

Cederlöf, Gunnel, and K. Sivaramakrishnan. 2006. Introduction to *Ecological nationalisms,* ed. Cederlöf and Sivaramakrishnan, 1–40. Seattle: University of Washington Press.

Centro Parchi. 1997. *Effetto parco/Park effect.* Public information leaflet. Roma.

Cerrina, Filippo. 1987. Alla ricerca del bosco perduto. *Gardenia* 43 (Nov.): 85–95.

Chambers, Iain. 2008. *Mediterranean crossings: The politics of an interrupted modernity.* Durham, NC: Duke University Press.

Chapin, Mac. 2004. A challenge to conservationists. *WorldWatch,* November/December 2004, 17–31.

Chatwin, Bruce. 1988. *The songlines.* London: Penguin Books.

Checker, Melissa. 2005. *Polluted promises: Environmental racism and the search for justice in a southern town.* New York: NYU Press.

Chironi, G. 1998. Superior Stabat. *Nuoro Oggi* 11 (3/4): 9–10.

Circolo Giovanile di Orgosolo. 1973. In nome dell'uomo: No al parco dei padroni. In *Giornale di Barbagia,* ed. C. Pirisi. Cagliari: Editrice Sarda Fossataro.

Ciriacy-Wantrup, S.V., and Richard C. Bishop. 1975. "Common property" as a concept in natural resources policy. *Natural Resources Journal* 15:713–27.

Clark, Mari H. 1983. Variations on themes of male and female: Reflections on gender bias in fieldwork in rural Greece. *Women's Studies* 10:117–33.

Clark, Martin. 1989. Storia politica e sociale 1915–1975. In *L'Età contemporanea.* Vol. 4: *Dal governo piemontese agli anni sessanta del nostro secolo,* ed. B. Bandinu et al., 389-456. Milan: Jaca Book.

———. 1996. Sardinia: Cheese and modernization. In *Italian regionalism: History, identity and politics,* ed. C. Levy. Washington, D.C.: Berg.

Clifford, James. 1988. *The predicament of culture: Twentieth-century ethnography, literature and art.* Cambridge, MA: Harvard University Press.

Cole, Jeffrey. 1998. *The new racism in Europe: A sicilian ethnography*. Cambridge Studies in Social and Cultural Anthropology. Cambridge: Cambridge University Press.

Collier, Stephen J. 2006. Global assemblages. *Theory, Culture and Society* 23 (2–3): 399–401.

Collier, Stephen J., and Aiwha Ong. 2005. Global assemblages, anthropological problems. In *Global assemblages*, ed. Ong and Collier, 3–21. Malden, MA: Blackwell Press..

Colombano, Giuseppe. 1993. Il parco come realtà dinamica. In *Il parco del Gennargentu: Un'occasione da non perdere*, ed. Scuola di Pubblica Amministrazione et al. Conference proceedings, June 6–7, 1993, Desulo. Cagliari: Edisar.

Colomo, Salvatore, and Francesco Ticca, eds. 1987. *Sardegna da salvare. Un sistema di parchi e riserve naturali per le grandi distese selvagge della nostra isola*. Vol. 1. Nuoro: Archivio fotografico sardo.

Comaroff, Jean, and John L. Comaroff. 1991. *Of revelation and revolution*. Vol. 1: *Christianity, colonialism, and consciousness in South Africa*. Chicago: University of Chicago Press.

Compaine, Benjamin M., ed. 2001. *The digital divide*. Cambridge, MA: MIT Press.

Conklin, Beth A. 1997. Body paint, feathers and VCRs: Aesthetics and authenticity in Amazonian activism. *American Ethnologist* 24 (4): 711–37.

———. 2002. Shamans vs. pirates in the Amazonian treasure chest. *American Anthropologist* 104 (4): 1050–61.

———. 2003. Speaking truth to power. *Anthropology News*, May.

———. 2006. Environmentalism, global community, and the new indigenism. In *Inclusion and exclusion in the global arena*, ed. M. Kirsch. London: Routledge.

Conklin, Beth A., and Laura R. Graham. 1995. The shifting middle ground: Amazonian Indians and eco-politics. *American Anthropologist*, n.s., 97 (4): 695–710.

Convegno Internazionale di Studi Gramsciani. 1967. *Gramsci e la cultura contemporanea*. Atti del Convegno internazionale di studi gramsciani tenuto a Cagliari il 23–27 aprile 1967. Roma: Editori riuniti; Istituto Gramsci [1969-70].

Corda, Elettrio. 1989. *Storia di Orgosolo. 1837–1953*. Milano: Rusconi.

Cowan, Jane K. 1989. *Dance and the body politic in northern Greece*. Princeton, NJ: Princeton University Press.

———. 1991. Going out for coffee? Contesting the grounds of gendered pleasures in everyday sociability. In *Contested identities: Gender and kinship in modern Greece*, ed. P. Loizos and E. Papataxiarchis. Princeton, NJ: Princeton University Press.

Cox, Paul Alan. 2000. A tale of two villages: Culture, conservation, and eco-colonialism in Samoa. In *Plants, people and justice*, ed. C. Zerner. New York: Columbia University Press.

Crehan, Kate. 2002. *Gramsci, culture and anthropology*. Berkeley and Los Angeles: University of California Press.

Cronon, William. 1995. The trouble with wilderness. In *Uncommon ground*, ed. Cronon. New York: W. W. Norton.

———. 2003. *Changes in the land*. 20th anniversary edition. New York: Hill and Wang.

Csordas, Thomas J. 1990. Embodiment as a paradigm for anthropology. *Ethos* 18 (1): 5-47.

———. 1993. Somatic modes of attention. *Cultural Anthropology* 8 (2): 135–56.

———. 1994. Introduction to *Embodiment and experience: The existential ground of culture and self*, ed. Csordas, 1-25. Cambridge: Cambridge University Press.

D'Acquino, Niccolo. 2000. Is Renato Soru Italy's Bill Gates? *Europe*, May 1, 2000.

de Certeau, M. 1984. *The practice of everyday life*. Berkeley and Los Angeles: University of California Press.

della Porta, Donatella. 1996. The system of corrupt exchange in local government. In *The new Italian Republic: From the fall of the Berlin Wall to Berlusconi*, ed. Steven Gundle and Simon Porter, 221–33. London: Routledge.

Del Piano, L. 1979. *Proprietà collettiva e proprietà privata della terra in Sardegna. Il caso di Orune (1874–1940)*. Cagliari: Della Torre.

Deplano, Andrea. 1997. *Tenores: Canto e communicazione sociale in Sardegna*. Cagliari: AM&D.

Diana, Gavino. 1998. Cinica partita sulla pelle delle popolazioni. *Nuoro Oggi* 11 (3/4): 7–8.

Diani, Mario. 1995. *Green networks: A structural analysis of the Italian environmental movement*. Edinburgh: Edinburgh University Press.

———. 1999. Social Movement Networks. Virtual and real paper for the conference "A New Politics?" CCSS, University of Birmingham, 16–17 September 1999. Downloaded from http://www.nd.edu/~dmyers/cbsm/vol2/bgham99.pdf, retrieved March 2009.

Diani, Mario, and Paolo R. Donati. 1999. Organisational change in Western European environmental groups: A framework for analysis. *Environmental Politics* 9 (1): 13–34.

di Chiro, Giovanna. 2004. Beyond ecoliberal "common futures": Environmental justice, toxic tourism and a transcommunal politics of place. In *Race, nature and the politics of difference*, ed. D. S. Moore, J. Kosek, and A. Pandian, 203–32. Durham, NC: Duke University Press.

Dickie, John. 1999. *Darkest Italy: The nation and stereotypes of the Mezzogiorno, 1860–1900*. New York: St. Martin's Press.

Doane, Molly. 2007. The political ecology of the ecological native. *American Anthropologist* 109 (3): 452–62.

Doolittle, Amity. 2005. *Property and politics in Sabah, Malaysia: A century of native struggles over land rights, 1881-1996*. Seattle, WA: University of Washington Press.

Dove, Michael. 2006. Indigenous people and environmental politics. *Annual Review of Anthropology* 35:191–208.

Doxtater, Michael G. 2004. Indigenous knowledge in the decolonial era. *American Indian Quarterly* 28 (3–4): 618–33.

Doyle, Timothy. 2005. *Environmental movements in minority and majority worlds: A global perspective*. New Brunswick, NJ: Rutgers University Press.

Dubisch, Jill. 1986. *Gender and power in rural Greece*. Princeton, NJ: Princeton University Press.

Durkheim, Emile. 1915. *The elementary forms of the religious life: A study in religious sociology*. Trans. Joseph Ward Swain. New York: Macmillan.

E. C. (European Community). 1988. *Programma Integrato Mediterraneo, Sardegna*.

Eckelmans, Jeanine, and Joelle Smeets. 1989. *Agriculture and the reform of the structural funds*. Luxembourg: Office for the Official Publications of the European Communities.

Edelman, Marc. 2001. Social movements: Changing paradigms and forms of politics. *Annual Review of Anthropology* 30:285–317.

El-Haj, Nadia Abu. 2005. Edward Said and the political present. *American Ethnologist* 32 (4): 538–55.

Ellen, Roy. 1986. What Black Elk left unsaid: On the illusory images of Green primitivism. *Anthropology Today* 2 (6): 8–12.

Ernst, Thomas M. 1999. Land, stories and resources: Discourse and entification in Onabasulu modernity. *American Anthropologist* 101 (1): 88–97.

Escobar, Arturo. 1994. Welcome to Cyberia. *Current Anthropology* 35 (3): 211–31.

———. 1995. *Encountering development: The making and unmaking of the Third World*. Princeton, NJ: Princeton University Press.

———. 1998. Whose knowledge, whose nature? Biodiversity conservation and the political ecology of movements. *Journal of Political Ecology* 5:53–80.

Fabian, Johannes. 1983. *Time and the other: How anthropology makes its object*. New York: Columbia University Press.

———. 2006. The other revisited. *Anthropological Theory* 6 (2): 139–52.

Fairhead, James, and Melissa Leach. 1994. Contested forests: Modern conservation and historical land use in Guinea's Ziama Reserve. *African Affairs* 93 (373): 481–512.

Fairhead, James, Melissa Leach, David Anderson, and Carolyn Brown, eds. 1996. *Misreading the African landscape*. Cambridge: Cambridge University Press.

Fancello, Tonino. 1992. Dentro il cambiamento culturale—protagonismo e marginalità dei giovani in Sardegna. *Nuoro Oggi* 4 (1): 11–14.

Farmer, Paul. 2004. An anthropology of structural violence. *Current Anthropology* 45 (3): 305–25.

Faubion, James. 1993. *Modern Greek lessons: A primer in historical constructivism*. Princeton, NJ: Princeton University Press.

Feeny, David, Fikret Berkes, Bonnie J. McCay, and James M. Acheson. 1990. The tragedy of the commons: Twenty-two years later. *Human Ecology* 18: 1–19.

Fennell, Rosemary. 1987. *The common agricultural policy of the European Community*. Oxford: BSP Professional Books.

Ferguson, James. 1994. *The Anti-politics machine: "Development," depoliticization and bureaucratic power in Lesotho*. Minneapolis: University of Minnesota Press.

———. 2005. Seeing like an oil company: Space, security and global capital in neoliberal Africa. *American Anthropologist* 107 (3): 377–82.

———. 2006. *Global shadows: Africa in the neoliberal world order*. Durham, NC: Duke University Press.

Ferguson, James, and Akhil Gupta. 2002. Spatializing states: Toward an ethnography of neoliberal governmentality. *American Ethnologist* 29 (4): 981–1002.

Fernandez, James W., and Mary Taylor Huber, eds. 2001. *Irony in action: Anthropology, practice and the moral imagination*. Chicago: University of Chicago Press.

Ferrer, Eduardo Blasco. 2002. *Linguistica sarda: Storia, metodi, problemi*. Cagliari: Condaghes.

Fortwangler, Crystal. 2003. The winding road: Incorporating social justice and human rights into protected area policies. In *Contested nature*, ed. Brechin et al., 25–40. Albany, NY: SUNY Press.

Foucault, Michel. 1977. *Discipline and punish: The birth of the prison*. Trans. Alan Sheridan. New York: Pantheon Books.

———. 1978. *The history of sexuality.* Vol. 1. New York: Vintage Books.

Furlong, P. 1996. Political Catholicism and the strange death of the Christian Democrats. In *The new Italian Republic,* ed. S. Gundle and S. Parker, 59–71. London: Routledge.

Gal, Susan. 1987. Codeswitching and consciousness in the European periphery. *American Ethnologist* 14 (4): 637–53.

Galtung, Johan. 1969. Violence, peace and peace research. *Journal of Peace Research* 6:167–91.

Garb, Yaakov. 1997. Lost in translation: Toward a feminist account of Chipko. In *Transitions, environments, translations,* ed. J. W. Scott et al. London: Routledge.

Gibson, Mary. 1998. Biology or environment? Race and southern "deviancy" in the writings of Italian criminologists, 1880–1920. In *Italy's "Southern Question": Orientalism in one country,* ed. J. Schneider, 99–116. Oxford: Berg.

Giddens, Anthony. 1979. *Central problems in social theory.* Berkeley: University of California Press.

Gilmore, David D. 1987. *Honor and shame and the unity of the Mediterranean.* Washington, D.C.: American Anthropological Association.

Gingrich, Andre. 2006. Conceptualizing identities: Anthropological alternatives to essentializing difference and moralizing about othering. In *Grammars of identity/alterity,* ed. G. Baumann and A. Gingrich, 3–17. Oxford: Berg.

Ginsborg, Paul. 1990. *A history of contemporary Italy: Society and politics 1943–1988.* London. Penguin.

———. 1996. Explaining Italy's crisis. In *The new Italian Republic,* ed. S. Gundle and S. Parker, 19–39. London: Routledge.

Gledhill, John. 2000. *Power and its disguises: Anthropological perspectives on politics.* London: Pluto Press.

Goddard, Victoria A. 1994. From the Mediterranean to Europe: Honour, kinship and gender. In *The anthropology of Europe,* ed. V. A. Goddard, J. R. Llobera, and C. Shore, 57–92. Oxford and Washington: Berg.

Goldman, Michael. 1998. *Privatizing nature: Political struggles for the global commons.* New Brunswick, NJ: Rutgers University Press.

———. 2005. *Imperial nature: The World Bank and struggles for social justice in the age of globalization.* New Haven, CT: Yale University Press.

Gordon-McCutchan, R. C. 1991. *The Taos Indians and the battle for Blue Lake.* Santa Fe: Red Crane Books.

Gramsci, Antonio. 1971. *Selections from the prison notebooks.* Ed. and trans. Quintin Hoare and Geoffrey Nowell Smith. New York: International Publishers.

————. 1995. *The Southern Question*. Trans. Pasquale Verdicchio. West Lafayette, IN: Bordighera.

Green, Sarah F. 2005. From hostile backwater to natural wilderness: On the relocation of "nature" in Epirus, northwestern Greece. *Conservation and Society* 3 (2): 436–60.

Greenblatt, Steven. 1990. Resonance and wonder. In *The poetics and politics of museum display*, ed. S. Lavine and I. Karp. Washington, D.C.: Smithsonian Institution.

Guha, Ramachandra. 1989a. Radical American environmentalism and wilderness preservation: A Third World critique. *Environmental Ethics* 11:71–83.

————. 1989b. The unquiet woods: Ecological change and peasant resistance in the Himalaya. Delhi and Toronto: Oxford University Press.

Guha, Ramachandra, and J. Martinez-Alier. 1997. *Varieties of environmentalism: Essays north and south*. London: Earthscan Publications.

Gupta, Akhil. 1998. *Postcolonial developments: Agriculture in the making of modern India*. Durham, NC: Duke University Press.

————. 2006. The Transmission of development: Problems of scale and socialization. In *Regional modernities*, ed. K. Sivaramakrishnan and A. Agrawal, 65–74. Stanford, CA: Stanford University Press.

Gupta, Akhil, and James Ferguson, eds. 1997a. *Anthropological locations: Boundaries and grounds of a field science*. Berkeley: University of California Press.

————. 1997b. *Culture, power, place: Explorations in critical anthropology*. Durham, NC: Duke University Press.

Haenn, Nora. 2005. *Fields of power, forests of discontent: Culture, conservation and the state in Mexico*. Tucson: University of Arizona Press.

Haensch, Dietrich. N.d. Sa lota de Pratobello/La lotta di Pratobello/Der Kampf von Pratobello 1969. Unpublished manuscript.

Hakken, David. 1999. *Cyborgs@Cyberspace? An ethnographer looks to the future*. New York: Routledge.

Hannerz, Ulf. 1996. *Transnational connections: Culture, people, places*. New York: Routledge.

Haraway, Donna. 1991. A cyborg manifesto. In *Simians, cyborgs and women*, 149–83. New York: Routledge.

————. 1997. *Modest_Witness@Second_Millennium.FemaleMan_Meets_ OncoMouse: Feminism and technoscience*. New York: Routledge.

Hardin, Garrett. 1968. The tragedy of the commons. *Science* 162:1243–48.

Harding, Sandra. 1986. *The science question in feminism*. Ithaca: Cornell University Press.

Harper, Krista. 2001. The environment as a master narrative: Discourse and identity in environmental problems. *Anthropological Quarterly* 74 (3): 101–3.

Harries-Jones, Peter. 1993. Between science and shamanism: The advocacy of environmentalism in Toronto. In *Environmentalism: The view from anthropology*, ed. Kay Milton. New York and London: Routledge.

Harris, W. V., ed. 2005. *Rethinking the Mediterranean*. Oxford: Oxford University Press.

Harrison, Faye. 1995. The persistent power of "race" in the cultural and political economy of racism. *Annual Review of Anthropology* 24:47–74.

———. 2002. Unraveling "race" for the twenty-first century. In *Exotic no more: Anthropology on the front lines*, ed. J. MacClancy, 145–66. Chicago and London: University of Chicago Press.

Harvey, David. 1989. *The condition of postmodernity: An enquiry into the origins of cultural change*. Oxford and New York: Blackwell.

Harvey, Penelope. 1996. *Hybrids of modernity: Anthropology, the nation state and the universal exhibition*. London: Routledge.

Heatherington, Tracey. 1999. Street tactics: Catholic ritual and the senses of the past in central Sardinia. *Ethnology* 38 (4): 315–34.

———. 2001. In the rustic kitchen: Real talk and reciprocity. *Ethnology* 40 (4): 329–45.

Heidegger, Martin. 1962. *Being and time*. San Francisco: Harper Collins.

Hellman, S. 1996. Italian communism in the First Republic. In *The new Italian Republic*, ed. S. Gundle and S. Parker, 72–84. London: Routledge.

Herzfeld, Michael. 1980. Honour and shame: Problems in the comparative analysis of moral systems. *Man* 15:339–51.

———. 1984. The horns of the Mediterraneanist dilemma. *American Ethnologist* 11:439–54.

———. 1985. *The poetics of manhood: Contest and identity in a Cretan mountain village*. Princeton, NJ: Princeton University Press.

———. 1987a. *Anthropology through the looking-glass: Critical ethnography in the margins of Europe*. New York: Cambridge University Press.

———. 1987b. "As in your own house." In *Honor and shame in the Mediterranean*, ed. D. Gilmore, 75–89. Washington, D.C.: American Anthropological Association.

———. 1991. *A place in history: Social and monumental time in a Cretan town*. Princeton, NJ: Princeton University Press.

———. 1997. *Cultural intimacy: Social poetics in the nation-state*. New York: Routledge.

———. 2004. *The body impolitic: Artisans and artifice in the global hierarchy of value.* Chicago: University of Chicago Press.

———. 2005a. Practical Mediterraneanism: Excuses for everything, from epistemology to eating. In *Rethinking the Mediterranean,* ed. W. V. Harris, 45–63. Oxford: Oxford University Press.

———. 2005b. Taking stereotypes seriously: "Mediterraneanism" reconsidered. In *The Mediterranean reconsidered: Representations, emergences, recompositions,* ed. M. Peressini and R. Hadj-Moussa, 25–38. Gatineau QC: Canadian Museum of Civilization.

Hess, David J. 1995. *Science and technology in a multicultural world: The cultural politics of facts and artifacts.* New York: Columbia University Press.

Hess, David J., and Linda Layne, eds. 1992. *Knowledge and society—The anthropology of science and technology.* Vol. 9. Greenwich, CT: JAI.

Hetherington, Kevin. 1996. The utopics of social ordering: Stonehenge as a museum without walls. In *Theorizing museums: Representing identity and diversity in a changing world,* ed. S. Macdonald and G. Fyfe, 153–76. London: Blackwell.

Heynen, Nic, and Paul Robbins. 2005. The neoliberalization of nature: Governance, privatization, enclosure and evaluation. *Capitalism, Nature, Socialism* 16:5–8.

Hirsch, Eric, and Michael O'Hanlon. 1995. *The anthropology of landscape: Perspectives on place and space.* Oxford: Clarendon Press.

Hobsbawm, Eric. [1959] 1971. *Primitive rebels: Studies in archaic forms of social movement in the 19th and 20th centuries.* 3rd ed. Manchester: Manchester University Press.

Hodgson, Dorothy. 2002. Precarious alliances: The cultural politics and structural predicaments of the Indigenous Rights Movement in Tanzania. *American Anthropologist* 104 (4): 1086–97.

Holmes, Douglass. 2000. *Integral Europe: Fast capitalism, multiculturalism, neofascism.* Princeton, NJ: Princeton University Press.

Honneth, Axel. 1995. *The struggle for recognition.* Cambridge, MA: MIT Press.

Horden, Peregrine, and Nicholas Purcell. 2000. *The corrupting sea: A study of Mediterranean history.* Malden, MA: Blackwell.

Hughes, David McDermott. 2006. *From enslavement to environmentalism: Politics on a southern African frontier.* Seattle: University of Washington Press.

Hume, Lynne. 1999. On the unsafe side of the white divide: New perspectives on the dreaming of Australian Aborigines. *Anthropology of Consciousness* 10 (1): 1–15.

IASM (Istituto per l'Assistenza allo Sviluppo del Mezzogiorno). 1983. *Gli usi civici in Sardegna,* document. Cagliari: Dipartimento EAT Assistenza Tecnica agli Enti Locali.

Igoe, Jim. 2004. *Conservation and globalization: A study of national parks and indigenous communities from East Africa to South Dakota.* Belmont, CA: Wadsworth.

Igoe, Jim, and Tim Kelsall. 2005. *Between a rock and a hard place: African NGOs, donors and the state.* Durham, NC: Carolina Academic Press.

Ingold, Tim. 1993. Globes and spheres: The topology of environmentalism. In *Environmentalism: The view from anthropology*, ed. Kay Milton, 43–58. London: Routledge.

———. 2000. *The perception of the environment: Essays on livelihood, dwelling and skill.* London: Routledge.

Ionta, Matteo. 2006. Regional media and identity in Sardinia. Online archive of the digital magazine *DiariuLimba*, Sotziu Limba Sarda, November 2006. www.sotziulimbasarda.net/novembre2006/RegionalMedia.pdf, retrieved June 2008.

———. 2008. Communicative construction of Sardinian identity on regional media. Presentation at Identity and Social Representations: Cultural and Mythical Dimensions. European Ph.D. on Social Representations & Communication Research Center and Multimedia LAB, Rome, Italy, April 26–May 4, 2008. http://www.europhd.eu/html/_onda02/07/13.06.00.00.shtml, retrieved June 2008.

IPCC (Intergovernmental Panel on Climate Change). 2007. *Fourth assessment report.* Electronic document at UNEP website, http://www.ipcc.ch/, retrieved December 2007.

IUCN (International Union for the Conservation of Nature). 1980. *World conservation strategy.* Washington, D.C.: World Wildlife Fund.

Jackson, Michael. 1983. Knowledge of the body. *Man*, n.s., 18 (2): 327–45.

———, ed. 1998. *Things as they are: New directions in phenomenological anthropology.* Bloomington: Indiana University Press.

Jacoby, Karl. 2003. *Crimes against nature: Squatters, poachers, thieves, and the hidden history of American conservation.* Berkeley: University of California Press.

Jaffe, Alexandra. 1996. The second annual Corsican spelling contest: Orthography and ideology. *American Ethnologist* 23 (4): 816–35.

———. 1999. *Ideologies in action: Language politics on Corsica.* Berlin: Mouton de Gruyter.

Jasanoff, Sheila. 1999. The songlines of risk. *Environmental Values* 8:135–52.

———. 2004. Heaven and earth: The politics of environmental images. In *Earthly politics*, ed. S. Jasanoff and M. Long Martello, 31–53. Cambridge, MA: MIT Press.

Joyce, Frank E., and Gunter Schneider. 1988. *Environment and economic development in the regions of the European Community*. Brookfield, VT: Avebury.

Judge, David. 1993. *A green dimension for the European Community: Political issues and processes*. London: Frank Cass.

Karlsson, Bengt G. 2006. Indigenous natures: Forest and community dynamics in Meghalaya, north-east India. In *Ecological nationalisms*, ed. G. Cederlöf and K. Sivaramakrishnan, 170–98. Seattle: University of Washington Press.

Katz, Cindi. 1998. Whose nature, whose culture? Private productions of space and the "preservation" of nature. In *Remaking reality*, ed. B. Braun and N. Castree, 46-63. London: Routledge.

Kertzer, David I. 1980. *Comrades and Christians: Religion and political struggle in communist Italy*. Cambridge: Cambridge University Press.

———. 1996. *Politics and symbols: The Italian Communist Party and the fall of communism*. New Haven, CT: Yale University Press.

Köhler, Axel. 2005. Of apes and men: Baka and Bantu attitudes to wildlife and the making of eco-goodies and baddies. *Conservation and Society* 3 (2): 407–35.

Kondo, Dorinne K. 1990. *Crafting selves: Power, gender, and discourses of identity in a Japanese workplace*. Chicago and London: University of Chicago Press.

Kottak, Conrad. 1999. The new ecological anthropology. *American Anthropologist* 101 (1): 23–35

Krauss, Werner. 2005. Of otters and humans: An approach to the politics of nature in terms of rhetoric. *Conservation and Society* 3 (2): 354–70.

Krech, Shepard. 1999. *The ecological Indian: Myth and history*. New York: Norton.

Kuhn, Thomas S. 1971. *The structure of scientific revolutions*. 2nd ed. Chicago: University of Chicago Press.

Laclau, Ernesto, and Chantal Mouffe. 2001. *Hegemony and socialist strategy: Towards a radical democratic politics*. 2nd ed. New York: Verso.

Lang, Andrew. 1994 [1912]. Introduction. In *Andrew Lang on totemism*, CSAC Monographs 8, ed. Andrew Duff-Cooper. Centre for Anthropology and Computing. University of Kent at Canterbury.

Langton, Marcia. 2003. The "wild," the market and the native: Indigenous people face new forms of global colonization. In *Globalization, globalism, environments, environmentalisms: Consciousness of connections*, ed. S. Vertovec and D. Posey, 141–70. The Linacre Lectures 2000. Oxford: Oxford University Press.

Langton, Marcia, Zane Ma Rhea, and Lisa Palmer. 2005. Community-oriented protected areas for indigenous peoples and local communities. *Journal of Political Ecology* 12:23–50.

Latour, Bruno. 1987. *Science in action*. Cambridge, MA: Harvard University Press.

———. 1998. To modernise or ecologise? That is the question. Trans. Charis Cussins. In *Remaking reality*, ed. B. Braun and N. Castree, 221–42. London: Routledge.

———. 2004. *The politics of nature: How to bring the sciences into democracy*. Trans. Catherine Porter. Cambridge, MA: Harvard University Press.

Lawrence, D. H. 2002. *Sea and Sardinia*. The Cambridge Edition of the Works of D. H. Lawrence, ed. M. Kalnins. Cambridge: Cambridge University Press.

Leavitt, John. 1996. Meaning and feeling in the anthropology of emotions. *American Ethnologist* 23 (3): 514–39.

Ledda, Gavino. 1975. *Padre padrone: L'educazione di un pastore*. Feltrinelli.

Li, Tania Murray. 2000. Articulating indigenous identity in Indonesia: Resource politics and the tribal slot. *Comparative Studies in Society and History* 42 (1): 149–79.

Lee, Richard Borshay. 2006a. Twenty-first century indigenism. *Anthropological Theory* 6 (4): 455–79.

———. 2006b. Indigenism and its discontents. In *Inclusion and exclusion in the global arena*, ed. M. Kirsch. London: Routledge.

Le Lannou, Maurice. 1971. *Patres et paysans de la Sardaigne*. Tours: Arrault et cie.

Li, Tania Murray. 2000. Articulating indigenous identity in Indonesia: Resource politics and the tribal slot. *Comparative Studies in Society and History* 42 (1): 149–79.

———. 2005. Beyond "the state" and failed schemes. *American Anthropologist* 107 (3): 383–94.

Ligas, M. 1990. *Indagine sulla Condizione Giovanile ad Orgosolo*. Comune di Orgosolo. Document.

Ligia, Mario. 2002. *La lingua dei Sardi: Ipotesi filologiche*. Ghilarza (Oristano): Iskra.

Lilliu, Giovanni. 2002. *La costante resistenziale sarda*. Nuoro: ILISSO Edizioni.

Liori, Salvatore. 1993. Saluti e interventi introduttivi. In *Il Parco del Gennargentu: Un'occasione da non perdere*, ed. Scuola di Pubblica Amministrazione et al. Conference proceedings of June 6–7, 1992, Desulo. Cagliari: Edisar.

Lohmann, Larry. 1993. Green Orientalism. Online publication from The Corner House website, http://www.thecornerhouse.org.uk/item.shtml?x=52179, retrieved September 2007.

Lowe, Celia. 2006. *Wild profusion: Biodiversity conservation in an Indonesian archipelago*. Princeton, NJ: Princeton University Press.

Lowenthal, David. 1988. *The past is a foreign country*. Cambridge: Cambridge University Press.

Lund, Katrín. 2005. Finding place in nature: "Intellectual" and local knowledge in a Spanish natural park. *Conservation and Society* 3 (2): 371–87.

Lury, Celia, Sarah Franklin, and Jackie Stacey. 2000. *Global nature, global culture*. London: SAGE Publications.

Lutz, Catherine. 1988. *Unnatural emotions: Everyday sentiments on a Micronesian atoll and their challenge to Western theory*. Chicago: University of Chicago Press.

Lutz, Catherine A., and Jane L. Collins. 1993. *Reading* National Geographic. Chicago and London: University of Chicago Press.

Lynch, Barbara Deutsch. 1996. Caribbean environmentalism: An ambiguous discourse. In *Creating the countryside*, ed. E. M. DuPuis and P. Vandergeest. Philadelphia: Temple University Press.

Macdonald, Sharon. 1993. *Inside European identities: Ethnography in Western Europe*. Providence, RI: Berg.

———. 1996. Theorizing museums: An introduction. In *Theorizing museums: Representing identity and diversity in a changing world*, ed. S. Macdonald and G. Fyfe, 1–18. London: Blackwell.

Macdonald, Sharon, Pat Holden, and Shirley Ardener. 1986. *Images of women in peace and war: Cross-cultural and historical perspectives*. Madison: University of Wisconsin.

Madau, Eric. 2005. La stagione delle "lotte popolari" e l'esperienza dei circoli barbaricini. In *Pratobello 1969: Una vittoria del popolo Sardo contro l'occupazione militare*, Sardigna Ruja, Atti del Convegno. Pisa/Firenze, December. Online at http://sardignaruja.altervista.org/content/view/27/2/, retrieved April 20, 2006.

Malaby, Thomas. 2003. *Gambling life: Dealing in contingency in a Greek city*. Urbana: University of Illinois Press.

Malinowski, Bronislaw. 1922. *Argonauts of the Western Pacific*. New York: E. P. Dutton & Co.

Mammarella, Giuseppe. 1995. Il Partito Comunista Italiano. In *La politica Italiana: Dizionario critico 1945–95*, ed. G. Pasquino, 287-310. Rome: Laterza.

Manca, Antonio Maria. 1995. *Gente di Orgosolo*. Cagliari: STEF.

Marcus, George. 1998. *Ethnography through thick and thin*. Princeton, NJ: Princeton University Press.

Marcus, George E., and Michael M. J. Fischer. 1986. *Anthropology as cultural critique: An experimental moment in the human sciences*. Chicago: Chicago University Press.

Marotto, Peppino. 1978. *Cantones politicas sardas*. Ghilarza: Quaderni degli Amici della Casa Gramsci di Ghilarza.

———. 1996 [1989]. *Su Pianeta 'e Supramonte. Cantadas in sardu*. Cagliari: Condaghes.

Mastino, Attilio. 1995. La Sardegna romana. In *Storia della Sardegna*, ed. M. Brigaglia. Sassari: Soter.

Mastroni, Franceschino. 1993. Diciamo sì al parco. In *Il Parco del Gennargentu: Un'occasione da non perdere*, ed. Scuola di Pubblica Amministrazione et al. Conference proceedings of June 6-7, 1992, Desulo. Cagliari: Edisar.

Mazzette, Antonietta. 2006. Fenomeni di criminalità in Sardegna note introduttive. In *La criminalità in Sardegna*, ed. Mazzette et al., ix–xliv. Centro di Studi Urbana, Università degli Studi di Sassari. Sassari: Edizioni Unidata.

McCarthy, J., and S. Prudham. 2004. Neoliberal nature and the nature of neoliberalism. *Geoforum* 35:275–83.

McCay, Bonnie J., and James M. Acheson. 1987. *The question of the commons: The culture and ecology of communal resources*. Tucson: University of Arizona Press.

McCay, Bonnie J., and Sven Jentoft. 1998. Market or community failure? Critical perspectives on common property research. *Human Organization* 57 (1): 21–29.

McLuhan, Marshall. 1994 [1967]. *Understanding media: The extensions of man*. Cambridge, MA: MIT Press.

McLuhan, Marshall, and Bruce Powers. 1992. *The global village: Transformations in world life and media in the 21st century*. Oxford: Oxford University Press.

McLuhan, Marshall, Eric McLuhan, and Frank Zingrone. 1996. *The essential McLuhan*. New York: Basic Books.

Meadows, D. H., Jørgen Randers, and Dennis L. Meadows. 2004. *The limits to growth*. Revised ed. London: Earthscan Publications.

Meloni, Benedetto. 1984. *Famiglie di pastori: Continuità e mutamento in una comunità della Sardegna centrale, 1950–1970*. Istituto superiore regionale etnografico. Nuoro: Rosenberg & Sellier.

Melucci, Alberto. 1989. *Nomads of the present: Social movements and individual needs in contemporary society*. Philadelphia: Temple University Press.

Mensching, Guido. 2000. The Internet as a rescue tool of endangered languages: Sardinian. Paper presented at MULTILINGUAE: Multimedia and Minority Languages International Conference. Nov. 8-9, 2000, Donostia-San Sebastian. http://www.gaia.es/multilinguae/, retrieved May 2008.

Menzies, Charles, ed. 2006. *Traditional ecological knowledge and natural resource management*. Lincoln: University of Nebraska Press.

Merleau-Ponty, M. 1964. *The phenomenology of perception*. London: Routledge and Kegan Paul.

Milton, Kay. 1996. *Environmentalism and cultural theory: Exploring the role of anthropology in environmental discourse*. London and New York: Routledge.

————. 2002. *Loving nature: Towards an ecology of emotion*. London and New York: Routledge.

Mitchell, Jon P. 1998. An island in between: Malta, identity and anthropology. *South European Society and Politics* 3 (1): 142–49.

————. 2002. *Ambivalent Europeans: Ritual, memory and the public sphere in Malta*. New York and London: Routledge.

Mitchell, Timothy. 1991. Everyday metaphors of power. *Theory and Society* 19: 545–77.

Moe, Nelson. 2002. *The view from Vesuvius: Italian culture and the southern question*. Studies in the History of Society and Culture 46. Berkeley: University of California Press.

Moore, Donald S. 1998. Subaltern struggles and the politics of place: Remapping resistance in Zimbabwe's eastern highlands. *Cultural Anthropology* 13 (3): 344–81.

————. 1999. The crucible of cultural politics: Reworking "development" in Zimbabwe's eastern highlands. *American Ethnologist* 26 (3): 654–89.

————. 2005. *Suffering for territory: Race, place, and power in Zimbabwe*. Duke University Press.

Moore, Donald S., Jake Kosek, and Anand Pandian, eds. 2003. *Race, nature and the politics of difference*. Durham, NC: Duke University Press.

Moore, Sally Falk. 1993. Introduction to *Moralizing states and the ethnography of the present*, ed. S. F. Moore. Washington, D.C.: American Anthropological Association.

Moore, Sally Falk, and Barbara G. Myerhoff. 1977. Secular ritual: Forms and meanings. In *Secular ritual*, ed. S. Moore and B. Myerhoff, 3–24. New York: Van Gorcum.

Morley, David, and Kevin Robins. 1995. *Spaces of identity: Global media, electronic landscapes, and cultural boundaries*. New York: Routledge.

Moro, Giovanni. 1982. Le lotte di Orgosolo (1966–1969). In *Lotte sociali, antifascismo e autonomia in Sardegna: Atti del convegno di studi in onore di Emilio Lussu: Cagliari, 4–6 gennaio 1980*. Edizioni della Torre.

Morphy, Howard. 1995. Landscape and the reproduction of the ancestral past. In *The anthropology of landscape: Perspectives of place and space*, ed. E. Hirsch and M. O'Hanlon, 184–209. Oxford: Clarendon.

Morton, Adam David. 2007. *Hegemony and passive revolution in the global economy*. London: Pluto.

Moss, David. 1979. Bandits and boundaries in Sardinia. *Man* 14:477–96.

Muggianu, Pietro. 1998. *Orgosolo '68–'70: Il triennio rivoluzionario*. Nuoro: Studiostampa.

Mühlhäusler, Peter, and Adrian Peace. 2006. Environmental discourses. *Annual Review of Anthropology* 35:457–79.

Myers, Fred. 1986. *Pintupi country, Pintupi self: Sentiment, place, and politics among Western Desert Aborigines*. Wash., DC: Smithsonian Institution Press

Myers, Norman, et al. 2000. Biodiversity hotspots for conservation priorities. *NATURE* 403 (Feb. 24, 2000): 853–58.

Naess, Arnold. 1989. *Ecology, community, and lifestyle: Outline of an ecosophy*. Cambridge: Cambridge University Press.

Nairn, Tom. 1982. Antonu su Gobbu. In *Approaches to Gramsci*, ed. A. S. Sassoon. London: Writers and Readers.

Nasdady, Paul. 2005. Transcending the debate over the ecologically noble Indian: Indigenous peoples and environmentalism. *Ethnohistory* 52 (2): 291–331.

Navarru, Giovanni. 1989. *Le strutture agricole della Sardegna nel quadro dell'integrazione europea*. Sassari: TAS.

Nazarea, Virginia. 2006. Local knowledge and memory in biodiversity conservation. *Annual Review of Anthropology* 35:317–35.

Netting, Robert McC. 1977. *Cultural ecology*. Menlo Park, CA: Cummings.

Neumann, Roderick. 1995. Local challenges to global agendas: Conservation, economic liberalization and the pastoralists' rights movement in Tanzania. *Antipode* 27 (4): 363–82.

———. 1998. *Imposing wilderness: Struggles over livelihood and nature preservation in Africa*. Berkeley: University of California Press.

———. 2004. Moral and discursive geographies in the war for biodiversity in Africa. *Political Geography* 23 (7): 813–37.

Neves-Graca, Katja. 2004. Revisiting the tragedy of the commons. *Human Organization* 63 (3): 289-300.

Niceforo, Alfredo. [1897] 1977. *La delinquenza in Sardegna*. Cagliari: Della Torre.

Niezen, Ronald. 2003. *The origins of indigenism: Human rights and the politics of identity*. Berkeley: University of California Press.

———. 2004. *A world beyond difference: Cultural identity in the age of globalization*. Malden, MA: Blackwell.

Oppo, Andrea. 2008. New research shows strong support for Sardinian language. *Europäisches Journal für Minderheitenfragen* 1:57–58.

Orgosolo Novembre 1968: 4 giorni di sciopero e di assemblee popolari. 1968. Pamphlet. Milano: Feltrinelli.

Ortner, Sherry. 1995. Resistance and the problem of ethnographic refusal. *Contemporary Studies in Society and History* 37 (1): 173–93.

Ortu, Gian Giacomo. 1981. *L'economia pastorale della Sardegna moderna: Saggio di antropologia storica sulla "soccida."* Cagliari: Della Torre.

Ostrom, Elinor. 1990. *Governing the commons: The evolution of institutions for collective action*. Cambridge: Cambridge University Press.

Palumbo, Berardino. 1997. *Identità nel tempo: Saggi di antropologia della parentela*. Lecce: Argo.

———. 2001. The social life of local museums. *Journal of Modern Italian Studies* 6 (1): 9–37.

Pasquino, Gianfranco, ed. 1995. *La politica Italiana: Dizionario critico 1945-95*. Rome: Laterza.

Patriarca, Silvana. 1998. How many Italies? Representing the south in official statistics. In *Italy's "Southern Question": Orientalism in one country*, ed. J. Schneider, 77–98. Oxford: Berg.

Paulson, Susan, and Lisa Gezon. 2004. *Political ecology across spaces, scales, and social groups*. New Brunswick, NJ: Rutgers University Press.

Peet, Richard, and Michael Watts. 2004. *Liberation ecologies: Environment, development, social movements*. 2nd ed. London: Routledge.

Peressini, Mauro, and Ratiba Hadj-Moussa, eds. 2005. *The Mediterranean reconsidered: Representations, emergences, recompositions*. Gatineau QC: Canadian Museum of Civilization.

Perley, Bernard C. 2006. Aboriginality at large: Varieties of resistance in Maliseet language instruction. *IDENTITIES: Global Studies in Culture and Power* 13 (2): 187–208.

Piattoni, S. 1998. "Virtuous clientelism": The Southern Question resolved? In *Italy's "Southern Question,"* ed. J. Schneider, 225–44. Oxford: Berg.

Piña-Cabral, Jose de. 1989. The Mediterranean as a category of regional comparison: A critical view. *Current Anthropology* 30 (3): 399–406.

Pintore, Gianfranco. 1993. Un progetto contrario agli interessi locali. In *Il Parco del Gennargentu: Un'occasione da non perdere*, ed. Scuola di Pubblica Amministrazione et al. Conference proceedings of June 6–7, 1992, Desulo. Cagliari: Edisar.

Pira, Michelangelo. 1978. *La rivolta dell'oggetto: Antropologia della Sardegna*. Milano: Giuffrè.

Pirastu, Ignazio. 1973. *Il banditismo in Sardegna*. Rome: Editori Riuniti.

Pirastu, Luigi. 1993. *Economia e società in Sardegna*. Cagliari: Editrice Democratica Sarda.

Podda, Luigi. 1976. *Dall'ergastolo*. Milan: La Pietra.

Posey, Darrell Addison. 2003. Fragmenting cosmic connections: Converting nature into commodity. In *Globalization, globalism, environments, environmentalisms: Consciousness of connections*, ed. S. Vertovec and D. Posey, 123–40. The Linacre Lectures 2000. Oxford: Oxford University Press.

———. 2004. *Indigenous knowledge and ethics: A Darrell Posey reader*. London: Routledge.

Pound, Christopher. 1995. Imagining in-formation: The complex disconnections of computer networks. In *Technoscientific imaginaries: Conversations, profiles and memoires*, ed. G. Marcus. Chicago: University of Chicago Press.

Povinelli, Elizabeth. 1995. Do rocks listen? The cultural politics of apprehending Australian Aboriginal labor. *American Anthropologist* 97 (3): 505–18.

———. 2002. *The cunning of recognition: Indigenous alterities and the making of Australian multiculturalism*. Durham, NC: Duke University Press.

Prato, Giuliana. 1993. Political decision-making: Environmentalism, ethics and popular participation in Italy. In *Environmentalism: The view from anthropology*, ed. K. Milton, 174-88. London: Routledge.

Pungetti, Gloria. 1999. From landscape research to ecological design and planning. In *Ecological landscape design and planning: The Mediterranean context*, ed. J. Makhzoumi and G. Pungetti, 32-154. London: E & FN Spon (Routledge).

Raffles, Hugh. 2002. *In Amazonia: A natural history*. Princeton, NJ: Princeton University Press.

Ramos, Alcida. 2003. Pulp fictions of indigenism. In *Race, nature and the politics of difference*, ed. D. S. Moore, J. Kosek, and A. Pandian, 356–79. Durham, NC: Duke University Press.

Ranco, Darren. 2005. Indigenous peoples, state-sanctioned knowledge and the politics of recognition. *American Anthropogist* 107 (4): 708–11.

———. 2006. The Indian ecologist and the politics of representation: Critiquing the ecological Indian in the age of ecocide. In *Perspectives on the ecological Indian: Native Americans and the environment*, ed. M. Harkin and D. R. Lewis. Lincoln: University of Nebraska Press.

Rappaport, Roy A. 2000. *Pigs for the ancestors: Ritual in the ecology of a New Guinea people*. 2nd ed. Long Grove, IL: Waveland Press.

Ridington, Robin. 1990. *Little bit know something: Stories in a language of anthropology*. Iowa City: University of Iowa.

Rocheleau, Dianne, Barbara Thomas Slayter, and Ester Wangari, eds. 1996. *Feminist political ecology: Global issues and local experience.* London: Routledge.

Rosaldo, Michelle. 1984. Toward an anthropology of self and feeling. In *Culture theory: Essays on mind, self and emotion,* ed. R. A. Shweder and R. A. Levine. Cambridge: Cambridge University Press.

Rosaldo, Renato. 1989. *Culture and truth: The remaking of social analysis.* Boston: Beacon Press.

Rosenblatt, Julius, Thomas Mayer, et al. 1988. *The Common Agricultural Policy of the European Community: Principles and consequences.* Washington, D.C.: International Monetary Fund. Document.

Rubanu, Pietrina, and Gianfranco Fistrale. 1998. *Murales politici della Sardegna: Guida, storia, percorsi.* Bolsena: Erre emme.

Rumsey, Alan, and James F. Weiner, eds. 2001. *Emplaced myth: Space, narrative and knowledge in Aboriginal Australia and Papua New Guinea.* Honolulu: University of Hawai'i Press.

Sachs, Wolfgang. 1991. *The development dictionary: A guide to knowledge as power.* Atlantic Highlands, NJ: Zed Books.

Said, Edward. 1978. *Orientalism.* New York: Vintage Books.

———. 1994. *Culture and imperialism.* London: Vintage.

Salis, Giovanni Battista. 1990. *Orgosolo tra storia e mito.* Cagliari: Ettore Gasperini.

Sanna, Giovanni. 1997. *Orgosolo: Diario di un Parroco 1955–1978.* Nuoro: Editrice "L'Ortobene."

Sardigna Ruja. 2005. Pratobello 1969: Una vittoria del popolo sardo contro l'occupazione militare. Atti del Convegno, Pisa, 6 dicembre 2005 & Firenze 9 dicembre 2005. Electronic document downloaded from Sardigna Ruja website, maintained by the Sotziu de Sos Emigrantes Sardos ("Pratobello 1969," http://sardignaruja.altervista.org/content/view/27/2/, accessed July 12, 2008).

Sassoon, Anne Showstack. 1987. *Gramsci's politics.* 2nd ed. Minneapolis: University of Minnesota Press.

———. 2002. *Gramsci and contemporary politics.* London: Routledge.

———, ed. 1982. *Approaches to Gramsci.* London: Writers & Readers.

Satta, Gino. 2001. *Turisti a Orgosolo: La Sardegna centrale come attrazione turistica.* Napoli: Liguori Editori.

———. N.d. Delinquenti nati: Stereotipi e teorie della razza nella *Psicologia della Sardegna* di Paolo Orano (1896). Unpublished essay.

Sawyer, Suzana. 2004. *Crude chronicles: Indigenous politics, multinational oil and neoliberalism in Ecuador.* Durham, NC: Duke University Press.

Schneider, Jane. 1971. Of vigilance and virgins: Honor, shame and access to resources in Mediterranean societies. *Ethnology* 10 (1): 1–24.

———. 1998. Introduction to *Italy's "Southern Question": Orientalism in one country*, ed. Schneider. Oxford: Berg.

———, ed. 1998. *Italy's "Southern Question": Orientalism in one country*. Oxford: Berg.

Schneider, Peter, and Jane Schneider. 1976. *Culture and political economy in western Sicily*. New York: Academic Press.

———. 2003. *Reversible destiny: Mafia, antimafia, and the struggle for Palermo*. Berkeley: University of California Press.

Schwartz, Katrina. 2006. *Nature and national identity after communism*. Pittsburgh: University of Pittsburgh Press.

Schweizer, Peter. 1988. *Shepherds, workers, intellectuals: Culture and centre-periphery relationships in a Sardinian village*. Stockholm Studies in Social Anthropology 18. University of Stockholm.

Scoppola, Pietro. 1995. La democrazia Italiana. In *La politica Italiana: Dizionario critico 1945–1995*, ed. G. Pasquino. Roma: Laterza.

Scott, James C. 1985. *Weapons of the weak: Everyday forms of peasant resistance*. New Haven, CT: Yale University Press.

———. 1990. *Domination and the arts of resistance*. New Haven: Yale University Press.

———. 1998. *Seeing like a state*. New Haven, CT: Yale University Press.

Scroccu, Gianluca. 1998. Gennargentu, un parco "storico." *Nuoro Oggi* 11 (3/4): 11–12.

Scuola di Pubblica Amministrazione e Governo Locale di Nuoro, Università degli Studi di Cagliari, and Assessorato all'Ambiente della Provincia di Nuoro. 1993. *Il Parco del Gennargentu: Un'occasione da non perdere*. Conference proceedings of June 6–7, 1992, Desulo. Cagliari: Edisar.

Seremetakis, C. Nadia. 1994a. Intersection: Benjamin, Bloch, Braudel, beyond. In *The senses still*, ed. C. N. Seremetakis, 19-22. Chicago: University of Chicago Press.

———. 1994b. The memory of the senses part II: Still acts. In *The senses still*, ed. C. N. Seremetakis. Chicago: University of Chicago Press.

Shore, Cris. 1990. *Italian communism: The escape from Leninism*. London: Routledge.

———. 1993. Inventing the "People's Europe": Critical approaches to European community "cultural policy." *Man*, New Series 28 (4): 779–800.

———. 2000. *Building Europe*. London: Routledge.

Sillitoe, Paul, ed. 2006. *Local science vs. global science: Approaches to indigenous knowledge in international development. Environmental Anthropology and Ethnobiology Series. Oxford: Berghahn.

Silverman, Sydel. 1975. *Three bells of civilization: The life of an Italian hill town*. New York: Columbia University Press.

Sio, Giovanni Francesco. 1996–97. *Gli istituti giuridici tradizionali in materia de lavoro nella pastorizia*. Tesi di Laurea, Università di Cagliari degli Studi.

Sivaramakrishnan, K. 2005a. Introduction to special issue. *American Anthropologist* 107 (3): 321–30.

———. 2005b. Some intellectual genealogies for the concept of everyday resistance. *American Anthropologist* 107 (3): 346–55.

Sivaramakrishnan, K., and Arun Agrawal. 2003. Regional modernities in stories and practices of development. In *Regional modernities*, ed. K. Sivaramakrishnan and A. Agrawal, 1–61. Stanford, CA: Stanford University Press.

Sivaramakrishnan, K., and Ismael Vaccaro. 2006. Postindustrial natures: Hypermobility and place attachments. *Social Anthropology* 14:301–17.

Slater, Candace. 2000. Justice for whom? Contemporary images of Amazonia. In *People, plants and justice*, ed. C. Zerner. New York: Columbia University Press.

———. 2003. *Entangled Edens: Visions of the Amazon*. Berkeley: University of California Press.

Smith, Anthony. 1998. *Nationalism and modernism*. London: Routledge.

Smith, Gavin. 2004. Hegemony. In *Companion to the anthropology of politics*, ed. D. Nugent and J. Vincent, 216–30. Oxford: Blackwell.

Smith, Mark. 1998. *Ecologism: Toward ecological citizenship*. Minneapolis: University of Minnesota Press.

Smith, Neil. 1990. *Uneven development: Nature, capital and the production of space*. Oxford: Basil Blackwell.

Spence, Mark David. 2000. *Dispossessing the wilderness: Indian removal and the making of the national parks*. New ed. Oxford: Oxford University Press.

Sponsel, Leslie. 2001. Do anthropologists need religion, and vice versa? In *New directions in anthropology and environment*, ed. C. Crumley. SAR Press.

Spotts, Frederic, and Theodor Wieser. 1986. *Italy: A difficult democracy*. Cambridge: Cambridge University Press.

Steedly, Mary Margaret. 1993. *Hanging without a rope: Narrative experience in colonial and postcolonial Karoland*. Princeton, NJ: Princeton University Press.

Stern, Nicolas. 2006. *Stern review on the economics of climate change*. London: HM Treasury.

Stewart, Kathleen. 1996. *A space on the side of the road: Cultural poetics in an "other" America*. Princeton, NJ: Princeton University Press.

Stoller, Paul. 1997. *Sensuous scholarship*. Philadelphia: University of Pennsylvania Press.

Strang, Veronica. 1997. *Uncommon ground: Cultural landscapes and environmental values*. New York: New York University Press.

Strathern, A. J. 1996. *Body thoughts*. Ann Arbor: University of Michigan Press.

Strathern, Andrew, and Pamela J. Stewart. 1998. Embodiment and communication. Two frames for the analysis of ritual. *Social Anthropology* 6 (2): 237–51.

Strehlow, Theodor Georg Heinrich. 1970. Geography and the totemic landscape in central Australia: A functional study. In *Australian Aboriginal anthropology*, ed. R. Berndt, 92–140. Nedlands: University of Western Australia Press.

Sutton, David E. 1994. Tradition and modernity: Kalymnian constructions of identity and otherness. *Journal of Modern Greek Studies* 12:239–60.

———. 2000. *Memories cast in stone*. Oxford: Berg.

Svašek, Maruska. 2005 Emotions in anthropology. In *Mixed emotions: Anthropological studies of feeling*, ed. K. Milton and M. Svašek. Oxford: Berg.

Swain, Tony. 1993. *A place for strangers: Towards a history of Australian Aboriginal being*. Cambridge: Cambridge University Press.

Sylvain, Renée. 2002. "Land, water and truth": San identity and global indigenism. *American Anthropologist* 104 (4): 1074–85.

———. 2006. Disorderly development: Globalization and the idea of culture in the Kalahari. In *Inclusion and exclusion in the global arena*, ed. M. Kirsch. London: Routledge.

Tassi, Franco. 1998. *Parchi nazionali in Italia. Missione impossibile?* Rome: Centro Parchi.

Taylor, Charles. 1994. The politics of recognition. In *Multiculturalism: Examining the politics of recognition*, ed. A. Gutmann. Princeton, NJ: Princeton University Press.

Theodossopoulos, Dimitrios. 2003. *Troubles with turtles: Cultural understandings of the environment on a Greek island*. New York: Berghahn Books.

Thompson, E. P. 1966. *The making of the English working class*. New York: Vintage.

———. 1975. *Whigs and hunters: The origin of the black act*. New York: Pantheon.

Tomaselli, R. 1977. Degradation of the Mediterranean maquis. In *Mediterranean forests and maquis: Ecology, conservation and management*. Man and Biosphere Technical Notes 2, pp. 33–72. Paris: UNESCO.

Touraine, Alain. 1988. *Return of the actor: Social theory in postindustrial society*. Minneapolis: University of Minnesota Press.

Tsetsi, Vula, and Ignazio Cirronis, eds. 1993. *Ambiente e sviluppo sostenibile: Il caso Sardegna*. Cagliari: CUEC.

Tsing, Anna Lowenhaupt. 1993. *In the realm of the Diamond Queen: Marginality in an out-of-the-way place*. Princeton, NJ: Princeton University Press.

———. 1997. Transitions as translations. In *Transitions, environments, translations*, ed. J. W. Scott et al. London: Routledge.

———. 2001. Nature in the making. In *New directions in anthropology and environment*, ed. C. Crumley. Walnut Creek, CA, and Oxford: Altamira.

———. 2005. *Friction*. Princeton, NJ: Princeton University Press.

Turchi, Dolores. 1981. *Dalla culla alla bara*. Nuoro: ARPEF.

———. 1990. Maschere, miti e feste della sardegna. http://www.mamuthones-mamoiada.it/docs/Maschere_miti_e_feste_della_sardegna.pdf, retrieved February 2008.

Turner, Terence. 2004. On "the return of the native." *Current Anthropology* 45 (2): 264–65.

UNCED (United Nations Conference on Environment and Development). 1992. *Convention on Biological Diversity*. Rio De Janeiro.

Urbinati, Nadia. 1998. The souths of Antonio Gramsci and the concept of Gramsci. In *Italy's "Southern Question": Orientalism in one country*, ed. J. Schneider, 135–56. Oxford and New York: Berg.

Vargas-Cetina, Gabriela. 1993a. "'Our patrons are our clients': A shepherds' cooperative in Bardia, Sardinia." *Dialectical Anthropology* 18:337–62.

———. 1993b. Cooperation in Sardinia: Production, exchange and cooperatives among highland pastoralists. Ph.D. diss., McGill University.

———. 2003. Representations of indigenousness. *Anthropology News* 44 (5) May 2003. http://www.aaanet.org/press/an/infocus/indigenous/0311_Vargas-Cetina.htm, retrieved March 2009.

Vertovec, Steven. 2001. Introduction to *Globalization, globalism, environments, environmentalisms: Consciousness of connections*, ed. S. Vertovec and D. Posey, 1–8. The Linacre Lectures 2000. Oxford: Oxford University Press.

Vivanco, Luis. 2002. Seeing green: Knowing and saving the environment on film. *American Anthropologist* 104 (4): 1195–1204.

Walley, Christine. 2004. *Rough waters*. Princeton, NJ: Princeton University Press.

WCED (World Commission on Environment and Development). 1987. *Our common future*. Oxford and London: Oxford University Press.

Weeks, Priscilla. 1999. Cyber-activism: World Wildlife Fund's campaign to save the tiger. *Culture & Agriculture* 21 (3): 19–30.

Weingrod, Alex, and Emma Morin. 1971. "Post-peasants": The character of contemporary Sardinian society. *Comparative Studies in Society and History* 13 (3): 301–24.

West, Paige. 2006. *Conservation is our government now: The politics of ecology in Papua New Guinea.* Durham, NC: Duke University Press.

West, Paige, James Igoe, and Dan Brockington. 2006. Parks and peoples: The social impact of protected areas. *Annual Review of Anthropology* 35:251–77.

West, Patrick C., and Steven R. Brechin. 1991. *Resident peoples and national parks: Social dilemmas and strategies in international conservation.* Tucson: University of Arizona Press.

Willems-Braun, Bruce. 1997. Buried epistemologies: The politics of mature in (post)colonial British Columbia. *Annals of the Association of American Geographers* 87 (1): 3–31.

Wilson, Alexander. 1991. *The culture of nature: North American landscape from Disney to the Exxon Valdez.* Toronto: Between the Lines.

Wilson, Thomas M., and M. Estellie Smith, eds. 1993. *Cultural change and the new Europe: Perspectives on the European Community.* Boulder, CO: Westview Press.

Woolard, Kathryn. 2004. Codeswitching. In *Companion to linguistic anthropology*, ed. Alessandro Duranti. Oxford: Blackwell.

Wright R., and D. Mattson. 1996. The origin and purpose of national parks and protected areas. In *National parks and protected areas: Their role in environmental protection*, ed. R. G. Wright, 3–14. London and New York: Blackwell.

WWF (World Wide Fund for Nature), Sezione Regionale Sardegna and Sezione Gennargentu. 1998. *Parco Nazionale del Golfo di Orosei e del Gennargentu: Facciamo chiarezza.* Public document.

WWF–Sardegna. 2000. Parco Nazionale del Golfo di Orosei e del Gennargentu, Internet portal, http://www.parcogennargentu.it/ParcoGennargentu1.htm, revised November 2000, consulted May 2002.

Yearley, Steven. 1993. Standing in for nature: The practicalities of environmental organizations' use of science. In *Environmentalism: The view from anthropology*, ed. K. Milton. London and New York: Routledge.

———. 1996. Standing in for nature: The practicalities of environmental organizations' use of science. In *Environmentalism: The view from anthropology*, ed. Kay Milton. London: Routledge.

Zerner, Charles. 2000. Culture and the question of rights. In *People, plants and justice*, ed. Zerner. New York: Columbia University Press.

Zizi, Onorato. 1994. *Nuoro a palazzo: Tradizioni di vita giudiziaria in Barbagia.* Cagliari: Edizioni Solinas.

Zucca, Pasquale. 1992. Il dovere di opporsi a operazzioni di colonizzazione. In *Il Parco del Gennargentu: Un'occasione da non perdere*, ed. Scuola di Pubblica Amministrazione et al. Conference proceedings of June 6–7, 1992, Desulo. Cagliari: Edisar.

————. 1989. Relazione Introduttiva al Convegno Regionale sugli Usi Civici. Presentation at conference, *Gli usi civici nella valorizzazione delle risorse e nella tutela dei territori comunali*. Baunei, Sardegna 1989.

INDEX

"aboriginal Europeans," xii, 248n20. *See also* Herzfeld, Michael
aboriginality, 8, 10, 24, 47–48, 53; in America, 144; Sardinian, 8, 53. *See also* indigeneity
Abruzzo National Park, 65–66, 69, 139
Abu-Lughod, Lila, xvi
age-mate, xiv, xx, 164–65
Agrawal, Arun, 146, 148, 232, 235. *See also* environmentalism: and subjectivity
agriculture, 33, 131, 137, 141, 164, 171–72, 212–13, 219–21; modernization of, 6, 130, 139–40, 200, 217; subsistence, xii, 15–16; and women, 164, 184, 199, 204. *See also* agricultural cooperative
agricultural cooperative, 70, 166, 176, 209, 218. *See also* agriculture
allochronism, 156, 159, 233, 264n33. *See also* Fabian, Johannes
alterity, 55, 159, 163, 252n38; and identity, 113–14, 138; discourse about, 31, 42–47, 50, 125, 155–56, 233; Sardinian, 33, 130–32, 141, 189. *See also* ecological alterity; otherness
Amazon, 32; conservation of, 43; indigenous people of, xv, 43, 51–52; representations of, 42–43, 132. *See also* Kayapo Indians
Angioni, Giulio, 131
anthropological advocacy, 4–6, 11, 47, 160, 207–10, 232–33

anthropological location, xiii, xv, 20, 86, 189, 260n13
anti-kidnapping movement, 115–17
anti-park movement, 86, 192, 196. *See also* Base Committee
Antonia Mesina, Blessed, 179, 184–85, 195, 255n5, 267n24, 269n9; as martyr, 187, 202–4. *See also* Roman Catholic Church; Sanguinetti, Don
Api, Gli, 177, 179
archaeological sites, 17, 59, 79, 137, 257n9, 264n33; as source of pride, 72
Aretxaga, Begoña, xxi, 101–2, 104
Argyrou, Vassos, 153, 231, 264n30
Armed Anti-Park Front, 185–86, 195, 197, 201–3, 209. *See also* Gennargentu Park
assemblies, 92, 98–100, 118, 199; political, 85, 166, 175, 181, 269n11
Australian Aboriginals, 47–49, 65, 244n21, 249n24. *See also* dreamtime, Australian Aboriginal
authenticity, 51–53, 76, 101, 189, 229, 232; cultural, 38, 73, 87, 133–34, 158, 181, 199, 201–2, 232–33; and environmentalism, 5, 43, 46, 49, 141; of nature, 68–69, 74–75, 81, 132, 141–42; representations of, 75, 158, 164, 192, 210, 222; and tourism, 92, 211
authority, 10, 67, 76, 81, 84, 89, 203; cultural, 24, 62, 70, 73–74, 76; local, 63, 181, 193, 198, 202; moral, 70, 95, 101,

106, 181, 201; over nature, 73, 132, 137, 141, 233; scientific, 70, 73–75, 204, 234

"backwardness," 44, 150; representations of culture as, xii, 30, 133–34, 155–57, 163, 207; as stereotype, 55, 103, 140; as stereotype about Sardinians, xii, 25, 41, 44–45, 66, 82, 114–15, 130, 136, 138, 141, 208. *See also* alterity
Bandinu, Bachisio, 226–27. See also *Pastoralismo, Il*
Banditi a Orgosolo (book): 89, 128–29. *See also* Cagnetta, Franco
Banditi a Orgosolo (film), xiv, 129–30, 164, 257n11
banditry: and Orgosolo, 40, 94, 173; as resistance, 103–4, 188–89; in Sardinia, 66, 115, 125–26, 129–31, 138, 141, 207. *See also* "backwardness"; bandits; criminality; kidnapping
bandits, xiii, 17, 41, 75, 128, 130, 189; stereotypes about, 115, 159, 173–74, 202. *See also* banditry; criminality; kidnapping
Barbagia, 79, 116, 127, 226, 253n18; development of, 77, 173, 176, 226; history of, 125, 204, 211
Base Committee, 180–81, 186, 191–201, 220, 225. *See also* anti-park movement
Bees, The. *See* Api, Gli
"black chronicle," 109, 113, 132, 223
Blessed Antonia Mesina. *See* Antonia Mesina, Blessed
Bourdieu, Pierre, 199, 254n21, 266n13, 269n11. *See also* symbolic capital
Braun, Bruce, 15, 35, 49–51, 79. *See also* epistemic erasure; Nuu-chah-nulth First Nation; "social nature"
Brosius, Peter, xiii

Cagliari (city), xv, xvii, 15, 98, 225; according to Lawrence, D. H., 29–30, 245n2; and politics, 130, 169, 176, 225; as Sardinian capital, 11, 30, 33; and wwf, 78
Cagliari (province), 11
Cagnetta, Franco, 40, 90–91, 93–94, 128–

29, 168; on criminality, 89, 128–29, 188–89
Calakmul (Mexico), 27
cantu a tenores. *See* tenores
cathedral of Orgosolo, 72–73, 81. *See also* Monte San Giovanni
Cau, Tonino, 211
Chambers, Iain, 31, 44
chapels, 58, 98, 125, 256n13; of Blessed Antonia Mesina, 184; ruins of, 61, 72. See also *priorissas*
Chipko movement, xi, 261n20
Christian Democrat Party. *See* Democrazia Cristiana
code-switching (language), xvii-xviii, 118–20, 200, 227, 241n4, 255n12, 256n4, 269n12. *See also* language
collective action, 31, 91, 93, 176, 201, 262n24. *See also* Pratobello
common lands. *See* communal territory
Commons (*su cumonale*), 96, 206, 258n7; connection to, 187; global, 8, 11, 20; as economic resource, 91, 96, 99; management of, 70, 83, 92, 98, 156, 216; of Orgosolo, 4, 15, 25–26, 58, 63, 68, 73, 91, 95, 98, 133, 181, 199, 203, 219, 268n3; question of the, xiii, 218, 222, 271n6; symbolic value of, 95–96, 220. *See also* communal territory
communal territory, 79, 93, 258n7; in Orgosolo, xiii, xv, 2, 4, 86, 91, 94, 99, 104, 198, 216, 255n11; loss of, 93–96, 102, 105, 172, 190, 221; uses of, xvii, 59–60, 66, 100–1, 116, 131, 135, 140, 157, 204, 214. *See also* Commons
Communist Refoundation Party. *See* Partito della Rifondazione Comunista
confini, 89, 91, 129, 264n1; example of, 88, 164, 265n1
Conklin, Beth, 51–52, 213, 233
conservation, xi-xiii, 141–42, 160, 216, 237; and biodiversity, 5, 33, 36, 146, 188, 259n8; critique of, 10, 17–18, 25, 48, 207, 229; enclosure movement as, 54, 125–26, 191, 255n9, 258n2; global, 8, 104, 204, 223; history of, 7, 13, 39; initiatives, 6, 9, 16–18, 22, 32, 145

conservation (*continued*)
219; and parks, 8–9, 86; policies, xiii,
34, 138; "sustaining," 27
Conservation International (CI), xi, 18,
239, 246n5
Convention on Biological Diversity. *See*
United Nations Convention on Biological Diversity
corruption: "Clean Hands" trials, 182;
perception of, 51, 63, 124, 167, 258n2
"cricca," xx, 165
criminal zone, 127, 132–33. *See also*
Niceforo, Alfredo
criminality, 79, 103, 115, 119–20, 185;
discourses on, 132, 138, 140, 208;
expectation of, 124–27, 134; as resistance to state, 41. *See also* banditry;
bandits; criminality
Cronon, William, 64–66, 144, 250n26,
252n5, 259n12. *See also* wilderness
cultural advocacy. *See* anthropological
advocacy
cultural difference, representations of, 41,
44, 46, 55, 114, 156
cultural ecology, 9, 15, 20, 64, 70–71,
207, 213, 217–18
cultural essentialism, 43, 114–15, 133–34,
208, 213, 249n21, 251n36; critique of,
26, 32–33, 51–53, 171, 232–34, 236,
252n38; and Gennargentu Park, 25,
204
cultural heritage, 5, 53, 137, 165, 212
cultural intimacy, 113, 207, 271n3. *See
also* Herzfeld, Michael
cultural revitalization, 53, 165, 210, 220,
223, 234, 267n23
cultural stereotypes, 113–14, 119, 124,
246n4; of Orgosolo, 122, 138
cultural translation, 138, 152, 230,
261n20; in Sardinia, 25, 149, 155–57,
160

dark frontier, 25, 31, 132, 138, 159
deep ecology, 234, 263n29
del Casino, Francesco, 128, 162, 177–80,
183, 267n19
Democratic Party of the Left. *See* Partito
Democratico di Sinistra

Democrazia Cristiana (DC), 165–68, 172,
174, 176, 239, 265n3
demonstrations, 3, 26, 63, 86, 225,
270n16, 272n1. *See also* Pratobello
Dickie, John, 124–25, 257n8
"discipline," 132, 139. *See also* Foucault,
Michel
dreamtime, Australian Aboriginal,
21–22, 231, 244n18. *See also* Australian Aboriginals; global dreamtime of
environmentalism

ecodevelopment, 62, 66, 71, 82; community-based, 39; opposition to, 41; in
Sardinia, 87, 190
ecological alterity, 17, 23, 26, 131–33,
149–50, 160; indigenous, 27, 48, 50,
54–55, 230
"ecological capital," 146, 260n15. *See
also* Escobar, Arturo
ecological citizenship, 152, 263n29
"ecological learning," 212, 234
ecological management, xii, 70, 85, 95,
137, 145, 190; traditional, 49, 55, 70
156, 237. *See also* land management
ecological modernity, 6
"ecological nationalism," 26, 45, 147;
and Gennargentu Park, 141–42, 226,
228
ecology, 31–32, 106, 208–9; and governance, 40; as objective knowledge, 32,
43, 69, 132, 142, 173, 217–19, 243n7
ecotourism, x, xii, 27, 81, 268n2; in Sardinia, 37, 59, 62, 65–66, 137, 217,
220. *See also* tourism
embodiment, 195: and experience, 86, 91,
101, 104–5, 194–95, 254n3; and identity, 194–96; and landscape, 98, 144,
187, 189, 200, 218; and subjectivity,
101, 103
"enclosure of the commons," 39,
93; in Sardinia, 16. *See also under*
conservation
ENGO, 17–20, 36, 50, 151, 209, 232–33;
ideology, 19, 81, 138, 156, 262n25. *See
also* WWF
environment: local understanding of 11,
59, 84; cultural construction of, 22, 114

Foucault, Michel, 132, 266n13. *See also* "discipline"; governmentality; power "frictions," 83, 149, 202–3, 247n10. *See also* Tsing, Anna

gender: and cultural identity, xvi-xvii, 85, 203; distinctions, 86, 102; and ethnography, xv, 31; identity, xvi-xviii, 203; and local politics, 25, 39, 198–99; and space, xvii, 42, 89, 198, 256n13
gendered discourse, 102, 116, 195–96, 202–3
Gennargentu Adventure, 153–55
Gennargentu Park, 3, 62, 74, 236; boundaries of, 16–17, 191; debate over, 6–9, 40, 84–87, 96, 99–100, 105–6, 119, 158, 191, 198; history of, 61–63; institutional framework for, 25–26, 36, 70, 78; on Internet, 80–83; legislation, 86, 92, 96, 137–38, 140–41, 196, 225; opposition to, 32, 133, 172, 181, 185, 188, 194, 220; promotion of, 69, 77, 137, 147–48, 150, 154, 203, 264n33; and symbolism, 154
geological features, 13–14, 17, 62–63, 69, 79, 137, 264n33
"global assemblages," 35–37, 247n10
global dreamtime of environmentalism, 9, 21–26, 62, 76, 78, 81–83, 133, 231, 236–37; and hegemony, 38, 149, 226; and indigenous peoples, 67, 133; and Internet, 51–52, 153–55; and post-environmentalism, 27, 209, 223, 231; and WWF, 138, 150, 160
"global hierarchy of value," 134, 231, 236. *See also* Herzfeld, Michael
governmentality, 149, 200; environmental, 208, 235. *See also* Foucault, Michel
Gramsci, Antonio, 37, 168–72, 175, 181, 189; and hegemony, 201, 223, 236, 266n12, 268n4; and Peppino Marotto, 178; background, ix, 37, 265n11; legacy of, 26, 40, 163, 178, 183. *See also* hegemony; "organic intellectuals"
grassroots mobilization, 17, 86, 133, 180, 186, 193–96, 198, 202, 220–23, 224, 235–37
"green politics," 7–8, 14, 188. *See also* environmentalism: and cultural politics; Latour, Bruno
Gruppo Rubanu, 173–74, 176. *See also* poetry; Pratobello
Gupta, Akhil, 52–53

Habitats Directive (European), 145, 147
Haenn, Nora, 26–27
Harrison, Faye, 133–34
Harvey, David, 152, 261n19
hegemony, 21, 31, 55, 80, 147, 168, 189, 223, 268n4; and governance, 150, 159, 170, 238, 266n12; and marginalization, 37–38, 51, 134, 150, 171; and resistance, 26, 83–84, 134, 172, 202–3; and values, 209. *See also* Gramsci, Antonio
herders. *See* shepherds
herding. *See* transhumance
Herzfeld, Michael, 37–38, 44, 71, 140–41, 245n3, 247n11, 271n3; "aboriginal Europeans," xii, 248n20; "global hierarchy of value," 134, 231. *See also* "global hierarchy of value"; monumental time; social time
historicity, 62, 189; of rural Sardinians, xv, 84, 105, 158, 181; as theoretical perspective, 8, 39, 86, 105 141, 254n2
Hobsbawn, Eric, 40, 103–4, 188–89
honor and shame, xvi, 241n2
honorary citizenship, 178–79. *See also* del Casino, Francesco; Sanguinetti, Don
"Horizon 2020," 34–35
hospitality, 17, 26, 105, 256n4, 257n6; as politics, 192–93, 200–2, 203, 268n5; for tourism, 61, 79; tradition of, 4, 17, 101, 185, 194, 222
human rights, 18, 54
hunting, 4, 75, 100, 128, 133, 207

Ibba, Gianmarco, 153, 155, 253n12
identity, 24, 50, 141, 235, 247n11; collective, 91, 151, 189, 196; community, 101, 118, 142, 218; cultural 8–11, 19, 41, 46, 55, 73, 83, 97–98, 138, 198, 208; embodied, 105; ethnic, 55, 133, 251n32; environmental, 22, 69, 81; European, 141, 147, 263n26; feminine, 85, 111, 184, 195, 269n10; formation,

x, 138, 141, 252n38; gendered, xvi–
xviii, 85, 105, 194, 203; indigenous,
50–52; local, 7–8, 76, 97, 105, 113,
182, 185–86, 192–93, 200–2; masculine, 92, 112; national, 7, 55, 141, 144,
259n10; political, 9, 33, 46, 133, 167,
182, 197, 199; regional, 115; religious,
58; Sardinian, 24, 26, 45–46, 114–15,
137, 184, 191, 194; self-, 69, 76; shepherd, 173
imagination: cultural, 48, 132, 138, 144;
environmental, 31, 49
imagined community, 11, 147, 231,
262n24
indigeneity, xii, xiv, 8, 50–53, 133, 213,
232–33, 249n21; African, 251n34,
251n36; framing of, 24, 28, 32, 43, 47,
50, 227; Sardinian, 53, 127, 159, 228–
29, 233; stereotypes about, 19, 38, 48,
55, 237, 261n21. See also aboriginality
indigenous knowledge, 18, 24, 222,
242n5, 247n12, 259n11; revitalization,
26, 234. See also local knowledge
indigenous peoples, 27, 133, 149, 272n3;
and claims for sovereignty, 49; and
marginalization, xiv, 21, 37, 43, 47,
54–55, 158; and social movements, 18,
232, 270n1; as symbols, 45, 48, 229
institutional narratives, 15, 47, 50, 188,
204, 210
International Union for the Conservation
of Nature (IUCN), 18, 151, 235, 239
Internet, xvi, 79–80, 84, 203, 253n19,
262n24; and cultural construction,
152; and environmental campaigns, 51,
64, 78, 137, 151–52, 155; and Gennargentu Park, 77; as communication,
20, 152, 263n28. See also media; virtual spaces
Italian Communist Party. See Partito
Comunista Italiano
Italian Popular Party. See Partito Popolare
Italiano
Italian Socialist Party. See Partito Socialista Italiano

Jasanoff, Sheila, 22–23, 244n21

Kayapo Indians, 43, 208, 232, 234. See
also "noble ecological Indians"
kidnapping, 17, 25, 41, 132 , 141, 211;
media coverage of, 25, 122–24; and
Orgosolo, 17, 25, 41, 75, 111, 115–19,
122–24, 133; solidarity with victims
115–17, 120, 196, 257n6. See also banditry; bandits; criminality

labor migration, xv, 13, 45, 178, 213–14,
255n7; to continental Europe, 16, 165,
233
land management, 63, 98, 156, 190, 208,
214. See also Commons; communal territory; ecological management; fallows
regulation
language: dual Italian-Sardinian, xvii; as
marker, xvii, 114, 120; and social identity, xvii, 17. See also code-switching
Latour, Bruno, 14
Law 394. See regional law 394
Lawrence, D. H., 29–31, 33, 45, 245n2
Legambiente, 64, 148
Life Natura. See LIFE-NATURE
LIFE-NATURE, 36, 77–78, 147–48, 155
Li, Tania, 52, 187, 235–36
local knowledge, 21, 84, 152, 156, 209–
10, 232–35, 272n5; in Orgosolo, 77,
115, 120, 132, 212, 223
"lunch with the shepherds," 59–60, 192,
219
Lussu, Emilio, 88, 91, 168, 175–76,
264n1, 265n10. See also Partito Sardo
d'Azione; Partito Socialista Italiano;
Partito Socialista Italiano d'Unita
Proletariano

macchia, 33, 135
Madonna Assumption Festival, 164–65
Manca, Antonio Maria, 89
Marotto, Peppino, 91–92, 168, 183, 204,
211–12, 267n20, 268n6; language initiative, 270n17; political views of, 168–
69, 176, 178, 212
media, xvi, 20, 37, 208, 213, 262n25;
and environmental narratives, 51–52,
80–81, 84, 151–52, 228; representations of backwardness, xii, 25, 103,

media (*continued*)
113–16, 131–33; representations of criminality, 113, 118–23, 135–36, 149–50. *See also* Internet; RAI; Sardegna Uno

Mediterranean: conservation, 32, 35–36, 55, 142, 246n9; ecosystem, xi-xiii, 13–14, 33–34; as object of study, xv, 31, 44, 245n3

Mediterranean Sea, xi, 33–34

metaphors, 268n4; of animals, 190, 193–94; of kinship, 85–86, 105; of marginality, 30–31, 89, 98, 142, 184, 195; of the Old West, 157–59

Mezzogiorno, 113, 124–25, 134; Fund, 165; poverty of, 171

Milton, Kay, 97, 145, 249n22, 250n29

Monte San Giovanni, 2, 59–63, 75–77, 157; as focus of cultural narratives, 66, 72–75, 81; geography of, 59, 68–69; as meeting place, 98, 116; as part of park, 60, 61–63, 68–69, 72–77, 81; as symbol, 62, 66, 73, 76

monumental time, 71. *See also* Herzfeld, Michael

Moore, Donald S., 39, 189–90, 268n4, 269n9; in 2003, 41–42, 249n22, 258n5

mouflon, 19, 59, 69, 173, 193, 207; slaughter of, 185–87, 201–2, 209; virtual, 153–55

mourning, 101–2, 135–36, 196. See also *priorissas*

multiculturalism, 27, 47, 49, 51, 133, 229, 250n25, 251n37

murals, xiii, 79, 109–10, 162–63, 179–80; as political commentary, 17, 114, 166, 172, 177–79, 183, 267n19, 267n22. *See also* del Casino, Francesco

"museum effect," 61–62, 67–69, 74–77, 81, 141. *See also* "way of seeing"

museumization of the landscape, 76–77

museums, 67–68, 74–76, 141; and Orgosolo, xvi, 164, 179, 267n24

narratives, 10, 78, 93, 95; environmental, 20–24, 32, 36, 43, 50–51, 65–70, 86, 159; global, 231; men's, 89–90, 212–13, 223; and representation, 202, 208; women's 89, 124, 198–99, 256n13

national parks, 6–7, 39, 95–96, 155–57, 268n6; compared to other cultural institutions, 68, 260n13; in Europe, 6, 38, 46, 71, 139, 142, 252n7; history of, 64–67, 71, 144–45; Sardinian plans for, 72–73, 103, 106, 131, 133, 137, 140–41, 148, 163, 186–91, 198, 208, 220, 225–27, 272n1; and tourism, 18, 63, 69. *See also* Abruzzo National Park; Gennargentu Park; parks

nationalism, 24, 125; and Gramsci, 171, 266n15; Sardinian, x, 168, 188, 204. *See also* "ecological nationalism"; ethnonationalism; Gramsci, Antonio

NATO, 180; demonstrations against base, 26, 140, 163, 173–76, 267n25. *See also* demonstrations

Natura 2000, 36, 142–43

Nature Conservancy (TNC), 18, 54, 239

nature excursions, 69; by locals, 73, 101; by tourists, 6, 69, 76; virtual, 153–55

"nature in the making," 10, 84. *See also* Tsing, Anna

Niceforo, Alfredo, 126–28, 171. *See also* criminal zone; evolution, conceptions of; Orano, Paulo

"noble ecological Indians," 48, 208, 232, 249n22

Nuoro (city), xv, 13, 30–31, 88

Nuoro (province), 11–15, 226, 258n5, 272n1; and the park, 139, 148, 188, 258n5, 261n18; stereotypes of, 17, 40–41, 126. *See also* Ogliastra (province); World Masterpieces of Intangible Cultural Heritage

Nuu-chah-nulth First Nation, 49–50. *See also* Braun, Bruce; epistemic erasure

Ogliastra (province), 12–13, 77, 224, 226, 272n1. *See also* Nuoro (province); World Masterpieces of Intangible Cultural Heritage

Old West (America), 64–65, 158–59

omertà, 117–18, 120, 123–24, 136

Orano, Paulo, 126–27. *See also* Niceforo, Alfredo

power *(continued)*
  231; and resistance, 145, 169, 189. *See also* Foucault, Michel
Pratobello, 174; demonstration (1969), 162–63, 173–77, 180, 197, 270n16; demonstration (1998), 108, 180–81, 192, 201, 220–21; as memory, 176, 178, 180–81, 186, 194. *See also* collective action; demonstrations
priorissas, 58, 116, 202, 221, 256n13; and the Commons, 123, 196, 220. *See also* mourning
processions, xiv, 116, 196, 221, 245n2, 267n23; for festivals, 72, 165, 253n18; to chapel, 58, 61, 98, 256n13. See also *priorissas*
protected areas, xi, 54, 67, 78

Raffles, Hugh, 43
RAI (Italian national television), 114, 119–20, 136. *See also* media
reforestation, 62, 68, 166
regional law 394 (Sardinia), 63, 180–81, 220, 225
representations, of culture, 5, 10–11, 61, 113–14, 147, 202; ethnographic, 210, 213, 238; negative, 17, 45–46, 132. *See also* media; narratives
resistance, xii–xiv, 173, 199; characteristics of, 8–9, 25, 169; collective, 97, 176, 188, 199; culture of, 32, 45, 93, 126–27, 130–33, 159, 169, 191, 201–4, 234–35; to ecodevelopment, 10, 25, 32, 74, 103, 185; and identity, 38, 164, 184; politics of, xiv, 37, 115, 163; as social construction, 40, 104, 194, 268n4; to the state, 25, 32, 38, 186, 194, 198
rights of usufruct, 139, 157, 242, 271n6; in Orgosolo, 4, 190, 214–16
Roman Catholic Church, 89, 125, 256n13; legacy of, 85, 195, 234; and local activities, 58, 102, 115–16, 119, 184, 195–97, 267n23; and politics, 168; priests, 121, 124, 168, 172, 174, 256n13; religious practices, 135, 165, 202, 222; teachings, 115, 199. *See also* chapels; *priorissas*

sacrifice, 87–90, 184, 196, 199, 203
Said, Edward, 244n1, 246n4, 248n17, 257n8. *See also* orientalism
Sanguinetti, Don, 179, 267n23. *See also* Antonia Mesina, Blessed
Sar Vaddes, 60, 252n1, 258n2
Sardegna Uno (television network), 114, 228. *See also* media
Sardinia, 224: ecology of, 13–14, 61, 68, 77, 141, 148, 234; economy of, 172, 248n14; geography of, 11–13, 62–63; history of, 6, 11–12, 29–31, 40, 73, 93, 125, 213; Region of, 6, 46, 94, 131, 146, 188; stereotypes about, xvii, 31, 40, 93, 130, 188, 208; traditions of, 53, 62, 93, 136, 222, 227, 234; virtual, 20–21, 53, 81, 153–55. *See also* Orgosolo
Sardinian Action Party. *See* Partito Sardo d'Azione
Sardinian language, 110, 118–19, 178, 227, 241n3, 242n4, 257n7; as traditional practice, xiii, xvii, 91, 194, 204, 221–22, 234
Sardinian Tenor Association, 227. *See also* Bandinu, Bachisio; tenores
Satta, Gino, 126–27
scarcity, 88, 105, 195
Schneider, Jane, 113–14, 246n4, 250n31, 258n6; and Peter Schneider, 236, 258n6
"science as practice," 9. *See also* Latour, Bruno
Scott, James C., 39, 139–40, 146, 187–88, 200–1, 258n4, 260n15. *See also* "everyday forms of resistance"; "seeing like a state"; "thin simplifications"; "weapons of the weak"
"seeing like a state," 140, 145, 147. *See also* Scott, James C.
shepherds, xiv–xv, 108, 176; as bandits, 126, 130, 134, 139; and class consciousness, 168, 255n9; and communal territory, 60–62, 214–15; and local identity, 95, 89–91, 185–86, 220; and loss of commons, 191; as symbol of tradition, 24, 97, 118–19, 131, 192; representations of, 75, 78, 129–31, 141,

153–54. See also "lunch with the shepherds"; pastoralism

Sio, Banne, 89–90, 255n6

Sivaramakrishnan, K., ix-x, 232, 269n14

Slater, Candace, 42–43, 248n19

social agency, 91, 105, 147, 170, 187–89, 245; of Sardinians, 14, 83, 193, 203. See also Gramsci, Antonio

social justice, 4, 9, 11, 208, 218. See also environmental justice

social life, 101, 110, 170, 256n4

social memory, 86–87, 97, 101–5, 110–11, 169, 248n17; gendered, 89; of resistance, 26, 163, 169, 189. See also historicity

"social nature," 25, 55. See also Braun, Bruce

social practices, of Sardinians, xv, 105, 197

social roles, 97, 166, 202, 215; of ethnographer, xvi-xviii, 3–4, 209, 229, 241n1, 242n5; of men, 157–58, 192, 227, 267n23; of Sardinians, 10, 187; of women, 85–86, 111, 157, 173, 194, 198, 202, 204, 256n13, 261n20

social time, 71, 109, 181. See also Herzfeld, Michael

Soru, Renato, 226, 272n1

Soru Law, 225–26

State Forestry Service, 14, 94. See also forestry service

strategic essentialisms, 51, 208, 222, 234

structural violence, 26, 54–55, 89, 184–85, 201–2, 210–11, 223, 233, 251n33

subsistence strategies, xii, 4, 15, 96, 164, 233

Supramonte, 15, 24, 61–62, 68–69, 86, 89, 141, 190; imagery of, 79–81, 92, 132, 151, 270n17

sustainable development, xii-xiii, 11, 18–19, 26–27, 96; and funding, 8, 34–35; critique of, 104, 260n15

symbolic capital, xvii, 45, 147, 200, 208, 217, 254n21. See also Bourdieu, Pierre

Telesardegna (Sardinian language news), 114, 119

television debate, 121–24

tenores, 92, 211, 227, 255n8

"thin simplifications," 140, 160, 250n30. See also Scott, James C.

totemism, 22, 185, 244n19–20

tourism, 3, 18, 31, 59, 61, 74, 151; and authenticity, 211; as development, 6–7, 13, 63, 91, 164; impacts of, 33–34, 46; in Orgosolo, xvii, 4, 16, 76, 79. See also ecotourism

tourists, xv, 18, 59–62, 74–77, 109; in Orgosolo, 159

transhumance, 24, 255n7; in Orgosolo, xii-xiii, 4, 15, 41, 46, 90, 94, 105, 127, 214, 267n20. See also Commons; Communal territory; shepherds

Tsing, Anna, 149, 237, 247n10, 254n4, 261n19. See also "frictions"; "nature in the making"

UNESCO, 53, 145–46, 226–28

United Nations, 18, 250n32, 251n35

United Nations Convention on Biological Diversity (CBD), xi, 5, 47–48, 147, 232, 239; commentary on, 5, 232, 242n3, 272n5

United Nations Educational, Scientific and Cultural Organization (UNESCO). See UNESCO

United Nations Environmental Programme (UNEP), 34–36

United Nations Environmental Programme Mediterranean Action Programme (UNEP/MAP), 34–35

usi civici. See rights of usufruct

vardau, su. See fallows regulation

Vargas-Cetina, Gabriela, 160, 248n14, 255n7, 258n5

virtual spaces, 20, 62, 78–81, 203, 253n19

visions of landscape, 6, 8–9, 31, 46, 61, 66, 74, 208; gendered, 101, 192; as sacred, 76, 95–96; Sardinian, 14–15, 86, 110, 141, 160, 203, 225

"way of seeing," 62, 67, 71, 79, 81. See also "museum effect"

"weapons of the weak," 186, 188, 200–1. *See also* Scott, James C.; "politics of the weak"; "thin simplifications"

West, Paige, 229, 243n15, 261n19

wilderness, 18, 42–43, 49, 61, 69, 81, 144; fiction of, 64, 142, 144, 147, 159, 259n12; representations of, 76, 132, 141, 149, 151, 155–56

World Conservation Union (WCU), xi, 239

World Masterpieces of Intangible Cultural Heritage, 226–27. *See also* UNESCO

World War II, 6, 87–88, 90–91

World Wide Fund for Nature. *See* WWF

World Wide Web (WWW). *See* Internet

World Wildlife Fund. *See* WWF

WWF, xi, 3–4, 18, 25, 208, 235, 246n5; conference in Orgosolo, 265n2; on Internet, 64, 78–79, 81–83, 137–38, 149–51, 153–56, 262n22; and Italy, 36, 64, 77, 138; narratives, 136–38, 155–57, 204, 264n33; and Sardinia, 51, 68, 148–49, 185, 194, 226, 261n18. *See also* ENGO

youth circle, 172–77

Zerner, Charles, 19, 217, 271n5